Commentary on
the Psalms

Commentary on the Psalms

Allan M. Harman

Mentor

To
Mairi

© Allan M. Harman
ISBN 1-85792-168-2

Published in 1998 by Christian Focus Publications Ltd
Geanies House, Fearn, Ross-shire
IV20 1TW, Scotland, Great Britain

Contents

Foreword

Anyone writing on the Psalms must be conscious of the rich heritage of literature we have on this book of the Bible. I want to acknowledge my indebtedness to the many authors from whom I have learned so much over the years. Looking back now I find it hard to locate many of the sources from which I have gained help and which have been so stimulating to me. Ideas from various books have become part of my own thinking and teaching on the Psalms, and I can only express deep thanks to all whose writings on the Psalms I have used.

I want to acknowledge the students to whom I have taught courses on the Psalms in various theological institutions. In particular I think of students in the Free Church College, Edinburgh, Scotland; the Reformed Theological College, Geelong, Australia; the Reformed Theological Seminary, Jackson, Mississippi, USA; and the Presbyterian Theological College, Melbourne, Australia. They have interacted with me as we studied the Psalter together, and again and again their responses have driven me back to the text.

Two friends, Bernard Secombe and Mark Tonkin, have been of great help in reading the manuscript and commenting on it, and I thank them warmly.

Finally, my wife Mairi has always encouraged me as we have worked together in the cause of the gospel for over 35 years. In this case she has often helped to keep me at the task amid many competing demands on my time in college and church life, and her comments have also improved the manuscript.

communal songs of praise, also involves an element of confession. In addressing God in words or song we are telling others what we know of him, and also confessing that he is the God whom we have come to honour and trust. Singing the Lord's songs then can be an acknowledgment of an allegiance to him.

1.3 Praise and the Wonderful Deeds of the Lord

The songs of praise in the Old Testament focus attention on what God has done. They are often long recitals of the great deeds of God. This is particularly so of the 'historical psalms' such as Psalms 78, 105, 106, and 136, while in many other psalms there are references to historical incidents. The psalmist, in Psalm 77, speaks of calling to mind the deeds of the Lord and remembering God's wonders of old (vs. 11-12). The use of the word 'wonder' is important in psalms like this, because it translates a Hebrew word which has the idea that it is something which only God can do. Telling out the 'wonders of the Lord' means to proclaim the great things God has done for the salvation of his people.

1.4 Praise and Commitment to God's Covenant

The praises of Israel have to be seen in the wider context of Israel's commitment to the Lord. There was a bond or covenant between God and Israel, and they were solemnly pledged to be the Lord's people. In all their worship they acknowledged the relationship; and numerous features of their life were said to be 'to the Lord' (e.g. the Passover, Exod. 12:11, 27, 48; the Sabbath, Exod. 16:23; the year of Jubilee, Deut. 15:2; the Nazirite, Num. 6:2). In singing to the Lord the people were in a verbal way paying their tribute to their great King and Saviour. It was another way of reaffirming the oath they had taken to him. This comes out strikingly in David's words, 'The LORD lives, praise be to my Rock' (Ps. 18:46). It is clear from Jeremiah 5:2 that the phrase 'as the LORD lives' was part of an oath formula. Here it appears in conjunction with a doxology to God.

Another way to see this same commitment is in regard to God's law. There are psalms such as Psalm 119 in which there is constant reference to God's word, or statutes, or testimonies. In other words, the praise of God's law is once again submission to God's covenant requirements. From the same perspective we can see that the laments, especially of a communal nature, are saying that the people have departed from God's covenant pattern for them.

1.5 Praise and Promise for the Future

Believers are able to sing contemporaneously with glorified believers in heaven. There is a union between saints on earth and saints in heaven (see Heb. 12:22-24). They sing a song on earth which echoes that of saints above. Believers still living on earth have access to the heavenly Zion of which they have become citizens. They are 'Blest inhabitants of Zion, Washed in the Redeemer's blood' (John Newton's hymn, *Glorious things of thee are spoken*), and so can sing in unison with the great company in heaven of redeemed sinners and angels who together sing praise to the Lamb who was slain (Rev. 5:12-13; 7:9-12).

Having learned of the grace of God in salvation, Old Testament psalmists also realised that it had implications for the future. The kingdom of God had not come to full expression. The Gentiles were hardly yet touched with the blessings of God, but they would yet experience the blessing of the Lord (Ps. 67). There are songs which express longing for the extension of God's kingdom, so that Messiah will reign from the River (i.e. the Euphrates) to the uttermost ends of the earth (Ps. 72:8-11), and all the ends of the earth will turn to the Lord, and all families of the nations will bow down before him (Ps. 22:27).

The fact that God has often intervened in human history and does great and wonderful things, encourages his people to sing of coming events. Believers have the confidence that the Lord will keep them and ultimately bring them into his glory (Ps. 73:24). At the end the LORD will come to judge the world in righteousness (Ps. 96:13). He has established a throne from which he will judge the world (Ps. 9:7-8), but he will vindicate his own people (Ps. 135:14).

2. THE USE OF POETRY

2.1 Poetry and Music

Jewish and Christian worship make extensive use of religious poetry. Such poetry involves two distinct features:

(a) It is a style of writing which is different from the normal style of narrative prose. For example, compare the account of God's covenant with David as recorded in 2 Samuel 7 with the poetical expression of it in Psalm 89; or Genesis 1 with Psalm 8. The same ideas can be conveyed in prose and poetry, but poetry contains music in words and this attracts us and is more memorable.

(b) This religious poetry is not only *said*, but it is *sung*, and such singing forms an important part of religious expression. Naturally we do not have examples directly from biblical times but there are many examples of synagogue music. Some of these are carried over into Christian worship, as for example the tune Leoni sung to the hymn 'The God of Abraham Praise'.

Music, like language, has its origin in the fact that man is a creature of God, and in making music man is imitating God himself. He has been created in God's image, and his ability to use both words and music is a result of his being an unique image bearer. Music is not given for pure entertainment but as a thing of beauty which directs attention to God's works of creation (creativity) and providence (order). When music and religious poetry are brought together in harmony there is a special appeal to the human mind and emotions. In itself music is not identical to language but it has some of the same abilities as poetical language to appeal to the imagination and to touch human emotions.

Creativity in language and music are brought together in psalmody and hymnody. A message is conveyed in both words and music which combine to produce an effect upon the hearer, which in turn heightens religious understanding and experience.

2.2 Characteristics of Poetry

The poetry of the Old Testament shares some features with Western poetry, but in other respects it is quite different from our understanding of poetry. Some of the features in common are:

(a) The normal patterns of word order can be varied in poetry. The impact of normal word order is important as we can often predict what the end of a sentence will be. However, an unusual pattern has the effect of pressing on our attention the idea being presented.

(b) The language of poetry is often much more conservative than popular speech, and unusual words are frequently used. Some words are even invented to fit a particular context. We have only to glance at an older hymnbook to see examples which would be very strange in ordinary conversation: 'inly', 'Bethlem', 'Christly', 'illuming', 'wert', 'cloys', 'lays', 'supernal', 'pent', 'till moons shall *wax*', 'riven', 'assuage'. It also retains words which have dropped out of everyday use, and thereby fossilises them in poetic form. For example, in modern Scripture in Song you will still find words like 'thee', 'thine', 'thou', 'realm', 'diadem' and many others.

(c) It uses many features of style such as playing on the initial sound in words (alliteration) or sound in other syllables (assonance). Poetry also uses similes (in which there is a comparison) and metaphors (in which something is said to be something else, e.g. the Lord is a rock). Metaphors are very important because they ensure that our minds are involved because we have to work out the meanings of the words of the poem. They also appeal to our imagination which is attracted by the total idea. Moreover, metaphors often touch our emotions for they appeal to our senses. Hence, because they combine an idea with a feeling, they express much more to us than the bare idea expressed without a metaphor.

(d) There is no sharp dividing line between prose and poetry, for sometimes elevated prose will contain features which are normally characteristic of poetry. There are distinctive characteristics of both prose and poetry, and many examples of literature share features from both. The distinction between poetry and prose may be one of degree, rather than an absolute division. For Old Testament poetry this can be illustrated by the following diagram:

Parallelism
Figurative language
Non-predictable word order

Prose ←————————————————————————→ Poetry

Narrative sequence
Non-figurative language
Predictable word order

2.3 The Distinctiveness of Old Testament Poetry
Other features of Old Testament poetry are quite different because they are part of Hebrew and therefore of Near Eastern poetic style.

The most important feature of Old Testament poetry is the use of phrases in a parallel way. Thus the psalmist says:

> *The eyes of the LORD are on the righteous*
> *and his ears are attentive to their cry* (Ps. 34:15).

There is a correspondence between the two phrases which may be similar as in this one, or which may express opposites as in Psalm 1:6:

> *For the Lord watches over the way of the righteous,*
> *but the way of the wicked will perish.*

Perhaps the most common pattern is where the second phrase adds something more to the expression. The poet introduces an idea, and then focuses more specifically on it in the following phrase. We can express this by calling the two phrases A and B. The pattern is:

> A, and what's more,
> B.

For example, Psalm 6 commences with the words:

> *O LORD, do not rebuke me in your anger*
> *or discipline me in your wrath.*

The psalm opens with a plea to God not to speak words of rebuke to him (A), but then in the second part of the verse (B), the psalmist asks that no action ('discipline') be taken against him. The phrases are clearly not identical, but show a progression of thought.

Hebrew poetry also uses a range of devices to draw attention to the ideas. These include features which are very stilted if we attempt to bring them over into English translations. For example, many poems in the Old Testament use acrostics, in which the letters of the alphabet appear in order at the beginning of lines. This can be done where a single line follows (Ps. 34) or where several lines follow (Pss. 9 and 10), or as in Psalm 119 in which every line of the twenty-two sections starts with the appropriate letter of the Hebrew alphabet. This explains why in English translations of this psalm the Hebrew letters are actually printed in our text (see also the NIV footnote). For native Hebrew speakers these devices would attract attention and make an appeal to the reader or listener. They can be likened to embroidery, which takes so many hours to do, but the result is a beautiful piece of work which attracts and delights.

2.4 Sung Praise in Old Testament Worship

From earliest times music was employed (Gen. 4:21) and songs of praise feature in the Pentateuch (Exod. 15:1-18, 21; Deut. 32) and the early historical books (Judg. 5; 1 Sam. 2). Music and religious poetry are inseparably connected from the time of David onwards. When the Ark of the Covenant was brought to Jerusalem David instructed the leaders of the Levites to appoint singers of joyful songs, who were to be accompanied with lyres, harps and cymbals (1 Chr. 15:16). For service in the house of God he appointed the sons of Asaph, Heman and Jeduthun to a ministry of singing (1 Chr. 25:1ff.; singing is called 'prophesying' in the Hebrew of this passage). On the day in which the Ark was brought to Jerusalem David committed to Asaph and his associates a song which is a combination of several psalms (cf. 1 Chr. 16:8-36 with Pss. 105:1-15; 96; 106: 1, 47-48), and to this song the people responded with 'Amen', and 'Praise the LORD'. Over 80% of the Psalms come from the period of David or later, and over 40% are attributed to David himself. There was song in the Temple especially when sacrifices were being offered, and at times the people responded with refrains (2 Chr. 7:3; Ezra 3:11).

3. INTRODUCING THE PSALTER

3.1 The Titles

The Hebrew Bible simply calls the Book of Psalms in Hebrew *tehillim*, 'Praises'. The Septuagint, the Greek translation of the Old Testament (commonly referred to as the LXX), produced by about 200 BC, called them 'Psalmoi', and it is from this word that ultimately we get our English word 'Psalms'. In the New Testament the collection of Psalms is called 'the Book of Psalms' (Luke 20:42; Acts 1:20) and from that expression we get our general descriptive title for the book. One early manuscript of the LXX translation has the title 'Psalterion'. This was the word used for an instrument like a zither, and from this Greek word we get another English title for the Psalms, 'the Psalter'.

Many of the individual psalms have titles given to them. These titles may not have originally been part of the psalms, but they are certainly very early. This is shown by the way in which songs outside the Book of Psalms have titles, such as David's psalm of thanksgiving (2 Sam. 22:1), Hezekiah's song (Isa. 38:9) and Habakkuk's psalm (Hab. 3:1, 19b). Also, the fact that the translators of the Old Testament into Greek had difficulties with the titles when they came to translate them suggests their antiquity. The titles can be grouped according to the type of information they contain. Some merely designate the type of psalm in question (e.g. hymn or song, Pss. 32, 83, 145), while others contain musical information (e.g. Pss. 4 and 5) or an indication of special use (e.g. Ps. 30, 'For the dedication of the temple'; Ps. 92, 'For the sabbath day'). Many of the titles relate to a person or groups of people (e.g. David, Ps. 3; Solomon, Ps. 72; Moses, Ps. 90) or give information relating the particular psalm to an historical situation, particularly with reference to David (e.g. Pss. 18, 56, 60, and 63).

3.2 Difficulties in Approaching the Psalms

The greatest difficulty we face is our familiarity with the Book of Psalms. For many Christian people the Psalms, or particular well-loved psalms, are the parts of the Bible that they know best. In many branches of the Christian tradition the Psalms are said or sung in a distinctive and traditional manner. Thus in Anglican churches, usually the Psalms are read or chanted. In Reformed churches, originating either on the European Continent or in Scotland, the Psalms for long formed either the major part of sung praise or in many cases the exclusive content of praise. Others are known because they are now part of the paraphrased poetry of the hymnbook. Simply because they are used so much does not necessarily mean that they are understood better than other parts of the Bible. A fresh look at the Psalms will bring us to a deeper appreciation of their content and meaning.

The Psalter is also a difficult book to study because it has an accumulation of problems which we do not face in the same way elsewhere in the Old Testament. For example, when we come to another book of the Old Testament, such as an historical book like Joshua, or a prophetical book like Ezekiel, we are able to put them in a distinct historical setting. When we are faced with the Psalter we have a tremendous range of historical settings, so that each psalm has to be interpreted individually. Moreover, we are not just dealing with one type of literature in the Psalms. While we can go to historical, prophetical, and poetical parts of the Old Testament in general, in the Psalter we have all these represented and more. For the Psalter, though, the absence of historical context for a particular psalm makes our task harder as we try to date the period from which it came, to see if the historical background helps us to interpret it better.

3.3 The Creed of Israel

The Book of Psalms brings together the faith of Israel into one book. The format in which it appears is new, but not the content. All the themes of the book are held together by the fact that it is the confession of Israel, for it is Israel's creed, sung not signed. That is to say, it expresses for us what believers in Israel of old knew and felt about the Lord in whom they trusted. It is a word from the heart, not the formal expression of a carefully composed credal statement to which they could have added their signature. The unity which it possesses is the unity which that faith gives to the whole book.

The Psalter is also important because it is virtually a theology of the Old Testament. Even without the other books which make up our Old Testament we could produce from the Psalms all the essential material from which we could write the theology. It contains long historical psalms which recount the history of God's people, while other psalms, as we know either by their titles or their contents, show us how the church in the Old Testament times reacted to particular situations. Their faith was on trial, and the songs they sang expressed their deepest religious convictions.

The theology of the Psalms, moreover, is popular theology. That is to say, it is not the theology or philosophy of a group of expert theologians discussing matters and formulating their conclusions in a very abstract way. The concreteness of the Psalms strikes us as we read them, as well as how down-to-earth they are. They display how life in response to God was lived in ancient Israel, and how believers 'through each perplexing path of life' (*O God of Bethel,* Paraphrase 2) put their trust in him. When we read other parts of the Old Testament we have to balance them with the underlying ideas about God contained in the Psalter, for it gives us what people were thinking and feeling in relation to their religious experiences. This is also another reason why the Psalms appeal to the broad Christian community. While many Christians feel they need special help to understand, for example, the Book of Leviticus, they are able to approach and appropriate the Psalms for themselves.

As we will see later, the groupings of psalms may well reflect some aspects of theological significance. That is to say, the way in which the Psalms are brought together in the one bundle may well have significance in that psalms with similar meanings are often placed in close proximity. Psalms 3 and 4 have similarities and are placed together, while Psalms 9 and 10 may well have originally been a single composition, for together they form in Hebrew a single acrostic poem. Other psalms, such as Psalms 42 and 43 and Psalms 142 and 143, are also brought together because of common themes.

It is also important to see the first two psalms as setting the pattern for the whole book. Psalm 1 contains the basic distinction between the righteous and the wicked and speaks of the blessedness or happiness of the person who delights in the Lord and his law (vs. 1-4). Jesus, in the Sermon on the Mount, also uses the idea of blessedness, when he expounds the same basic principles even more fully and carries on the teaching concerning the two ways (Matt. 5-7). The second psalm carries on the theme of the two ways by emphasising how nations set themselves against the Lord and his anointed, which came to pass at the crucifixion (see the quotation from this psalm in Acts 4:25-26). Both psalms refer to 'the way' (1:1; 2:12). The anointed king of Psalm 2 transcends any of David's successors, and the presentation of this figure points to Jesus as the appointed Son and Servant (see Matt. 3:17; 17:5; 2 Pet. 1:17).

3.4 The Prayer Book of the Bible

At times the Book of Psalms has been called the prayer book of the Bible. This, however, suggests that all the psalms are addressed to God, but yet there are some which are not (e.g., 1, 2, 32, 45, etc.). It is better to think of the Psalms as showing us the true nature of prayer, and how believers can respond to the great saving acts of God. To what God does in an objective way, his people give their subjective response in the meditation and prayers of the Psalter.

The Psalms help us to understand the true nature of prayer because of their main characteristics.

(a) For men to pray to God using human words can only be the response to God's words to us. Thus when the psalmists are praying to God, they are praying back to him what he had spoken. They also appeal to God to remember the word which he has given (Ps. 119:49). The whole principle of meditation rests upon the fact that God has both spoken and acted.

(b) The focus of attention is God himself. This holds true even when the psalmists are praying concerning their own needs. So many of the psalms are declarations of God's gracious character, and they are therefore basically songs of praise. It is not surprising, therefore, that the Jews called the whole book *tehillim* ('praises'). The very act of prayer to God is a recognition who he is, and in coming to him in this way we are proclaiming that we acknowledge that he is precisely who he claims to be.

(c) The Psalms also teach us that a mark of true prayer is humility before God. The descriptions we have of human sin and guilt in the Psalms are not accidental. Rather, these descriptions go to the very heart of prayer with the recognition that we have no right to stand our ground before a holy God (Ps. 24:3), for none living is righteous in his sight (Ps. 143:2). We are reminded that those who pray come as humble servants, waiting till the Lord shows mercy (Ps. 123:2). The constant references in the Psalms to the need for God's intervention are another aspect of their humility before him. They know that in need or in deliverance the glory is to be to God's name on account of his love and faithfulness (Ps. 115:1).

4. THE PSALMS AND SPIRITUAL LIFE

4.1   The Psalms – The Most Comprehensive Book of the Old Testament

The Book of Psalms is very different from every other Old Testament book. To use the illustration of Athanasius (c. 295-373 AD), all the other books are like gardens which grow only one kind of fruit. However, the Book of Psalms, in addition to growing its own special fruit, also grows some from all the other gardens. Thus it includes history and prophecy as well as praise and prayer. As Luther expressed it: 'You may rightly call the Psalter a Bible in miniature.'

There is no other Old Testament book which has such an historical range. Psalm 90 is attributed to Moses, while the bulk of the book comes from the period of David and Solomon. There are psalms such as 74, 79 and 80 which are clearly written after the destruction of Jerusalem. In them the psalmists recount something of the city's destruction (74:3-8; 79:1-4; 80:4-6, 8-16) and appeal to God to visit his people again and restore them. Psalm 137 pictures the exiles being mocked in their captivity in Babylon, while Psalm 126 rejoices in what the Lord has done in restoring the people to their own land.

In the Psalms we have a representative sample of the faith of Israel over centuries. This helps us to see how enduring was the commitment of the people to the Lord, and how their trust in him sustained them during periods of testing. Clearly too the psalmists saw the responsibility of parents and elders to pass on the faith to coming generations. They wanted succeeding generations not only to know about the great deeds of the Lord, but also to put their trust in him for themselves (Ps. 78:7). Generations yet unborn had to be told about the Lord and his righteousness, so that they too would serve him (Ps. 22:30-31). Children were encouraged to learn of the fear of the Lord and to know that his eyes were on the righteous (Ps. 34:11-16).

4.2 The Psalms – The Most Personal Book of the Old Testament

The Psalter is markedly different from the other books of the Old Testament. In them the human author is normally writing in the third person of events, even those concerning himself. We see this illustrated by the way in which Moses reports the conflict between himself and Aaron and Miriam (Num. 12:1ff), or in the manner in which Amos speaks in the third person in connection with his own conflict with Jeroboam and Amaziah (Amos 7:10-17). There are brief biographical elements in some of the prophets such as Isaiah (6:1-13) and Jeremiah (1:4-19), but in the main the Old Testament is written in the third person.

However, the Psalter uses the first person throughout. It speaks of 'I' or 'we', which points out straightaway that they are expressions of personal religious life. The Psalms are not abstract writings about theology, or anything approaching a philosophical discussion of religious themes. They are really an expression of the knowledge about God and his ways which is rooted in personal experience of a vital relationship with him. If knowledge of God was revealed so all in Israel would profit from it, then that knowledge should be grasped and used by all. The Psalms articulate that theology for ancient Israel, and so we see in them the popular religious feeling of redeemed sinners.

Another amazing feature of the Psalms is that they portray all the varied experiences and emotions of the human heart, with all its ups and downs. They describe real life in which the psalmists bare their souls for others to see and express their deepest emotions and longings. We not only see them at the heights of joy, but they express their honest feelings of despair and doubt.

4.3 Identification with the Psalmist

The Psalms also provoke a response in us because of our similar spiritual experiences. They are in themselves a response to God and truths concerning him. They stimulate us as we pass through similar experiences and find that we can identify with the psalmists in their day. Their words become our words, and we find that we can take over their expression of religious faith and use it as if it were our own.

This also means that the Psalms serve as a mirror of the soul. Calvin expressed it like this: 'This book I am wont to call an anatomy of all the parts of the soul, for no-one will find in himself a single feeling of which the image is not reflected in this mirror.' Here Calvin is echoing the words of Athanasius who said: 'It seems to me, moreover, that because the Psalms thus serve him who sings them as a mirror, wherein he sees himself and his own soul, he cannot help but render them in such a manner that their words go home with equal force to those who hear him sing, and stir them also to a like reaction.' The Psalms both serve as a suitable means for us to express our own feelings, and also stimulate us further as we crystallise our thoughts regarding God's dealings with us. In this way, the Psalms not only speak to us, but they also speak for us.

The variety of experiences described by the psalmists also meets us in our needs. Whatever the situation in which we are, we can turn to the Psalms knowing that something appropriate for us will be found there. This is why Martin Luther found such comfort in the Psalms during his own spiritual agony, for he found in them his own innermost feelings. If Luther was mad, then so was the psalmist; if Luther was hungry and thirsty for God, then so was the psalmist! Luther said that in the Psalms 'everyone, in whatever state he is, finds words that fit his case and suit him exactly, as though they were put there for his sake alone .... Then he becomes sure that he is in the communion of saints.'

The emotional element of poetry and song enables us to express with power and feeling our response to God in the words of the Psalms. The Psalms are directed towards the emotions of men and women, because they are the expressions of human beings as they passed through crises in their lives. One of the ways in which we can classify the Psalms is by the emotion expressed in them. Thus we can think of songs of joy, or cries of despair, or laments of abandonment, or the calm peace of confident trust. Emotions are grounded in our faith, and thus our present relationship with God will affect our emotions. The Psalms help us to see how Old Testament believers wrestled with their emotional response to situations, and how their changed understanding of God and his ways impelled them to action.

4.4 The Faith of the Psalmists

We must not make any distinction between the faith of Old Testament believers and believers in the New Testament period in respect to trust in God and his Word. The same principle applies even to us today. When the New Testament writers wish to illustrate the nature of faith they appeal to Old Testament examples (see Rom. 4; Gal. 3; Heb. 11; Jas. 2:20-26). Those believers are part of the great cloud of witnesses whose testimony should stimulate us to run with patience looking unto Jesus (Heb. 12:2). While they did not have the fullness of New Testament revelation, yet they responded to what God had revealed up to their day, and they believed it

When we turn to the Psalms we see frequent expressions of trust in the Lord. Those whose trust is in him display an entire self-commitment to him, coupled with expressions of obedience to his Word and commands. A wide variety of language is used to describe this relationship. The people of God are said to act in certain ways including 'believe', 'trust', 'take refuge in', 'rely upon', 'wait for', and 'wait patiently for'. Some of these expressions are used in contrast to putting trust in substitutes like military weapons, princes, idols or even man himself (Pss. 44:6; 146:3; 135:15-18; 52:7). The words of Psalm 62:8 express the basic message of the Psalms regarding faith: 'Trust in him at all times, O people.'

In all their experiences the psalmists were relying on the character of God as he had made himself known. There was no special word of revelation to help them in their time of need. Because there was no personal message they had simply to rely on God's love and mercy revealed previously. In times of great perplexity, it was knowledge of God's existing revelation which broke through and brought light into a dark situation. Thus in Psalm 73 the psalmist was in turmoil about the prosperity of the wicked until he came into God's house and then he understood the end of the wicked (vs. 16-17). In the Book of Psalms faith is like faith elsewhere in the Bible; it is reliance on him and his character as revealed in earlier periods of the Old Testament.

5. DEVELOPMENT OF THE PSALTER

5.1 The Groupings

Clearly the Psalms have been arranged in some order, but certainly this is not chronological. While we do have psalms from the period of the exile or later (such as 126 or 137) coming towards the end of the Psalter, they do not come at the very end. The most that can be said is that the psalms of David appear predominantly in the first half of the Psalter, though just after a song of the exile (137) a psalm of David follows (138). Neither is the arrangement by author or by content, though some sections do bring together psalms by a particular author or linked by a theme. However, this is not done consistently throughout the whole book.

What is apparent is that while the Psalms have been brought together into a complete book, actually there are five separate books which have been combined to make the whole. The division into five may well be in imitation of the five books of Moses (Genesis to Deuteronomy). This division can be set out in a table like this:

The Complete Psalter

Book 1: Psalms 1-41
Book 2: Psalms 42-72
Book 3: Psalms 73-89
Book 4: Psalms 90-106
Book 5: Psalms 107-150

Each of these divisions ends with a doxology. Thus the first book ends with the words of Psalm 41:13:

> *Praise be to the LORD, the God of Israel,*
> *from everlasting to everlasting.*
> *Amen and Amen.*

Similar doxologies occur at the end of Books 2, 3, 4 (72:18-19; 89:52; 106:48). There is no doxology of that kind to end the final book, but the whole of Psalm 150 is a doxology, which fittingly concludes the whole Psalter with the call: 'Let everything that has breath praise the LORD. Praise the LORD.'

This division is old, because the Greek translation (LXX) contains it. The doxology which ends the fourth book is also quoted in 1 Chronicles 16:36 in connection with the ark of the covenant being brought into Jerusalem.

5.2 The Development of the Psalter
The gradual development of the Psalter is shown by several facts:

(a) In addition to the doxology at the end of the third book there is also a note, 'This concludes the prayers of David son of Jesse' (72:20). As psalms of David do come later than this (cf. 108-110, 138-145) it seems that Psalm 72 must have been the ending of an earlier collection later incorporated in the present Psalter.

(b) There are various psalms or portions which are repeated in the Psalter. They are:

Psalm 14	=	Psalm 53
Psalm 40:13-17	=	Psalm 70
Psalm 57:7-11	=	Psalm 108:1-5
Psalm 60:5-12	=	Psalm 108:6-13

Duplication is not unknown in the prophetical books where the same passage can occur in two different prophets (cf. Isaiah 2:2-4 with Micah 4:1-3) but very rare within the same book. Here it suggests that collections of psalms were in use prior to the present full Psalter.

(c) Within the Psalter there are clearly defined blocks of material, which appear to have been collected together prior to their being brought into the full Psalter. There are various smaller groups but the main subsidiary collections can be seen from the following table:

Groups of songs within the Psalter

Davidic Psalms   3-41; 51-72; 108-110; 138-145
Korahite Psalms   42-49; 84-85; 87-88
Elohistic Psalms   42-83
(using the name
Elohim in reference
to God)
Asaphite Psalms   73-83
Kingship Psalms   93-100
Praise Psalms   103-107
Songs of Ascent   120-134
(used on pilgrimage
to Jerusalem or on
return from Exile)
Hallelujah Psalms   111-118; 146-150
(beginning or ending
with 'Hallelujah')

(d) The use of the names for God in the Psalter also suggests stages in development. Psalms 1-41 (Book 1) mainly uses the covenant name *Yahweh* (taken into English as 'Jehovah'), with *Elohim* only occurring rarely. In Psalms 42-72 (Book 2) the main word for God is *Elohim*, while in Book 4 only *Yahweh* is used. The preference for one name for God over another comes out very clearly in the duplicate psalms. Whereas Psalm 14 uses the name *Yahweh*, its duplicate Psalm 53 has *Elohim* instead (there are some other minor alterations as well). The Jews felt great reverence for the name *Yahweh* and did not even pronounce it, substituting the Hebrew word *Adonai* (Lord) instead. Where the word *Yahweh* appears in the Hebrew text, nearly all English translations print the translation as LORD, whereas *Adonai* is printed as Lord. This practice regarding the use of 'Lord' carries over into the New Testament, where Lord is used of God and of Christ.

Clearly the Psalter is a collection of songs which was brought together over centuries, and finally, some time after the return from Exile, was put into their present form. It has often been called 'the hymnbook of the second temple', that is to say, the book used for song in the restored temple in Jerusalem (completed in 516 BC) and which remained in use until the destruction of Jerusalem in AD 70. While definitive proof of this is lacking, the evidence certainly points to the use of the Psalter in the Jewish observances before and after Christ, and the continuing use of the Psalms in early Christian worship (see Matt. 26:30; 1 Cor. 14:26; Jas. 5:13). The Psalter should not be compared to the building of a magnificent palace, but rather to the development over centuries of a cathedral. It bears the marks of various styles, distinctive development in stages, and yet an overall beauty as a whole book of the Bible.

There is another movement in the Psalter and that is towards a climax of praise. With all the varied moods of the human heart being apparent in earlier songs, it is clear that towards the end of the Psalter the exultant joy of God's people come to the fore. The final songs (144-150) are all ones of joyous praise which culminate in the call: 'Let everything that has breath praise the LORD. Praise the LORD' (150:6). The emphasis on praise towards the end of the Psalter seems deliberate, and this movement may well be the reason why the whole book was called *tehillim, songs of praise*.

5.3. The Numbering of the Psalms and Verses

While the numbering does not affect our understanding of the Psalms it does affect our use of the Bible and also commentaries on the text. There is a difference between the numbering of verses in the printed Hebrew Bible and most English versions. The reason for this is that in the Hebrew Bibles the titles of the Psalms are often regarded as a verse, and therefore the numbering of what we regard as the first verse will be verse 2. This means that for many psalms the Hebrew text shows one more verse than corresponding English versions. A few commentaries, especially those working from the Hebrew text, follow this system.

There is also a difference in the numbering of the Psalms themselves. The explanation for this lies in differences between the Hebrew Bible and the way in which the Psalms have come over into English. The Greek Bible subdivided two of the psalms (116 and 147) and twice joined two of them together (9/10 and 114/115). The Greek Bible also contains an additional psalm (151) which has never been reckoned by others as part of the Psalter. It is specifically noted in the title that this psalm is 'outside of the number'. The table below shows the two systems of numbering the psalms.

The Numbering of the Psalms

Hebrew and Protestant Bibles	Greek and Roman Catholic Bibles
1-8	1-8
9	9
10	
11-113	10-112
114	113
115	
	114
116	115
117-146	116-145
	146
147	147
148-150	148-150
	151 (Greek)

6. THE PSALMS AND GOD'S COVENANT

6.1 God and Covenant

The Bible speaks of God's relationship with his people as being a covenant. This relationship is the concept which gives unity to the whole of the biblical revelation. A covenant is a bond between God and man, and it is given by a sovereign God as an expression of his grace. In a formal way he expresses the relationship which exists between himself and his people. The central core of the covenant is that God promises, 'I will be your God and you shall be my people.' There is a progressive unfolding of this covenant throughout the Old Testament in various stages. The arrangement entered into by God at creation (Gen. 1-2) is reaffirmed after the flood (Gen. 6:18; 9:1-7). The call of Abraham is followed by a formal covenant arrangement (Gen. 12, 15, 17) which is supplemented by the covenant at Sinai (Exod. 20–23), following the Exodus from Egypt. After the introduction of kingship there is a special covenant in which the Davidic family is chosen (2 Sam. 7). Finally the Old Testament speaks about a new covenant which will come to pass (Jer. 31:31ff.; and see Heb. 8:7-13; 10:11-16).

From archaeological discoveries we know that God used a form of covenant which was familiar to the people. Kings who conquered another people forced them to enter into a covenant bond, in which they pledged themselves to serve him as their overlord. Many of the expressions used in the Old Testament of the covenant relationships can be paralleled from extra-biblical sources. The treaties or covenants from these sources follow a formalised pattern which has many similarities to the biblical covenants. The language employed in connection with them and various aspects of the ceremony of entering into a covenant or of enforcing one has its counterpart in the Old Testament.

6.2 Covenant in the Psalms

The word 'covenant' is not common in the Psalms, occurring only in the Hebrew text twenty-one times (25:10, 14; 44:17; 50:5, 16; 55:20; 74:20; 78:10, 37; 83:5 [NIV 'alliance']; 89:3, 28, 34, 39; 103:18; 105:8, 10; 106:45; 111:5, 9; 132:12). This is very similar to its use in the prophetical books of the Old Testament where it does not appear frequently. However, in both there are many other indications of the presence of the whole idea of covenant which underlies all the expressions of religious faith and feeling.

The Psalms contain many references to the earlier parts of the Old Testament and especially to the relationships between God and the patriarchs and with the people of Israel after they had been redeemed from Egypt. There is also reference to the covenant with David which is set out in 2 Samuel 7. A summary of the references is as follows:

Covenant with Abraham	105:1-22
Exodus and the Sinai Covenant	50:4-6, 16; 66:5-12; 78:12-53; 80:8-11; 81:1-16; 86:5; 99:7; 103:7; 105:23-38; 106:6-33; 114; 135:4, 8-9
Covenant with David	78:70-72; 89:1-52; 132:1-18

A series of other expressions also draws attention to the covenant relationship. Many of these expressions echo passages from the Pentateuch which speak of God and his people. Attention can be focused on a few of these terms.

(a) Israel is often spoken of as the people of God (Pss. 29:11; 81:11; 100:3). They were the inheritance of the Lord and often this phrase is used in conjunction with reference to them as God's people (Pss. 28:9; 78:62, 71; 94:5; 106:4-5). The phrase, 'I will be your God and you shall be my people', is echoed in passages like Psalm 95:7 which declare: 'for he is our God and we are the people of his pasture, the flock under his care.'

(b) The fact that God had chosen Israel to be his covenant people is emphasised in the Psalter. The word 'choose' is first used in Deuteronomy to describe Israel as God's choice (Deut. 7:6). The Psalms use it when recalling the wonder of God's election of Israel, and link it with other words which also point to the same sovereign choice. For example Psalm 33:12 speaks of Israel being chosen as God's inheritance, while Psalm 135:4 says that he chose Israel as 'his treasured possession'. This latter word is a rare one, being used to denote the utterly special position which Israel occupied before God (Exod. 19:5; Deut. 7:6; 14:2; Mal. 3:17).

(c) A variety of other terms associated with the covenant also make their appearance in the Psalter. The repeated use of the word 'servant' recalls how this expression is used of an inferior submitting to some great king. Thus King Ahaz sent word to the king of Assyria and said: 'I am your servant and your vassal' (2 Kgs. 16:7). Reference is also made to the oath by which the covenant was sworn, and also to such features as the ark of the covenant. There is also constant reference to God's faithfulness, which is not just expressing trust in God's character in general but in the specific form in which he revealed it in the covenant relationship. He was the God who even in the Ten Words declared that he would show his 'love to a thousand generations' of those who love him and keep his commandments (Exod. 20:6; Deut. 5:10).

6.3 The Covenant Relationship

The Psalms are not just individual expressions of religious understanding but rather they are distinctly expressions of faith which come out of a community of faith. The sphere from which the songs of Israel come was the covenant community, bound in common allegiance to the Lord. Some of the psalms are clearly communal because they use the first person plural ('we', 'our'), but even the majority, which use the first person singular ('I', 'my'), stem from a common commitment to the God of Israel.

The Psalms also show how vital the covenant relationship was, for the various songs put into poetry reveal the depth of the relationship with God. The faith of the psalmists is built upon God's word to his people, not upon individual personal promises. Knowledge of God's character and his works provided the common basis upon which individuals could live. The singers knew that God was concerned with their personal lives and with the good of each one of his covenant children. Psalm 84 puts it like this: 'For the LORD God is a sun and a shield; the LORD bestows favour and honour; no good thing does he withhold from those whose walk is blameless. O LORD Almighty, blessed is the man who trusts in you' (vs. 11-12; notice the connection with passages such as Gen. 15:1; 17:1). It is not surprising that they wanted to sing and rejoice in this relationship, for those who feared the Lord lacked no good thing (Ps. 34:9).

The central feature is God's kingship over his people. As covenant servants the people had to reaffirm in various ways their allegiance to the Lord. They paid their tribute of praise to him in extolling his creation or his great acts of redemption. In speaking of the majesty of his person they were offering spiritual sacrifices of praise to their King. When they sang of the beauties of God's law, this was another affirmation of the manner in which they were submitting to his claims upon them. The Psalter, therefore, served the broad purpose of reminding the people that they were God's people, the people who made up his flock (100:3). It also assisted them in maintaining a right relationship with him.

God's presence with his people in their history and also with them as individuals is reaffirmed in the Psalms. The long historical psalms in particular are recitals of the ways in which God's power had been shown in the life of Israel. At important times Israel had to repeat summaries of what God had done for her (see the declaration at the time of bringing the firstfruits [Deut. 26:3-10] and at the time of covenant renewal [Josh. 24:16-18]).

Finally, the Psalter emphasises the grace of God in forgiving and restoring an erring covenant people. Thus one psalmist can say to God: 'You were to Israel a forgiving God, though you punished their misdeeds' (Ps. 99:8). This was simply a reaffirmation of the declaration which God had made of himself when he proclaimed his own name to Moses on the occasion of the second giving of the tablets of stone (Exod. 34:6-7). David says that 'all the ways of the LORD are loving and faithful for those who keep the demands of his covenant'. Then on the basis of God's covenant he pleads: 'For the sake of your name, O LORD, forgive my iniquity, though it is great' (Ps. 25:10-11). A covenant God was true to his word of promise and would forgive and restore.

7. TYPES OF PSALMS

7.1 Identifying Types
In English we have various types of literature, just as we have various types of spoken language. To illustrate the latter first of all, we know that there are different styles in keeping with different occasions. Thus when a bridegroom stands up to speak at his wedding we can often predict the style his speech will take and some of the standard expressions which will be heard. There is an expected format to the speech and we are almost disappointed if it does not occur. Other similar types of speeches could be a politician conceding an election defeat or a speech presenting a gift to a fellow employee on his retirement.

The same thing holds true concerning written English. We adopt a particular style depending on the complete set of circumstances which has led to our writing. A letter written to one's mother will be quite different from a formal letter to one's solicitors concerning some property matter. The form in which a newspaper report on a traffic accident is written will be quite different from the style of the same paper's editorial. A variety of situations demand a known and predictable style.

We very quickly identify particular forms of writing, and subconsciously read them with that in mind. This is important because our mental approach to the form will often determine our attitude to the text. If, for example, we recognise a particular piece as a novel, we know we can read it quickly and even miss out some parts without affecting the flow of the story. However, if we try that with other pieces of writing, for example, a set of instructions on how to construct an unassembled piece of furniture, we could run into great difficulty and create problems for ourselves.

So it is when we come to the Psalms. There are various types of psalms and we have to recognise the differences. Look at these three quotations from successive psalms:

O LORD my God, I take refuge in you;
            save and deliver me from all who pursue me,
or they will tear me like a lion and rip me to pieces with
            no-one to rescue me (Ps. 7:1-2).

O LORD, our Lord,
            how majestic is your name in all the earth!
You have set your glory above the heavens (Ps. 8:1).

I will praise you, O LORD,
            with all my heart;
I will tell of all your wonders.
I will be glad and rejoice in you;
            I will sing praise to your name,
                        O Most High (Ps. 9:1-2).

They are all quite different and are indicative of different styles. The first is from a lament in which an individual is asking God for protection as he faces false accusations from his enemies. The second comes from a hymn of praise, and particularly one which is praising God for his creation. The third example is from a hymn in which there is mention of rejoicing and exaltation of God's name. As we note the different types of psalms it helps us to recognise other psalms of a similar nature and to read them accordingly.

There are several benefits to be gained by looking at the Psalms in this way. It means above all else that we are viewing them as whole units, rather than just individual verses. That is to say, we are considering them as a total piece of literary composition and reading them in that light. We come to them knowing that they are not like a telephone directory, in which there is no necessary connection between successive entries; any connection which might appear is quite accidental, not by design. In the Psalms however, the connection is there simply because each psalm is a poem which holds together as a unit, and therefore we must interpret it in that way. To extract a single verse and isolate it from its context in the psalm is to distort the meaning. Thus a phrase such as 'I will fear no evil' (Ps. 23:4) should not be taken out of that psalm and used as an isolated encouragement. Its meaning can only be seen in the light of the whole psalm and the certainty of God's care as a shepherd of his people. Similarly the opening verse of Psalm 89, 'I will sing of the LORD's great love for ever; with my mouth I will make your faithfulness known through all generations', is not an isolated promise concerning God's faithfulness. It comes in a psalm which is putting into poetry the covenant which God made with David (see 2 Sam. 7). To extract the one verse and apply its teaching without reference to the setting in the psalm is to teach contrary to the express message of the psalm itself. This principle of interpreting a verse within the unit of which it forms a part, applies, of course, to the whole of the Bible.

This type of approach also lets us ask questions regarding the function of any particular song. From the Books of Chronicles we know that particular songs were appropriate to special occasions such as the bringing of the ark of the covenant into Jerusalem (1 Chr. 16:7-36, and cf. Pss. 96, 105:1-5 and 106:1, 47, 48), or for use at the dedication of the Temple (2 Chr. 5-7 and especially cf. 5:13 and 7:3, 6 with Ps. 136). If we can find out something about the function which a particular psalm fulfilled, that helps us to understand it better. Sometimes this may be apparent from within the psalm itself, or the title may show how the psalm was used. Clearly the psalms were meant to be sung and many were used in appropriate settings during the religious life of the people. We can compare this to the way in which modern Christian hymnbooks not only list hymns according to content but also show the appropriate hymns for particular occasions (e.g. Easter, Pentecost, Christmas, Baptism, the Lord's Supper, harvest thanksgiving).

A word of warning is also needed. This method of listing psalms according to type should be used as a valuable tool to help our understanding but should not be pressed to an extreme. There is the

constant danger that a psalm will be classified according to a specific
type, and in so doing its individual distinctiveness may be overlooked.
The characteristics of a particular psalm have to be taken seriously so
that common features of a group do not cause us to overlook important
variations.

7.2 Classification of Types of Psalms

An outline will now be given to show some of the main types of psalms
and briefly to indicate their main characteristics. It should be remembered that any classification has to be fluid, and we need to recognise
that certain groups of psalms overlap in their characteristics.

Hymns Many psalms come into this category, for the Psalter contains
a great number of songs of joy in the Lord. Typical examples are
Psalms 92, 103, and 113. Nearly all of them share some common
features:
  a) they begin with a call to worship
  b) they give reasons why God is to be praised
  c) they have other calls to worship, many of which conclude the psalm.
It is the second feature which takes the greatest space, for the psalmists
draw attention to the concrete things which God has done and which
should provoke praise.

Laments These are cries of distress, either by an individual (e.g. Pss.
3, 7, 13, 17, 26) or by the community as a whole (e.g. Pss. 12, 44, 60,
74). Enemies are mentioned but rarely are they identified clearly.
These psalms may have several features:
  a) the psalmist pleads for help from God
  b) complaints are made which show why the psalmist is calling on God
  c) either a confession of sin, or a profession of innocence
  d) often there is an expression of confidence in God's power to help
  e) a song of praise may conclude the psalm.

Thanksgiving Psalms When they respond to God's answer to a cry of
need, the psalmists extol him for the answered prayer. Psalms in this
group (such as 18, 32, 34) are characterised by:
  a) praise of the Lord or a blessing
  b) testimony to God's goodness in his life
  c) often there is a restating of the lament
  d) a description of God's salvation.

Psalms of Remembrance Song was clearly used as a medium to recount the wonderful deeds of the Lord (cf. Moses' song, Deut. 32) and the Psalter has several story-telling psalms which recount the history of Israel. The psalms of this type are often much longer than others (e.g., Pss. 78, 105, 106, 135, 136) and they are distinguished by:

    a) retelling the great events in Israel's history
    b) focusing attention particularly on the Exodus from Egypt
    c) stressing the faithfulness of God to his covenant promises
    d) doing this to elicit praise, or to encourage future generations to trust in the Lord.

Wisdom Psalms There are psalms which share some features in common with the so-called Wisdom books like Proverbs, Ecclesiastes, Job and the Song of Solomon. These psalms (such as 37 and 73) have as their characteristics:

    a) a concern for the practical issues of life
    b) a clear distinction between the two ways which face us in life
    c) a struggle with the problem of why the wicked seem to prosper as compared with the righteous
    d) hints that the final solution lies in the life to come.

Kingship Psalms There is a group of psalms which all speak of God as King (29, 47, 93, 95-99). These psalms (with which some others may be associated (e.g., 24, 110) have among their characteristics:

    a) the assertion that the LORD ('Yahweh') reigns
    b) that this rule was from of old
    c) that this rule is not only over Israel but the whole world
    d) in Zion the God of Israel is extolled as universal King.

Psalms of Trust The Psalms are full of expressions of confidence in the God of Israel. However, a group of psalms (including 11, 16, 23, 27, 91, and 125) share in a specific way several features in common:

    a) while their structure is not the same they share a common content
    b) in the face of enemies there is calm trust in the LORD
    c) their declarations have a ring of certainty about them
    d) they use a variety of metaphors to describe God ('refuge', 'rock', 'shepherd', 'help').

8. GOD IN THE PSALMS

8.1 Reverence in Worship

Any teaching of the Psalter has to be considered in relation to the fact that the Psalms are songs of worship. The presentation of teaching about God and his ways is given in the context of worship of him. Thus all the psalms are God-centred because they are prayers *to* him or songs *about* him. Our response in studying the Psalms should be one of worship, and our love to him should be deepened through understanding better their message. 'How my love for God is kindled by the Psalms!' exclaimed Augustine.

The Book of Psalms is a tremendous testimony to the living God, and its use throughout centuries by the Christian church has had a far greater influence than is often realised. In the liturgies of the Christian church the language of the Psalter features very prominently, while the thought of the Psalter has been influential either through its direct use or through hymnology based on Psalter passages. Much of our Christian understanding of God and our relationship with him is based on the Psalter.

In their focus on God the Psalms show us how vital he was in the life of Israel. Our knowledge of that relationship comes largely from the Psalms and when God's attributes are being set forth, it is in the context of prayer and praise. We should not think, though, that the type of understanding of God revealed in the Psalms was universal in Israel. The fact that the prophets had to direct condemnatory speeches against the people shows a different picture.

8.2 The Majestic God

The Psalms are full of praise of God, and this praise takes two forms. In some passages the psalmists simply declare God's praise, but in many of them they describe who the Lord is and what he has done. Thus the opening and closing of Psalm 103 voices praise to God:

> Praise the LORD, O my soul;
> > all my inmost being, praise his holy name (v. 1).

> Praise the LORD, all his works everywhere in his dominion.
> > Praise the LORD, O my soul (v. 22).

In between these two exclamations of praise is the main body of the psalm which contains descriptions of God and his works like this:

who forgives all your sins
and heals all your diseases;
who redeems your life from the pit
and crowns you with love and compassion;
who satisfies your desires with good things,
so that your youth is renewed like the eagle's (vs. 3-5).

The language of praise is accompanied by content, which tells us things about the God who was being worshipped. The Psalms are not empty liturgy but are full of words which direct attention to the glorious person of the living God.

The picture which the Psalms present of God is that of a sovereign God before whom we all must come. The greatness of God is stressed in various ways including the use of a distinctive name. He is said to be *Elyon*, the Most High. This word occurs almost only in poetical passages in the Old Testament, and most of these are in the Psalms (18 occurrences out of 30). At times it is used in parallelism with *Elohim* (God) or *Shaddai* (the Almighty), but other times by itself. Psalm 47:1-2, one of the songs of the sons of Korah, provides a good example of its usage:

Clap your hands, all you nations;
Shout to God with cries of joy.
How awesome is the LORD Most High,
the great King over all the earth!

God's character is stressed at times in contrast to the heathen gods, who are only lifeless idols. When the nations say, 'Where is their God?' Israel can reply, 'Our God is in heaven, and he does whatsoever pleases him' (Ps. 115:2-3). The response which is called for when one is confronted with the greatness of God is to bow down in worship before him (Ps. 96:4-9).

But though God is so high, yet he stoops to make himself known to men. 'He made known his ways to Moses, his deeds to the people of Israel' (Ps. 103:7). The same psalm goes on to liken God to a father who has compassion on his children, and who knows their frailty (vs. 13-16). In him David also found a substitute father and mother (Ps. 27:10). The picture of God presented in the Psalms is of one involved in the life of his children so that he is a shepherd for them (23:1; 80:1); or like a bird who protects her young under her wings (91:1, 4); or a judge who dispenses justice (50:4, 6); or a warrior who is a shield to them (18:2). The great wonder is that the God who calls the stars by name is the same God who heals the broken-hearted and binds up their wounds (Ps. 147:3-4).

8.3 God the Creator

The doctrine of creation as set out in Genesis 1 is reaffirmed in the Psalter. God had only to speak the word and the world came into being:

> *By the word of the LORD were the heavens made,*
> *their starry host by the breath of his mouth....*
> *For he spoke, and it came to be;*
> *he commanded, and it stood firm* (Ps. 33:6, 9).

Genesis 1 is turned into a prayer in Psalm 8, and man's role as vice-regent is again proclaimed. All of creation has been placed under him, and God has made him ruler over everything which has been created (Ps. 8:5-8). Psalm 104 comprises a long song in praise of creation, in which there are many echoes of Genesis 1.

Throughout the Psalter the creation is depicted as God's handiwork, not something divine in itself or originating by itself. Hence there is no worship of nature, only worship of the Creator. He is the God who has shown his power in the creation of the world. The inference drawn from this is that because God is so powerful, then he will care for his own. There is a formula in use in the Psalms which joins together the thought of the Lord as the Maker of heaven and earth with the idea of blessing for his people. This formula may well go back very early in the Old Testament for Melchizedek blessed Abram saying, 'Blessed be Abram by God Most High, Creator of heaven and earth' (Gen. 14:19). By the right of creation the Lord controls the world, and is therefore able to bring blessing and protection to Israel (Pss. 115:12-15; 121:2; 124:8; 134:3; 146:5-6).

There are also hymns of praise to God as the Creator who sustains all his creatures, animals as well as mankind. A group of psalms (104:24-30; 136:25; 145:15-16) speak of God as opening his hand to provide for the needs of his creatures, and they even speak of his 'steadfast love' for them. This term occurs often of God's covenant love for his own people, but it can be applied to his gracious concern for all his creatures (Pss. 33:5; 119:64; 136:25). This usage of covenant terminology may surprise us, yet God made a covenant not just with Noah but with all living creatures (Gen. 9:9-17). The scope of God's concern is as extensive as his creation in its entirety.

8.4 The Compassionate God

Special attention needs to be given to this aspect. The very fact that the psalmists come in prayer to God is a recognition of their need of him and his forgiving grace. They come because they know of his righteousness, and how they have offended against him. David, in his cry for mercy in Psalm 51, recognises that his sins against Uriah and Bathsheba were horrendous in the sight of God, and includes them in his confession to the Holy One of Israel: 'Against you, you only, have I sinned and done what is evil in your sight' (Ps. 51:4). Repeatedly the psalmists confess the sinfulness of man in the strongest terms. Humans are sinful right from their mother's womb (51:5; 58:3), and all their actions are corrupt and vile (14:1). In the New Testament, when Paul comes to convince his readers of the universal sinfulness of humanity, he does so by citing from six psalms and one passage from Isaiah (Rom. 3:10-18), and even his conclusion in that passage echoes a psalm: 'Therefore no-one will be declared righteous in his sight by observing the law' (Rom. 3:20; cf. Ps. 143:2b).

The Psalms do not only paint the extent of sin, but they also point to the grace of God shown in the forgiveness of sins. There is a group of psalms which Luther once called 'the Pauline Psalms' (32, 51, 130, 143) because they teach the same truths which Paul has in his epistles. Luther said of these psalms: 'They all teach that the forgiveness of sins comes, without the law and without works, to the man who believes. ... and when David sings, "There is forgiveness with you, that you may be feared," this is just what Paul says, "God has concluded them all in unbelief, that he might have mercy upon all" (Rom. 11:32). Thus no man may boast of his own righteousness. That word, "That you may be feared", dusts away all merit, and teaches us to uncover our heads before God, and confess, *it is mere forgiveness, not merit at all; remission, not satisfaction.*' We are brought into a relationship with God in which we enjoy the forgiveness of sins solely by the free grace of God. The teaching that we are forgiven by faith alone is one which is imbedded in the Psalms: 'Blessed are they whose transgressions are forgiven, whose sins are covered. Blessed is the man whose sin the Lord will never count against him' (Rom. 4:7-8, quoting Ps. 32:1-2). God will not despise a broken and a contrite heart (Ps. 51:17), and those who come to him will find that their cry for mercy will be answered by his declaration of forgiveness (Ps. 130:1-4).

The God who forgives sin is the one who works in the hearts of the penitent. Many of the psalms reveal the profound spiritual experiences through which the writers went and they lay the foundation for truths which the New Testament develops more fully. Profound sorrow for sin accompanied confession to God (38:18), and there is a recognition of the need for a profound spiritual change. Psalm 51 highlights this in the case of David, who pleaded for a clean heart and an internal change by the work of the Holy Spirit (v. 10). This experience is described more fully in the New Testament in terms of the new birth (John 3:5, 6; 2 Cor. 5:17; Gal. 6:15). Those who experienced it could sing for joy because God gives his forgiven children a new song to sing, 'a hymn of praise to our God' (Ps. 40:3).

9. THE KINGSHIP OF GOD

9.1 The Idea of Kingship

The idea of God's kingship is central to the Bible. It appears from the beginning of Genesis, even though the actual words 'king' and 'kingdom' do not appear till later. The basic idea underlying the Bible's presentation of the relationship between God and humanity is that the Creator God is a sovereign who exercises his rule over his world and over his human creatures in particular. The kingdom of God is concerned with God's people, in God's place, and under God's rule. Living under God's covenant rule, men were directed in their response to God by the various commandments he gave them. As loyal servants they yielded obedience to him as their master.

At the time of the Exodus from Egypt the children of Israel were brought into a formal relationship with God and with one another by the formation of the nation of Israel. At Mount Sinai God entered into a covenant with them, which regulated the life of the nation. By this covenant God set the conditions under which his people would live. He initiated the covenant and he was sovereign in the relationship.

As noted above, the pattern which the covenant at Sinai takes has been shown to be similar to other covenants in the ancient Near East. Political treaties were entered into by countries, especially when one had been conquered by another. The king of the more powerful country (the conqueror) initiated a new relationship with the less powerful (the conquered). The Great King set out his demands on his new subjects, and in turn promised to defend them if they were attacked. In the Book of Exodus God is the Great King who establishes a new form of covenant relationship with his people Israel.

When God redeemed his people from Egypt, Moses and the people sang a song extolling his triumph. The song tells of the LORD's power over Pharaoh (Exod. 15:1-7), the sea (15:8-12), and the nations generally (15:13-18). The Lord is a mighty warrior who saves (v. 2), destroys the enemy (v. 6), does wonders (v. 11), guides his redeemed people (v. 13), and who reigns for ever and ever (v. 18). This last verse is important because it speaks of the eternal reign of the LORD: *The LORD will reign for ever and ever.* The fitting outcome of the victor's conquest is that he rules his people. How that takes place is spelled out in detail later in Exodus. The people have become a royal priesthood and a holy nation (19:6). Everyone in Israel was to be a priest to God, while the nation as a whole was to be consecrated to God. The detailed laws which follow in Exodus and Leviticus show how the King desired his subjects to live under his authority. Specific details were given of the structures in life which were to regulate their lives. The kingdom of God from the period of Moses can be illustrated in the following diagram:

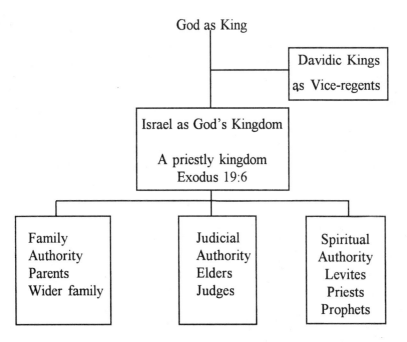

God as King

Davidic Kings as Vice-regents

Israel as God's Kingdom

A priestly kingdom
Exodus 19:6

| Family Authority Parents Wider family | Judicial Authority Elders Judges | Spiritual Authority Levites Priests Prophets |

This form of government, which is often called 'a theocracy', continued until the appointment of the first king of Israel in the person of Saul. When he was succeeded by David, God entered into a special covenant with him, adopting the Davidic family and appointing them as his vice-regents. During the period of the monarchy God was still the ultimate King, but the Davidic kings were to display his rule among men, and they were also to point to the coming of the Messiah as the final King.

9.2 The LORD's Kingship in the Psalms

It is hardly surprising that the central fact of Israel's faith, that the Lord was their King, should be so prominent in the songs of the people. They proclaim him as their own LORD and call upon others to acknowledge him also (96:10).

The Psalms speak of God as the one who is King for ever and ever (10:16). He is seated on his heavenly throne (11:4; 29:10) and as the Creator is clearly the 'king from of old' (74:12). Thus he is rightly King over all the earth (47:2, 7) and all nations are to be told, 'The LORD reigns' (96:10).

But more particularly he is the King of Israel, and many of the psalms which speak in this way of him link his Kingship with Zion (Jerusalem). Zion is called 'the city of the Great King' (48:2) and the declaration is made: 'Great is the LORD in Zion' (99:2). It is striking the number of times that God is called 'the Great King' or reference is made to his greatness. Several psalms proclaiming his kingship are grouped together in the Psalter (93, 95-100). These psalms use the expression, 'The LORD reigns' (or, 'is King'). This recalls the shout which went up when Absalom assumed the kingship: 'Absalom is king in Hebron' (2 Sam. 15:10). When used of the LORD this acclamation has something of a dynamic ring about it, rather like the triumphant Easter hymn, 'Jesus Christ is risen today, Alleluia!'

He is also the King who made Israel his own flock, and he calls them 'my people' (50:7; 81:8, 11). He created Israel, and the people can say, 'We are his people, the sheep of his pasture' (100:3). The LORD chose 'Jacob to be his own, Israel to be his treasured possession' (135:4, and cf. Exod. 19:5).

Some psalms also fix attention on the final outcome of human history, when the Lord will be seen to be King of all nations. He will come to judge 'the world in righteousness and the peoples in his truth'

(96:13). Because he reigns, even the distant isles can be called upon to rejoice (97:1). It is as if the psalmist is picturing the result after the final judgment when God's universal dominion will be established.

9.3 The Davidic Kingship

There are also many psalms which speak of the kingship of the line of David. They show how the covenant with David (2 Sam. 7) was understood in Israel. If we follow the titles of the psalms, David himself calls God 'my King' (5:2), and recognises that his own authority came from God. Two of the psalms (89 and 132) are expositions of the covenant which God made with David (2 Sam. 7), and they show the special place which the Davidic kingship occupied in Israel. In psalms such as 18, 20, 21 David acknowledges that his strength comes from God and that his victories are really God's victories.

The king also speaks of the people as not his own, but as God's. He can appeal to God in these terms for them: 'Save your people and bless your inheritance; be their shepherd and carry them for ever' (28:9). The evil doers are described as crushing 'your people, O LORD; they oppress your inheritance' (94:5).

This attitude of the king also helps us to explain some of the difficult passages in the Psalter in which there is appeal to God to destroy the enemies. The contexts make it clear that the enemies were not the king's personal enemies but really they were enemies of God. Thus in Psalm 5 David prays for his enemies to be banished for their sins, and he gives as the reason, 'for they have rebelled *against you*' (v. 10). For a fuller discussion of these passages see pp. 60-62.

9.4 Our Response to the Kingship of God

Two important aspects come out of the Psalter in relation to the impact that the teaching about God as King should have upon us.

Firstly, our response should be one of worship. Repeatedly in the kingship psalms the thought of worship appears, especially because God is not only a King, but is also a holy God.

> *Come, let us bow down in worship,*
>   *let us kneel before the LORD* (95:6).

> *Ascribe to the LORD the glory due to his name;*
>   *bring an offering and come into his courts.*

Worship the LORD in the splendour of his holiness;
   tremble before him, all the earth.
Say among the nations, 'The LORD reigns' (96:8-10).

Exalt the LORD our God
     and worship at his footstool;
     he is holy.

Exalt the LORD our God
     and worship at his holy mountain,
     for the LORD our God is holy (99:5, 9).

In a similar way the message of Revelation 19 concludes with the mighty shout: 'Hallelujah! For our Lord God Almighty reigns. Let us rejoice and be glad and give him glory!' John in response to this fell at the angel messenger's feet, but the angel said: 'Do not do it! Worship God!' (Rev. 19:6-10). A knowledge of God as King should bring us to his footstool in worship.

Secondly, the thought of the kingship of God should be a stimulus to us in regard to missionary work. The Psalms present to us the picture of the nations of the world being subject to our God. God is so great that the nations must come and worship before him. This picture is not just a vision of the future, but something which stirs the psalmists with a real missionary urge. They call upon the world at large to come and worship the LORD (see Pss. 57:8-11; 66:1-4; 67:2-5; 96:3, 7-13; 99:2-3; 100:1-3; 108:3; 113:3-4; 117:1-2; 145:21). There is an eagerness about their longing to see all nations bowing before the King and being subject to his rule. The vision of the ultimate kingdom of God impels them with a real missionary spirit.

10. GOD'S LAW IN THE PSALMS

10.1 A Sovereign and His Laws

The laws of the Old Testament are not abstract moral laws, but the requirements of a covenant God. They are the demands of a personal, sovereign God upon his subjects. God spoke his law on Mount Sinai and then it was given in written form, both as the tablets of stone and also as the book of the covenant (Exod. 24:7) and the Book of Deuteronomy (Deut. 31:9). The personal character of the law is emphasised by the exhortations which occur so often, encouraging

Israel to keep the law and to be holy because the LORD is holy (Lev. 20:26).

The way in which the law was given to Israel places stress on the fact that it was given to a redeemed people. They had been brought out of slavery in Egypt by the Lord, who had shown great favour and grace to them in their need. There could be no thought that salvation was going to be based on their obedience to God's law. Even at Mount Sinai the people had sinned against him and provoked him to anger. They had not, and could not, merit God's favour (Deut. 7:7-8; 9:4-6).

Israel was taught that God's covenant was unchangeable. The promises to the patriarchs, Abraham, Isaac, and Jacob could not be broken (see, for example, Exod. 3:15-17). This meant also that the basic requirements of the covenant, God's law, were also unchangeable. The psalmists say that God remembered his covenant (105:42; 106:45). Moreover, he brought his people into the land of Canaan so 'that they might keep his precepts and observe his laws' (105:45).

To enforce his law upon the people, God promised blessings if they obeyed. Following an initial experience of God's grace when they were redeemed from slavery, further obedience would result in greater experience of God's grace. God's choice of Israel came first, and then as the people obeyed God a fuller appropriation of the blessings of salvation became theirs.

The opposite truth was that curses were expressed against the people if they were unfaithful to God's covenant (for the curses see especially Leviticus 26 and Deuteronomy 28). The Psalms reflect both these aspects, since blessings are pronounced on those who walk in the way of the LORD (1:1-2; 119:1), and often judgments are expressed against those who have gone their own way (1:6).

10.2 God's Law in the Psalms

We saw earlier that the Psalter came out of the covenant community. Hence it is quite understandable that a community which sang about God as their Great King would also sing about his law. In Psalm 81 God challenges his people to listen to his warning, and says:

> *You shall have no foreign god among you;*
> *you shall not bow down to an alien god.*
> *I am the LORD your God, who brought you up out of Egypt*
> (vs. 9-10).

These words, of course, are taken from, or echo, the opening of the Decalogue, and contain parts of the preface and the first two commandments (cf. Exod. 20:2-4). They are used to re-assert the claims which the Redeemer God had upon his people. They had to own him as their god, and not yield obedience or worship to any other.

There is a group of psalms which concentrates on God's law, and they focus particular attention on the blessings which come to those who obey it. They make God's law the object of thanks and praise, and they teach us especially the blessings of the law. Three of them in particular stand out because of their emphasis on walking in the way of God's law.

(a) Psalm 1 sets the pattern for the whole Psalter, as we have already seen (section 3.3). It opens with the word of blessing on those whose delight is in the law of the LORD. The contrast with the wicked is brought out in a very striking way:

[positive]	1. Blessed is the man who does not walk . . . Rather . . . Result
[negative]	2. Not so the wicked! . . . Rather . . . Result
	3. Summary For the LORD ...

(b) The thought of this psalm is extended in Psalm 19, which first of all refers to the declaration of God's glory in his creation (vs. 1-6) before it goes on to speak of the preciousness of God's law. The language used about the law is deliberate and most revealing. A variety of nouns is employed to describe God's revealed will (law, statutes, precepts, commands, and ordinances). The adjectives used in reference to them highlight the nature of God's law (perfect, trustworthy, right, radiant, pure, sure), while the succession of verbs (e.g. reviving, making wise, giving joy, giving light, enduring) tell of the impact which God's law has on his children.

(c) The high point of praise of the law comes in Psalm 119, which is the longest song in the Book. It is an acrostic psalm divided into twenty-two sections, with every verse in each section beginning with the same letter of the Hebrew alphabet. This is not a sudden outpouring of the heart such as other psalms are, for it is not the sort of poem which could be composed quickly. The psalm is a beautiful work of art singing the praise of God's law, for every verse but three (vs. 84, 121, 122) contains a virtual synonym for 'law' ('word', 'statutes', 'testimonies' etc.). The psalmist varies the expressions to portray how wonderful God's law is, and to show yet again how it serves as a lamp to the feet and as a light to the path (119:105).

10.3 The Response to God's Law

God's law was clearly precious to the psalmists. This contrasts with the modern view of law which may respect God's demands and try to obey them but hardly think of them as exhilarating. But that is precisely the way believers in the Old Testament considered God's laws.

> *The ordinances of the LORD are sure*
> *and altogether righteous.*
> *They are more precious than gold,*
> *than much pure gold;*
> *they are sweeter than honey,*
> *than honey from the comb* (19:9-10).

> *How sweet are your words to my taste,*
> *sweeter than honey to my mouth!* (119:103).

> *Because I love your commands*
> *more than gold, more than pure gold,*
> *and because I consider all your precepts right,*
> *I hate every wrong path* (119:127-128).

God's law directed the ways of his people. At the time of renewing the covenant just before entry into the land of Canaan Moses said: 'What other nation is so great as to have such righteous decrees and laws as this body of laws which I am setting before you today? ... Teach them to your children and to their children after them' (Deut. 4:8-9). Thus the psalmists can ask for God to teach his way (25:4-5; 119:33) and also make mention of God's command to teach succeeding generations (78:5-8). In pleading for forgiveness David promised that if this was granted he would then 'teach transgressors your ways, and sinner will turn back to you' (51:13).

God's law was the object of meditation. As the children of Israel went into the promised land, they did so with Joshua's words ringing in their ears: 'Do not let this Book of the Law depart from your mouth; meditate upon it day and night, so that you may be careful to do everything written in it' (Josh. 1:8). The Psalms show us how the people had taken this command to heart and practised it.

> *Blessed is the man ...*
> *[whose] delight is in the law of the LORD*
>   *and on his law he meditates day and night* (1:2).

> *I will remember the deeds of the LORD;*
>   *yes, I will remember your miracles of long ago.*
> *I will meditate on all your works*
>   *and consider all your mighty deeds* (77:11-12).

> *I meditate on your precepts*
>   *and consider your ways* (119:15).

Meditation, according to the Psalter, consists of three things. It is firstly grounded in the *truth* of God. God has spoken in his word, and that word is to be hidden in the heart (119:11). Meditation stimulates thought about it and heightens the meaning of a passage. Secondly, meditation is a response to the *love* of God. Faith in God is evidence of a personal relationship with him, and love to him is stimulated by meditation upon his word. Thirdly, meditation is really an aspect of *praise* of God. It is worship of the living God and consists of adoration of God and his works. In meditating on his word our attention is directed to God himself.

11. SPECIAL TYPES OF PSALMS

11.1 Hymns

In this and the following three sections we look more closely at four specific types of psalm. A hymn is a song which extols the glory and greatness of God. Songs other than those in the Psalter also come into this category. The Song of Moses and the Song of Miriam (Exod. 15:1-18, 21) are good examples, as are Hannah's Song (1 Sam. 2:1-10) and Hezekiah's Song (Isa. 38:10-20).

The hymns have a definite structure like this:

A. Introduction: Call to Worship

Usually the hymn commences with a call to worship in the form of an imperative in the second person plural. Sometimes it can be a form in which the person calls upon his own soul to praise the Lord, such as in Psalms 103 and 104, 'Praise the LORD, O my soul.'

B. Main Section: The Reasons for Praise

Often this section is introduced by a clause beginning with the word 'for', followed by the explanation of the motives behind the praise. Sometimes this is disguised in English translation for the Hebrew word which is normally used (*ki*) can be translated by more than one English word (e.g. in Psalm 8:3 it is translated by 'when': *when I consider your heavens* ...). If this 'for' is omitted in the Hebrew, there will be other words which serve the same function, such as can be seen in Psalm 103:3ff. or 104:2ff.

C. A Repetition of the Opening Call to Worship

Frequently the same sort of call resounds again at the end of the song.

A good example of the hymn is Psalm 117, the shortest song in the book.

A. *Praise the LORD, all you nations;*
   Extol him, all you peoples.

B. *For great is his love towards us*
   and the faithfulness of the LORD endures forever.

C. *Praise the LORD.*

Martin Luther wrote a long commentary on this shortest of all psalms because he thought that these two verses were basic to our understanding of the love of God. They stress the covenant love of the LORD to his people and the missionary vision of reaching out to the nations.

Three major topics provide the motive for praise of the Lord in these psalms. Firstly, there is a group of psalms (66:1-12; 100; 114; 149) which praise God for the fact that he created (or redeemed) Israel. They have much in common with songs outside the Psalter such as Exodus 15:1-8, Deuteronomy 32:1-43, Habakkuk 3:2-19, and Isaiah 52:7-10. Secondly, another group of psalms sing the praise of God as Creator of the world, either in a brief form such as in Psalm 8, or much more extensively as in Psalm 104. In this latter psalm even the order of Genesis 1 is preserved as the psalmist describes poetically the wonder of God's creation (104:2-4 = 1:6-8; 104:5-9 = 1:9-10; 104:10-13 = implied in 1:6-10; 104:19-23 = 1:14-18; 104:24-26 = 1:20-22; 104:27-30 = 1:24-30). Thirdly, the final group of hymns sing of God as the Creator and covenant God who is the ruler of history (33; 103; 113; 117; 145; 146; 147; 150).

11.2 Lamentations

The lamentations form the largest group in the Psalter. This term is rather misleading, as it suggests that these psalms are full of sadness and are completely pessimistic in spirit. That is not altogether true as many of them contain strong affirmations of trust in the Lord. Other terms such as 'complaint', 'confidence in distress', or 'appeal for help' may be closer to the mark in describing them, because they are appeals to God to come and intervene in particular situations and to bring his deliverance. In this way they are songs of praise, however muted, because the psalmists know of God's power to help.

As with other types of psalms the lamentations have similarities with various parts of the Old Testament outside the Psalter. Job even cursed the day he was born and wonders why it was that he did not perish at birth (Job 3:1-26). The Book of Jeremiah contains several long laments by the prophet (1:18-12:6; 15:10-21; 17:14-18; 18:19-23; 20:7-13; 20:14-18).

The question arises as to why so many psalms are of this kind, as they far outnumber any other type of psalm. What they emphasise is the reality of religious experience, and the fact that believers do not always have periods of great joy. In this way these psalms are so realistic of the experiences of God's people. They pass through times when events overwhelm them, as they are not immune to the changing situations of human life.

There is a considerable amount of individual variation, depending upon the particular situation of the psalmist. The psalms which have been designated as the penitential psalms since the early Christian centuries are also included in this grouping (Pss. 6, 32, 38, 51, 102, 130, 143). The following features are characteristic of this type of psalm, though not all may necessarily be present or there may be variation in order:

A. Address to God
This can be very brief or expanded into a longer form.

B. Complaint

The form of complaint varies depending on whether it is a song of the community, who mainly complain about famine or attack by enemies; or an individual complaining from sickness or from fear. The penitential psalms refer to the psalmist's awareness of sin and his plea for forgiveness.

C. Confession of Trust

In midst of complaints the psalmists often express confidence in God as the one who can help, and frequently they introduce this with words like 'but' or 'nevertheless'.

D. Petition

Appeal is made to God to help in the particular situation which the psalmist is facing. At times reasons are given why this should happen.

E. Words of Assurance

The psalmist expresses certainty that his prayer is heard and that God will come to his aid.

F. Vow of Praise

In the confidence that God has heard, the psalmist pledges himself to call on God's name and to tell what God has done for him.

A good example is Psalm 13, which has this pattern:

A. *How long, O LORD? Will you forget me forever?*
How long will you hide your face from me? (v. 1)

B. *How long must I wrestle with my thoughts*
and every day have sorrow in my heart?
How long will my enemy triumph over me? (v. 2)

C. *But I trust in your unfailing love;*
my heart rejoices in your salvation (v. 5).

D. *Look on me and answer, O LORD my God.*
Give light to my eyes, or I will sleep in death;
my enemy will say, "I have overcome him,"
and my foes will rejoice when I fall (vs. 3-4).

E. *I will sing to the LORD,*
for he has been good to me (v. 6).

The setting of some of these psalms of complaint suggests that they may have been said or sung at the Temple in conjunction with some form of sacrificial offering. When Hannah prayed in the building housing the tabernacle at Shiloh, Eli watched her praying and accused her of drunkenness. In reply she spoke of how she was pouring out her heart before God. She said: 'I have been praying here out of my great anguish and grief.' Eli then responded: 'Go in peace, and may the God of Israel grant what you have asked of him' (1 Sam. 1:9-17). It may have been customary to give such a benediction in response to similar complaints, including many of the complaints recorded in the Psalter. There is often an abrupt change in mood in the psalm, with the indication in some that a similar declaration by the LORD's servant has been made. Thus the 85th Psalm has a series of petitions by the psalmist followed by the words:

> *I will listen to what God the LORD will say;*
> *he promises peace to his people, his saints –*
> *but let them not return to folly* (85:8).

An assurance like that could well have been made to the psalmist by the person, like Eli, ministering at the altar, and this may explain the more joyful note at the end of the psalm.

11.3 Thanksgiving Psalms

There is a close connection between the thanksgiving psalms and both the psalms of lamentation and the hymns of praise. The lamentations often have a concluding note of praise. In comparison with them the thanksgiving psalms expand that type of song considerably. There is also the difference that in the complaints the song of praise is in *anticipation* of the deliverance of the Lord, while in the thanksgiving psalms the praise is for the deliverance which has *already come*.

The comparison with the hymns is also helpful to see the essential difference between them and the thanksgiving psalms. There are two ways in which God is praised in the Psalms. He is praised in general terms simply for what he is in himself or as he is manifested in his creation. On the other hand, he is praised for specific acts of deliverance. In the first case the praise is describing something wonderful about God, while in the second case there is a declaration of what he has done.

Like the laments, the songs of thanksgiving come in two forms.

There are several which are a form of thanksgiving by the whole community. The most specific is Psalm 124, which rejoices in a deliverance which God brought to his people. Other community thanksgiving songs are Psalms 65, 67, 75, 107, and 136. The more common form, however, is the individual song of thanksgiving in which individuals give testimony to what the Lord has done in their life. These are typical examples:

You have granted him the desire of his heart,
   and not withheld the request of his lips (21:2).

O LORD, you brought me up from the grave;
   you spared me from going down into the pit (30:3).

He put a new song in my mouth,
   a hymn of praise to our God (40:3).

Come and listen, all you who fear God;
   let me tell you what he has done for me (66:16).

The pattern which the individual thanksgivings takes is as follows:

A. Address to God
There is direct address to God, frequently brief but sometimes more extended.

B. Description of the Psalmist's Experiences
Usually this includes an account of the trouble which the psalmist faced, an indication of his cry for help, and then finally the deliverance which God has provided for him.

C. Testimony to the Lord
The psalm finishes with a proclamation of the goodness of the Lord. There may also be other features such as a request for future help.
   Psalm 116 provides an excellent illustration of this pattern:

A. Address to God
The psalmist calls to the LORD (vs. 1-2), and gives the reason why he is praising him (notice the clause beginning with *for*).

B. Description of the Psalmist's Experiences
Verse 3 gives the circumstances which the psalmist faced, followed by his cry for help (v. 4). As he thinks over what has happened he

expresses his confidence in the LORD, who is gracious and righteous (vs. 5-7).

C. Testimony to the LORD
The psalmist rejoices in what God has done for him.

> *For you, O LORD, have delivered my soul from death,*
> *my eyes from tears,*
> *my feet from stumbling,*
> *that I may walk before the LORD*
> *in the land of the living* (vs. 8-9).

The psalm ends with the psalmist pledging himself to the Lord and making his vows in the presence of the congregation (referred to in verses 14 and 18). He is the Lord's servant (v. 16), and he ends his song with a 'Hallelujah' (v. 19).

Since the Psalms are so personal in their authorship, clearly there is blessing in our personal appropriation of them.

11.4 Wisdom Psalms
Within the Old Testament there are several books which are often called 'the wisdom books'. They include Job, Proverbs and Ecclesiastes, and are so-called because their main emphasis is not on the great facts of God's redemption, but with the practical outworking of life which is lived in the fear of the LORD. This phrase, 'the fear of the LORD', occurs both in the Book of Proverbs and in the Psalms (e.g. Prov. 1:7; 8:13; 14:26; 15:33; Pss. 19:9; 34:11; 111:10). It does not describe the abject fear of a slave before a master, but rather the devotion of a loving heart towards one's sovereign Lord. The wisdom literature shows how such a fear displays itself in practical life, so that it is really 'godliness in working clothes'.

Much of the wisdom literature appears in the form of proverbs, which are marked out by the following characteristics:

(a) Proverbs are brief, usually consisting of fewer than twenty-five words. The best proverbs are often the shortest. The brevity comes from a desire to put the wisdom saying into as short a form as possible, and also as an aid to memorisation. Sometimes there is a repetition of a word or sound which is a further help to the memory.

(b) Proverbs use figurative language. They are dealing with truth, but they put it in a form which is easy to grasp and retain. They take an experience from everyday life and use it to teach a lesson. Because they paint pictures the vividness of the proverb is retained in spite of repeated use.

(c) Proverbs have many different applications. They do not refer to just one situation in life. Rather, their general nature enables them to be applied in a variety of situations. Thus the proverb, 'like father, like son' can be applied to the relationship between a teacher and a pupil, or even between a mother and a daughter.

(d) Proverbs express general truths. They are not promises of God which apply without exception. Rather, they are generalisations based on human experience, and there may well be exceptions to the general truths contained in them.

There are several psalms which fit into the general pattern of the wisdom literature, while parts of other psalms reflect something of that same approach to life or share in matters of style and form. Among the former are Psalms 37, 49, and 73, while psalms such as 25, 34, 78, 111, 112, 127 and 128 have features which resemble wisdom literature. Of these Psalm 78 starts with the words:

O my people, hear my teaching;
  listen to the words of my mouth.
I will open my mouth in parables,
  I will utter hidden things, things from of old (vs. 1-2).

There are several features in this opening which are typical of wisdom literature, such as the call to hear and the words 'teaching', 'parables' and 'hidden things'.

In contrast to other types these wisdom psalms do not display a structure which remains constant to them all. Rather, they are distinguished by characteristics which mark them out as distinctive. These characteristics include:

a) the knowledge that the fear of the LORD is the beginning of wisdom

b) a concern for the practical issues of life

c) a clear distinction between the two ways which face us in life, so that a clear distinction is drawn between the righteous and the wicked.

d) a struggle with the problem of why the wicked seem to prosper as compared with the righteous

e) hints that the final solution lies in the life to come.

The first of the major wisdom psalms is Psalm 37, whose eleventh verse ('But the meek will inherit the land and enjoy great peace') was picked up by Christ and appears as the third beatitude (Matt. 5:5). The psalm is an acrostic, with each second verse commencing with a consecutive letter of the Hebrew alphabet. The teaching of this psalm has come over into English through John Wesley's translation of Paul Gerhardt's hymn *Put thou thy trust in God* (Gerhardt's hymn *Befehl du deine Wege* is also an acrostic, with each of its twelve verses commencing with a successive word from Psalm 37:5, 'Commit your way to the Lord ...'). The psalm points to the source of true wisdom and blessedness and encourages readers to follow the way of the Lord.

The second of the psalms which are strongly in the wisdom type is Psalm 73. It presents teaching very similar to Job and Ecclesiastes and it is clearly a teaching poem. When faced with the arrogance of the wicked and their prosperity, the psalmist did not understand the situation until he went into the sanctuary of God. There in the temple he realised what was to be their ultimate destiny (vs. 16-17).

12. PSALMS OF REMEMBRANCE

12.1 Israel's Historical Faith

The faith of Israel was rooted in the events of Old Testament history. God acted in the world and especially in redeeming his people from their bondage and slavery. It was the real world to which God came and the events were calendar events in human history. Thus the happenings in the Old Testament are not fictitious accounts composed to teach a certain message, but the record of actual events. There are serious consequences for any professing Christian to maintain that these events were fictitious. If we accept that the historical confession of Israel's faith does not have its roots in history, then we deprive the Christian faith of its foundation.

Israel expressed her faith over and over again in the Old Testament, and in doing so, recounted the historical developments of the nation. Some of these opportunities were provided in the annual ceremonies, such as the Passover. In this annual commemoration the children of Israel were reminded of the origin of the nation at the momentous time of the Exodus. When their children asked them, 'What does this ceremony mean to you?' they were to reply: 'It is the Passover sacrifice to the LORD, who passed over the houses of the Israelites in Egypt and spared our homes when he struck down the Egyptians' (Exod. 12:25-27). This was one way in which parents were to teach their children each year the historical facts which were the basis for the Passover. This was developed over the centuries into the Passover Haggadah which is still used to the present day. Jewish people still confess in the Passover ceremony that not only their forefathers but they themselves were brought out of Egypt.

> It was not alone our fathers whom the Holy One, blessed be He, redeemed, but also us whom He redeemed with them, as it is said, 'And *us* He brought out thence that He might lead *us* to, and give *us*, the land which He swore to our fathers.'

Similar communal aspects of a confession of faith occur in the declaration required in the presentation of the firstfruits. After Israel came into Canaan, at the time of presenting the firstfruits they had to confess that their father (Jacob) was a wandering Aramean who had gone down into Egypt and become a great nation. The confession continued:

> But the Egyptians ill-treated us and made us suffer, putting us to hard labour. Then we cried out to the LORD, the God of our fathers, and the LORD heard our voice and saw our misery, toil and oppression. So the LORD brought us out of Egypt with a mighty hand and an outstretched arm, with great terror and with miraculous signs and wonders. He brought us to this place and gave us this land, a land flowing with milk and honey; and now I bring the firstfruits of the soil that you, O LORD, have given me (Deut. 26:6-10).

This confession was not a private one, for it was performed by all Israelites as they brought the firstfruits to the sanctuary. It was, therefore, a very public acknowledgment and reminder of the great events of the Exodus from Egypt. Moreover, each Israelite had to make the confession not just for himself but for others as well. He identified himself as part of the total community of Israel ('the Egyptians ill-treated *us*', '*we* cried out', 'the LORD heard *our* voice', 'he brought *us*'). The central intent of it was to bring praise to the God of Israel who had done such wonderful things for his people. It sets a pattern of recounting the distress of the people and then extolling the great deeds of the LORD.

It is important to note that the people even sang their history at the command of the Lord himself. Moses was told to write down a song which the Lord would give him, and to teach it to the people; they were to sing this song so that it might be a witness against them. Moses did as he was instructed (Deut. 31:19, 22). In this act Moses was joined by Joshua, so that the outgoing leader of the people was acting in conjunction with the incoming leader (Deut. 32:44). It was really the covenant commitment expressed in the form of a song, with the warning that the departure from God's requirements would result in his judgements coming upon the nation. The importance of the song of Moses is highlighted by the way in which in Revelation 15:3-4 'the song of Moses the servant of God' is linked with 'the song of the Lamb'.

12.2 The Purpose of the Historical Psalms

There are a group of psalms (especially 78, 105, 106, 114, 135, 136) which are essentially story-telling psalms. The story is not like those in English which begin with 'Once upon a time', for these songs are proclaiming the great deeds of the LORD. They are story-telling in the sense that they are narrative psalms which recount the history of Israel.

Just as the confession on the occasion of the presenting the firstfruits was intended to be praise of God, so also with the narrative psalms. They were intended to teach the people the events of their history and to point them to the significance of those events so that they would praise the LORD. This is especially true of psalms such as 105 and 106 which both end with a song of praise to the LORD.

Within them there is a pattern of declaring the distress which God's people experienced at particular times, and then of proclaiming the deliverance which God afforded them.

> *But he brought his people out like a flock;*
> *he led them like sheep through the desert* (Ps. 78:52).

> *For he remembered his holy promise*
> *given to his servant Abraham.*
> *He brought out his people with rejoicing,*
> *his chosen ones with shouts of joy* (Ps. 105:42-43).

The historical songs of Israel were clearly to magnify the deeds of the Lord and remind the people whenever they used the songs that their God alone was the deliverer of his people.

12.3 The Stories of the Lord
The main historical psalms are these:

Psalm 78: A summary of the history of Israel which recounts the story from the Exodus until the time of David and the choice of Jerusalem.

Psalm 105: An account of Israel's history from the Exodus till the occupation of Canaan and surrounding territory.

Psalm 106: Another narrative of Israel's history, but carrying the story further to tell of the sins of the people after they came into Canaan.

Psalm 135: A song which includes references to God as Creator, and one whose power was shown in Egypt and in giving Israel the land of Canaan as an inheritance.

Psalm 136: Another song which refers to creation, and then recounts the history of Israel in antiphonal form.

The narrative style is also displayed in parts of many more psalms. Using the Pentateuch (Genesis to Deuteronomy) as a guide, we can reconstruct from the Psalms the history from the time of Abraham up till the time of occupation of Canaan and later. The events include:

Israel, the offspring of Abraham	105:6
Israel goes into Egypt	105:16ff.
God delivers from their oppression	77:15; 81:6
He inflicts plagues on Egypt	78:44ff.; 105:27ff.; 135:8f.; 136:10
He led them through the sea	77:16ff.; 78:13, 53; 114:3, 5
He guided them in the wilderness	68:7f.; 78:14ff.; 105:39ff.; 106:6f.; 114:8
Canaan was their heritage	44:2; 47:4; 60:7f.; 135:10ff.; 136:17ff.

However, what is different about these references and the major story-telling psalms is that in the latter there is a chronological record of the events of Israel's history.

12.4 The Faithfulness of God
The historical psalms hark back to the great salvation of God seen in the redemption from Egypt. They record his great deeds in order that his people might have their faith strengthened, and that the record of

past deliverance would serve as a model of hope for the believing community. Just as God had acted in this way before, so would he act again to save his people.

Ultimately this idea of hope for the future is based on the faithfulness of God. The fundamental theme of Israel's praise in this group of psalms is the fact that God is utterly faithful to his word of promise. There is frequent mention of the fact that God has remembered his covenant:

> *He remembered that they were but flesh,*
> *a passing breeze that does not return* (Ps. 78:39).

> *For he remembered his holy promise*
> *given to his servant Abraham* (Ps. 105:42).

> *For their sake he remembered his covenant*
> *and out of his great love he relented* (Ps. 106:45).

> *He remembered us in our low estate* (Ps. 136:23).

God's relationship with his covenant people is characterised by his utter steadfastness. He has spoken and he will perform it. There is no variableness with him, but complete integrity towards his people. The New Testament reinforces this Old Testament teaching. As Christians we will be kept 'strong to the end', so that we 'will be blameless on the day of our Lord Jesus Christ. God, who has called you into fellowship with his Son Jesus Christ our Lord, is faithful' (1 Cor. 1:8-9).

13. THE PROBLEM SONGS

13.1 Introduction
One group of psalms stands out above all others because of the difficulties they have created for Christian people. These psalms are often called 'the imprecatory psalms'. The word *imprecation* comes from a Latin word *imprecatio*, which describes calling down harm on someone. Thus the English word is used in this connection to describe the psalms in which curses are expressed on others. Often it is not a whole psalm in question but only some verses from it. The psalms in which these passages mainly occur are 55, 59, 69, 79, 109, and 137.

The problem which they present is one of reconciling the curses and prayers for destruction of the wicked with the teaching of the New

Testament. For some the problem is so acute that they assert that no New Testament Christian can use or approve of the imprecations in the psalms. This kind of judgement is often made without realising the full picture which must be taken into consideration.

There are some facts we have to remember before we look at the solutions to the problem.

Firstly, this is not just a pressing problem for those who use the Psalter as a songbook in worship. It is just as real a problem for those who merely want to read the Psalms in private devotions or in public worship.

Secondly, the fact that there are other portions of the Bible which contain similar curses must be borne in mind. These occur in passages such as Nehemiah 6:14 and 13:29; Jeremiah 15:5; 17:18; 18:21-23; 20:12. They also occur in New Testament passages such as Acts 8:20; Galatians 1:9; 5:12; 2 Timothy 4:14; Revelation 6:10.

Thirdly, Christ quoted freely from the Psalms. He used the Messianic psalms most frequently, and quoted most often from the psalms with curses in them. Thus in his lament over Jerusalem he referred to dashing the little ones to the ground, taking the words from Psalm 137:9 (in the LXX version). He also repeatedly used Psalm 69 (see John 2:17; 15:25). The fact that these psalms were endorsed and appropriated by our Lord does not remove their difficulty, but it should warn us not to judge them rashly.

Fourthly, some of these psalms are expressly referred to in the New Testament as having been given by inspiration as the psalmists spoke under the guidance of the Holy Spirit. In the case of Psalm 109:8 the apostle Peter quoted from it and said: '... which the Holy Spirit spoke long ago through the mouth of David concerning Judas' (Acts 1:16).

13.2 Suggested Solutions

Various solutions to the problem have been proposed, and some of these can be reviewed.

An obvious solution which some have adopted is simply to reject the teaching of these psalms and to pretend they are not there. This is done by avoiding any use or recognition of them. This presents us with the problem that the curses often come in psalms with other wonderful sayings, to which we wish to cling. Also, these psalms and many others, were part and parcel of our Lord's use of the Old Testament. The problem has to be faced, not avoided.

It has been claimed that the Psalter belongs to the Old Testament dispensation, not the New Testament dispensation of grace; and therefore it teaches a lower morality than the New Testament with its injunction to love one's enemies (Matt. 5:44-45). But this would make Scripture contradict itself, for the Old Testament does not teach hatred towards one's enemies (see, for example, Exod. 23:4, 5; Lev. 19:17, 18). Also, when Paul was condemning the sin of a revengeful spirit, he does so by quoting in Romans 12:18-20 from two Old Testament passages (Deut. 32:35; Prov. 25:21, 22).

Others have suggested that these psalms merely predict the doom of the wicked but are not to be understood as desiring their destruction. While there is an element of truth in this explanation, yet it does not explain many of the cases which go far beyond mere prediction. They ask God to carry out the destruction of the wicked (see, for example, 55:9 and 59:12-13).

Another view has been that the curses are to be understood in a figurative or spiritual sense. Thus the enemies spoken of are really our temptations, and when we use these psalms we are praying that our temptations may be put to death or removed from us. But the persons spoken about give every appearance of being real persons, not just some desires or emotions that we may have.

Some have the idea that the imprecations are cries stemming from personal vindictiveness and they are seeking personal vengeance. Such utterances were wrong, but because of the circumstances in which the psalmists were placed they may be excused for speaking such curses. This theory does not fit the facts, as they show that in David's history there is no such spirit of vindictiveness. The real answer is deeper.

13.3 The Curses of the Covenant
Earlier we saw that the Psalms have to be placed in their true setting within God's covenant. It is striking that the cursing psalms strongly emphasise the relationship between Israel and the Lord. They stress the kingship of God over his people, and appeal to the God who is enthroned for ever to hear the cry of his people and to afflict their enemies (Ps. 55:19). The relationship to God is stressed by use of the term 'servant' (Pss. 69:17; 109:28) and also by the claim of the community to be God's people (Ps. 79:13).

In almost all the imprecatory psalms the context is one of judgment.

The appeal is to God to act as judge, and to be the vindicator of his people. In Psalm 109, for example, there is explicit reference to blessing and cursing (vs. 17-19, 28). This seems to be a clear allusion back to Genesis 12:3: 'I will bless those who bless you, and whoever curses you I will curse, and all peoples on earth will be blessed through you.' Psalm 137 is different because there is no reference to a judicial procedure. However, two passages from the prophets (Hos. 13:16; Isa. 13:16) provide the background for the curse in this imprecatory psalm. The psalmist speaks a word of cursing against the arch-enemy of Israel, Babylon, in language which is clearly reminiscent of these two prophets. In particular Isaiah 13:16 had already prophesied the downfall of Babylon.

The imprecatory psalms also show that the enemies were indeed God's enemies, not just the enemies of the psalmists. Thus Psalm 5 calls on God to declare the wicked guilty because, he says, 'they have rebelled against *you*' (v. 10). Similarly Psalm 79 asks God to repay 'the reproaches they have hurled at *you*, O Lord' (v. 12). Even Psalm 137 must be understood to imply that the enemies are the enemies of the Lord. It is Babylon as the opponent of Israel which is in view. Just as Jeremiah cried: 'Do to her as she has done to others' (Jer. 50:15), so the psalmist was asking for divine visitation on her.

The concept of cursing was central to the whole idea of covenant, both in the biblical record and outside it. In the extra-biblical treaties a person entering into a treaty was obliged to treat the other party's enemies as his enemies. The principle was, as one Hittite treaty puts it, 'with my friend you shall be friend, and with my enemy you shall be enemy'. In the Old Testament itself the word 'curse' could be employed as a virtual synonym for 'covenant' (Deut. 29:13, 18). When the prophets speak judgement against Israel, they echo the curses of the covenant from passages such as Leviticus 26 and Deuteronomy 27 and 28. Rebels, whether within the covenant nation or outside, came under the same curses. In this respect the curses in the Psalter are typical of the covenantal approach of the Old Testament both in regard to relationships between humans and relationships between God and humanity.

Finally, we should remember that the Bible consistently marks a sharp distinction between those who are for God and those who are against him. There is a final judgement day coming when the Son of Man will separate the sheep from the goats (Matt. 25:31-33). The picture the New Testament gives us of heaven is that nothing sinful or unclean will ever enter it (Rev. 21:27). As elsewhere in the Bible, the psalmists look at life from the perspective which will prevail at the last day. In appealing for God's vindication they are virtually asking for God's final judgement to be advanced in time and made a reality here and now.

14. A CHRISTIAN READING OF THE PSALMS

14.1 An Open Songbook

The Psalter developed over a long period of time. In its early stages it was an open songbook of God's people, in the sense that it was growing by the addition of new psalms. Moreover, it was in constant use by individuals and the collective group of believers as it was growing. There must have been many other songs which were not incorporated, but those we have were especially written under the influence of the Holy Spirit and brought together as the special songbook of the Old Testament church.

The Psalter is an open songbook in another sense as well. While the psalms come out of the individual experiences of their authors, they often lack clear indications which would enable us to say exactly what those experiences were. Thus, to say that the Lord has delivered our eyes from tears does not specify anything more than that the Lord has removed our sorrow or grief. It does not tell us the details of the experience which caused such sorrow. This is in marked contrast to other Old Testament songs such as the Song of the Sea (Exod. 15) or the Song of Deborah (Judg. 5). The lack of specific details is important, however, as it enables us to identify all the more closely with the psalms. Because they are general in character we can use them so readily and apply them to our own specific need.

The New Testament sets a pattern of use of the Psalms for Christians in that it appropriates them and uses them for believers passing through similar experiences. Their pastoral use and application was realised, and, when in trouble, New Testament Christians found comfort in them. Thus when Paul is describing his deliverance on the occasion of his preliminary hearing he says he 'was delivered from the lion's mouth' (2 Tim. 4:17). This is an apparent reference to Psalm 22:21, and may indicate that he had used that lament in prayer at the time of his trial. In the letter to the Hebrews the writer quotes a word from the psalms which had relevance for his experience and for his readers: 'The Lord is my helper; I will not be afraid. What can man do to me?' (Heb. 13:6; cf. Psalm 118:6). These and many other quotations and allusions are applied on the principle given by Paul in Romans 15:4: 'For everything that was written in the past was written to teach us, so that through endurance and the encouragement of the Scriptures we might have hope.' He has just quoted from a psalm (Ps. 69:9) and his readers are encouraged to place their trust in the Lord, for the Old Testament Scriptures gave ample evidence of his faithfulness.

14.2 The Psalms and the New Testament
We cannot read the Psalms today as believers in the Old Testament read them, for we live *after* the coming of Christ. Jesus himself was brought up in a Jewish environment in which the Psalms were extensively used. Augustine said of Jesus, *iste cantator psalmorum*, 'He, the singer of the psalms.' On occasions of pilgrimage to Jerusalem (cf. Luke 2:41f.) and at the Passover, he would have been part of the community who sang from the Psalter. During the washing of his feet he quoted from Psalm 41:9 (John 13:18), while on the Cross he used several phrases from the Psalms ('My God, My God, why have you forsaken me?', Ps. 22:1; 'It is done', cf. Ps. 22:31 ['he has done it']; 'Father, into your hands I commend my spirit', Ps. 31:5).

Moreover, Jesus is the focus of both Old and New Testaments, and in his own ministry he gave indications of how we are to understand the Old Testament (including the Psalms) in reference to himself. Twice following his resurrection he spoke of how the Old Testament pointed to himself as the promised Messiah. To Cleopas and his friend he began with Moses and all the prophets and 'explained to them what was said in all the Scriptures concerning himself' (Luke 24:27). Then to the assembled disciples in Jerusalem Jesus appeared and said: 'Everything must be fulfilled that is written about me in the Law of Moses, the Prophets and the Psalms' (Luke 24:44). Clearly Jesus expounded the Psalms to the disciples and explained them in terms of his own coming and work.

Jesus' use of the Psalms also explains their extensive use throughout the New Testament. This is so with the early sermons of the apostles as recorded in the Book of Acts. Peter uses Psalms 110 and 16 in his speech on the Day of Pentecost (Acts 2:25-28; 34), while in his later speech to the rulers he quotes Psalm 118:22 (Acts 4:11). When

Paul spoke in the synagogue at Pisidian Antioch he quoted from Psalm 2, and like Peter also used Psalm 16 (Acts 13:33-35). Clearly the apostles preached and taught on the basis of the instruction which they had received, and Jesus had assured them that the Holy Spirit would bring to their remembrance the things he had spoken (John 14:26). Hence the meaning and intent of Jesus' words, along with his use of Old Testament passages such as those from the Psalms, is developed in the New Testament writings. There are about 360 quotations from the Old Testament in the New, and of these about one-third are from the Book of Psalms.

14.3 Messianic Element

What Jesus himself and his apostles saw in the Psalms his followers also wish to see. In our discussion of the Messianic element in the Psalms we must be guided by the way in which the New Testament uses and applies specific psalms. Some Christians have taken the position that there are no psalms which directly prophesy of the Messiah. This would be very strange because Messianic prophecies occur in many other places in the Old Testament. It is also very difficult to uphold this position when we consider the words of quite a few of the psalms, for they speak of a king in a way which goes far beyond anything that a king in David's line could ever be.

It is probably best to view the Messianic psalms under several categories. Most of the Messianic psalms take their starting point from the promise to David in 2 Samuel 7. In the first group are those which refer to this promise, yet speak of the enduring nature of David's kingdom in such a way that points to the ultimate Messianic kingdom. Psalms 89 and 132 expound 2 Samuel 7, while many other psalms, including 18, 21, and 61, celebrate the grace which God shows to David and his dynasty. The past deliverances of David form the basis on which he looks ahead so confidently to the exaltation of the Lord among the nations (Ps. 18:46-50).

There is another group of psalms which comprises those which are directly related to the coming of the Messiah. While a song like Psalm 2 may be couched in language which echoes 2 Samuel 7, yet the words used point with distinctiveness to the one in whom the promise would find its final fulfilment. The way in which Paul used this psalm in his speech in Pisidian Antioch confirms this understanding of Psalm 2. From the vision of David and his kingdom, the eye was directed to a greater son of David who would ultimately be lord of all. So Psalms 2 and 110 speak of a Messiah who is David's Lord and whose kingdom includes all the earth.

There are also psalms which take their starting point from Solomon's kingdom, and yet point far beyond it. Thus while a psalm such as Psalm 45 was probably composed on the occasion of a royal wedding, yet the eyes of the inspired psalmist were suddenly lifted up to see the glory of the Messianic ruler who is even called 'God' (v. 6). Psalm 72 presents us with the true prince of peace whose kingdom is going to far transcend the limits of the Davidic/Solomonic empire. His kingdom is going to extend from the River (i.e. the Euphrates) outwards! This same reference to Messiah's rule occurs in another Messianic passage in Zechariah 9:10.

The final group of Messianic psalms are those which are typically Messianic. That is to say, their primary reference is not to Jesus, but he is the one who fulfils the descriptions which they give. They are psalms of righteous people; he is the *only* righteous one. The idea of a righteous person undergoing suffering and putting his trust in God is fully realised in the life and ministry of Jesus. These psalms include 6, 16, 22, 35, 40, 41, 69, 70, 71, 102, and 109. In this sense many of the psalms (or perhaps all) are Messianic. Some of this group of psalms had in view not only David but also his descendants (102, 109), and in this way a link is formed with the psalms specifically based on 2 Samuel 7.

15. USING THE PSALMS TODAY

15.1 The Psalms and Spiritual Life
As we have seen in our earlier studies, the Book of Psalms serves two great purposes, which can be expressed in these statements:

> The Book of Psalms speaks *to us*.
> The Book of Psalms speaks *for us*.

Each of these aspects is important and has practical consequences for us today. The Psalter came from God and it leads to God. We receive blessing as we read and use the Psalms and as we are instructed by them. They speak *to* our hearts and bring spiritual truths to our minds and consciences. But they also speak *for* us, as we utilise them in praise and prayer as if we were their author. They come out of real life situations and, because they are facing the variety of human needs, we are able to respond to God by using their words as our own.

15.2 Personal Devotions

Christians today need the richness of the Psalter to aid them in their spiritual life. It is *the* devotional book of the Bible, and as such continues to be our devotional book and our guide. In using it we are served by the thoughts and prayers it contains, and in turn we voice our praise and adoration of God, and our petitions, in its words. Very often the Book of Psalms has been published along with the New Testament so that Christians can have ready access to it for their devotional use.

The Christian church throughout the centuries has found spiritual nourishment in the Book of Psalms. It was common in the early church for the whole Psalter to be memorised by those who were seeking to become pastors. Jerome tells that in his time (c. 347-420) it was common to hear the Psalms being sung in the fields and in the gardens. The same phenomenon occurred at the time of the Reformation, when the Psalms again became prominent in the life of the church. The Reformation movement is the reason why the reading and chanting of the Psalms became customary in Anglican churches, while metrical psalters became central in the worship of Dutch and Scottish churches. The Psalms should fill a central place, not only in the life of individuals, but also in the collective worship of the church.

There is the need to let the word of Christ dwell in us richly. Paul, in writing to the Colossian Christians says: 'Let the peace of Christ rule in your hearts, since as members of one body you were called to peace. And be thankful. Let the word of Christ dwell in you richly as you teach and admonish one another with all wisdom, and as you sing psalms, hymns and spiritual songs with gratitude in your hearts to God' (Col. 3:15-16). The various types of Christian songs, including psalms, are regarded as 'Christ's word'. It is to take up its abode in our hearts and it is to be used as we teach and admonish each other. That indwelling word builds us up in our faith and it counsels us, and it also forms part of our praise and thanksgiving to God.

15.3 Praise

There are various ways in which the Psalms have been and can be used in our worship. Chanting of prose psalms has a long history, though it is frequently associated with Anglican worship. It has the advantage of allowing the words to be dominant, and it usually only requires a restricted number of chants to be known. Many in our cultural setting prefer a greater variety of tunes to be used in worship than is normally the case with chanting.

'Scripture in Song' is a phenomenon of the modern church, though the principle of setting short passages of Scripture to music is very old. This practice means that many Christian people are singing portions of psalms and it is good to hear this use of God's Word. The disadvantage is that the selections are often taken out of their context, and sometimes they are interpreted by users of 'Scripture in Song' in a way which is not supported by the context in the particular psalm. We need to remember that the psalms are poetic pieces *as a whole*, and that simply to select a verse or two can distort their essential message.

The Reformation, which in some respects brought a revolution in worship, in other ways continued the practices of the pre-Reformation church though in a new form. The use of the Psalms not only continued but took on a new role as their use was popularised during the Reformation movement. Luther wrote in 1523: 'I plan after the example of the prophets and ancient fathers of the Church to make German psalms for the people, that is to say, spiritual songs, so that the Word of God may dwell among the people by means of song also.' To this he added that the words were to be 'all quite plain and common, such as the common people may understand, yet pure and skilfully handled'. Calvin also regarded music as a gift of God and encouraged the use of the full Psalter, and he himself attempted to translate some of them into French, though the work of Clement Marot (1497-1544) and Theodore Beza (1519-1605) was much more extensive and influential. Wherever the Protestant Reformation reached, the Psalms were used in worship, and they became so popular that even Roman Catholics were known to sing them.

This tradition of psalm singing continues to this day. The Scottish Metrical Psalter of 1650 has been widely used, and has often been employed alongside modern revisions or alternative versions. The Irish Presbyterian Church undertook a light revision and added twenty-seven additional versions in 1880. The United Presbyterian Church of North America produced complete Psalters in 1871 and 1912 which have been widely used, especially in the United States. *The Book of Psalms with Music* (1950) and *The Book of Psalms for Singing* (1973) of the Reformed Presbyterian Church of North America have also been extensively used. In modern English Anglicanism there has been renewed interest in the Psalter and *Psalm Praise* (1973) and the later *Psalms for Today* and *Songs from the Psalms* are representative of this approach. The variety of versions available testifies to the abiding character of the Psalter as *the* songbook of the church and one which has helped to give vitality to the worship of Christians in many countries and situations.

The Psalter has also been most influential in serving as a model for the church's hymnology, and often individual psalms have been used extensively as the basic of many hymns. There are hymns from the Reformation period such as Luther's *A mighty fortress is our God* (based on Psalm 46), but it is especially from the period of Isaac Watts (1674-1748) and Charles Wesley (1707-1788) that the attempt was made to use the content of the Psalms but to infuse distinctively New Testament teaching into it. Watts in particular carried this too far, but some of his hymns based on psalms remain in constant use today (e.g. *Jesus shall reign* from Psalm 72, and *O God our help in ages past* from Psalm 90). Wesley makes no claim that his hymns are translations of psalms, but rather they are Christian hymns based on the Psalms, just as he based other hymns on other parts of the Bible or on Christian writings. Thus his hymn *O for a heart to praise my God* uses the ideas of Psalm 51, while *Jesu, mighty to deliver* is Psalm 70 expanded as a Christian song of praise. Many other hymns clearly reflect the influence and pattern of the Psalter, and this is good for the church.

15.4 Epilogue

Study of the Psalms should never be an end in itself. The purpose should be to direct us back to the Psalms with fuller understanding and greater interest. The use of the Psalms should be a vital part of our spiritual growth, as we use them to pray to God and as they speak to us. In turn that study should provoke us to use them all the more in praise to God and adoration of him and his works. Our song should be like the one that ends the Psalter:

> *Praise the LORD ...*
> *Let everything that has breath praise the LORD*
> *Praise the LORD* (Ps. 150:1,6).

Suggestions for Further Reading

Commentaries

J. A. Alexander, *The Psalms Translated and Explained* (Evangelical Press, 1975).

J. M. Boice, *Psalms*, Vol. 1, Psalms 1-41 (Baker, 1994)

John Calvin, *Commentary on the Psalms* (Baker, 1979).

P. C. Craigie, *Psalms 1-50* (Word, 1983).

Walter C. Kaiser, *The Journey Isn't Over: The Pilgrim Psalms* [Pss. 120-134] *for Life's Challenges and Joys* (Baker, 1993)

F. D. Kidner, *Psalms: An Introduction and Commentary*, 2 vols. Tyndale Series (IVP, 1973)

H. C. Leupold, *Exposition of the Psalms* (Baker, 1969).

J. J. Stewart Perowne, *The Psalms*, 2 vols. (George Bell and Sons, 1886).

W. VanGemeren, 'The Psalms', in *Biblical Expositor* (Zondervan), vol. 5, pp. 3-880)

E. J. Young, *Psalm 139: A Study in the Omniscience of God* (Banner of Truth, 1965).

General

James E. Adams, *War Psalms of the Prince of Peace: Lessons from the Imprecatory Psalms* (Presbyterian and Reformed, 1991).

R. Dean Anderson, Jr., 'The Division and Order of the Psalms', *Westminster Theological Journal* 56, 2 (Fall, 1994), 219-241.

E. Calvin Beisner, *Psalms of Promise: Celebrating the Majesty and Faithfulness of God* (Presbyterian and Reformed, 2nd ed. 1994).

C. Hassell Bullock, 'The Book of Psalms' in *An Introduction to the Old Testament Poetic Books* (Moody Press, 1988), pp. 111-145.

Robert B. Chisholm, Jr., 'A Theology of the Psalms', in *A Biblical Theology of the Old Testament* (Moody Press, 1991), pp. 257-304.

Raymond B. Dillard and Tremper Longman III, 'Psalms', in *An Introduction to the Old Testament* (Zondervan, 1994), pp. 211-234.

Tremper Longman III, *How to Read the Psalms* (Intervarsity Press, 1988).

J. B. Payne, 'Book of Psalms', *Zondervan Pictorial Encyclopedia of the Bible*, 4, pp. 934-947.

N. H. Ridderbos and P. C. Craigie, 'Psalms' in *The International Standard Bible Encyclopedia*, fully revised, vol. 3, pp. 1029-1040

Bruce K. Waltke, 'A Canonical Approach to the Psalms', in *Tradition and Testament: Essays in Honor of Charles Lee Feinberg*, ed. Paul Feinberg and John Feinberg (Moody Press, 1981).

BOOK 1

PSALM 1

The manner in which the Book of Psalms opens is important. The first
two psalms are not strictly prayers but declarations. The first prayer is
actually Psalm 3. Together, Psalms 1 and 2 form two keys to help us
understand the whole book. This first key starts by contrasting the two
ways in which people can live. This opening is intended to challenge
readers as to their commitment to the LORD and to his law.

1. *Near to God (verses 1-3)*

The book opens with a pronouncement of blessing. 'Blessed is the
man,' says the psalmist. In Hebrew there are two words for blessing,
one used by God when he is expressing a benediction, and the other
(used here) by men when referring to other men. To merit the word
'blessed' used here, man has to do something, or, as in this case, not
do something, for which he can be commended.

Here the character of the blessed man is defined by three negative
terms – 'who does not walk in the counsel of the wicked or stand in the
way of sinners or sit in the seat of mockers' *(verse 1)*. With mounting
emphasis the psalmist describes the character of those whose trust is
in the LORD. They do not look to ungodly men as a source of wisdom;
their path is not that taken by sinners; their company is not with those
who mock God or who are self-satisfied and proud. On the contrary,
the blessed man is marked out because 'his delight is in the law of the
LORD, and on his law he meditates day and night' *(verse 2)*. God's
instruction forms the basis of his conduct and is the treasure of his
heart. The word 'law' does not mean a list of rules and the appropriate
punishments, but the fullness of God's teaching for his children. This
instruction, which included the history of God's dealings with his
people, was to be passed on from generation to generation (see Psalm
78:1-8). The Hebrew word translated 'meditates' implies something
more than silent reflection. It means to whisper or to murmur.

The result of such meditation is that the blessed man is like a
transplanted tree *(verse 3)*, set alongside an irrigation canal. The
thought of being transplanted recalls the imagery of God transplanting
a little vine from Egypt into Canaan, where it became a great tree (Ps.
80:8-16). It may also reflect the situation prevailing when the whole
Psalter was brought to completion, soon after the experience in exile,
in which the exiles knew so much about the irrigation canals of
Babylon. In its well-watered position the tree brings forth its fruit, and

its location ensures that it will not fade. So it is with the believing child of God who endures to the end (Phil. 1:6) and who brings forth fruits of righteousness (Gal. 5:16-26).

2. *Far from God (verses 4-6)*

How different are those whose trust is not in the LORD! The lines of demarcation between God's children and the children of the world are clearly drawn. The contrast is clear. Instead of being like a living tree, the wicked are as unstable as chaff. They are without root and without fruit. Such people will not be able to stand their ground at God's judgment seat, neither have they any right to be among God's people. Their experience will be one of exclusion from the company of God's people on earth, and exclusion from the presence of God in eternity.

The final verse of the psalm sums up the contrast. The way of the righteous is overseen constantly by the LORD, whereas the way of the ungodly has no future. It is going to perish utterly. This is a poetic form of the challenge of Moses to the children of Israel in Deuteronomy 30:11-20. By implication the psalmist echoes Moses' command: 'Now choose life, so that you and your children may live.'

PSALM 2

The second key to the Book of Psalms is Psalm 2, and it is linked to the first by two words, 'plot' (in Psalm 1:2 translated as 'meditate') and 'blessed'. In this psalm the focus is on the ungodly and specifically on the Gentile nations who reject the LORD's rule. The only solution to their situation is to accept the rule of God's chosen Messiah, and then they will know the blessedness of trusting in him *(verse 12)*. Just as Psalm 1 begins with the word 'blessed' *(verse 1)*, so Psalm 2 ends with this word. It is possible that these two psalms were, in fact, regarded as one, for in some early Greek manuscripts of the New Testament Paul's quotation from Psalm 2 in Acts 13:33 is said to be from 'the first psalm'. Some early church writers like Origen (c.185-254) also refer to it in the same way.

1. *Rebellious Nations (verses 1-3)*

Whereas the godly meditate on God's word (Psalm 1:2), the ungodly rulers of the Gentile nations meditate in the sense of plotting. The word 'anointed' is the Hebrew word from which we get the English word

'Messiah'. Antagonism is not only shown against the LORD, but also against his chosen servant, whose appointment is spoken of later in this psalm *(verses 6-9)*. What these kings and rulers did not realise is that their plans are in vain in God's sight. When they take their stand and gather together they make a declaration of their independence: 'Let us break their chains,' they say, 'and throw off their fetters' *(verse 3)*. Sinful men never want to walk within the limitations which God places on his creatures. In their arrogance they declare their supposed freedom, and they claim to be master of their own destinies.

2. *Divine Rule (verses 4-6)*
In contrast to the feverish activity described in verse 1, the LORD is able to view the plottings of men from his heavenly throne. He does not laugh to ridicule them *(verse 4)*, but because he views their planning from his sovereign security, and because he knows that *his* day is coming (Ps. 37:13). Almost the same expression occurs in Psalm 59:8.

When the LORD does speak, it will be in anger for he will terrify them. The declaration he makes concerns the place of his king, against whom the heathen rulers have been plotting. Kingship in Israel was an institution which God had given for his people (see Deut. 17:14-20, and for its introduction 1 Sam. 8-12). From the time that David captured the fortress of Zion (2 Sam. 5:7) it became the centre of both religious and political life in Israel. Each Davidic ruler typified the coming of the final Messianic king who is spoken of here.

3. *God's Declaration to His Son (verses 7-9)*
It is now the Messianic king who speaks of his own appointment. 'I will proclaim the decree of the LORD: He said to me, "You are my Son; today I have become your Father" ' *(verse 7)*. Elsewhere in the Psalms the LORD's decree refers to the establishment of his orderly rule in the universe (Ps. 148:6). Here it is used of the sovereign appointment of his Son. The words are echoed at Jesus' baptism (Matt. 3:17) and at the transfiguration (Matt. 17:5). Paul also uses the words in reference to the resurrection (Acts 13:33). Jesus entered this stage of his sonship when through the Spirit of holiness he was 'declared with power to be the Son of God by his resurrection from the dead' (Rom. 1:4).

'Ask of me, and I will make the nations your inheritance, the ends of the earth your possession. You will rule them with an iron sceptre; you will dash them to pieces like pottery' *(verses 8-9)*. A command to ask of the LORD was given to Solomon at Gibeon (1 Kgs. 3:5), but now it is said to a far greater than Solomon. Just as the kingly rule in Psalm 72 extends to the ends of the earth, so here also. Messiah's rule is one which ensures that the nations become his inheritance and the ends of the earth his possession. Rebellious kings ('them' in verse 9) have already been mentioned in verse 2. They will find that his sceptre is not just a symbolic staff, but an iron sceptre which is able to shatter them into pieces.

4. *A Call to Allegiance (verses 10-12)*

A sovereign call now goes to these kings. Earthly rulers can only find blessing for themselves and their subjects when they are subservient to the claims of Christ. 'Serve the LORD with fear and rejoice with trembling' (*verse 11*) is the call which goes to them. They must become his vassals (for so the word 'serve' implies). Furthermore, they have to 'Kiss the Son, lest he be angry and you be destroyed in your way, for his wrath can flare up in a moment. Blessed are all who take refuge in him' *(verse 12)*. In the Hebrew text the word used here for 'Son' is not the usual word *(ben)*, but an Aramaic form *(bar)*. Aramaic was the common language for much of the Ancient Near East over many centuries, and it is appropriate that such a word is used in a context in which Gentile kings are addressed. They are called to perform an act of homage before the LORD's anointed king, lest his anger burn against them and they be destroyed. Just as the first psalm commenced with the concept of blessing, so this second psalm ends on this same reassuring note. All who take refuge in the LORD will find true blessing and satisfaction in him. He is the only refuge from the storm of God's anger.

In addition to the quotations of this psalm in the New Testament already noted above, it is important to realise how often it is alluded to in the Book of Revelation (see e.g. 2:27; 12:5; 19:15). Christians see in Psalm 2 the picture of the Messianic king who is ruling now in the world, and who is going to rule until he subdues all other rulers, and delivers the kingdom to the Father (1 Cor. 15:24). The Book of Revelation shows us the ultimate picture of Christ ruling with an iron sceptre, and bearing the name 'King of kings, and LORD of lords' (Rev. 19:15-16).

PSALM 3
A psalm of David. When he fled from his son Absalom.

For the context of this psalm, we have to look back to the account in 2 Samuel 15ff. where we read of Absalom's conspiracy against his father David. Absalom had plotted a rebellion and won over the hearts of many in the country (2 Sam. 15:1-6). When the rebellion became known to David he fled, and the historical narrative gives a graphic picture of the king weeping as he went up the Mount of Olives, barefooted and with his head uncovered (2 Sam. 15:30). Here David makes his appeal to God. This is the first of a collection of Davidic psalms (3-41).

1. *A Forlorn Cry (verses 1-2)*
This is the first prayer of the Book of Psalms, and the threefold mention of 'many' attracts attention straight away. David feels the pressure which has been put upon him by his numerous opponents, and cries out to his covenant God. The verb 'rise up' can be used of rebellions, but it also has the wider connotation of any opposition coming against someone. Not only did he recognise the extent of opposition against him, but he also knew that numerous others were talking *about* him. What they were saying touched the very honour of God himself, for they were claiming that there was no salvation with God.

This is the first of seventy-one appearances of the word 'Selah' in the Psalter. It only occurs in psalms which are divided into three sections, and always comes at the end of a section, sometimes of all three. It is a technical term which probably denotes louder musical accompaniment.

2. *Certain Protection (verses 3-4)*
In spite of the opposition against him, David knew how sure the LORD's protection was. The opening words of this section stand in marked contrast to what the enemies have been saying. The LORD is indeed the protector, for he is David's shield. The expression goes back to Genesis 15:1, where God reassures Abraham that he will safeguard him from danger. Here, David knew that his 'Glorious One' (see Psalm 4:2 for the similar use of this title) would lift him up out of the dust. This term is rich in theological meaning for it speaks of the redemptive presence of God. David's cry was constantly to the LORD, and he had

received repeated answers. These had come from God's holy hill, Mount Zion, to which site David had brought the ark of the LORD (cf. 2 Sam. 6).

3. *Sure Deliverance (verses 5-8)*

Quiet sleep was possible for David because his salvation was from the LORD *(verse 5)*. Moreover, the fact that Absalom had so many followers was not the point. Because the LORD was his shield, David could rest securely at night, and the support he received meant that 'God's hand was his pillow' (Delitzsch).

'I will not fear the tens of thousands drawn up against me on every side' *(verse 6)*. We know from the historical record that the majority of the people had followed Absalom (2 Sam. 15:13; 17:11; 18:7), but David makes a confident appeal to his protector *(verse 7)*. It is not only the enemies who arise (see verse 1), but the LORD. This is a typical anthropomorphic expression (one describing God in human terms), calling on him to bring help quickly as he had done in the past.

The conclusion of the psalm is a confident expression of trust and hope in the LORD *(verse 8)*. The word 'deliverance' in Hebrew is *yeshu'a* from which the word 'Jesus' comes. David knew that this deliverance of God was not only a personal truth, but one which applied to all the people. Hence he prays for the LORD's blessing to be granted to the nation as a whole. Personal problems did not outweigh his spiritual vision for the people.

PSALM 4
For the director of music. With stringed instruments.
A psalm of David.

There are various connections between Psalms 3 and 4. Jointly they give us morning and evening prayers, even to the extent of repeated key words as the table on the next page shows.

1. *A Cry in Need (verse 1)*

David appeals to his righteous God, i.e. the God who does right, and who keeps his covenant word. David desires relief by having his distress removed far from him. There is the recognition of his need for undeserved grace so that God may hear and answer his prayer.

3:1 LORD, how many are my *foes (tsar)*	4:1b from my *distress (tsar)*
3:2 *Many* are *saying* of me	4.6 *Many* are *asking*
3:3b my *Glorious One (kebodi)*	4:2b my *glory (kebodi)*
3:4 To the LORD I *cry* aloud *(qara')* and he *answers ('anah)* me	4:1a *answer ('anah)* when I call *(qara')* to you 4:3b The LORD will hear when I *call (qara')* to him.
3:5 I lie *down (shakab)* and *sleep (shanah)*	4:8a I will *lie down (shakab)* and *sleep (shanah)*
	4:4a on your *beds (mishkab)*

2. A Description of His Enemies (verses 2-6)

Now David speaks to his enemies and accuses them of forsaking the true God and seeking after false gods *(verses 2-3)*. 'Glory' is here a title for God (as in Psalm 106:20). The action of men is ever the same, for as Paul says, sinful men always want to exchange the glory of the immortal God for man-made images (Rom. 1:21-23). But godly ones, like David, are set apart by the LORD. Anyone who shows covenant commitment *(chesed)* is a godly one *(chasid)*, and can assuredly say that God will answer his prayers.

The enemies are then encouraged to consider their evil deeds *(verse 4)*. The Hebrew verb rendered by 'in your anger' conveys the idea of trembling. David wants his enemies to be deeply moved before the LORD, and not to continue in their sin. Rather, they should heed his words and in the quietness of the night reflect upon their ways. Paul uses this verse in Ephesians 4:26, using the Septuagint rendering. 'Selah' adds emphasis to this call.

They need to be like the righteous and put their trust in the LORD *(verse 5)*. Those who do so, will also bring the proper and appropriate offerings to the sanctuary. The phrase 'right sacrifices' is first used in Deuteronomy 33:19, and here it probably indicates that they would need to make an offering for their past sin.

Spectators who had seen all that had happened to David, now speak *(verse 6)*. They desire to share in the blessing, and pray for themselves in terms of the Aaronic benediction (Num. 6:24-26; cf. also Pss. 31:16; 80:3, 7, 19).

3. *An Evening Prayer (verses 7-8)*

God provides for his servants, such as David, joy in the midst of distress. His enemies could have their festive occasions at harvest, but God-given joy was something far greater. Christians are called to rejoice in sufferings (1 Pet. 4:13), and believing in Christ brings 'inexpressible and glorious joy' (1 Pet. 1:8). Peaceful sleep comes because God was David's protector. The emphasis at the end of *verse 8* is definitely on the LORD: 'Indeed, it is you, LORD, you alone ...' The contrast with the false gods of verse 2 is plain. Only in the LORD is there safety.

PSALM 5
For the director of music. For flutes. A psalm of David.

This psalm is clearly an appeal for help, but no precise indication is given of the circumstances which lay behind it. Throughout the psalm, in almost every verse, there is mention of the words which the psalmist was addressing to God, and also some indication of the evil with which he was contending. It begins with the address to God, and ends with acclamation of him.

1. *A Cry to the King (verses 1-3)*

Now there is an urgent appeal to God, though the psalmist had for long been sighing in his affliction (*verses 1-2*). The word for sighing (*hagig*) only appears here and in Psalm 39:3 in the Psalter. It is connected with the word for murmuring or meditating (see Pss. 1:2; 2:1). There is inaudible prayer to God as well as direct and loud appeals. However, there is confidence in the psalmist's approach, as he is coming to his King and his God. From the time of the Exodus onwards God was regarded as the King of Israel (see Exod. 15:18).

Just as there were morning sacrifices, so also prayers were directed to the LORD at that time (*verse 3*). The language of sacrifice is carried over here, for 'lay my requests' represents the verb used of laying in order the wood (Lev. 1:7) or the victim for sacrifice (Lev. 1:8; 6:12). He then waits in anticipation for God's answer.

2. *God and Evildoers (verses 4-8)*

Emphasis in the Hebrew text of *verse 4* comes on the words, '*But* you ...'. God does not delight in wickedness, and with him is no haven for wicked men because his holiness is to them a consuming fire (Isa.

33:14). Those coming to his holy hill must have God's righteousness (cf. Pss. 15 and 24:1-6).

Those who reject the wisdom of the LORD and live by their own folly cannot stand their ground before him (*verses 5-6*). Here the wicked are characterised as liars, murderers, and deceivers. God's attitude towards them is one of abhorrence and hate, and their ultimate destiny is destruction.

The words 'But *I*' in *verse 7* match the words 'But *you*' in verse 4. The psalmist is not shut out from God's presence or God's house. He goes there on one ground only – God's abundant covenant love to him, and therefore he can enter into the holy place. The epistle to the Hebrews points to the fact that because Jesus has gone before us into heaven we have an anchor for the soul in the inner sanctuary of God (Heb. 6:19-20).

3. *God and Judgement (verses 9-10)*

After the character of the holy God and that of the righteous worshipper comes the character of the evildoer. Here the concentration falls on the sins of the tongue (cf. Jas. 3:6-12). Paul uses the words of the second part of *verse 9* as he sets out the universal sinfulness of mankind in his list of quotations from the Old Testament in Romans 3 (see verse 13a). David asks the LORD to 'declare them guilty'. This is one word in Hebrew, coming from the root *asham*, which is used of the sacrifice for sins of inadvertence (cf. Lev. 4:2f). Guilt must lead to atonement, or alternately to destruction. That David was not asking for personal vengeance is made clear by the closing words of *verse 10*: 'they have rebelled *against you.*' As a loyal covenant servant he asks God to exercise his judgement on his rebel subjects. For fuller discussion of the psalms of cursing see the Introduction, pp. 58-62.

4. *Protection and Joy (verses 11-12)*

The character of God's people as those who take refuge in the LORD is illustrated in this psalm by David's own attitude. Those who live under God's protection can sing for joy for he provides the screen which overshadows them. Probably the idea is that of the mother bird protecting her young with her wings (cf. Ps. 91:4). Another description of the righteous is that they love God's name, i.e. his character. He had revealed himself as the Redeemer of Israel, and the sanctuary of which the psalmist had already spoken (verse 7) was the place where God had made his name dwell (Deut. 12:5).

The idea of protection in *verse 12* is carried on from the preceding verse. God surrounds his people with a protective shield so that they are safe from the enemy. Moreover, it remains true that blessing from the LORD is the portion of his believing children.

PSALM 6
For the director of music. With stringed instruments.
According to sheminith. A psalm of David.

Though an individual composition, yet this psalm was intended for corporate singing. The term *sheminith* in the title is difficult, as the literal meaning is 'an eighth'. If this means an octave, then it is possible the term indicates that it should be accompanied at a lower octave, in keeping with the solemn note of the psalm, or sung by the male voices. This psalm is a complaint to God, and exhibits not only appeal to him but also confidence in the midst of distress. It should be compared to other similar appeals in the Psalter and to Hezekiah's prayer after his illness (Isa. 38:10-20). This is the first of the penitential psalms (cf. comments on Psalm 51).

1. *A Cry to a Gracious God (verses 1-3)*
Each section of the psalm opens with an imperative, and the first two follow on with a question. The psalmist does not confess any sin here, as compared with Psalm 38 which opens with almost the same words. Hence the opening request may mean: 'Don't be angry with me raising this matter with you in prayer.' He goes on to plead for God's intervention in his case. The full extent of his trouble is disclosed by the reference to both bones and soul. In body and spirit he is greatly troubled. The unfinished question 'how long?' appears about thirty times in the Bible and of these, sixteen are in the Psalms. In his distress he breaks off in the midst of the sentence. During his last painful illness, John Calvin uttered no word of complaint, but raising his eyes heavenward he would say in Latin, 'Usquequo Domine' ('Lord, how long?').

2. *His Need Described (verses 4-7)*
He feels that God has been absent from him (a frequent experience of distressed believers), and he wants him to return *(verse 4)*. The 'how long?' of the previous verse now becomes an urgent request for deliverance. The basis of his call is God's unfailing covenant love.

Verse 5 finds its parallel (or its echo) in Hezekiah's prayer (Isa.

38:18). It is the living who are the testimony to God's power and grace.

The distressing condition is not specified. All we know is that the night hours were particularly difficult for him *(verses 6-7)*. Because of physical illness and also the sense of separation from God, he wept so copiously that it seemed as if he flooded his bed with tears. Moses' eyes had not failed even near his death (Deut. 34:7), but David's eyes failed because of his grief and also because of his enemies. His friends may well have forsaken him at this time, and so appeared as if they were enemies.

3. *A Prayer Heard (verses 8-10)*
The sudden change in tone in *verse 8* is surprising. This may indicate either that the psalmist reached an understanding of God's help, or that a priest ministered a word of encouragement, such as Eli gave to Hannah (1 Sam. 1:17). Probably the former is the case, and twice he says that God has heard him. This leads on to the triumphant declaration in verse 9. The tenses are important here: the LORD *has heard* my cry, the LORD *will accept* my prayer. The final verse has a lot of music in the Hebrew text, in that there is repetition of words and sounds. This helps to reinforce the message. Presumably the evildoers and his enemies are the same people, and he longs to see them put to shame. Early in the psalm his bones and soul had been disturbed (verses 2-3). Now he uses the same verb of his enemies in *verse 10* ('dismayed'), while his desire for them is expressed ('turn back') using the same verb he has used earlier of God's seeming return to him ('turn', verse 4).

PSALM 7
A shiggaion of David, which he sang to the LORD
concerning Cush, a Benjamite.

In the midst of distress David calls on the LORD. Though his situation is serious, yet at the end of the psalm he is singing praise to his God. The precise details of the incident(s) concerning Cush are unrecorded in the biblical history. We do know, however, that David faced many problems from the Benjamites (see 1 Sam. 24, 26; 2 Sam. 16:5; 20:1). David protests his innocence in the face of false accusations and asks God to arise to help him. *Shiggaion* in the title is only used here in the Psalter, though another related word occurs in Habakkuk 3:1. It probably meant 'a lamentation'.

1. God – A Safe Refuge (verses 1-2)

David starts with a confident assertion of his hope. He appeals to his God, saying, 'In you [alone] I take refuge.' In the midst of all their troubles, God's children know where their help is to be found, and they turn to the LORD. They can confidently sing:

> All my hope on God is founded;
>> He doth still my trust renew.
> Me through change and chance He guideth,
>> Only God and only true.
>>> God unknown,
>>> He alone
> Calls my heart to be His own.   (Joachim Neander)

Though David's problem seems to have been slander, he feels that he is being torn apart like a lion's victim. Hence he asks God for salvation, for if that does not come, there will be no other salvation ('deliver' and 'to rescue' in these verses are from the same Hebrew verb, *natsal*).

2. God – A Just Vindicator (verses 3-9)

We meet protestations of innocence like this (*verses 3-5*) on the part of psalmists quite often (e.g. 17:3; 18:20-24; 26:1). These should not be taken as claims to sinlessness. Rather they assert a practical and relevant life of obedience as over against their wicked oppressors. They affirm that their lifestyle shows devotion to God, and therefore they are worthy recipients of his protection. The accusation seems to have been that he has not been faithful to a covenant partner ('him who is at peace with me'). If that were true, he invites death from the LORD.

Following Moses' example (Num. 10:35), David requests God to take action against his foes, using three synonymous expressions, 'arise', 'rise up' and 'awake' (*verses 6-8a*). These terms relate both to military and judicial action. He pictures a judgment scene in which God has gathered the nations on earth before him, and then from on high he carries out his judgement. The psalmist is happy to rest in that judgment.

The psalmist now comes back to his own need (*verses 8b-9*). As over against his enemies he stands in integrity before the LORD, who alone can search the inner recesses of the heart (cf. Ps. 17:3; Jer. 11:20; 17:10; 20:12; Rev. 2:23). Repetition of the idea of righteousness marks the confidence of the psalmist before God's judgment. He knows that

the righteous God, who establishes the righteous, will confirm his
righteousness in the face of his opponents.

3. God – A Certain Saviour (verses 10-16)

The military language is carried on first of all by referring to God as
his shield, the protector of the upright in heart. Then it is continued by
reference to God getting his weapons (sword, bow, and flaming
arrows) ready to attack. God is 'sifting out the hearts of men before his
judgment seat', and he has 'loosed the fatal lightning of his terrible
swift sword' (Julia Ward Howe).

The metaphor of a pregnant woman is taken over and applied to the
sinner plotting against the righteous. He conceives the plan, only to
find that it does not eventuate. Like a hunter who digs a trap for an
animal, he falls into it himself. Whatever action he takes, he discovers
that it comes back on himself. This last thought is often alluded to in
the Old Testament (cf. Ps. 37:14-15; Prov. 26:27).

4. God – Worthy of Praise (verse 17)

No mention is made of the ultimate outcome of the distress. While the
psalmist wanted immediate action to free him from his troubles (see
verses 6-9), yet he may have been disappointed if the answer did not
come speedily. But what was most important (and we need to learn this
lesson as well) is that he was given a new perspective on the problem
by taking it to God in prayer. He could rest in the confidence that God
would deal justly and would vindicate him. No wonder that he can sing
a doxology to the LORD! That praise was in honour of God's righteousness. Here, the additional name for God is the 'Most High'. This title
for God occurs thirty times in the Old Testament, of which eighteen are
in the Psalter. It emphasises the majesty of God. In confidence he sings
praise to the name of his God. That does not mean simple repetition of
God's name, but praise for the revelation that God has made of his
nature. He is indeed a Saviour and a righteous Judge.

PSALM 8

For the director of music. According to gittith. A psalm of David.

Creation is the focus of this hymn of praise. It is the latter part of
Genesis 1 turned into a song. Biblical Hebrew has no word for 'thank
you', but it manages to express thanks in a way rather like many of our

English expressions are used when a gift is received ('It's the very thing I wanted!'; 'How beautiful it is!'). As psalmists and prophets understand more of God's character and works, they extol them. The expressions of delight in God's works, as here in verse 1, are themselves a mode of thanking him for them. Here a joyful song praises God's creative activity. The term *gittith* in the title may indicate a musical instrument (a Gittite lyre) or a bright melody to which it was sung. *Gittith* is probably from the name of the town Gath in the south-west of Israel.

1. God's Majesty (verses 1-2)

The psalm opens with a declaration of the majesty of God's name. God is addressed by the use of the covenant name, LORD (Yahweh), to which is added 'our Lord', using the common word for 'Lord'. The pronoun 'our' most probably relates to Israel, rather than to mankind. God's character is seen in the created world, and to believing eyes the whole world manifests God's glory.

> Heaven above is softer blue,
>   Earth around is sweeter green;
> Something lives in every hue,
>   Christless eyes have never seen.
>   (George Wade Robinson)

There is a fuller explanation of God's glory in creation in verses 3ff. Even young children can mouth his praise, and such praise is able to quieten that of his enemies. God is able to use the weak things of this world to confound the mighty (1 Cor. 1:27). Jesus quoted *verse 2* (cf. Matt. 21:16) when rebuking the authorities who wanted him to quieten the children shouting his praise when he entered Jerusalem.

2. Man's Insignificance (verses 3-5)

In comparison with the majesty of all creation, and behind that the majesty of God (cf. '*your* heavens, the work of *your* fingers'), man's position seems so very insignificant. The words chosen for 'man' in this verse (*'enosh* and *ben 'adam*) seem to be deliberately chosen to highlight his frailty. The expected answer to the question the psalmist asks has to be, 'Nothing!'

'You have made him a little lower than the heavenly beings and crowned him with glory and honour' *(verse 5)*. It is better to follow the

NIV margin and accept the Massoretic Hebrew text which has 'God' instead of 'heavenly beings'. Man occupies a special position in creation, in that he alone of all the creatures was made in the image and likeness of God (Gen. 1:26-27; 5:1). Because of his creation he has to reflect God's glory in a special way as he rules as God's vice-regent.

3. Man's Role in Creation (verses 6-8)
Man was given dominion over the rest of creation (Gen. 1:28-30; 9:1-3), and these verses show how comprehensive this rule was. The words 'you put everything under his feet' find their fullest meaning in Jesus' dominion through his resurrection and exaltation (1 Cor. 15:27; Eph. 1:22; Heb. 2:6-8). What is pictured here of man in respect to creation is yet to have its fullest significance in the great re-creation.

4. God's Praise Renewed (verse 9)
Just as the psalm begins, so it ends. It started on the note of praise, the reasons for praise were unfolded, and finally ends with more praise.

PSALM 9
For the director of music. To the tune of
'The Death of the Son'. A psalm of David

Psalms 9 and 10 form a unit, as they together comprise an acrostic (see Introduction, p. 13). The acrostic pattern is not complete, as several letters of the Hebrew alphabet are missing and some letters are not in the usual order. The use of an acrostic clearly appealed to some poets, and it must also have brought responsive appreciation from hearers or readers. Acrostics may well have served a teaching purpose in that they were a device to assist in memorising a poem. The emphasis in Psalm 9 is on praise of God, while in Psalm 10 the main focus is an appeal to God in distress. The words translated 'The Death of the Son' do not occur elsewhere in the Psalter.

1. A Song of Thanksgiving (verses 1-2)
These verses contain several terms which concentrate on praise, probably public praise in the sanctuary: *praise, tell, be glad, sing praise*. To the opening one is added, *with all my heart*, to indicate the depth of his 'praise'. The 'wonders' were the deeds which the LORD alone could and did perform, such as the great redemptive acts

connected with the Exodus. The 'name' is a reference not to a title for the LORD but to the revelation he had made of himself. The psalmist sings praise to his covenant God *(LORD)* and to his exalted sovereign *(Most High)*. Similar language is used at the opening of Psalm 75.

2. *Acknowledgment of Personal Help (verses 3-6)*
These verses refer back to historical incidents which are the foundation of praise. God had intervened, and the psalmist's enemies had perished before him. The verb 'to stumble' often occurs in the poetical books in this metaphorical sense of being brought to ruin. Judgment had been executed on his behalf by God, who from his kingly throne carried out just judgment. Even the Gentile nations had felt God's 'rebuke', a word elsewhere applied to dramatic actions of God such as the flood (cf. Ps. 106:9; Isa. 54:9). Nations had been blotted out before him so that no recollection of them remained. The duration of the ruin is stressed by the use of 'for ever and ever' and 'endless'.

3. *The Rule of the King/Shepherd (verses 7-10)*
The thought of God as judge leads on to statements concerning his general rule and his protective care. In contrast to the enemies, the LORD sits enthroned for ever *(verse 7)*. Here the picture seems to move to the scene at the end of time, when all shall appear before the LORD's throne of judgment. The action of judgment occurred in the past (verse 5), but future judgment is still in store. Unlike human judges, God judges righteously *(verse 8)*. His administration will not be marred by the flawed justice of human systems. The whole of the inhabited world *(tebel)* will be subject to his rule. This verse is used again in the later Royal Psalms to describe the end-time judgment of the divine king (Pss. 96:13; 98:9).

For any afflicted there is the assurance that God is a 'refuge' or 'stronghold' (in the NIV translation these words render the same Hebrew word which occurs twice in *verse 9*). The main idea of the Hebrew word is a place with high fortifications (cf. Isa. 25:12). There in times of trouble the oppressed find refuge. 'Oppressed' is a synonym for 'afflicted' in verse 12. The character of those who take refuge is described as 'those who know your name'. Unlike the names of the wicked which are blotted out (verse 5), God's name is the revelation of his person. Those who love him have come to a personal knowledge of him, and therefore they put their confidence in him.

None of those who seek him ever find themselves left in the lurch. The verb 'to seek' appears often in the Psalms, especially in the general sense of asking help or assistance from the LORD (cf. Ps. 14:2).

4. A Doxology (verses 11-12)

The psalmist in verses 11 and 12 returns to the theme of praise found at the beginning of the psalm (verses 1-2). He who is enthroned in Zion (the presence of the ark in Jerusalem is intended) is to be praised, and his deeds declared to the Gentile nations. What his deeds consist of is made clear in verse 12. God was the one who would take vengeance on those who took (or attempted to take) the life of others (cf. Gen. 4:10; 9:5). His sovereign deliverance of his people would be proclaimed as his 'wonders' (verse 1). Not till later in the Psalms is there fuller expression of this wish that all the nations might know the LORD's deeds (cf. Pss. 18:49; 57:9, and the Introduction, pp. 10, 41-42).

5. An Appeal for Help (verses 13-14)

The tone of the psalm changes at this point to become more like a lament, with appeals to God for his mercy and deliverance. These appeals are going to be repeated at the end of the psalm (verses 19-20).

Stemming out of the assurance given in the preceding verse that God is the avenger, the psalmist appeals in respect of his own case. Statements of God's character often form the basis for individual prayer. David's persecution by his enemies had reached the point where he felt he had reached the gates of death itself. Death is looked at as if it were a territory, or a city with doors (cf. Rev. 1:18, 'the keys of death and Hades').

The psalmist wants mercy to be shown to him so that he in turn can declare God's praises. The highest desire he has is not just his own deliverance but the opportunity to praise his deliverer. Those delivered by God desire to declare the praises of him who called them out of darkness into his marvellous light (1 Pet. 2:9). 'The Daughter of Zion' is a personification of Jerusalem as a young girl, perhaps better rendered as 'Daughter Zion'. There, surrounded by the inhabitants of Jerusalem, he longs to sing and rejoice in God's salvation.

6. The Wicked Ensnared (verses 15-16)

Attention now comes back to the nations (see verse 5). The outcome for the wicked is described in terms of their being caught in their own snares. What they wanted to do to Israel has become their own portion. They were to know the consequences of their own plotting, not on others, but on themselves (cf. Ps. 5:10). The work of their own hands turns on them. The opening of *verse 16* makes it plain that God's hand was also in this. 'The wicked' (synonymous with 'nations' in verses 5, 15, 17 and 19) are the subjects of God's justice, which turns their plots against themselves.

'Higgaion' comes from a Hebrew root which means to murmur, sigh, meditate. Hence it probably denotes that the last part of the psalm is to be rendered softly in keeping with the solemnity of the subject.

7. *The Destiny of the Wicked (verses 17-18)*
Those who forget God return to Sheol. Earlier in this psalm there is mention of 'forgetting' (verse 12, NIV 'ignore'). Here it means people who do not think about the true God or serve him, but rather strive against his people. The verdict expressed against them may not mean here immediate judgment and death, but that which is treasured up for them in the future (see verse 20). The verb to forget appears again in *verse 18*, but with what a great contrast! God will never forget his poor and afflicted ones. He will never allow their hope to perish. Their expectation is based on God's sure word to his children.

8. *A Final Appeal (verses 19-20)*
It is clear that the opposition to the righteous (and especially to the psalmist himself) was still present, and therefore he asks for God's speedy help (for 'arise' cf. Psalm 7:6). The language used here goes back to Moses' words in Numbers 10:35 when the ark was moving: 'Rise up, O LORD! May your enemies be scattered; may your foes flee before you' (cf. also Ps. 68:1-2). The psalmist does not want frail man to be able to rejoice in triumph. The Hebrew word translated 'man' (*'enosh*) carries with it implications of human frailty and weakness, especially as here in contrast to God's power.

What was needed was a fresh demonstration of God's power such as had been shown at the Exodus. The word 'terror' implies this, for it is used in Deuteronomy 4:34 of God's awesome deeds when he brought Israel out of Egypt. By a repetition of such divine action the nations would truly know their own frailty and insignificance before the LORD. An appearance of God would fill his enemies with apprehension as they realised that they could not stand before him.

PSALM 10

Almost all the psalms in the first book (Psalms 1-41) have a title. The only exceptions are 1, 2, 10 and 33. The fact that a title is missing for this psalm is another indication that it is to be considered in conjunction with Psalm 9, whose title also covers this psalm. The note of appeal to God is much more prominent here, though at the end of the psalm there is an affirmation that God the King is also a prayer-hearing God.

1. *A Heartfelt Cry (verses 1-2)*

The psalmist is in deep trouble and turns to the one who is a stronghold at such times (see 9:9). The introductory word is 'Why?' This speaks of the hurt and disappointment he feels, but it also includes the idea of expectation of God's help. There is also the note of puzzlement at the treatment believers receive from persecutors. Later psalms such as 37 and 73 help to provide the answer to that puzzle.

'In his arrogance the wicked man hunts down the weak, who are caught in the schemes he devises' *(verse 2)*. This short statement of the situation is explained more fully later in the psalm (see especially verses 7-10). In the second clause of this verse the subject of the verb 'caught' is 'they'. This could refer to the wicked being caught in their own snares, but more probably the NIV is correct to take it as meaning the poor are entrapped.

2. *The Pride of the Wicked (verses 3-6)*

It is part of the routine of sinners to glorify themselves *(verses 3-4)*. Right from the time of the first sin they have wanted to elevate themselves to be as God (Gen. 3:5). Sin also causes wrong understanding of the deeds of other sinners, as well as of God's character. Hence the sinner praises greedy and ruthless men, while God is blasphemed. He makes no attempt to seek after God and shuts him out of all his thoughts. Part of the nature of sinful man is to suppress the knowledge he has of the truth and to fail to glorify and give thanks to God (Rom. 1:18-21).

The wicked enjoy prosperity, but it makes them even more arrogant *(verses 5-6)*. They live in seeming freedom from divine judgment (it is better to take the Hebrew word *mishpat* as 'judgment' rather than as the NIV's 'law'). Towards their enemies they show contempt and make the boastful claim that they will always stand firm. The second part of verse 6 is difficult to translate and interpret, and an awkward verse division complicates it further. A literal rendering would be: 'From generation to generation [I will have] happiness and not trouble; he has sworn.' It is part of the wicked man's arrogance to claim exemption from trouble and from judgment. He considers himself unassailable.

3. *The Character of the Wicked (verses 7-11)*

A description of sinful man now follows, with emphasis on his role as an oppressor *(verses 7-8)*. The description at the start of verse 7 of sinful man (with a tongue that is always speaking lies) is taken over by Paul from the LXX and used in his description of the utter sinfulness of man without Christ (Rom. 3:14). Continually the wicked pour out their evil words against others. In addition to words, they act with violence against others.

There is no reason to suggest anything other than a literal understanding of the description here *(verses 9-11)*. They act like lions in attacking their prey. Similar imagery occurs quite frequently in the Psalter (cf. 17:12; 37:32; 56:6; 59:3; 64:4). The spiritual conditions behind these verses are unknown to us. However, we have enough evidence from the prophets to confirm the accuracy of the description given here. There were clearly many occasions when force was used against the poor and needy in Israel (see Isa. 1:15-17, 21-23; Jer. 7:9; Ezek. 22:2ff.; Hos. 4:2; 6:8-9). Sheer brute force had been used and the helpless were felled. In verse 11 the thought of verse 6 is taken up and developed further. The inner thoughts of the wicked are exposed, for what has taken place outwardly is only the expression of inward godlessness. The wicked are depicted as claiming that as God does not see them, they can act sinfully with great boldness. Jesus, in his teaching, developed the whole concept of inner sin coming to expression in outward actions (see Matt. 5:21-30; Mark 7:14-23).

4. *A Call to God (verses 12-13)*

The appeal to God is urgent. This is emphasised both by the call to him to 'arise', but also the use of three different names for God in these verses. He is first of all addressed as Covenant LORD (Hebrew, *yhwh*), then as God (Hebrew, *'el*) and finally by another word for God (Hebrew, *'elohim*). To lift up the hand clearly means to punish (cf. verse 15), or to put it positively, to rescue his afflicted ones (as in Psalm 138:7). Those who reviled God thought that he would not seek them out. They had already declared themselves as atheists (verse 4), and now they proudly boast that they will be left alone to carry out their evil deeds. Sinners ever need to be reminded that ultimately they will be called to account before the judgment seat of God (2 Cor. 5:10).

5. *A Song of Confidence (verses 14-18)*

How different were things in reality *(verses 14-15).* God saw everything that happened, in contrast to the claim that he neither saw (verse 11) nor punished (verse 13). The orphan is singled out as representative of that group for whom the LORD ever showed great care (Exod. 22:22-24; Mal. 3:5). Those in need have the reassurance that God sees their trouble and that he acts as their helper. In verse 15 the psalmist asks God to break the powerful arm of the wicked so that he cannot continue in his evil way. God is said to seek out for punishment the wicked (Hebrew, lit. 'you seek [to punish] his wickedness. Surely you can find it!').

The psalmist ends with a song of complete confidence in the LORD *(verses 16-18),* and he was so certain of being heard by him that he describes the result of his prayers as a present reality. He recognises that the LORD exercises his kingship over the whole land, and will even destroy the enemies from it. That thought is remarkable, because in the psalm the enemies are opponents within Israel. However, the concept of judgment on the enemies reminds him that God will also deal with the external enemies of Israel. Verse 17 contains the assurance that the prayers he has already expressed for the afflicted are indeed heard by God. Notice the variety of terms he uses for the needy: *weak,* verse 2; *innocent,* verse 8; *helpless,* verse 12; *fatherless,* verses 14 and 18; *afflicted,* verse 17; *oppressed,* verse 18. Man, who boasts of his might, is but frail man ('*enosh,* cf. Ps. 9:19) who will no longer be able to terrify others. He is 'of the earth' and cannot stand before the judge of all.

This psalm reminds us that under persecution and oppression we must turn to God for relief. Our pattern is Jesus of whom it is written, 'when they hurled their insults at him, he did not retaliate; when he suffered, he made no threats. Instead, he entrusted himself to him who judges justly' (1 Pet. 2: 23). The same epistle counsels us that if we suffer we are to commit ourselves to our faithful Creator and continue to do good (1 Pet. 4:19).

PSALM 11
For the director of music. Of David.

This is a song of confidence, probably composed when David fled from Absalom. If that is so, verse 1 may contain the advice his friends were giving him. They were telling him to flee for safety as he had done when Saul was persecuting him to 'the Crags of the Wild Goats' (1 Sam. 24:2). But he knew that his protection was only with the LORD.

1. *The Needy Situation Described (verses 1-3)*
The Psalm opens and closes on a confident note: 'In the LORD I take refuge ... the LORD is righteous.' The opening words give the basic theme of the psalm – confident trust in the LORD. In his crisis situation friends were giving advice. They were suggesting he should fly or escape like a bird to a mountain hideout. The verb is plural, so perhaps his friends and associates were intended to flee as well. The designation 'your mountain' has been taken by some to indicate the well-known retreat which David had previously used.

The thought of the bird fleeing is carried over from verse 1, and now the imagery is of a hunter out after the birds with his bow *(verse 2)*. Elsewhere the wicked are also described as bending the bow (Psalm 37:14). The language of fleeing to the mountains to escape may well be a reflection of the advice to Lot (Gen. 19:17; and see verse 6 later in this psalm). The godless are ready to shoot their arrows at the upright without being seen.

There was so much upheaval that even the foundational principles of society were being shaken *(verse 3)*. There was no truth or justice any more. The final sentence could refer to the past: 'What has the righteous done?' i.e. to deserve this. However, it is better to follow the NIV and take it as a question of despair: 'What can the righteous do?'

2. *The Source of Confidence (verses 4-7)*
The question of despair asked by the psalmist's friends now finds its answer. 'The LORD is in his holy temple; the LORD is on his heavenly throne. He observes the sons of men; his eyes examine them' *(verse 4)*. Normally there is a spoken prayer after an expression of great need, but one is lacking here. Rather the psalmist points to the LORD on high, seated on his judgment throne. There was the visible presence of God in the Tabernacle, but he was also the exalted heavenly ruler. From

heaven he saw all that happened, and with penetrating gaze, he was able to test the works of all mankind. The verb translated 'examine' is often used of testing metals by fire and is a favourite word in the Book of Jeremiah (11:20; 17:10; 20:12). Even the actions in darkness (*verse 2*) were open to his sight.

Both righteous and unrighteous come under God's judging eye (*verses 5-6*, cf. Paul's words, 'we must all appear before the judgment seat of Christ', 2 Cor. 5:10), though God's attitude is quite different regarding the two groups. His innermost being ('his soul') hates the violent man, presumably an indication that the psalmist's enemies were of this kind. The thought of fire used for testing metals changes in verse 6 to become a picture of the fiery judgment. For believers the fire will test the quality of their work (1 Cor. 3:13), while for unbelievers the fire will come as the exterminator of evil. 'Fiery coals and burning sulphur' reminds us of what happened to Sodom (Gen. 19:24). A similar fate awaits the wicked. The reference to the scorching wind is a description of the east wind which blows over Israel, bringing with it the desert heat.

How differently God will act towards the righteous *(verse 7)*! He himself is righteous and he loves justice, i.e. the righteous deeds done by his people. The phrase 'loves justice' could mean that God loves to do righteous deeds, but this is less likely in the context. The final outcome is that the upright in heart will see God's presence manifested in his saving deliverance of them. The psalmist returns at the end of the psalm to the same confession he made at the beginning.

PSALM 12
For the director of music. According to sheminith.
A psalm of David.

Psalms like this one show the contrasts in spiritual life within Israel. So many had turned away from obedience to the LORD that it seemed to the righteous that the godly had disappeared altogether. The other contrast in the psalm is between the lying words of the ungodly and the sure words of the LORD.

1. The Vain Speech of the Ungodly (verses 1-4)
The opening word is a cry of desperation. The Hebrew word used *(hoshi'ah)* is normally followed by an object: 'help *me*'. Here, and also

in the Hebrew text of Psalm 118:25, the shout is never finished. It is like a drowning person calling out, 'Help'. The Hebrew verb is the one from which the names Joshua and Jesus come. The urgency of the request concerns the apparent disappearance of the faithful from the land. They are described by use of the words for covenant loyalty (*chasid*) and faithful (*'emunim*; cf. the fanatical Israeli group *gush 'emunim, assembly of the faithful*). The spiritual division of society was recognised later by Elijah (1 Kings 19:9-18), and manifested particularly in Jesus' rejection by his own (John 1: 10-11).

Life was marked by deceit, so that everyone spoke against his neighbour *(verse 2)*. No society or church fellowship can continue if this is the case (cf. Eph. 4:25). With double hearts (Hebrew, *a heart and [still another] heart*) they spoke, so that their words did not agree with reality.

The psalmist adds to his cry for help (verse 1) an appeal for the LORD to intervene by cutting off all deceivers and those who boast in their arrogance *(verses 3-4)*. The verb 'cut off' goes back to the threat in Genesis 17:14 that an unfaithful covenant person will be 'cut off'. Rather than cutting a covenant with the LORD, they will be cut off, i.e. executed. These people are described further as proud boasters. Their lips are at their service and they challenge anyone to prevail against them. Later, the prophets had to rebuke the people for the sins of the tongue (Hos. 4:1-2; Jer. 12:6), while the New Testament reaffirms how the tongue is a fire corrupting the whole person (Jas. 3:6).

2. *The Sure Speech of the LORD (verses 5-8)*

Prayer was made and speedily answered *(verse 5)*. No indication is given of how the LORD's words came to the psalmist. It could have been by the ministry of a priest, just as Eli ministered God's word to Hannah (1 Sam. 1:17). The answer is more direct than English translations are able to convey. The cry for help in verse 1 *(hoshia')* is followed now by an assurance that the LORD is going to bring salvation to them (*yesha'*, from the same root, *yasha'*) for him. God hears the cry of the weak and needy and arises to help (cf. Pss. 7:6; 9:19; Isa. 33:10). He is the deliverer of the oppressed (Pss. 72:12; 103:6).

The contrast of the Lord's words with the words of the deceivers is so clear *(verse 6)*. The LORD's words are pure, i.e. they have been purified like silver in the furnace, and so they stand forever (cf. the use of the same expression for the law of the LORD in Psalm 19:9). They have no dross, and so can be relied upon. The implication is that the words of the deceivers are all dross!

The message from the LORD has brought reassurance to the psalmist *(verse 7)*. Protection will be provided from 'such people' (the Hebrew has 'from this generation'; cf. Jesus' words in Matthew 17:17, 'O unbelieving and perverse generation'). 'Generation' is used in the broad sense of a type of people who share the same mind-set, a group bound together by common interests.

The psalm returns in its conclusion to its opening ideas. The ungodly are still parading around and 'among men' (repeated from verse 1); what is vile is still highly regarded *(verse 8)*. The end of the psalm is a reminder that believers have to persevere in believing prayer, even as wickedness continues or even abounds. Our pattern has to be that of Jesus who suffered at the hands of liars (John 8:44-47) and who 'offered up prayers and petitions with loud cries and tears to the one who could save him from death, and he was heard because of his reverent submission' (Heb. 5:7).

PSALM 13
For the director of music. A psalm of David.

This short psalm has all the characteristics and structure of a lament or appeal for help. It moves from the desolation of the opening verses to the strong confidence in God's abiding mercy in the closing ones. It is a reminder that as many as the LORD loves he rebukes and chastens (Rev. 3:19).

1. *A Cry of Distress (verses 1-2)*
The fourfold cry, 'How long?' dominates the opening stanzas. The psalmist feels himself forgotten by God, and even suggests that it is for ever. 'How long?' is a phrase of urgency, even of desperation. God can reach the end of divine endurance as he did with Israel: 'How long will these people treat me with contempt? How long will they refuse to believe in me, in spite of all the miraculous signs I have performed among them? I will strike them down with a plague and destroy them ...' When Moses pleaded God's covenant mercy, God relented and forgave the people (Num. 14:11, 12). Here we have the same link made between 'How long?' and God's covenant mercy (verse 5). The personal feelings which predominate in a situation like this are inward

thoughts of sorrow. They occur all the time as the psalmist faces the foe, which seemingly is illness and death (see verse 3).

2. *A Plea to the Lord (verses 3-4)*

In his opening lament the psalmist has spoken of God hiding his face (verse 1). Now his plea is for the LORD to 'look' (i.e. to consider, scrutinise) and to answer his questions. Illness is understood as a darkening of the eyes. Hence the psalmist prays for light to dawn on him so that he will not experience death. There is a tender note in the way he makes his plea. He says 'O LORD my God.' The pronoun 'my' injects an affectionate aspect into the prayer and also a note of believing confidence. Those who approach God in prayer 'must believe that he exists and that he rewards those who earnestly seek him' (Heb. 11:6). If his God does not answer him he will die, and all his foes will then take joy in gloating over what has happened to him (cf. Ps. 38:16).

3. *A Certain Confidence (verses 5-6)*

There is a marked difference between the psalmist's foes and himself, and the opening of verse 5 sets them over against each other. 'But I,' he says, 'trust in your unfailing love; my heart rejoices in your salvation. I will sing to the LORD, for he has been good to me.' His confidence is in the covenant love of the LORD which expresses itself in his deliverance. Hence he can overflow with loving praise and he asks God to let his heart rejoice when that salvation appears. This understanding of verse 5 (that his deliverance is yet in the future) is confirmed by the Hebrew idiom in the final verse, which means that he will sing praise 'as soon as he has dealt bountifully with me'. Deliverance, though yet to come, is acknowledged and praised in believing trust. Believers can always look forward in anticipation of God's deliverances.

PSALM 14
For the director of music. Of David.

Psalms 14 and 53, while not exactly identical, are so close that one is basically a replica of the other. The main differences lie in the use of divine names (Psalm 14 uses LORD *[yhwh]* four times; Psalm 53 consistently uses God, *'elohim*), slight verbal differences in the opening verses, and more major differences in the closing verses (14:5-6

=53:5). Most probably Psalm 14 is the earlier version, but the importance of its teaching must have been recognised and an alternative version used in worship. Finally, both forms were incorporated into the present Psalter.

The style of the psalm is closest to Psalms 1 and 2, or to the wisdom literature, especially illustrated by the Book of Proverbs. Psalm 14 is not concerned with intellectual atheism. Its focus is rather on the person who is a practical atheist because he has renounced the covenant and therefore the covenant God. The New Testament points more fully than the Old Testament to the ultimate wisdom of God which is found in Jesus Christ (1 Cor. 1:23-25).

1. A Description of the Fool (verses 1-3)

The Hebrew word for fool or folly *(nabal)* marked out those who had renounced their allegiance to the covenant God and consequently to one another *(verse 1)*. It was used, for example, of the nation in Isaiah 9:13-17. The fool lacks the wisdom with which the fear of the LORD begins. He not only says but lives as if 'There is no God'. The second part of verse 1 clearly shows the normal character of such fools. Their actions are corrupt and an abomination to the LORD. They do not do what is good. The reference may be to more than just general goodness. More specifically it might indicate a failure to follow covenant commitments.

An anthropomorphic description (one in terms of human characteristics) of God's actions is given to emphasise how he sees everyone *(verses 2-3)*. He looks out for those who 'understand'. The Hebrew word stands in contrast to 'fool' in verse 1, and is a synonym for 'wise', 'spiritually understanding'. Another expression for the godly is used at the end of verse 2. They 'seek God,' i.e. they approach the face of God in prayer. The divine verdict is given in verse 3. The godless, far from seeking God, have turned aside and they have become corrupt. The words 'there is no one who does good' are repeated from verse 1, with the addition of the emphatic, 'not even one'. Paul employs words from verses 2 and 3 to give further confirmation of his assertion that none are righteous before God (Rom. 3:10-12).

2. The Oppression of the Righteous (verses 4-6)

It becomes clear that not everyone has turned aside from the LORD, for there are those whom he can call 'my people' *(verse 4)*. They are the objects of oppression on the part of 'fools', or as they are called here, 'evildoers'. Their problem is that they do not have spiritual knowledge, and consequently they 'do not call on the LORD'. This last phrase can be used in the Old Testament in the sense of proclaiming the LORD (cf. what God himself does for Moses, Ex. 33:19), but it also means, as here, to use God's name in prayer (Gen. 4:26).

Verses 5-6 are difficult verses to interpret. In both of them there is a contrast between the evildoers in the first part of the verse, and the righteous in the second. There does not seem to be any direct connection between the two clauses other than direct contrast. The evildoers live in fear as a result of their folly and they oppress the poor. On the other hand, the righteous have God in their midst, in their assembly. They also have the assurance that while they are being oppressed, the LORD is their refuge.

3. A Prayer for Deliverance (verse 7)

The psalmist longs for the coming salvation of the LORD. Clearly the psalm dates from a time when Zion was the religious centre (i.e. after David's bringing of the ark there). The words 'restoring the fortunes' need not be a reference to the coming return from exile. Rather, the Hebrew phrase (lit. *restores the captivity*) can be taken in a general way as speaking of a real change in the people's circumstances. Salvation would come from the LORD. Every saving action of God in the Old Testament was a precursor of the far fuller salvation which Jesus would bring. It is not surprising that the psalm ends on a note of joy, for salvation brings forth a song from the people of God. When the ultimate redemption is completed, a great multitude will sing: 'Salvation belongs to our God who sits on the throne, and to the Lamb' (Rev. 7:10).

PSALM 15
A psalm of David.

Psalm 15 and Psalm 24 have much in common. They both ask about coming into the presence of the LORD at his holy hill, and they both answer in a similar way. The character of the godly worshipper is set out clearly. Both psalms probably originate with the removal of the ark of the covenant to Jerusalem by David (2 Sam. 6).

1. *The Question Asked (verse 1)*

'LORD, who may dwell in your sanctuary? Who may live on your holy hill?' The two clauses are clearly used in parallel with one another. Two different verbs are used ('dwell', 'live') and two different descriptions of God's dwelling place are given ('sanctuary', 'holy hill'). The mountain of the LORD has been spoken of in the Song of Moses (Exod. 15:17). When David captured Mount Zion (2 Sam. 5:7) he took up residence there and brought the ark of the LORD to dwell there. The worshipper now asks who can sojourn as the LORD's guest. The verb 'dwell' does not just imply temporary dwelling (cf. its use in Psalm 61:4). To 'live' is a verb used of living in a tent and from it one of the names for the tabernacle was derived *(mishkan)*.

2. *The Answers Provided (verses 2-5a)*

The answer comes in a pattern of two sets of positive conditions, with two corresponding sets of negative conditions.

Positive	Negative
Verse 2a	Verse 3a
Verse 2b	Verse 3b
Verse 2c	Verse 3c

Positive	Negative
Verse 4a	Verse 5a
Verse 4b	Verse 5b
Verse 4c	

The first group of positive conditions does not include sacrificial requirements, nor do any of the others *(verse 2)*. The concentration is on moral characteristics. The first one, walking blamelessly, is virtually a synonym for being godly, and speaks of the wholeness of the person. The second one starts to be more specific, demanding righteous actions, while the third one asks for truthful speech.

The negative conditions now follow *(verse 3)*. The first one implies no wrong use of his tongue. Literally it is, 'he has not spied with [or possibly, tripped over] his tongue.' Nor has he done any harm to his neighbour or made fun of the faults or situations of his friends (or possibly relations).

The second set of positive conditions includes honouring those who fear God and despising those who are rejected by God *(verse 4)*.

Thus spiritual attitudes are important in the worshipper. The third condition in this verse is difficult to translate and interpret. The NIV rendering is one possibility. It is also possible that it means 'he has sworn to do no wrong and does not alter,' i.e. he keeps his pledged word without any change.

The final two conditions are negative and both relate to money *(verse 5a)*. It was forbidden for an Israelite to lend with interest to a fellow Israelite (Lev. 25:36-37; Deut. 23:19). It was, however, permissible to lend with interest to a foreigner (Deut. 23:20). Also, no bribe could be taken to ensure the conviction of the innocent (cf. Exod. 23:8; Deut. 16:19). Passages in the prophetical books such as Isaiah 33:14-16 and Micah 6:6-8 may well be building upon these conditions given in verses 2-5a.

3. *The Promise (verse 5b)*
The final word in the psalm is one of reassurance. The person who fulfils its conditions will not be moved, i.e. be removed from the house of the LORD and from the LORD's presence. The answer to the opening question in effect is: 'Whoever does these things shall dwell in his sanctuary for ever.'

PSALM 16
A miktam of David.

The title attributes the psalm to David, and both Peter and Paul in the New Testament confirm this (Acts 2: 25-32; 13:36). The word *miktam* is most probably from a verb which means 'to inscribe', and therefore a *miktam* is a song which is to be inscribed. The word occurs here and in the titles of five other psalms (56, 57, 58, 59, 60), and only here and in Psalm 58 is there omission of details linking this particular psalm with incidents in David's life. It is a song of confidence, and in the final verses David prophesies the resurrection of Jesus.

1. *An Opening Prayer (verse 1)*
As no details are given of any particular crisis in David's life, it is best to take this appeal at the beginning of the psalm to be for continuing divine protection. Those who have already experienced that protection know how to pray, for, like David, they have taken refuge with him. This is a favourite expression with him (see Pss. 7:1 and 11:1).

2. *The Words of an Idol Worshipper (verses 2-4a)*

There are problems in giving a good English translation of *verses 2-4a* and fitting them satisfactorily into the psalm as a whole. The verb at the beginning of verse 2 is not first person singular (as given in the NIV, '*I* said'), but second person singular ('*you* (fem.) said'). The following comments assume that the words are those of an idol worshipper who claimed allegiance to the LORD but who followed other gods. He tried to maintain a spoken commitment to the LORD ('my Lord') and to claim that all his goodness was to be found in him ('apart from you I have no good thing'). However, the reality was that he followed foreign gods, calling them in verse 3 'holy ones' (NIV, 'saints') and 'mighty ones' (NIV, 'glorious ones'). His real pleasure was solely in them. The psalmist gives his verdict on all those who follow this example (verse 4a). The word rendered 'run' in the NIV is better taken as meaning 'acquire' or 'exchange' (cf. Ps. 106:20; Jer. 2:11). Those who swap the true God for idols will always increase their sorrows. This may be an allusion to the fertility rites practised in the heathen religions (cf. Isa. 57:7-8).

3. *A Song of Confidence (verses 4b-6)*

Heathen worship holds no attraction for a true believer *(verse 4b)*. David says emphatically that he will not share in their false sacrifices, nor even take their names on his lips. He will shun any association which might link him with such false beliefs.

Verses 5-6 is the reaffirmation of the blessings which the LORD had given him, and which stand in such contrast to the sorrows which the idol worshipper experiences (verse 4a). 'Portion and cup' refers to the overflowing bounty which God had given him. The imagery is related to that concerning God's provision for the Levites (Num. 18:20; Deut. 10:9; 18:1-2). His allocated territory was certain, and the places where the lines had been marked for him were pleasant. He is not speaking of an earthly inheritance, such as the tribes received, but of God's gift of himself.

4. *The Reward of Confidence (verses 7-11)*

The psalmist breaks out into a song of thanksgiving for the wisdom which has come to him from the LORD *(verses 7-8)*. At night time (or possibly the plural form in Hebrew denotes dark nights) he considers and meditates on this instruction. True meditation is never with a blank mind, but is based on God's revealed word. 'Heart' is literally the kidneys, which the Hebrew people considered to be the seat of the emotions. Verse 8 gives further expression to the thought of refuge in verse 1. The LORD is always before his eyes, and he is ever at his right hand. This is the position which is mentioned as the place of the helper (Pss. 109:31; 121:5). Because the LORD is with him, he knows assuredly that he will not be moved.

Safety with the LORD produces a further song of praise from David *(verses 9-10)*. Various synonyms for 'I' appear in these verses: 'my heart', 'my glory' (the NIV follows the LXX text and reads 'my tongue'), 'my body', and 'my soul' (NIV 'me'). David is not separating soul from body, but simply indicating that the whole person is living securely.

Verse 10 occupies a special place in biblical thought because it is quoted in reference to Jesus' resurrection. David is asserting that the LORD will not abandon his life to Sheol, nor let his faithful one (i.e. David) see corruption. He knows that his prayer of verse 1 ('help me') is answered and that he will not die, or alternately, that he will be preserved from a premature death. But David also speaks prophetically by the Holy Spirit and looks to the resurrection of the Messiah. His eye is on one of his descendants (see Acts 2:27) and his words have a far deeper meaning than the surface reading of them would suggest.

The final verse (*11*) uses words and ideas already employed earlier in the psalm ('make known,' 'life,' 'joy,' 'your presence,' 'pleasure,' 'eternal'). David wants to experience God's leading in the path through life (cf. the path of peace, Luke 1:79). Fullness of joy is to be found where the LORD reveals his presence (cf. Pss. 4:7; 21:6), and the pleasant places and things (see verse 6) from the LORD's hand will last right through life. Hence 'lasting pleasures' would be a preferable translation to the NIV's 'eternal pleasures'.

PSALM 17
A prayer of David.

A psalm such as this shows how strongly the covenant hope supported troubled and persecuted believers in the Old Testament period. The psalmist calls on God and asks for a further display of covenant mercy, such as God had shown in acts of deliverance at the time of the Exodus. There is dependence upon words from the Song of the Sea (Ex. 15:1-

18) and also from the Song of Moses (Deut. 32). There are also many points of connection between Psalms 16 and 17. Some of these are: the prayer, 'keep me' (16:1; 17:8); communion with God at night (16:7; 17:3); the use of the Hebrew word *'el* for God in prayer (16:1; 17:6); the reference to the right hand of God (16:8; 17:7,14); and the pleasures of God's presence (16:11; 17:15). The two psalms may well form a pair composed near the end of David's life.

1. *A Prayer from an Innocent Person (verses 1-5)*

The request which David makes is given in three forms: 'hear,' 'listen,' and 'give ear' *(verse 1)*. Likewise his description of his plea is threefold: '[my] righteous [plea]'; 'my cry'; and 'my prayer'. The varied language draws attention immediately to the intensity of his requests and the deep need in which he found himself. He disclaims any deceitfulness on his part. This type of protestation of innocence is common to the Psalter (cf. 18:20-24; 26:1). These should not be understood as self-righteous claims to sinless perfection. They are affirmations that the writers were essentially devoted to God, that they were innocent of the slanderous accusations of their enemies, and hence they were worthy of God's protection. The psalmist knows that right judgment will come from the LORD and he is quite prepared to leave his life open before his all-seeing eye *(verse 2)*. He is willing to have sentence passed by his judge.

David claims that all of God's testing, however probing it may be (two of the terms, 'probe', and 'test', are from metallurgy), will find no dross in his life *(verse 3)*. He knew the dangers of the sins of the tongue, as he was the victim of accusations. However, he set himself to refrain from transgressing with his mouth.

The psalmist isolates himself from the wicked for, in contrast to them, he has kept to God's word and his steps have followed God's paths *(verses 4-5)*. His enemies were clearly violent in action as well as in word. By following God's directions he had shunned their way of life and had not deviated from God's paths.

2. *A Fresh Appeal in the Face of Danger (verses 6-12)*

From pressing dangers the psalmist turns again to God *(verse 6)*. The 'I' with which this verse begins is emphatic. He has just described himself in the previous verses and he now calls urgently to his God, whom he knows will answer. Certainty as to this fact encourages expectancy. The second half of the verse is virtually an abbreviated form of verse 1.

The basis of his appeal is the covenant bond *(verses 7-9)*. He longs for a fresh manifestation of God's power and redeeming mercy as was shown during the Exodus. The language here echoes that in the Song of the Sea (Ex. 15:11-13). Historical recollection often forms the basis for present prayer in the Psalms. David knew that God saves those who take refuge in him.

Allusion to the Exodus continues in verse 8. God found Israel in the wilderness and guarded her as the apple of his eye (Deut. 32:10). The idiom 'apple of the eye' used there of the people as a whole is taken over here, when an individual Israelite prays for himself. The thought of being protected under the LORD's wings is probably taken from Deuteronomy 32:11, whence the imagery of the eagle is introduced. God provides protection from all the dangers (cf., for use of the idea of God's wings, Pss. 36:7; 57:1; 61:4; 63:7; and 91:4). The danger is from enemies (also called the wicked) who attack his life.

They come against him with murderous intent *(verses 10-12)*. A fuller description is given of these enemies. They shut up their hearts. The Hebrew text says 'they shut up their fat'. Probably this is another allusion to Deuteronomy 32 and specifically to God's little Jeshurun (Israel), who grew fat and kicked (32:15). The idea of rebelliousness carries over here, for the enemies will not bow before God's majesty and they attack his servant David. He felt surrounded on every side (verse 11) for they were waiting for their chance to overthrow him. The most threatening enemy is singled out in verse 12 (cf. with the use of the plural in verses 10-11), or perhaps the leader of the band. He is likened to a crouching lion who is ready to leap out at his prey from his secret hiding place. It is not surprising that the New Testament depicts the devil as a roaring lion (1 Pet. 5:8).

3. *Another Urgent Prayer (verses 13-15)*
The military language, already noted in Psalms 3:7; 7:6; 10:12, is again used by David in *verse 13*. He appeals with urgency to his divine protector to come as a warrior ('your sword') and subdue his enemy, delivering him from his enemy, rescuing him from his clutches.

The enemies are described as being 'men of this world' who will only know rewards in this life *(verse 14)*. They will know nothing of having the LORD as their portion, which is the condition of the righteous

(Ps. 16:5). The New Testament speaks of the same type of people who belong to the world (John 15:19), who are people of this world (Luke 16:8), and whose mind is on earthly things (Phil. 3:19). From such men David seeks rescue. The final part of this verse speaks of God's blessings on his cherished ones. They have plenty to eat, they have many children (taking 'sons' as the object of the verb), and are able even to pass on the superabundance to their children.

In *verse 15* the contrast with the worldly men of verse 14 is most obvious. Any satisfaction they get has to be in this life. For David there was the prospect of satisfaction beyond the grave, because he gives us in this verse a glimpse of eternity. The language is similar to that used by Moses when speaking of his relationship with the LORD (Num. 12:8). David grasps something, however tenuous, of a doctrine of resurrection, which is spoken of elsewhere as an awaking from sleep (see Isa. 26:19; Dan. 12:2). The LXX translation clearly understood the verse in this way in pre-Christian times for it added the words 'in the vision of your glory'. God's actual presence would then be his joy and satisfaction. It is the pure in heart who will see God (Matt. 5:8).

PSALM 18
For the director of music.
Of David the servant of the LORD. He sang to the LORD the words of this song when the LORD delivered him from the hand of all his enemies and from the hand of Saul. He said:

This psalm is tied into historical circumstances both by its title and by the fact that it occurs in a duplicate form in 2 Samuel 22:1-51. The essential text is the same in the two songs, though there are numerous minor differences. In form it is similar to victory songs like Exodus 15:1-18 and Judges 5, though the details of any specific victory are not given. David achieved many victories, and this song seems to be a royal thanksgiving psalm in which he looks back on all that the LORD has done for him. The psalm speaks of how God prepared and preserved David for kingship, and then established him in his kingship.

1. *An Introductory Song of Praise (verses 1-3)*
The psalm begins with an unusual word for 'love' (*racham*) which in the form used here occurs nowhere else in the Old Testament. Another form of the verb occurs often with God as the subject. David expresses

his heartfelt love to the LORD (cf. Ps. 116:1) and confesses that he is his 'strength', i.e. his strong helper. This is the first of eight titles for God which are clustered together, all with the personal suffix 'my'. This fact points to the faith from which David speaks and of the bond between himself and the LORD.

In *verse 2*, the first two titles point to the majesty of God as David's hiding place. He has his refuge in the cliff (Hebrew uses a different word for 'rock' later in the verse) and it is a fortress for him. Linked with those first two titles, the third one could be expected to be 'a place of refuge', but the vowels in the Hebrew text make it the participle 'my deliverer' (*mephalet* instead of *miphlat*). 'Rock' is an old title for God (Deut. 32:4, 15, 18, 31, 37), while 'shield' reminds one of God's words to Abraham (Gen. 15:1). 'Horn' is descriptive of power in battle (only here is it a title for God); finally 'stronghold' completes the list by giving added emphasis to God's protective care for his servant.

God is worthy of praise (the Hebrew word comes from the same root as 'Hallelujah'), and David expresses his settled conviction that he can call on God and he will answer *(verse 3)*. He knows (and what follows in this psalm is a testimony to the fact) that God can save him from his enemies.

2. A Divine Appearance (verses 4-19)
Death came very near to David *(verses 4-5)*. He felt tied by its cords and terrified by its torrents. The Hebrew text says 'torrents of Belial'. 'Belial' occurs in Deuteronomy 13:13, for example, and is probably an abstract noun meaning 'destruction'. The cords of Sheol (NIV, 'grave') were pulling him there and he felt entrapped by death. David must have felt his life to be in danger for many years, and in this poetic description he expresses his feelings in the face of constant deadly situations.

A prayer of faith comes from his lips *(verse 6)*. He says, 'my God' (cf. verse 2). In his need he knew to turn to the God with whom he had a living relationship. God heard from his 'temple', a word which describes both the place where God is honoured and worshipped, and where he sits enthroned in majesty (cf. Isa. 6:1-7). The description of his rescue which follows is given in poetic terms as a theophany (a visible manifestation of God). God came to him in a way similar to his coming to Sinai of old (Exod. 19:16-19), or to Elijah on his visit there (1 Kings 19:11-12). Similar descriptions of a theophany are given in Psalms 68:7-8 and 77:14-20. God's great acts of salvation are pictured in similar terms by psalmist and prophet alike (Ps. 97; Hab. 3).

Firstly, there is an earthquake. God had heard his servant's cry and was ready to do battle with those who were attacking him. His anger was aroused and he was preparing to come as he had done at Mount Sinai *(verses 7-8)*. The description points to the powerful reality of God's presence.

The theophany moves on from the earthquake to the picture of dark clouds enveloping the earth *(verses 9-11)*. God brought storm clouds down, while he himself flew on cherubim. Because of the parallelism in verses 9-10 'cherubim' may here be a poetic term for clouds. In the midst of the storm the LORD was there, controlling all the forces at his disposal. He comes with majesty to bring deliverance.

The storm now breaks *(verses 12-15)*. Thunder and lightning come from the LORD's presence. However, the light which streams from the LORD becomes a consuming fire for his enemies. The bolts of lightning are likened to a warrior's arrows with which he attacks and routs the enemies. The representation of the LORD's voice as being thunder is common in the Old Testament (cf. Ps. 29:3-4; Joel 3:16). The use of the divine title 'Most High' in verse 13 serves to designate how exalted he is over all, including the enemies. Earth experiences turmoil as God's breath pours forth as a storm. Even the very foundations of the earth are uncovered as the storm blows upon it.

The hand of the LORD was then stretched out to save David *(verses 16-19)*. The figurative language describes a divine arm which reaches down to rescue David from the overwhelming flood. At the end of verse 16 the theophany ceases and the description then reverts to ordinary description. The LORD delivered him from his powerful enemy. This is probably a reference to Saul, while the plural 'my foes' may very well include Saul's henchmen. When he was confronted by them he found that the LORD was his support. In the context the Hebrew word used *(mish'an)* suggests not only support or stay but also provider. He found that the LORD brought him out of his narrow and confined situation into a place where there was much liberty. God's delight in his servant was because he was indeed his anointed kingly servant. The following verses which deal with David's integrity before the LORD point to his life and obedience as being also part of the reason for God's delight in him.

3. *The Goodness of God (verses 20-30)*

David is not claiming sinless perfection (see the comments on Psalm 17:1) but is asserting his own integrity before the LORD *(verse 20)*. He was walking in righteousness and his hands were clean. According to his character God had rewarded him. Even the king was not exempt from showing obedience to the LORD's commands.

He had not turned aside from the ways of the LORD, but had guarded his steps carefully *(verses 21-22)*. Never had he acted rebelliously and departed from his God. The judgments and ordinances of the LORD were constantly before him, as if placarded before his eyes. At no time had he turned away from God's commands and consciously set his requirements aside.

The word 'blameless' (*verse 23*) should not be read as if it meant 'sinless'. It speaks rather of the legal obedience of a covenant servant, and it reappears later in this psalm in verses 25, 30, and 32. The reference to guarding is a reminder of the watch which the Bible teaches believers to have over their lives ('Keep yourself pure', 1 Tim. 5:22; 'keep oneself from being polluted by the world,' Jas. 1:27). *Verse 24* repeats again the thought of verse 20. Such repetition of the opening thought of a section at its close was a typical poetic device which calls attention to a major idea or theme.

Verses 25-27 confirm what has been already said of God's character and his way of dealing with his servants. To the faithful covenant servant *(chasid)* God shows himself merciful *(chasad)*. To the man of integrity, he acts with integrity towards him. To the pure, God responds with a demonstration of his own purity. Other Old Testament passages give the full doctrine. God dealt with Israel in terms of his covenant and thus not according to their sins (Ps. 103:10; cf. also Ps. 143:2).

After these assertions about the godly, one assertion is dedicated to the ungodly with an introduction which sets it over against what has preceded ('*but*, to the crooked ...'). It may not seem good to call God 'shrewd'. The Hebrew word can have a more neutral meaning closer to 'inscrutable'. David is saying that God will deal with the person who mocks him over his covenant dealings, just as he has already dealt with his own personal enemies.

This section of the psalm points to the way in which God deals with men according to their character. It is only divine grace which makes the difference in God's attitude to the godly and the ungodly, and which, therefore, determines the abiding destiny of both at the final judgment (Rev. 22:11).

A summary statement is given in verse 27 which ties together much of what David has been speaking about. God shows his gracious character in delivering the afflicted, whereas the proud and arrogant are humbled by him. 'He mocks proud mockers but gives grace to the humble' (Prov. 3:34), words which are quoted by Peter with the added instruction: 'Humble yourselves, therefore, under God's mighty hand, that he may lift you up in due time' (1 Pet. 5:6). David goes on to describe his deliverance in terms of God's providing a lamp for him, and giving him light in his darkness. A special application of the idea of David's lamp is made in 1 Kings 11:36 when God promised through Ahijah the prophet that David would always have a lamp in Jerusalem.

In *verses 29-30* David returns to the theme of the opening of the psalm and specifically to God's help for him in his battles. With confidence he could attack an enemy troop (or possibly, following NIV margin, 'run through a barricade'), or leap over a wall. The thoughts which have preceded lead David to praise his God. He extols the LORD's ways, i.e. his actions, his dealings with David, and proclaims them as complete. Along with his actions his word is mentioned. It has been tested and shown to be flawless (the word comes from metal-working), and almost the same language is used of God's spoken word in Psalm 119:140. The final statement in this section is virtually a brief summary of verse 2. For all who, like David, put their confidence in the LORD and trust him as their refuge, he proves to be a shield.

4. *The Character of God (verses 31-45)*

David as king had good reason to praise the LORD for the help he provided him. He does so in words extolling him as the only God, and the one who blessed him greatly during his military campaigns *(verses 31-32)*. The rhetorical questions are an important way of emphasising that there was no other God except the LORD (cf. the way Isaiah in particular uses similar language and style in chapter 40ff.). The language concerning God as a 'rock' has already been used by David in verse 2, in dependence on Deuteronomy 32. This is one of many allusions to Deuteronomy throughout this song. The word for God (*'eloah*) is a relatively uncommon word, but it seems to be employed to give variation in the use of the divine names. God had indeed strengthened David for his battles and made his way perfect. This last expression must mean that God had so assisted David that his life turned out well and especially that his kingship was a fulfilment of God's purposes.

Like a swift and sure-footed deer he was able to escape his enemies and stand upon the heights, i.e. upon mountain strongholds he had captured *(verses 33-34)*. Almost the same expression comes at the conclusion of the Book of Habakkuk (3:19). God gave to David the physical strength he needed to engage in battle. This line from verse 34 is used again in Psalm 144:1. So strong was David that he could even use a bow which required considerably more than normal strength.

David recognises that it was not his own strength which won him victories *(verses 35-36)*. God had provided for him a shield and constantly supported his servant. The last part of verse 35 is a remarkable anthropomorphic expression, for David says that God's condescension has made him great. God had stooped to David and taken a humble shepherd boy and made him king. All of God's acts of mercy to his children and expressions of his condescension came to fullest expression in Jesus' coming in human flesh. David's path was made plain and broad before him so that he was able to go along it without impediment and also he did not suffer any injury.

In a psalm of thanksgiving for his victories, David now details some of the events surrounding them *(verses 37-38)*. He had pursued his enemies and had not turned back till his mission was completed. His armies had so smitten the enemies that they were unable to arise, and hence they were in subjection under his feet.

Once again David acknowledges that his victories did not come from his own strength or from that of his army *(verses 39-40)*. It was the LORD who had girded him for war (see verse 32 for the earlier use of the same expression), and his opponents have been made to prostrate themselves before him. The word used for his 'adversaries' can mean opponents in general, though it could also designate rebellious subjects. Verse 40 contains a Hebrew idiom which is not brought out in the NIV translation. The meaning is that God gave the enemies into his hands so that he could put his foot on their necks. This was the sign of victory in the Near East. The Authorised Version rendering is correct: 'Thou hast also given me the necks of my enemies.' An illustration of the practice is provided by Joshua's action regarding the kings of Jerusalem, Hebron, Jarmuth, Lachish and Eglon (Josh. 10:22-24).

In their distress David's enemies prayed to the LORD *(verses 41-42)*. The fact that they prayed to Israel's God does not necessarily mean that the enemies were people within Israel. At times of crisis heathen people could use the name of the LORD in prayer (see Jonah 1:14). There was no answer from the LORD and David continued his attack until they were destroyed.

David's victories had not only been internal to Israel but external as well *(verses 43-45)*. He subdued surrounding nations and so became their head. This meant that he was sovereign over them, hence the saying they were subject to him, i.e. they became his servants. It is not clear if the foreigners in verses 44-45 are those subdued through further foreign victories or those already conquered. Probably the former is correct. Kings like Tou of Hamath heard of David's victories and quickly made peace with him (2 Sam. 8:9-10). The accounts of David's battles were enough to cause them to come trembling from their strongholds.

5. David's Doxology to the LORD *(verses 46-50)*

Having reviewed his past victories, David now sings out triumphantly, 'The LORD lives!' *(verse 46)*. That was so evident from his past experience, for not only does the LORD live but he reveals that to his own believing people. Seeing that this is a statement it is probably best to take the following words as a statement too: 'My rock is worthy to be praised!' Likewise the third phrase: 'God my Saviour is exalted!' All three statements stem from David's own experience of the LORD.

Vengeance is something which belongs to the LORD (Deut. 32:35), and room must be left for God's wrath (Rom. 12:19). Here David acknowledges that God had indeed avenged him, and that he had brought foreign nations under his sovereignty *(verses 47-48)*. God was his Saviour who had also exalted him over all his enemies.

Assuming that such foreign nations were brought under his authority, David says that he will praise the LORD among these Gentiles *(verse 49)*. He wants to make public proclamation of what the LORD has done for him. Quotations from Deuteronomy 32:43, Psalm 117:1, and Isaiah 11:10 are used, along with this verse, in Romans 15:9-12 to show that participation of the Gentiles in gospel blessings was anticipated in the Old Testament.

The final verse of the psalm changes from first person ('I') to third person ('his anointed,' 'David'). This could be a later addition by another inspired poet, or else David referred to himself in this way.

Two things are said about the LORD. Firstly, he had given and was still giving great victories to David. This may be another pointer to the fact that the psalm was composed much earlier than its position in 2 Samuel would suggest. Secondly, the LORD shows covenant mercy to his anointed. It cannot be doubted that 'his anointed' is defined by the word 'David' which follows. David was the anointed king to whom great promises were given concerning his seed (see 2 Sam. 7). The mention of 'seed' points even to Christ in whom the promises to David's house find their ultimate fulfilment (Luke 1:30-33; Rom. 1:2-4). David, in his varied experiences set out in this song of thanksgiving, is a pointer to Jesus who bears the name 'Christ', the 'anointed one'.

PSALM 19
For the director of music. A psalm of David.

God has manifested himself clearly. His great power is seen in the created world around us. But the revelation which comes from that display of his power is not in words. For revelation in words, we have to turn to the Scriptures, which are indeed the Word of God. Both forms of revelation are celebrated in this nineteenth psalm, though the focus is more on the wonder and beauty of God's Word.

1. *God's Glory in Nature (verses 1-6)*
The beautifully balanced opening sentence sets the theme for the first section. The first part of the verse has the subject ('the heavens'), the verb ('declare'), and the object ('the glory'). Then in typical Hebrew poetic style it has parallel expressions in the second half with the word order reversed (object, verb, subject). The created world declares in an on-going way the glory of God. Its testimony is never finished. Night by night the majesty of the stars is a witness to the Creator. The second verse continues the same ideas and does so with similar poetic artistry. Day by day the message of creation bubbles forth. Creation cannot contain itself, but day and night proclaim the glory of God.

Nowhere in the world is isolated from this message, for it penetrates everywhere *(verses 3-4a)*. The voice of creation is a universal messenger. The voice (or call) of the heavens and earth has gone to the uttermost part. This is a proclamation or a summons from God to mankind. Nonetheless this is a muted message for it cannot say anything about God's grace or the way of approach which he has provided to his throne.

The picture is enlarged with a description of the sky as the tent which God has provided for the sun *(verses 4b-6)*. Just as the bridegroom comes out from under his canopy, or the virile athlete runs his race, so the sun comes forth to run its daily course. It has a daily circuit which it covers, and from the standpoint of our observation it goes from one edge of the heavens to the other. Its heat penetrates everywhere. The description of the sun is clearly based on Middle Eastern experience.

How many receive the message of creation? Paul says in effect: 'Very few.' For although men 'knew God, they neither glorified him as God nor gave thanks to him, but their thinking became futile and their foolish hearts were darkened' (Rom. 1:21). It is only a believer who can truly see in creation the hand of God, and give him praise for the wonder of his works.

2. *God's Glory in His Word (verses 7-10)*

The last clause in verse 6 serves as a bridge between the first and second parts of the psalm. Just as the sunshine reveals everything, so does God's Word search out our hearts. It is 'sharper than any double-edged sword, it penetrates even to dividing soul and spirit, joints and marrow; it judges the thoughts and attitudes of the heart' (Heb. 4:12).

There are several noteworthy things about *verses 7-9*.

Firstly, instead of the word God (*'el*) used when speaking of creation, the psalmist now uses the covenant name LORD (*yhwh*) when speaking of the Scripture.

Secondly, he uses six parallel expressions to describe the Scriptures (law, statutes, precepts, commands, fear, and ordinances). While each name adds something more to the description, together they form a multifaceted picture of God's word.

Thirdly, we have a balancing list of six attributes (perfect, trustworthy, right, radiant, pure, and sure).

Fourthly, accompanying each title is a descriptive phrase telling what the Scripture does (reviving the soul, making wise the simple, giving joy to the heart, giving light to the eyes, enduring forever, altogether righteous).

The description starts in verse 7 with the revelation of the LORD being called his perfect law. That is, it was divine instruction (the

Hebrew word used here comes from a verb meaning to teach or instruct) which brought refreshment in weakness or despair.

Likewise the LORD's statutes are trustworthy, and they bring wisdom to those who lack it. The psalmist is not indicating a special class of people, for he would certainly include all in the description of 'simple' (cf. our Lord's words in Matthew 11:25).

In verse 8 he moves on to speak of the righteous precepts which are a source of joy and satisfaction. From another angle they are sincere commands which bring light to the eyes.

When he speaks of the fear of the LORD in verse 9 he is not speaking of the inward experience of a believer. As it is in parallel with other terms relating to Scripture it must mean the 'law', which had as one of its purposes to bring men to fear the LORD (cf. Deut. 4:10). Moreover, this 'fear' stands in perpetuity as the abiding manifestation of God.

The final concluding statement in verse 9 sums up the character of the law – it is altogether righteous since it comes from the righteous God himself.

This section concludes with the assurance of how precious and sweet is God's Word *(verse 10)*. It is far more valuable than purified gold; it is far sweeter than honey. For those in the ancient world who did not have an abundance of sugar, there was nothing sweeter than honey. Similar expressions about God's law are found in Psalm 119 (gold, verses 72 and 127; honey, verse 103).

3. *The Response to God's Word (verses 11-14)*

Now comes the reflection on what has been said about God's precious words *(verses 11-12)*. They brought meaning (or perhaps better, 'enlightenment') to David, as they continue to do to us, and there is great blessing in walking in the pathway of God's commands. David knew that there was no complete and perfect obedience to be given to God's law and therefore he asks concerning his 'errors'. The Hebrew word he uses here *(shegiot)* is related to the word used for the sins for which atonement could be sought *(shegagah,* Lev. 4:1ff., 4:13ff., 4:22ff.). His plea is for forgiveness for even inadvertent sins. There has to be sensitivity of heart before the LORD so that we can pray this prayer with David. A true response to his truth is to seek cleansing even from faults not obvious to our eyes.

The danger of sin was present with David *(verse 13)*. Hence he asks for preservation from presumptuous and wilful sins, which have a tendency to rule over people. Such sins are like a wild animal waiting to catch its prey, as Cain found out to his cost (Gen. 4:7). They take hold of a person and make him their slave (John 8:34). If kept from such sins David would be wholehearted in his commitment to the LORD and not guilty of the 'great transgression'. Elsewhere in the Old Testament this phrase commonly referred to adultery (see Gen. 39:9), but here it probably means sin in general.

The psalm opened with the thought of the heavens speaking. It closes with the psalmist asking that *his* words would be pleasing to the LORD *(verse 14)*. He is referring to the words of this song in particular, and acknowledges that it is his speech and meditation which he desires to be acceptable to his Rock and his Redeemer. The psalm which began on the note of the glory of all God's creation, closes on the note of a personal relationship with the Saviour.

PSALM 20
For the director of music. A psalm of David.

Before battles it was customary in Israel and Judah to pray to the LORD and to seek an answer from him. Thus Jehoshaphat prayed before his battle with Moab and Ammon, a Levite responded, and then all the people worshipped (2 Chr. 20:5-19). Psalm 20 seems to come from a similar situation and to be intended as a song to be sung before a battle. The early part may have been sung by all the people after the king had offered sacrifices. They look forward to rejoicing in his victory (verse 5), and then an individual (probably a Levite) makes a declaration, and finally all the congregation respond in praise.

1. *A Prayer Before Battle (verses 1-5)*
The psalm begins and ends with similar words (closer in Hebrew than the NIV translation suggests). 'Answer in the day of ...' is clearly a key term in the psalm. The appeal is to the LORD, or as he is also described, 'the God of Jacob'. This term occurs again in an abbreviated form in Psalm 24:6, and it is common elsewhere in the Psalter (46:7,11; 75:9; 76:6; 81:1; 84:8; cf. also Isaiah's term, 'The mighty one of Jacob,' 49:26; 60:16). 'The name' of the LORD is clearly God himself (cf. Isa. 30:27) through whom enemies were overcome (Ps. 44:5).

The date of writing was clearly after the ark was brought to Jerusalem, and the establishment of the sanctuary on Mount Zion *(verse 2)*. The following verse, with reference to sacrifices, shows that it is the earthly and not the heavenly sanctuary which is meant. Their plea is that when they leave for battle they would go with the LORD's help and sustaining power.

The sacrifices *(verse 3)* could be all those of the past, but probably what is meant are those offered on the particular occasion of going into battle (cf. 1 Sam. 7:9; 13:9). The first word for sacrifice is a general term which covers many types, while the second is the burnt offering, in which everything was consumed as a symbol of dedication to God.

What is intended is that the plans of the king for the battle would come to fruition *(verse 4)*. His heart's desire and his counsel were that he would overcome the enemy, and for that the people pray: 'May God give it!'

The scene moves now to the future when those at present praying would be among those rejoicing in victory *(verse 5)*. Songs of rejoicing would be heard as the people celebrated God's salvation or victory. They would also erect or wave banners, possibly the tribal banners under which they camped when in the desert on the journey to Canaan (Num. 1:52). The final clause in the verse repeats the idea of verse 4 in describing full realisation of the king's requests.

2. *God's Declaration of Victory (verse 6)*

The introductory 'now' is important, as it is an adverb which often indicates a change in the narrative and, especially in the prophetical books, introduces imminent activities of the LORD, either in blessing or cursing (see, for a good example, Isa. 43:1). Here it precedes the declaration that the LORD saves his anointed. The deliverance is still in the future, but the assurance is given that the LORD hears and answers the cry of the king. He does so from his holy throne on high. His 'right hand' describes in anthropomorphic terms God's power and ability to deliver.

3. *A Song of Thanksgiving (verses 7-9)*

Without trusting in the LORD the use of horses and chariots was useless *(verse 7)*. There was a constant temptation for God's people to trust in human might or agencies to bring deliverance. Even Moses had to learn the lesson in this respect (see Exod. 2:11-14, and Stephen's comment, Acts 7:23-29). There could be no trusting in honour, chariots, bows, or swords (Ps. 44:5-7), but only in the LORD himself (see the use of 'name' already in verses 1 and 5) who was their God.

The outcome of battle, if the LORD was on their side, was that their enemies would be humbled and fall *(verse 8)*. The word 'fall' often occurs in military contexts as here and denotes falling to death (see the account of Sisera's death in Judg. 5:27: 'At her feet he sank, he fell; there he lay. At her feet he sank, he fell; where he sank, there he fell – dead'). In contrast the Israelites would arise and stand their ground.

Again the whole congregation joins in singing, as they repeat the opening intercession *(verse 9)*. They want God to show his power in delivering the king in battle. This cry of the people lies behind the British expression of loyalty to the sovereign, 'God save the King/ Queen!' The New Testament use of Hosanna particularises this cry and does so by way of its use in Psalm 118:25. The psalm, which began with the cry of 'answer', finishes on the note of entreaty.

PSALM 21
For the director of music. A psalm of David.

This psalm is closely connected in theme with the preceding one. It is a song which recounts past victories which the LORD gave, and which expresses trust that he will do the same yet again for his people. It is also a psalm with strong covenant overtones. This is best seen in verse 7. On the LORD's part he shows covenant commitment *(chesed)* to his people; on the people's part (represented by the king) they respond in trust *(batach)*. The former never altered, but time and again the people had to be challenged in regard to their commitment to the LORD. At the heart of the psalm is this fresh affirmation of the covenant faith, and this is confirmed by the blessings in verses 2-7 and promised divine protection in verses 8-13.

1. *Rejoicing in the LORD's Victories (verses 1-7)*
The people join in a song of praise to the LORD because of the assistance he has provided for the king *(verse 1)*. The LORD's strength has been manifested in the battles of the past. At the end of the psalm reference is made again to this aspect (verse 13). So much of the history of Israel and Judah was dominated by battles, as the people extended or endeavoured to maintain their boundaries. All these victories were the LORD's, and the king and people together rejoiced in them.

Prayer before battle was customary in Israel (verses 1-4 in the previous psalm). Now the people acknowledge that when the king had prayed, God had answered him *(verse 2)*. In time of need, the LORD had not refused to listen to the request which the king had made.

The blessings of kingship are described, using the crown as a symbol of all the good things which the LORD bestowed upon the king *(verses 3-4)*. It is just a poetical figure to sum up the many gifts which God gave to the Davidic kings. In regard to verse 4 we can ask: 'When was the request made, and when was the answer given?' Most probably before going into battle the king asked that his life would be spared. When he came back after the battle he knew that God had prolonged his life in accordance with his prayer. The expression 'length of days, for ever and ever' does not mean eternal life. The expression is used even of heathen kings (Neh. 2:3; Dan. 2:4), and here it means prolonged life extending into the foreseeable future, or possibly continuation of the Davidic line.

After the God-given victories the king received not only life but 'splendour and majesty' *(verses 5-6)*. These are attributes of God himself, but the king reflected these characteristics as he occupied the divinely appointed office. As in verse 4 the thought is not of the blessing of eternal life, but of lasting or enduring blessings. While it is not expressly stated, the thought behind the expression is that the king was a mediator of God's blessings to others.

Verse 7 is the key verse of the psalm, and the one connecting verses 1-6 with verses 8-13. It is in the third person, not in the second person as is the rest of the psalm. Covenant love shown by the Most High is the foundation of the whole relationship. The response of the people has to be one of trust in the LORD.

2. Confidence in the LORD's Future Victories (verses 8-12)

Now the focus switches to the future, and to deliverances which the LORD will provide. It is the king who is being addressed. Just as verses 2-7 described the *blessings* of God on the king, so now verses 8-12 set out the *curses* which the king visits on his enemies. When the king appears (using language which is often used of God himself) he will destroy his enemies with the aid of the LORD *(verses 8-9)*. Just as the contents of a burning oven are destroyed, so shall the enemies perish.

The destruction of the enemies would be so complete that they would leave no descendants behind them *(verse 10)*. This was a curse often expressed in the Ancient Near East (cf. Jer. 22:30 in reference to

King Jehoiachin). However much they devise plans, they will not succeed, for the King has them on the run so that their backs are exposed to him (*verses 11, 12*).

3. *The Prayer of the Congregation (verse 13)*
The psalm ends with a prayer asking for God to reveal his strength and majesty. There are military overtones here in keeping with the subject matter of the psalm (cf. Num. 10:35). The request for God to be exalted is echoed later in the Psalter (see 57:5, 11). The might of the LORD is to be the subject of praise by the people as a whole ('we'), just as verses 2-7 were such praise regarding past victories.

PSALM 22
For the director of music. To the tune of
'The Doe of the Morning.' A psalm of David.

This is a priceless psalm, and in many ways the supreme example in the Psalter of an appeal for help. According to the title, it is a cry from David to the LORD, and there are features in the psalm which point to it being connected with incidents in David's life (see verse 2, which shows that the appeal was made over a considerable period of time). He calls on God in whom 'our fathers put their trust' (verse 4), which seems to be a reference to earlier fathers of the nation, or possibly even to the patriarchs, Abraham, Isaac, and Jacob. It may be, as Calvin claims, that David sums up here various incidents of suffering and persecution in his life.

There are strong connections between this psalm and Jeremiah's writings (cf. 6b with Jer. 49:15; 7a with Jer. 20:7b; 7b with Lam. 2:15 and Jer. 18:16; 9-10 with Jer. 1:5; 15:10; 20:14, 17-18). Yet the fact that it is quoted thirteen times in the New Testament, and nine times alone in the account of Jesus' suffering and death, points to a fuller meaning realised only in our Lord's Messianic affliction. This explains why in the North African churches in Augustine's time (c.354-430) this psalm was sung at the Easter celebration of the Lord's Supper. Similarly, this psalm is also traditionally associated with communion services in the Scottish churches since the Reformation.

1. *Invocation and Call for Help (verse 1-2)*
The psalm opens with a despairing cry: 'My God, my God, why have you forsaken me?' *(verse 1a)*. The ultimate expression of desolation

is Jesus' use of these words on the cross (Matt. 27:46; the words quoted, *Eloi, Eloi, lama sabachtani*, are the Aramaic equivalent of the Hebrew words here in verse 1). The idea of being forsaken by God occurs several times in the Old Testament, especially in passages in which God accuses his people of sinning against him (Judg. 10:13; 1 Sam. 8:8; 1 Kgs. 11:33; 2 Kgs. 22:17). Neither here nor in Psalm 44, a communal lament on being forsaken by God, is there any suggestion of sin on the part of the speakers.

Even though the speaker has called God 'my God', yet he feels that salvation is so far away from him *(verses 1b-2)*. The words of his groaning are addressed to God day and night, and yet no answer seems to come. A sense of abandonment comes over the psalmist, and God's silence troubles him. The word 'far' is repeated in verses 11 and 19, which helps to maintain throughout the psalm the sense of isolation.

2. The Basis of Faith (verses 3-5)

Verse 3 can be translated as the NIV does ('Yet you are enthroned as the Holy One; you are the praise of Israel'), or we can follow ancient translations (LXX, Vulgate) and render: 'You the Holy One are enthroned on the praises of Israel'. Whichever option is taken, the idea is present that God is the object of Israel's praise, and the explanation of this is that their forefathers had put their trust in him. Three times the verb 'to trust' is used (*batach*), and this is one of the great 'faith' words of the Old Testament. All who trust or take refuge in the LORD will never be put to shame, for he will save them (cf. Ps. 71:1).

3. Lament (verses 6-8)

The psalmist now bemoans his condition, that he is barely left as a man *(verse 6)*. There are many similarities here to the language of Isaiah, who calls Israel a 'worm' (Isa. 41:14), and who says of the Servant of the LORD that he is so disfigured that people can hardly recognise him as a man (Isa. 52:14; 53:2-3).

All who see his suffering take delight in it *(verse 7)*. They shake their heads, not in compassion, but out of joy that he has been brought to this condition, and they cast reproaches in his face. What they say to him is: 'He trusts in (Hebrew, *gol*, which is an imperative: lit. *roll on*) the LORD; let the LORD rescue him. Let him deliver him, since he delights in him' *(verse 8)*. Of course, it is said in jest, with no expectation that God would intervene and save his servant. But later in the psalm we see that the prayer of the psalmist was indeed answered, for God did not turn his face away and refuse to listen (verse 24).

4. *A Confident Appeal (verses 9-11)*

All the songs of appeal have as a characteristic an expression of trust in the LORD and of commitment to him. It comes here in the words: 'Yet you brought me out of the womb; you made me trust in you even at my mother's breast. From birth I was cast upon you; from my mother's womb you have been my God. Do not be far from me, for trouble is near and there is no one to help.' The words of the mockers are now turned against them, as the psalmist says that from infancy he has been trusting in the LORD. The same verb for 'trust' is used as has already appeared in verses 4-5. The God in whom he trusts is said to be 'my God', echoing the appeal to God in verse 1. The request, 'Do not be far from me', also echoes verse 1, as he pleads with God to reverse the present seeming separation between them.

5. *Another Lament (verses 12-18)*

The imagery in these verses is dramatic, for various metaphors are used to describe graphically the ordeals he has been through *(verses 12-16a)*. Such metaphors are part of biblical poetry, for they serve to engage the mind and to stir emotions (see Introduction, pp. 12). We can feel for the psalmist as he describes his enemies as bulls, lions, and dogs, while he himself has a heart of wax, strength as dry as a potsherd, a tongue stuck to his palate, and feels as if he is already in the grave.

'They have pierced my hands and my feet' *(verse 16b)*. This part of verse 16 has for long provided difficulty for commentators as the Hebrew text does not seem to make good sense. It reads literally, 'like a lion, my hands and my feet'. All the early translators into Greek, Latin, Syriac and Arabic found this verse a problem, and instead of 'like a lion', they all insert a verb: 'they pierced', or 'they bound', or 'they put to shame'. Unless we propose some textual change and read something like, 'My hands and feet are exhausted', we are left with the problem. If so, then the word normally translated 'lion' may well be a verb 'to bind'. Hence, the translation would be, 'they bound my hands and feet'. The only other alternative would be to understand a verb, e.g. 'like a lion [they maul] my hands and feet'. The New Testament quotes Psalm 22 often, yet never once is this verse referred to the crucifixion.

The final act of indignity is that the sufferer, who can count all his bones which are out of joint (see verse 14a), is the laughing stock of his persecutors, who strip him of his clothing *(verses 17-18)*.

6. *A Further Appeal (verses 19-21)*

Once more the psalmist cries to his God, commencing with the same language as at the end of his previous appeal in verse 11: 'But you, O LORD, be not far off; O my Strength, come quickly to help me' *(verse 19)*. There has been a progression in the psalm in regard to this idea of God being far off. First, there was the recognition of this fact (verse 1); then, the appeal for him to come near, noting there was none to help (verse 11); and, finally, with an added emphasis ('But you' is emphatic), an urgent appeal for God to come quickly.

The enemies are again depicted as wild animals ('dogs', 'lions', 'wild oxen'), crowding in on him waiting for his death *(verses 20-21)*. But now he knows with assurance that God has heard him (following NIV margin), and this leads to the final songs of thanksgiving which conclude the psalm.

7. *Two Songs of Thanksgiving (verses 22-26, 27-31)*

What a contrast between the beginning and end of the psalm! Now that God has heard, he wants to proclaim God's character ('name' often has this connotation in Hebrew) to his fellow Israelites *(verses 22-24)*. The reason for this praise is that God has remembered his afflicted one, and answered his call for help. The synonymous expressions for the people of God are important: 'my brothers', 'the congregation', 'you who fear the LORD', 'all you descendants of Jacob/Israel'. He even adopts a missionary spirit, as he encourages others to honour and revere the LORD. Deliverance by the LORD is the greatest, and most basic, motivation to missionary service. David refers to himself in the third person here, calling himself 'the afflicted one', in order to bring into sharper focus God's mercy to him. Other humans would turn their faces away from the afflicted, but God, who is not a man, had listened and heard his cry. The words of verse 22 are used in Hebrews 2:12 in reference to Jesus not being ashamed to call believers his brothers. Furthermore, the psalmist unites with other sufferers as they together praise the LORD.

He acknowledges that from the LORD alone comes the reason for his praise; it is all of his doing *(verses 25-26)*. As in verses 22-23, after his deliverance by the LORD he sings his praise at the sanctuary in the presence of other God-fearers. He also brings a thankoffering which he had vowed during his trouble (Lev. 7:16), and in accordance with the custom in reference to the tithes (Deut. 14:28-29; 26:12) and at the harvest (Deut. 16:11), the widows, orphans and poor in the community share in the meal. The final phrase in verse 26 may well have been a customary expression used at meal times, asking for divine provision to be always the portion of those present at that time.

David widens his vision at the end of this psalm and prophesies that all the nations and even children yet to be born will join in praise to the LORD *(verses 27-29)*. In the context the primary meaning is that even far off nations will hear about David's deliverance and turn to the LORD in repentance. Gentile nations will come and bow in subjection to him who has all dominion and authority (cf. Pss. 72:8-11; 96:10-13). These words are part of the missionary vision of the Old Testament, as prophets and psalmists sing of God's kingdom being extended to incorporate Gentile believers. The thought of verse 29 is that rich and poor alike will join in worship of the LORD. There will be no separation of rich and poor in that day, for the wealthy and those so poor that they are on the brink of the grave will both bow in submission to their Saviour.

Within Israel coming generations will serve the LORD, for there shall be generation after generation who are told of the wonderful deeds of the LORD *(verses 30-31)*. Those yet to be born will in their day hear of the LORD's righteousness (cf. Ps. 78:1-7). In this context 'righteousness' has the idea of 'salvation', 'deliverance'. The final words of the psalm stress that salvation is indeed of the LORD alone: 'for he has done [it]'. Neither the subject nor the object is expressed in the Hebrew text, but the preceding references to the way in which the LORD heard the cry of the psalmist make it plain that it is the deliverance by the LORD that is in view. The psalm which began on such a sorrowful note ends with the theme of universal joy in God's redemption.

David's experiences as set out in this psalm are not his alone, but they are a pointer to the coming sufferings of the Lord Jesus. On the Cross our Lord used both its opening words ('My God, My God, why have you forsaken me?') and also its closing words ('It is finished', cf. 'for he has done it'). He is the one who has identified with us in our sufferings, a fact which the writer to the Hebrews stresses in his exposition of the work of Jesus (2:10-18; 4:15-16; 5:7-10). Having been made perfect through suffering, he is able to be a merciful and faithful high priest for his people, and even to unite with them in singing praise for God's salvation.

PSALM 23
A psalm of David.

Probably no psalm is better known nor more universally loved than this one. Because of its lack of details it is impossible to date this psalm, or to link it with any specific event. Its general nature, however, helps us to identify with it as it proclaims the depth of personal relationship between the LORD and a believer. It is steeped in covenant language, and it has many affinities with descriptions of the Exodus experience. It uses the metaphor of the shepherd to speak of God's loving concern for his sheep and the richness of provision he makes for them.

1. *The Divine Shepherd (verses 1-4)*
The covenant nature of the psalm is emphasised by the fact that the opening word is the distinctive covenant name for God. The psalmist declares that this LORD is his own shepherd. He is appropriating language for himself which applied to the nation as a whole (see Pss. 79:13; 95:7; 100:3; Isa. 40:11; Ezek. 34). In the same way Christian believers can speak in personal terms of Christ's work (cf. Gal. 2:20b: he 'loved *me* and gave himself for *me*'). Just as God saw to it that the children of Israel lacked no good thing after the Exodus, so also the individual believer will lack nothing (cf. Deut. 2:7).

The function of the shepherd with respect to the flock as a whole is now particularised to his care for the individual sheep *(verses 2-3)*. He leads to pasture and to water, and thus brings what seems like new life to the soul. The first part of verse 3 defines further what has already been said in verse 2. All the paths of the LORD are paths of righteousness, and he leads in these paths 'for his name's sake'. The verb 'leads' re-echoes the use of the same verb of the Exodus (Exod. 15:13), while 'for his name's sake' is also used of the Exodus experience (Ps. 106:8).

The many ravines in Palestine suggest the metaphor of *verse 4*. In all the facets of life, including the most feared ('the valley of the shadow of death', or alternately, 'the valley of deepest darkness'), the shepherd's rod and staff give comfort and assurance. If God is with believers, then why should they fear? (cf. Rom. 8:31ff.).

2. *The Gracious Provision (verses 5-6)*
The scene changes from food and water for sheep to banquet fare for
humans. While it is possible that the psalmist is thinking of the special
meals at sacrifice time, yet it is more probable that he is thinking of the
other meal times or special feasts. The shepherd lavishes his care on
his children. He anoints the head, and gives so liberally that it is like
an overflowing cup. Oil was used on festive occasions and, along with
perfumes, symbolised joy (cf. Ps. 133:2). All this is because of the
covenant relationship.

The psalmist is sure that the blessings of the covenant and God's
steadfast love will pursue him to the end of his life. He commits
himself to come back constantly to God's house. The Hebrew text has
'I will return', while the commonly accepted English translation ('I
will dwell', NIV) follows the LXX. God's house (the tabernacle or
later the temple) would be the constant abode of his people. The final
phrase in the Hebrew text is simply 'length of days', which parallels
'all the days of my life' in the first part of the verse. A lifelong
experience of God's tender care brings a commitment to be always
found in the LORD's house.

PSALM 24
Of David. A psalm.

From Jewish tradition we know that this psalm was sung every Sabbath
morning in the Temple when the wine offering was made. The LXX
evidence agrees with this as it adds to the title the words, 'for the
seventh day of the week'. The psalm opens with an affirmation of the
LORD's sovereignty over everything. It moves on to describe the
character of the true worshipper, and then ends on the theme of the
Kingship of God as the ark is brought into Jerusalem. The use of *Selah*
marks out the three divisions.

1. *The Lord of Creation (verses 1-2)*
The opening words of this psalm are quoted by Paul (1 Cor. 10:26) to
show that all foods can be eaten, because they all come from the Lord.
The LORD is not only the God of Israel, but the God of the whole world.
To him it belongs, as do all who live in it. It is his, because he is its
Creator. The founding of the earth is described in terms reminiscent of
other Ancient Near Eastern creation accounts. Other passages in the
Old Testament use similar language (Pss. 104:5-6; 136:6; Job 38:4ff.).

2. The Character of True Worshippers (verses 3-6)

The questions in *verse 3* are very like those in Psalm 15:1. They may well have been asked as the ark was being brought into Jerusalem, but they also clearly have a wider connotation. The psalmist is enquiring about the character of the worshipper who approaches God's dwelling and stands his ground there. The answer specifies four characteristics.

Purity of action and purity of desire are both demanded *(verse 4)*, which Jesus later spoke of when he said: 'Blessed are the pure in heart, for they will see God' (Matt. 5:8). Likewise there could be no compromise with idolatry. The Hebrew word translated 'idol' is simply 'vanity', but this word is applied to false gods in the Old Testament. The phrase clearly refers to an Israelite who is not living a life of obedience to the LORD. The final characteristic describes a life of falsehood by singling out one special form which it takes – false swearing.

What is impossible for sinful man to do is ultimately received as a gift of God *(verses 5-6)*. The content of the blessing becomes much clearer in the New Testament, where it is seen as spiritual and eternal gifts (see Matt. 25:34; Gal. 3:14; Eph. 1:3). God the Saviour is also the vindicator of his people, as he lives up to his part of the covenant and faithfully blesses them. 'Seekers' is a common Old Testament expression for true worshippers who seek the LORD in prayer and who turn to him in their need. The description of God at the end of verse 6 is awkward in the Hebrew text, as it simply says 'Jacob'. This is probably a case of ellipsis, so that we have to insert the words 'God of' to complete the meaning.

3. The Triumph of the King of Glory (verses 7-10)

This psalm either dates from the bringing of the ark to Jerusalem (see 2 Sam. 6), or the return of the ark after a victorious battle. In the midst of the people is the ark, 'which is called by the Name, the name of the LORD Almighty, who is enthroned between the cherubim that are on the ark' (2 Sam. 6:2; cf. also Num. 10:35). It represents God himself, and therefore the call goes out for the gates of Zion to receive the LORD. The removal of the ark to Jerusalem marked the end of the battles to obtain possession of the land. The LORD comes as a mighty warrior to his rightful dwelling place *(verses 7-8)*.

The words of verse 7 are repeated almost exactly in *verse 9* (the only change is from 'be lifted up' to 'lift up'). The final question draws

attention to the character of this triumphant king. The King of glory is
the LORD Almighty. The expression 'LORD of hosts' or 'LORD Almighty' can mean the LORD of the armies. This would be most fitting
here, as the LORD leads his armies into Jerusalem. The LORD of creation
(verses 1-2) is also the exalted King of salvation (verses 7-10).

PSALM 25
Of David.

This beautiful psalm reads well in English, but our translations
disguise another aspect of it. In Hebrew it is an acrostic like Psalms 9-
10, with each successive verse beginning with the next letter of the
Hebrew alphabet. Two of the exceptions are that the letter *vav* is
missing, and after the final letter of the alphabet is used in verse 21,
another verse follows introduced by the letter *pe*. This too may be
deliberate, because the first letter *(aleph)*, the middle letter *(lamed)*
and the final letter *(pe)* form the Hebrew word which means 'to learn'
or 'to teach'. The theme of teaching is so central to the psalm, with its
repeated mention of being taught God's ways. The background of this
instruction is God's covenant love, which the psalmist wants to make
known. The psalm breaks up into three sections. In the first (verses 1-
7) he addresses God in the second person, while changing to the third
person in the second section (verses 8-15). The final section (verses
16-22) reverts to direct address to God in the second person.

1. *Prayer to the LORD (verses 1-7)*
A word of prayer is addressed directly to God *(verses 1-2)*. The close
relationship between the psalmist and his God is indicated by the way
in which he addresses him and by the confident appeal he makes. He
claims the LORD as '*my* God', which is the language of faith. He
couples this with a declaration of trust in him. Because of that
relationship he can go on to make his appeal to God. What he wants is
help against his enemies. Later in the psalm he is going to describe
more closely his affliction (verses 16-18). If there is no help from God
an audience of gloating enemies will rejoice over his downfall. For
Christians there is the assurance that by faith in Christ we come to
possess a hope which will never disappoint us (Rom. 5:1-5).

In *verse 3* a different word is used to express confidence in the
LORD. No-one who truly 'waits on' the LORD will find their prayer
disregarded, for they are displaying confidence in him. On the other

hand, those who deal treacherously with God (the verbs 'wait' and 'deal treacherously' stand in contrast, with God as the object) will find that there is no deliverance for them.

Two things especially are needed by the psalmist. He needs to have enlightenment regarding God's ways, and then he needs God's help to rescue him from his present troubles *(verses 4-5)*. He looks for further instruction from the LORD, and acknowledges that he is the God of his salvation or deliverance ('God my Saviour'). The use of this description of God is in reference to his distress. Constantly he looks in trust to his God.

There is a threefold use of 'remember' in *verses 6 and 7*. David asks for forgiveness of past sins, for God not to remember his sins, and finally for God to remember him as an individual. His past sins troubled him, even the rash sins of youth, and he did not want them held against him. He can pray confidently because he is basing his prayer on the character of God. He is the covenant God who displays covenant love to his people, and acts towards them with generous compassion.

2. *The Goodness of the LORD (verses 8-15)*

The final statement of verse 7 is amplified at the start of *verse 8*. God is good, and one way in which he shows that goodness is in teaching sinners his ways. He desires that they know his ways and so be guided in true paths. He wants all men to come to a knowledge of the truth (1 Tim. 2:4) and repent of their sinful ways. God's scholars should always be humble, for 'he mocks proud mockers but gives grace to the humble' (Prov. 3:34; also quoted in 1 Pet. 5:5).

Being in covenant with the LORD always brought with it demands *(verses 10-11)*. The same is true of Christians who have to show their love to Jesus by obedience to his commands (John 14:15). Here the psalmist says that God's ways reflect his character in that they are also loving and faithful. The NIV rendering is a little free at the end of verse 10 because the Hebrew text uses two synonyms to describe the formal relationship with the Lord – 'his covenant and his testimonies'. This is a reminder that the relationship binding the believers to the LORD was of a formal nature with a solemn ceremony in which they swore allegiance to him. Because God is both 'good and upright' the psalmist asks for forgiveness. God cannot overlook sin, but in his mercy can forgive (verse 11). Today he remains just and the justifier of the person who believes in Jesus (Rom. 3:26).

Already the psalmist has described what fearing the LORD involves – including praying and receiving his instruction. Now he says that that instruction will be in the way of God's will (*verse 12*). He himself will enjoy rest and safety, while his descendants will continue to occupy the land of Canaan (*verse 13*). Elsewhere the psalms teach that the wicked will be uprooted from the land and perish (Psalms 37:10-11; 1:5).

The covenant also meant a close bond of friendship with the LORD *(verses 14-15)*. There existed a reciprocal relationship in which believers feared the LORD (with a child's, not a slave's fear) and the LORD disclosed more of himself and his covenant. It also meant that in times of trouble, such as that which the psalmist presently faced, the believer fixed his eyes on the LORD. Only the LORD could deliver from all the traps which the enemies laid.

3. A Tender Appeal (verses 16-21)

Again the psalmist returns to direct address to God in the second person *(verses 16-18)*. He was facing troubles from within (his own sins) and troubles from without (hatred from his enemies). From both he pleads for release. He senses his loneliness, i.e. he was without a helper, and consequently he makes his appeal for God's graciousness to be shown to him. He feels hemmed in by his troubles and he wants to be taken out of his distress. Knowing that God would forgive for his own name's sake (see verse 11), he asks again for the removal of his sins along with help in his troubles.

The call for God to 'see' is really a call to help (*verse 19*). The trouble surrounding him was not just verbal abuse. He was facing physical danger from the enemies. That is why he asks for God to rescue him, lest his enemies be able to gloat over him (*verse 20*). As his song draws to a close he returns to the theme of trusting in the LORD. He had no other helper, for his trust was in the LORD alone.

God's character ('integrity and uprightness') was the basis for his plea (*verse 21*). There is no reference to God's answer in the psalm itself, but clearly the praise portion which has preceded (verses 8-14) suggests an expectancy on the part of the psalmist.

4. A Prayer for the Nation (verse 22)

Because this verse begins with the letter *pe* (like *P* coming after *A-Z* in English), it has led many to think that it was added when the psalm began to be used in formal worship situations. The fact that it uses the name 'God' and not 'Lord' also supports this possibility. On the other hand, the references to the covenant in the psalm may well have led into this final verse with reference to all Israel. What was true of the psalmist, was also true of the whole nation, or to put it in another way, the whole psalm was applicable to Israel. If an individual could appeal for help in his personal troubles, why should Israel not appeal for deliverance as well?

PSALM 26
Of David.

This psalm does not appear to be an individual complaint to God, for there is no mention of illness or of persecution. Rather, the context suggests worship at the tabernacle. The psalmist renounces connection with ungodly men (verses 4-5, 9-10), and longs to be in the assembly of the righteous proclaiming the wonderful deeds of the Lord (verses 6-8, 12). His love is for God's altar (verse 6), God's house (verse 8), and God's people (verse 12). Possibly this song was later used as worshippers came individually to the temple precincts to worship at the Lord's altar.

1. A Confession of Trust (verse 1)
The psalmist expresses his confident trust in the Lord, for he has maintained his confidence without slipping from his ways. His appeal to God is for vindication as he comes to the temple again to worship. He knew that all authority was of God, who was going to preside at the last great judgement (Ps. 96:13). To him he cries again for vindication because the central issue of his life is his relationship with his God.

2. A Prayer and an Affirmation (verses 2-5)
Stemming from his confession of trust in verse 1, the psalmist moves on to make his request from the Lord to test him (verses 2-3). Three synonyms are used to describe putting to the test. The first of these (test) is commonly used of God, and often has a very spiritual connotation. The second (try) is the general word for testing or refining, while the third (examine) is the most specific, being a term from metallurgy meaning 'smelt' or 'refine'. The psalmist is so confident of his standing that he is willing to submit to the all-seeing eye of the Lord. His trust was continually fixed on God's covenant

love and his whole conduct (his 'walk') was based on God's truth.

Anyone like the psalmist, committed to the LORD and his truth, shuns association with those who show no love to the LORD *(verses 4-5)*. There is no desire to be in constant contact with them as individuals, nor to identify with them when they gather together.

3. *Approaching the Place of Worship (verses 6-8)*

Coming to the temple the psalmist now speaks of the nature of true worship *(verses 6-7)*. The idea of washing one's hands probably comes from Exodus 30:17-21, where Aaron and his sons were commanded to wash their hands and feet before they did service at the altar. Here the idea is figurative. Nowhere is such a ceremony of going round the altar commanded in the law, but apparently such an occasion involved singing songs of thanksgiving to the LORD. It may be that the king had a special function at this ceremony. It was an opportunity for praise and proclamation.

Past association with the place of worship, which is intended especially as the place of God's presence, meant that David could speak of his love for it *(verse 8)*. It was where God's glory took up an abiding presence, and it is noticeable that God's glory is specially mentioned in connection with the ark of the covenant (see Ps. 24:7; 1 Sam. 4:21; 1 Kings 8:10f.).

4. *Another Prayer (verses 9-10)*

The thought of entering into God's house immediately suggests the contrast – being with ungodly sinners. Any evildoer who attempted to draw near to God would be destroyed (Ps. 5:6-7). David does not want to be killed along with ungodly people by God's judgment, and so he prays that God will not take away his life. The sins he mentions were probably intended as a general description of sinful actions, though they could also have been things of which he was unjustly accused.

5. *Continuing Trust (verses 11-12)*

At the close of the psalm, reference is made back to verse 1, picking up again the theme of integrity before the LORD. Entry into God's presence was not to be determined by merit, but only by grace. Hence the psalmist prays for redemptive mercy to be shown to him. The reference to 'level ground' could be to the floor of the tabernacle, or else the phrase could be a metaphor for uprightness of life. When, by grace, he entered the assembly of God's people, the psalmist would there bless the LORD. The psalm, which began on a note of trust (verse 1), ends on a note of praise.

PSALM 27
Of David

This personal appeal to the LORD is made in the face of pressing attacks. There are expressions of a military nature in the psalm which suggest that David is speaking as king. Especially in verse 3 is seen the picture of a battle situation in which he and his country are facing serious attacks. Yet his trust is in the LORD and he can encourage himself and others to take heart and to wait for him.

1. Confidence in the LORD (verses 1-6)

David sums up what the LORD was to him in three words – 'light', 'salvation', and 'stronghold' (verse 1). 'Light' may well have carried overtones of a military nature, for it is used in Psalm 18:28-29 of military victory. 'Salvation', in a context like this, can be virtually equivalent to deliverance and victory. 'Stronghold' notes the safety which the LORD affords, and the protection he was to David and his people. Is it surprising then that by his two questions he can assert his complete trust in his deliverer?

It is not clear if 'devouring the flesh' is to be taken as a metaphor for destruction, thus comparing his enemies with wild animals (verse 2). It could also refer to personal attacks of a verbal kind, such as false witnesses could make (see verse 12). Whatever the oppression, he was certain of God's intervention and that no attack would succeed. God would ensure that the enemies stumbled and fell.

Verse 3 is an expansion of the idea of verse 1, 'Whom shall I fear?' Even if faced with a siege against Jerusalem, or a bold attack on him, the psalmist will trust in what God is to him. He had promised himself as a deliverer, and on that David stakes his confidence.

The opening of verse 4 has no parallel anywhere in the Old Testament. It is a statement of exclusive trust in the LORD. His faith is such that he wants to live continually in God's presence. In particular he wants to see the glory of the LORD symbolised by the ark of the covenant and the associated ceremonies of worship, and to be able to see the LORD at the sanctuary. Such 'seeking' may well have been in connection with the military dangers he faced, when advice from the priest concerning the will of the LORD would be sought. Confident trust enables the psalmist to express in *verse 5* how safe he felt. Probably the references to 'dwelling' and 'tabernacle' are general in character, and are not directed specifically to the dwelling place of the ark. The final words of the verse support this interpretation, because lifting high on a rock suggests safety and protection in general (cf. Ps. 3:3).

The outcome of the LORD's protection is that the psalmist knows deliverance from his enemies, and with thankful heart he wants to sacrifice and praise the LORD *(verse 6)*. Sacrifices of thanksgiving would be offered after military victories, and with joyful song the LORD would be praised. If this psalm was used in later worship situations in the Old Testament church, it may have been that a sacrifice would be offered at this point in its recitation.

2. *Prayer for Divine Assistance (verses 7-13)*

The flow of thought from the first part of the psalm continues on into the second part, with several key words being repeated. Now the psalmist cries to God to hear his request and to show compassion to him in his need *(verse 7)*. Praise has turned into prayer. Here he prays in general terms, while later (see verse 11) he becomes more specific.

The translation of this *verse 8* is difficult, as all the ancient translations show. The main problem is that in Hebrew the imperative 'seek' is second person plural, while the context requires second person singular. The NIV margin provides an alternative which may be the best solution at the moment: 'To you, O my heart, he has said, "Seek my face"'. The expressions 'seek God' and 'seek his face' may go back to Deuteronomy 4:29. If so, the psalmist is acting in the spirit of that verse, as he indicates that he is indeed seeking admission to God's presence in order to ask a favour.

He wants God's presence to be manifest to him, not hidden as when God is angry with his children *(verse 9)*. He acknowledges that God has been his helper, using a Hebrew expression which suggests God's abiding nature as his helper. What he was in the past, he continues to be to David. He pleads that his Saviour will not thrust him away in his need.

This expression – 'Though my father and mother forsake me, the LORD will receive me' *(verse 10)* – is not to be taken literally, as though David's parents were abandoning him. Rather, it expresses the new relationship which David as king had with the Lord. God now filled the role which his parents previously had occupied. He was adopted as God's son (Ps. 2:7) and therefore sheltered by him.

The specific request he makes is for guidance in God's way *(verses 11-12)*. He wants to be kept in God's paths, though his oppressors are attacking him. He fears their designs on him, for they are speaking lies against him and their purpose is to destroy him. The opponents could well be foreign nations who did not want Israel's king to be walking in the ways of the covenant LORD.

All hope would have gone for him if he had not been convinced that he would see God's salvation *(verse 13)*. He knew that he would not be cut off in the midst of his days (Ps. 102:24, literally 'in the half of my days'). The land of the living is simply the opposite of the land of the dead (see Pss. 52:5; 116:9; Isa. 38:11).

3. *A Call to Wait (verse 14)*
The final verse appears to be a call to others to follow the psalmist's example, though it is possible that it is addressed to himself as a word of self-encouragement. The repetition of the word 'wait' gives particular force to the idea. From a strong faith in the LORD flows mighty deeds in his name. The 'heart' stands for the centre of his whole life. With all of his being he is willing, like Joshua (Josh. 24:15), to serve the LORD.

PSALM 28
Of David.

The setting of this psalm seems to be very similar to that of Psalm 26. It may be that the period of Absalom's rebellion against David is the historical background of both. The peril of the psalmist, his enemy's hypocrisy, and the mention of the sanctuary all point in this direction. It is an appeal on behalf of the people and their anointed king (God's anointed one, 'his messiah', verse 8).

1. *A General Plea (verses 1-2)*
There is but one 'rock' for the psalmist and that is the LORD (cf. Ps. 18:2). To him he makes his appeal and asks that he will not refuse to listen to him. He doesn't want God to remain deaf to his plea. This would really mean being 'inactive', 'not helping'. If God doesn't intervene, then death stares him in the face. 'To go down to the pit' is

an Old Testament expression for death (cf. Pss. 30:3; 88:4; 143:7). The poet recognises that he needs mercy, for his situation is desperate. He has his hands lifted up, as it were, out of the pit, waiting for God to rescue him. The 'Most Holy Place' was the inner sanctuary of the tabernacle/temple, the place which symbolised God's earthly presence.

2. Deliverance from his Enemies (verses 3-5)

The psalmist did not want to be associated with wicked people *(verse 3)*. He characterises them in three ways. They practise evil, on the surface they speak peacefully to their neighbours, and in their hearts they treasure up evil. 'To practise evil' is a phrase which occurs about twenty times in Job, the Psalms and Proverbs. It may designate men who were skilled in magic or idolatrous ritual, because the Hebrew word for evil in this phrase (*'awen*) sometimes denotes idolatry (cf. Beth-aven, Hosea 5:8; 10:5, 8).

Words such as these, calling for vengeance on enemies, seem to some as contradictory to the Christian belief in love and forgiveness *(verses 4-5)*. However, a much broader view has to be taken of them (see the fuller discussion in the Introduction, pp. 58-62). David is asking for the covenant curses to be visited on those who are in breach of covenant requirements. To repay what people deserve is a technical, legal expression. The LORD is a God of retribution (Jer. 51:56) who gives to the wicked their due. The form of the cursing here echoes Deuteronomy 28 and it has many similarities to passages in Jeremiah (cf. verse 5b with Jer. 24:6; 42:10; 44:6).

3. Praise for the Deliverer (verses 6-9)

There is a direct link between the words of thanksgiving in *verses 6-7* and the earlier part of the psalm. The psalmist had asked, 'Hear my cry for mercy' (verse 2a). Here he says that the LORD has heard his cry for mercy. He has received the assurance of the LORD's intervention on his behalf (verse 5), and now he praises him for deliverance. This, in concise form, is a song of thanksgiving. It starts with an introduction (verse 6a) and ends with a conclusion (verse 7c, d). It has a confession in verse 7a, and a recounting of the deliverance in verses 6b and 7b. He acknowledges his refuge, and he can sing a jubilant song about him, now and always. Even in his great need he did not cease to trust in the LORD, and in deliverance he confesses where his help lies.

His confession continues with the acknowledgment that the LORD is not only the psalmist's strength, but that of his people in general *(verse 8)*. What he is to the king as an individual ('his anointed one'), he is also to the believing community as a whole.

Verse 9 confirms the impression that the setting of the psalm is a time of national danger. David prays for the salvation of the people of Israel, and for blessing for God's inheritance. The concept of Israel as God's special, chosen heritage (Deut. 4:20; Exod. 34:9) is carried over into the New Testament (see Eph. 1:3ff.). The idea of the loving shepherd is reminiscent of Psalm 23:1 and Isaiah 40:11.

PSALM 29
A psalm of David.

This is a mighty song of victory, and an exaltation of the power of the LORD. It has often been pointed out that this psalm has certain similarities to poetry that we know from Canaanite sources. However, it could be a polemical psalm directed against the heathen notions of the Canaanites, and in particular a denial of the place of Baal in the world of nature. The LORD is the mighty Creator who has all the forces of nature in his control. The psalm also has similarities to other victory songs such as Exodus 15:1-18 and Judges 5:2-31, which also use storm imagery to describe victory in battle. A Jewish tradition, as early as around 250 BC, associated this psalm with the Feast of Tabernacles.

1. *A Call to Praise (verses 1-2)*
The opening call is for the LORD's glory and strength to be acknowledged. The word 'strength' is often associated with victory in battles, as is the reference to God's name (see Exod. 15:3, for example). Those addressed are most probably the angels, so that the speaker requests the angelic host to join in praise of the LORD. What is fittingly his, should be rendered to him in praise and adoration. The final phrase of *verse 2* could refer to the manner in which the LORD was worshipped (as in NIV translation), or it could refer to the garments which the servants wore. Some commentators have suggested that it refers to the dress which the priests wore on special occasions.

2. *The Mighty Voice of the LORD (verses 3-9)*
Mention is made seven times of the LORD's voice in this central section of the psalm. Thus it is clearly the focal point, as the psalmist uses the language of the storm to refer to God's power and glory. Over all the

mighty waters he reigns supreme, and he speaks as with a clap of thunder *(verse 3)*.

The reference to Lebanon is interesting, because it marked the border with the Canaanitish territory to the north *(verses 4-5)*. The cedars of Lebanon were well-known, and they represented the strength of Lebanon itself. But they could be shattered by the majestic voice of the LORD. When he commanded, they split in pieces.

Now Lebanon itself and nearby Sirion come directly into the picture *(verses 6-7)*. 'Sirion' is Mount Hermon (see Deut. 3:9), and here it is used as basically synonymous with Lebanon. God's voice makes these great mountains skip like young animals, for the Creator has power over his creation. Perhaps an earthquake is in view. The likening of the LORD's voice to lightning is in keeping with Near Eastern ideas, for lightning was often used in visual depictions to denote weaponry used in battle.

It is hard to know whether a specific desert is in view in *verse 8*, or whether it is just a general reference to the semi-desert steppe country. The locality could be the Kadesh situated about 50 miles south-west of Beersheba (Kadesh Barnea), or it could be Kadesh on the Orontes, a Hittite capital about 80 miles north of Damascus. More probably it just denotes the control which the LORD has over vast territories.

Verse 9 presents a contrast between what is happening outside (thunder, lightning, earthquake) with what is happening in God's sanctuary. It is not clear if this sanctuary is the heavenly one, or the one situated in Jerusalem. Perhaps the two were combined in the thought of the people, the earthly sanctuary being made after the fashion of the heavenly one. In the sanctuary there is peace, and a cry of 'Glory' arises. This provides a beautiful ending to this part of the psalm, for there is no parallel expression accompanying it and it calls attention to the way in which the psalm opened (verse 1, 'ascribe to the LORD glory').

3. *A Concluding Song of Praise (verses 10-11)*

The final verses of the psalm rejoice in the fact that the LORD is the eternal king. There seems to be a reference back to the creation account in Genesis 1, and to the manner in which God is sovereign over his creation, including the waters. What God is in himself (verse 1), he gives to his people, and having won victory for them he bestows his peace. The psalm which starts with 'glory to God in the highest' ends with 'peace upon earth'.

PSALM 30

A psalm. A song. For the dedication of the temple.
Of David.

This song of thanksgiving is a joyful response to what God has done. Wailing has turned to dancing (verse 11), and there is praise to the LORD for the fact that he spared his servant, delivering him from death. The title is ambiguous. The Hebrew word translated 'dedication' could possibly mean 'initiate, begin to use', while the word 'temple' is the Hebrew word for 'house' or 'palace'. It is possible that this is a Davidic psalm intended for use in his palace, or possibly for the temple when it was built. It is a song which concentrates on the LORD, using that title nine times, while twice he is called 'my God'. It is also much more concrete in its description of the danger from which he has been delivered than in many other psalms.

1. A Grateful Song (verses 1-5)

The verb 'exalt' *(verse 1)* in a setting like this has the meaning of praising (cf. Ps. 99:5). The 'depths' from which the psalmist is lifted is clearly sickness, as is evident from the following verses. Had he succumbed to that illness and died, then his enemies would have taken great delight.

The psalmist directed his cry for help to God, and he found that he was restored *(verse 2)*. The verb 'to cry for help' is found more often in the psalms than in any other Old Testament book, and it is usually used in autobiographical settings such as this one. In *verse 3* 'Sheol' (or the grave) and 'the pit' are used in parallelism to describe death. What was involved in calling on the LORD is spelt out in more detail in verses 8-10.

The psalmist wants the whole congregation to share with him in praising the LORD for his deliverance *(verse 4)*. He calls the members of the congregation 'saints' or 'holy ones'. The word used is clearly related to the Hebrew word *chesed* (mercy), and they were probably called this because, having received God's mercy, they also were characterised by it in their lives. 'His holy name' is literally 'his holy memorial', which is an echo of Exodus 3:15: 'This is my name for ever, the name by which I am to be remembered from generation to generation.'

Sorrow is depicted as if it were a guest which intruded into our lives *(verse 5)*. It takes up temporary lodging, but is eventually replaced by joy. The light of God's love chases away the night of sorrow and gloom.

2. A Detailed Description of His Deliverance (verses 6-12)

The detailed description of the trouble from which the LORD had delivered him starts here *(verse 6)*. Looking back on his life before the onset of sickness, the psalmist realises that in his health he had been complacent and self-sufficient. This was something that a member of the covenant community should not have been (see Deut. 8:17-18). Prosperity and safety both came from the Lord.

David has already spoken of 'favour' in verse 5. It is the response of God to repentance and faith on the part of his people. The contrast he presents is between being firmly established by God (as though set firm on a mountain) and trembling when God removes his favour. He was perplexed when God took away the signs of his gracious presence *(verse 7)*.

He now recalls his prayer to the LORD at the time of his trouble *(verses 8-9)*. These words show how, when realising his true condition, he turned to the LORD, seeking mercy from him. His argument was that his death would not be any profit to God. All it would do would be to rob God of an offering of praise and confession.

Verse 10 is the outcome of the reasoning of the psalmist in the preceding verse. He now knew that his former feelings of self-sufficiency were gone. Instead he recognises that he needs the LORD's mercy if he is to recover from his sickness and join in praising him again. The only helper he has is the LORD.

In an expansion of verse 5b, the psalmist describes the complete reversal in his circumstances. Here the allusions are to the outward signs of sorrow (wailing and wearing of sackcloth) being removed *(verses 11-12)*. Instead, he has God-given joy and his whole being (his heart, his soul) is able to sing and praise the LORD. Death would have brought silence. Recovery brings praise. The final verse is a re-affirmation of the praise with which the psalm began. It can be compared with the final verse of Hezekiah's song after he received mercy from the LORD and was spared: 'The LORD will save me, and we will sing with stringed instruments all the days of our lives in the temple of the LORD' (Isa. 38:20).

PSALM 31

For the director of music. A psalm of David

The indications, within the psalm itself, of its setting are not precise enough to allow certainty. Clearly the psalmist faced scheming enemies, who were slandering him. It may even have been a warlike situation, as there are various expressions which suggest the need for defence in the heat of battle. It is typical of songs of complaint in that while the urgent needs come to the fore, yet there is thankful recognition of the wonderful love of the LORD shown to him.

1. A Prayer for Deliverance (verses 1-8)
This opening is very like that of Psalm 71:1-3. The NIV translation captures well the emphasis at the commencement of the psalm. The psalmist points away from himself to the LORD, in whom he had taken refuge. This is accentuated by the fact that there is no parallel expression to match it, and therefore it stands as an introduction to the whole psalm. In a context such as this, 'put to shame' has the idea of being confused and disappointed. 'Righteousness' is not a reference to God's justice, but rather to his power to save. It often has this meaning in prophetical passages such as in Isaiah 40ff.

The opening prayer is expanded in *verse 2*, as the psalmist appeals for speedy help. In a pressing situation he asks that God would listen to him, and then hastily answer. The terms he uses in the second part of the verse point to a military situation, for he is asking for protection and safety from a fierce enemy.

After asking for God to be his fortress, he now declares that that is exactly what God is to him! *(verse 3)*. This conviction is a fruit of his praying. He calls him 'my rock' and 'my fortress', and requests that for the honour of his name he will take him to a safe place. The reference to 'name's sake' seems to go back to the experiences of the Exodus, when God, for his name's sake redeemed his people from their bondage and showed his mighty power (see Ps. 106:7-8).

For the first time in the psalm specific mention is made of the enemies, and he asks for deliverance from their snares *(verse 4)*. Again the overtones of the Exodus deliverance are here, with the expression 'free me' being one of the common expressions to describe God's bringing his people out of Egypt (see Exod. 13:3, 9, 14, 16; 20:2). He has already declared that God is his rock and fortress, and now he says that God is his refuge.

Verse 5 is well-known because of the use of the first part of it by the Lord Jesus upon the Cross: 'Father, into your hands I commit my spirit' (Luke 23:46). Jesus used these words in a similar spirit of trust to that of the psalmist here. The words should not be taken to mean that the psalmist was simply resigning himself to his fate. Rather, they indicate the strong faith of one who has complete confidence in God's ability to save and to keep. 'Redeem' is a further allusion to the Exodus, and just as God had acted in this way for his people (see Deut. 7:8), so now the psalmist asks for similar redemption for himself at that hand of the faithful God ('God of truth').

The phrase 'worthless idols' occurs only in *verse 6* and in Jonah 2:8. It refers to false gods which disappoint their worshippers. Calling them vanities goes back to Deuteronomy 32:21. Later it was to become a favourite expression of Jeremiah to describe the idols (see Jer. 2:5; 8:19; 10:15; 14:22; 16:19). The contrast between those people and the psalmist is made plain in the final clause. The true source of help was the LORD, and he expresses his trust in him. This was the response which covenant commitment required, and it is just another way of expressing the confession the psalmist had made in his opening words (verse 1).

God's covenant love had been the psalmist's stay *(verses 7-8)*. He records how God had heard his cry and delivered him, putting him into a broad place. This last phrase is a favourite one with David (see Ps. 18:19, 36). It describes the release from oppression into a condition of freedom. He had not been abandoned to the enemy, because the LORD had intervened, and song and joy are but the rightful response to his dealings with him.

2. *A Description of Sorrows (verses 9-18)*

The central part of the psalm is a description of the psalmist's sorrows and afflictions. The appeal he makes for mercy is set over against the oppressive situation in which he lives *(verse 9)*. Whereas he had pled on the basis of God's righteousness earlier (verse 1), he now pleads on the basis of God's mercy. He sets out in detail before the LORD his misery and anguish. His whole body is consumed with grief, so that he feels all strength is gone.

In *verse 10* it is better to accept the NIV marginal reading of 'guilt' in place of 'affliction'. This is the only place in the psalm in which mention is made of the psalmist's own sin. It is a blessing when suffering turns the heart inward to see one's true condition before the LORD. He pictures himself as an old man, stumbling along in his weakened condition, whereas he previously had been so strong.

The psalmist faces problems on every side – enemies assail him, neighbours shun him, even friends turn away from him in public places as if he had a dreadful, infectious disease *(verse 11)*. This is all because he is facing such opposition from his enemies, and no-one wants to associate with him any longer.

The hurt of his situation is described in *verse 12*. He is so shunned by his acquaintances that it is as if he were dead. He thinks of himself as just being a cast-off piece of pottery, broken and of no more use!

The first part of *verse 13* is like Jeremiah 20:10, though there the expression 'Terror on every side' is what the people were saying. The phrase 'terror on every side' *(magor missabib)* is a frequent one in Jeremiah's writing (see Jer. 6:25; 20:3; 46:5; 49:29; Lam. 2:22). Here the picture is simply of backbiting enemies who attack from all sides and who plot together to take his life. The same phrase is used in Psalm 2:2 of the rebellious rulers plotting against the LORD. Not just slander, but death threats come against him.

Yet in the midst of all his afflictions the psalmist can turn to the LORD and make confession of his faith in him *(verse 14)*. The sudden transition between this and the preceding verse is remarkable. What matters most in his situation is the relationship between himself and the LORD. The pronouns 'I' and 'you' stand next to each other in the Hebrew text, and emphasise the bond between the psalmist and the LORD.

By 'times' *(verse 15)* the psalmist means all the circumstances of life. The same word is used in 1 Chronicles 29:30 of the circumstances of David's lifetime. Because all of his life is in God's control, he can appeal to him to come and rescue him from his present distress. Having made his confession of trust, he is on even surer ground as he renews his cry for deliverance.

'Let your face shine on your servant' *(verse 16)* is an allusion to the priestly blessing in Numbers 6:24-25: 'The LORD bless you and keep you; the LORD make his face shine upon you and be gracious to you....' The psalmist then appeals for saving mercy to be shown him in his distress. The basis of his request is the unfailing covenant love of the LORD.

But in *verse 17* the appeal is for a completely different result to

come for the psalmist than for his enemies. He wants them to be put
to shame. In English the idea of shame stresses the inner feelings,
whereas in Hebrew thought it is more outward disgrace. 'To lie silent
in the grave' is equivalent to saying 'dead'. Those in Sheol are both
inactive and silent.

The reference to lying lips in *verse 18* goes back to the thought of
verse 13. In their arrogance the ungodly speak against the righteous,
such as the psalmist. He now asks for an end to their slander, so that
no longer would the deceitful words of his enemies be a trouble to him.

3. *Praise and Thanksgiving (verses 19-24)*

The psalm draws to a close with a beautiful acknowledgment of the
LORD's mercies and with a call to all God's saints to love him *(verse
19)*. The psalmist extols the wonderful goodness of God, which is
displayed to his servants. They are described by the parallel expressions 'who fear you' and 'who take refuge in you'. The LORD has stored
up his love, but then the demonstration of that love to his servants is
done publicly.

God himself is a place of refuge and protection for his people *(verse
20)*. Just as God stores up love for his people (verse 19), so he stores
them up (using the same Hebrew verb) in a secure place, and protects
them against the slander of men. This is one particular way in which
God's love is shown to them.

The expression 'praise' or 'blessed' often comes at the beginning
or at the end of a psalm of thanksgiving (cf. 66:20; 144:1). The reason
for such ascription of praise to the LORD is because of an unique and
sovereign display of his covenant love. 'Showed his wonderful love'
attempts in English to convey the idea that God has acted to manifest
his love in a way which belongs to God alone *(verse 21)*. It is hard to
know whether the reference to a besieged city is a true historical
allusion (to a city such as Ziklag) or a metaphorical description of the
acute distress in which he was. *Verse 22* tells the story of his
deliverance. The cry for mercy (verse 9) has been heard. When in a
state of disquiet ('alarm') he had claimed that he was cut off from
God's sight. The Old Testament describes being cut off from God's
care (Ps. 88:5), from God's house (2 Chr. 26:21), and from the land of
the living (Isa. 53:8). The reality was that God heard his cry for help.

An experience of God's mercy leads to a desire to see others sharing
in it *(verses 23-24)*. He calls on all of God's saints, that is, all who have

been objects of his mercy, to respond in love to him. This word for saints (*chasid*) occurs most often in the Psalms, and later it became the word for the orthodox party in Judaism in pre-Christian times (the Chasidim). All who firmly rely on the LORD will be guarded by him. On the other hand, those who vaunt themselves in their pride will find that the LORD renders to them just punishment.

The final call is for believers to strengthen themselves as they hope in the LORD. 'To hope' is practically synonymous with 'to trust'. The ultimate expression of believing trust is set out for the Christian in Romans 8:28-29.

PSALM 32
Of David. A maskil.

The central theme of this psalm is the free grace of God in forgiving sin. Paul speaks of it as illustrating 'the blessedness of the man to whom God credits righteousness apart from works' (Rom. 4:6). No precise mention is made here of the nature of the sin itself. David clearly had been through a deep experience of knowing God's disfavour and of suffering illness at his hand. But with a fresh experience of God's unfailing mercy, he can sing this song of thanksgiving. This psalm forms another of the penitential psalms of the early church (cf. comment on Psalm 51).

1. *The Blessing of Pardon (verses 1-2)*
Three terms for sin are used. 'Transgressions' refers to acts of rebellion against God, while 'sins' is the broadest term for sin in the Old Testament. It denotes in general a missing of the mark, and hence an offence against God. The third term, also translated as 'sin' in the NIV, has the idea of distortion or twisting from the right way. The wonderful thing which the psalmist can sing about is that all three kinds of sin can be forgiven by God – he can remove sin as far as the east is from the west (Ps. 103:12). The psalmist is not speaking of forgiveness in general. Rather, he is relating his own experience of the grace of God. For us today, the New Testament makes it plain that forgiveness comes through the same free grace of God displayed in the death and resurrection of Jesus. 'He was delivered over to death for our sins and was raised to life for our justification' (Rom. 4:25).

2. *A Personal Confession (verses 3-5)*

We now have a glimpse back to the period before the psalmist came to repentance and made his confession to the LORD *(verses 3-4)*. The time of silence was the time prior to his confession of guilt. The psalmists repeatedly speak of God being silent, but God also has cause to complain of the silence of his children. The physical effects brought on by David's spiritual condition included a wasting of bones and a sapping of strength. The verb used of his bones ('wasted away') is one normally used of clothes wearing out (cf. Josh. 9:13). Other psalms, such as 6:2-7; 102:3-5; and 119:82, also describe the physical effects of spiritual conflict. Constantly he was aware of God's hand upon him, but resisted the promptings of his conscience to turn to the LORD in repentance.

The three words for sin already used in verse 1 also appear in *verse 5*, while the phrase 'the guilt of my sin' is a combination of two of these terms. The silence is broken and the psalmist recounts abruptly his change of heart. When God's Spirit brings true repentance there is no attempt to cover our sin and guilt. The psalmist had openly confessed his sin, and he knew the reality of God's forgiving mercy. The confession and the forgiveness are simultaneous (cf. 1 John 1:9).

3. *Instruction for the Godly (verses 6-10)*

Having experienced forgiveness for himself, the psalmist now wants others to seek the LORD as well *(verses 6-7)*. The godly can find God (Isa. 55:6), whereas proud sinners discover that God has withdrawn himself from them (Prov. 1:28; Hos. 5:6). The person, who in faith prays to the LORD, will find him, and know that he keeps his children safe, even when the mighty waters look like overwhelming them. There may be an allusion here back to the flood in Noah's day. A believer will be safe because he has found a sure hiding place with the LORD (cf. Pss. 27:5; 31:20). When God protects his people he also gives them a joyful spirit and enables them to sing songs of deliverance (lit. 'songs of escape').

Some have taken the words of *verse 8* – 'I will instruct you and teach you in the way you should go; I will counsel you and watch over you' – to be what God said to David. But in the context they appear to be part of David's response to the LORD. Elsewhere he pledged himself to teach sinners the ways of the LORD (Ps. 51:13). Here he assures another godly person that he will both give instruction and also keep a watchful eye upon him. If another believer was caught in a similar set of circumstances to those which had overtaken him, he would be able to instruct him in the ways of the LORD.

Verse 9 could be advice against stubbornness in general, but in the context it may well be suggesting that there should be none of the hesitancy which David had in confessing his sin (see verses 3-4). A sinner should not be constrained like a rebellious animal to come to the LORD. Out of a sense of need he should make his confession and seek pardon.

The contrast is drawn between the sinner and the person constantly trusting in the LORD *(verse 10)*. The one knows many distresses (possibly 'sicknesses', cf. the use of the same Hebrew word in Isaiah 53:3, 'man of sorrows'), whereas the other has the knowledge of God's covenant love. Trust is the abiding characteristic of a believer.

4. *A Call to Praise (verse 11)*
The call to praise concludes the psalm. It is very similar to other calls such as Psalm 97:12. It fits in well with the thought of the psalm because of the place 'the righteous' have in it (see especially verse 6). The verb 'sing' is first used in the Old Testament in connection with a divinely appointed sacrifice (Lev. 9:24). In its later usage it normally denotes joy in connection with God's great saving acts. 'Righteous' and 'upright in heart' are parallel terms describing the condition of those who have received God's mercy.

PSALM 33
This is a hymn of praise to the LORD, and it is his creative work which is especially in focus. It is firstly a short commentary on Genesis 1 (see particularly verses 6-9). Then the implications of the LORD's mighty power for Israel are applied. The Creator of the world is the Creator of Israel, and he is able to keep and deliver a people whom he chose for his own. The psalm falls into the normal pattern for hymns (see the Introduction, pp. 46-48), having an introductory call to praise the LORD, followed by the reasons for this, and a conclusion which expresses confident trust in the covenant love of the LORD. This is the last of the psalms in Book 1 which does not have a title.

1. A Call to Praise (verses 1-3)

Praise is something appropriate for the righteous *(verse 1)*. The word rendered 'fitting' by the NIV occurs again in Psalm 147:1: 'How good it is to sing praises to our God, how pleasant and fitting to praise him!' In that context, because of the parallelism, the word seems to suggest that praise is lovely. Such an idea fits in well here too. Praise is to be expected from the righteous, but when rendered it is also a lovely thing. 'Righteous' and 'upright' occur as parallel terms to describe the believing community.

The choice of but two instruments in *verses 2-3* is meant to be representative of the whole range of instruments used in ancient Israel (see Psalm 150 for a fuller list). The thought of a 'new song' can be interpreted in two ways. The use of the word 'new' has suggested to some commentators that it designates an eschatological or end-time song, just as 'new heavens and new earth' designate the great physical change which is coming. This would be in agreement with the use of the expression in Psalms 96:1 and 98:1, and it would also suit the use of the same phrase in Revelation 5:9. However, the phrase appears to be sometimes more general in its use (here and in Psalm 149:1), so that it marks out the freshness of praise which is rendered to the LORD.

2. The Reasons for Praise (verses 4-19)

The first reason given for praise concerns the word of the LORD (*verse 4*). The use of the word 'for' is one of the distinctive characteristics of psalms such as this, as it marks out the things for which praise is to be given to the LORD (see also verse 9). The things which mark out God's word are those which first of all distinguish him (uprightness, truth, righteousness, justice, and covenant love). Then in the work of creation, as he speaks the word and the world comes into being, his love is seen displayed there. He always acts in a manner consistent with his own character, for he cannot deny himself.

Verses 6-7 are the start of a description of the creative work of God, for it was the LORD's word which caused the heavens to come into existence. The word 'host' has a variety of meanings in the Old Testament. It can be used for an army, for the angelic beings, or as here for the stars. The NIV correctly identifies its meaning here by adding the word 'starry'. The gathering of the waters (see Gen. 1:9-10) is described in poetical language as if God gathered all the water into a bottle, or as if he put the deeps (cf. Gen. 1:2) into stores.

By God's powerful word the world came into being. Since then, as Paul teaches in Romans 1:20, 'God's invisible qualities – his eternal power and divine nature – have been clearly seen, being understood from what has been made, so that men are without any excuse'. God's voice was heard, and creation resulted. It is not expressly called 'creation out of nothing', but that certainly is the implication of what is taught here and elsewhere in the Old Testament about creation (*verse 9*). As this revelation is universal, then everyone in the world should bow in adoration and reverence before him (*verse 8*). In a context such as this 'fear' does not mean 'to be afraid', but rather to 'adore' or 'revere'.

The second reason for praise comes in *verses 10-11*. God is not only great in his creative work, but also in the outworking of his providence in history. The Bible ties together very closely the ideas of creation and providence. Nations may plot, but God intervenes to work out his own purposes. Israel was to see various kingdoms rise and fall. Through Isaiah, the LORD told the surrounding nations that their strategies would be thwarted, and their purposes would not stand (Isa. 8:10). God's purposes are sure, and his plans continue generation after generation. The contrast is so marked. Human schemes are temporary and fail; the LORD's plans are enduring and succeed.

After speaking of creation and providence, the psalmist now reaches the point where he speaks of the unique position of Israel (*verse 12*). It was part of God's purpose that he chose Israel to be his people, and his inheritance. The truth stated here is reiterated in Psalm 135:4: 'For the LORD has chosen Jacob to be his own, Israel to be his treasured possession.' The verb 'choose' in the Old Testament always involves the idea of careful, well thought-out choice, and mostly (as here) it is used to designate the choice which expresses God's eternal purpose. God chose Israel to be his 'inheritance' (see Deut. 4:20; Exod. 34:9), and how happy should Israel be knowing that!

The third reason for praise is that God's eye is over all his creatures (*verses 13-15*). The fact that it is 'from heaven' that he looks down, emphasises the rule which he has over everything. The LORD can see much more than just the outworking of sinful purposes by men (cf. verses 10-11). He can even see their hearts. He is the Creator of those hearts, and this action is described using a word ('form') which is used in Genesis 2:7ff. of the original creative work (see also its use in Pss. 74:17; 94:9; Isa. 45:18; Jer. 10:16). It is a word which describes the divine potter forming man from the dust of the ground.

The fourth reason for praise is that God's might delivers his people *(verses 16-17)*. Firstly, there is reference to displays of human strength which fail. It is not simply the size of a king's army which guarantees success in battle. Nor does an individual warrior manage to escape by his own ability. The horse was noted for its strength in battle, but Israel was warned not to trust in it for military victories (Isa. 30:15-16; 31:1). The Egyptians had learned at the Exodus that the horse and its rider could be overthrown by the LORD, for the LORD fought for his people (Exod. 15:1-14).

The 'but' (*hinneh*, behold) at the beginning of *verse 18* marks out the transition to the opposite idea. The LORD does not only look down on all mankind (verse 13), but he has a special interest in the God-fearing community. The parallel description of them (they who fear the LORD and who hope for his covenant love) also occurs in passages such as Psalm 119:74. The verb 'to hope for' has the idea of expectant looking for something. In this case, it is that the God-fearers look to the LORD's covenanted mercy to deliver them in time of trouble. He is able to save from death (from enemies) or to preserve alive in times of famine. This seems to mean more than just to be kept alive. Rather it is preservation to enjoy God's presence and blessing, and to henceforth live in relationship with him.

3. *A Declaration of Trust in the Lord (verses 20-22)*

Now the song of confidence sounds again from the psalmist *(verse 20)*. The NIV rendering 'wait in hope' aptly captures the sense of the Hebrew verb used here, for it denotes eager expectation and confident trust. The assertion that follows about the LORD is taken up as a refrain in Psalm 115, 'He is their help and shield' (verses 9, 10, 11). Both descriptions of God are fitting in a psalm which has spoken about battle. God supports and strengthens his people, and because he is their protector it is not surprising that he is called their shield.

After the acknowledgment which has just been made of the LORD's help, the psalmist now shows that the response to that was one of joy *(verse 21)*. Where there is believing trust in God's character, then there can be songs of joy which extol what he is to his people. The aspect of God's holiness is most important, for he is distinguished from his creatures in his character and his works.

The psalm concludes with a prayer for covenant mercy to rest upon the believing community *(verse 22)*. This is putting verse 18b into the form of a prayer. The song of joyful trust, evident at the outset of the psalm, continues right through to its close.

PSALM 34
*Of David. When he pretended to be insane before Abimelech,
who drove him away, and he left.*

This is an acrostic psalm, with each of its verses beginning with a letter of the Hebrew alphabet. The only irregularities are that one letter is omitted *(vav)* and that an extra *pe* is added to commence the last verse. Using an acrostic pattern placed certain restrictions on an author, but the thought pattern flows well throughout this psalm. It is a song of thanksgiving, though it is hard to be certain what the precise situation was in which the psalmist was placed. There is no reason to doubt the accuracy of the title, and to relate the psalm to that specific period of David's life. The word 'Abimelech' (which means, 'my father is king') may well have been a title for the Philistine kings, just as Pharaoh was for the Egyptians. If that was so, then the king referred to would be Achish (1 Sam. 21:10).

1. *An Introductory Hymn (verses 1-3)*
As part of his thanksgiving the psalmist pledges himself to bless the LORD always, and to have his praise constantly on his lips *(verse 1)*. This is a vow which he is making, and he does so to the covenant LORD of Israel. The constant repetition of the name of the LORD is a striking feature throughout the psalm (see verses 1-4, 6-11, 15-19, 22). So great has been the LORD's mercy to him that he pledges himself to praise him repeatedly.

The experience of joy which David had was one which he wanted others to know as well *(verse 2)*. He wanted his fellow afflicted ones to listen to this call and also rejoice in the LORD. Some have thought that he is referring to those who have come to worship at the sanctuary, but this seems too restrictive. Elsewhere the psalmist says that all who swear by God's name will rejoice (Ps. 63:11).

Human praise can never make God any greater than he is, but David desires praise which calls others to magnify God's name in public acknowledgment of him *(verse 3)*. Most probably 'his name' is to be understood as the object of the verb 'glorify', for the Hebrew has, 'glorify for the LORD with me'. It is common in Hebrew poetry not to repeat the same phrase in both parts of a verse. What is sought is a united song of praise to the LORD.

2. A Testimony to Deliverance (verses 4-10)

Now the psalmist relates his own experience of seeking the LORD and finding him *(verses 4-5)*. The verb 'sought' often suggests a diligent seeking. His cry had been heard and had received a ready answer from the LORD, and he had found deliverance from the fears which had oppressed him. To look to God is the same as seeking him, and those who do look will not do so in vain. None who cry to him will know disappointment. Instead, there is a radiance about their faces as they receive from the LORD's hand.

Verses 6-7 form a parallel with the preceding pair. Thinking back on his own condition David refers to himself as a poor man who cried to the LORD. That cry was heard and salvation or deliverance resulted. The outcome was he knew that deliverance or salvation was from the LORD, who then stations himself around his people as their protector.

Resulting from his own experience of the LORD the psalmist now calls to others to enter into a similar experience *(verse 8)*. 'Taste' is used here, as in Proverbs 31:18, of discernment (lit. 'She [the wife] sees [Hebrew, tastes] that her trading is profitable'). In the early church, because of the idea of tasting, this verse was appropriated to the Lord's Supper. The reference to knowing that the LORD is good fits in well with the psalm as a whole, which, by its constant use of the divine name, emphasises the covenantal character of the relationship. It is significant that 'good' or 'goodness' are terms used in the Old Testament to describe the things promised by a covenant. The person who takes refuge in the LORD will know indeed the blessedness which he bestows on his children.

The expression 'the fear of the LORD' *(verse 9)* is one of the most comprehensive terms which the Old Testament has to describe a true believing attitude to the LORD. It is the devoted reverence of a trusting saint. Those who do trust him will find that he fulfils his word to them and they do not miss out on any of the good things he has promised in his covenant. Even a powerful animal like the lion may go hungry, but none of God's children will lack *(verse 10)*.

3. *Instruction Offered (verses 11-20)*

The style now becomes very like the wisdom style of the Book of Proverbs. The children *(verses 11-13)* addressed are students or pupils rather than literal sons, and the phrase is commonly used in the Book of Proverbs in this sense (cf. Prov. 1:8; 4:1). Hence the teacher is called a father (2 Kings 2:12; Matt. 23:9). In the Hebrew text, verses 12-13 form a question which finds its answer in verses 14 and following. The question relates to the fundamental question of the meaning of life. In 1 Peter 3:10-12, verses 12-16 are quoted to enforce the lesson that we must not repay insult with insult.

The life lived in the fear of the LORD is not just a state of heart and mind, but one which translates into action. It involves shunning evil and seeking good *(verse 14)*. Moreover, peace is to be sought as a harmonious relationship, and here it is largely relationship with other human beings rather than peace with God. God desires that his children will 'make every effort to do what leads to peace and to mutual edification' (Rom. 14:19).

The LORD keeps watchful guard over his children, and he is ever willing to heed their cry *(verse 15)*. The evildoers of *verse 16* seem to be those who are righteous in name only, and against them God will display his anger if they set themselves to follow evil ways. The ultimate result is that they will perish from the earth, and no memory of them will remain.

In the Hebrew text the subject of the verb 'cry out' is simply 'they' *(verse 17)*. The context at first suggests that the subject should be the evildoers, but as the main thrust of the passage concerns the righteous it is best to follow the NIV and understand the reference as being to them. Verse 17 is then to be understood as stating a general and abiding truth. The LORD ever hears the cry of his people and is ready to free them from their troubles. He is also ready to help. Two synonyms are used in *verse 18* to describe the righteous – 'brokenhearted' and 'crushed in spirit'. Both are virtually equivalent to describing them as humble or contrite. God's promise through the prophet Isaiah was that he would dwell 'with him who is contrite and lowly in spirit, to revive the spirit of the lowly and to revive the heart of the contrite' (Isa. 57:15). He is nearby for all who call upon him in truth (Ps. 145:18).

Verses 19-20 are very similar in style to the Book of Proverbs, as they both state general truths, not promises to individuals. Trouble is the norm for the life of the righteous, but there is another norm applying as well, and that is that God is their deliverer. Verse 20 puts the truth in a pictorial way. God will not allow his people to be brought into an extreme situation of danger, nor allow his people to be made objects of derision and shame. When the soldiers came and found Jesus dead they did not break his bones, so that this scripture would be fulfilled (John 19:33-37). That was the highest expression of the idea of verse 20.

4. Concluding Summary (verses 21-22)

Just as verses 15-16 contained a contrast, so there is another here. Those who give themselves to evil will find that in time they are destroyed by that evil. The enemies of the righteous will perish (taking the Hebrew verb 'asham here and in the following verse in this sense). On the other hand, the LORD redeems his servant.

This final verse stands outside the acrostic pattern, just as the last verse of Psalm 25 does. There is another similarity between these two psalms in that the letter pe is introduced to commence the final verse and in both cases it is the verb redeem which is used. Whereas the wicked perish, God saves his servants, and none perish who trust in him. All who seek refuge with him will find that they are preserved.

PSALM 35
Of David

At first glance this appears to be an individual song of complaint. However, on closer examination it seems to be a psalm sung by the king. He appeals to God to intervene in a situation in which some treaty partners have proved false to their commitments. There are various phrases in the psalm which have either a legal or a military connotation. In general it is similar to the much shorter Psalm 20.

1. A Request for Help (verses 1-10)

Verse 1 is very terse in Hebrew. It can be rendered, 'Contend, O LORD, with my contenders, and fight with my fighters'. The Hebrew verb translated 'contend' often occurs in a legal or covenant setting (cf. Jer. 2:9, 'I bring charges'; Mic. 6:1, 'Plead your case before the mountains'). The psalmist wants God to fight his legal battles and also to defend him against his attackers. If the attack was caused by a treaty partner who had gone back on a formal agreement, then both battles were in fact identical.

Shield and buckler were two different types of shields used in battle. The shield was the smaller round shield carried by infantry, while the buckler was a larger rectangular shield which protected the whole body. The appeal is for God to enter into battle for him, lifting up weapons both to defend and to attack. He also longs for reassurance from God by means of a declaration that he is his deliverer *(verses 2-3)*.

In *verse 4* there is a change from direct address to God (verses 1-3) to indirect appeal in the form of curses on his enemies. Curses such as these are not to be regarded as expressions of personal vindictiveness. They are best taken as expressions of a covenant servant desiring that God deal with his enemies (see Introduction, pp. 60-62). Here David prays that his enemies will be disgraced and shamed. These two verbs often occur together in the Old Testament. In English 'shamed' has the idea of inner feelings, whereas the Hebrew verb conveys the idea of public disgrace. His enemies were seeking his life, and he wants them to be put to open shame.

The reference to 'chaff before the wind' *(verse 5)* suggests complete worthlessness (cf. Ps. 1:4). The idea of the angel of the LORD pursuing the enemies *(verse 6)* probably comes from the role which the angel played in the defeat of the Egyptians (Exod. 14:19ff.). In the previous psalm the angel of the LORD was the guardian of his people (Ps. 34:7). Here he is the one who brings destruction on the enemies.

As often in psalms like this, the psalmist proclaims his innocence *(verses 7-8)*. His enemies have acted against him without just cause. Their actions are unprovoked on his part (cf. similar assertions in Psalms 109:3 and 119:161). He feels trapped by their plots, but prays that these plots will turn upon themselves and that his enemies will be caught by their own craftiness.

The psalmist anticipates that his prayer will be heard and answered *(verses 9-10)*. Thus he is able to express his delight in the LORD as his Saviour and Deliverer. He is confident that his present situation will be overturned, and that the judgement he has invoked on his enemies will come to pass. The question, 'Who is like you, O LORD?' is typical of victory songs, and the one here is probably an echo of the one sung after the Exodus: 'Who among the gods is like you, O LORD? Who is like you – majestic in holiness, awesome in glory, working wonders?'

(Exod. 15:11). The psalmist is conscious of his own weakness ('poor and needy'), yet he knows that his salvation rests with the LORD alone.

2. A Description of the Enemies (verses 11-18)

This new section of the psalm sets out the psalmist's innocence in the face of the persecution he is facing *(verses 11-12)*. He urges this as a reason why God should intervene and help him. The phrase 'ruthless witnesses' is literally 'witnesses of violence' (cf. Exod. 23:1; Deut. 19:16). The scene is that of an irregular court. He is questioned by these violent men about crimes he knows nothing about. The result is that he is punished for things he has never done, and so is left desolate. He is like a child who has lost his mother.

Verses 13-14 contain several of the Old Testament terms for mourning. Sackcloth was an outward sign of mourning, and worn against the skin it was very uncomfortable. Fasting was practised in dangerous and sorrowful situations. 'To go about in mourning' is a phrase to describe mourners who show their deep grief by going about without washing and wearing soiled clothes. To pray with bowed head (lit. 'my prayer returns to my bosom'), like the tax collector did (Luke 18:13), meant that physical posture and inward agony were seen to be united. How different was the psalmist's attitude to his enemies than theirs to him! Even if his enemies had been the closest of family, he could not have shown more grief for them.

A very unusual word is used for attackers *(verse 15)*. It seems to come from a Hebrew verb meaning to strike, but in form it should be passive ('stricken', 'crippled'). It is used in Isaiah 66:2 of those who are crushed in spirit. If this meaning is taken here, it implies that even those who were in a similar state as the psalmist did not try to console him. Rather, they gloated over his condition, and wounded him further with their bitter words *(verse 16)*.

In *verses 17-18* there is direct appeal to the LORD to step into the situation and deliver him. The phrase 'How long?' occurs when there is a feeling of utter abandonment (Pss. 13:1; 79:5; 89:46). David wants his life delivered from the present bitter attacks by these evil men. The reference to 'my precious life' may suggest that he was very self-centred, but the word almost invariably is used of those loved by God. Such love by God brought protection (cf. Benjamin, Deut. 33:12). Our attitude to our own lives must be taken in Christian terms, and like Paul we must only view it in relation to God's purpose for us (Acts 20:24).

3. *A Call for God's Help (verses 19-27)*

Direct appeal to the LORD is now made, replacing the curses earlier in the psalm. Once more the innocence of the psalmist is maintained for he is being persecuted 'without cause' and 'without reason' *(verse 19)*. He does not want such people to be able to gloat (lit. 'rejoice') over his trouble. The Hebrew verb translated 'wink' has the idea of pinching something together. 'Wink' is probably too much associated with merriment in English. It would be better to use an expression like 'narrow the eyes' which may better depict the hostility.

Further indication comes in *verse 20* of the treaty or covenant background to the psalm. The term 'peace' was used in international treaties of the Ancient Near East to designate the relationship between the parties. Thus Joshua made peace with the Gibeonites, establishing a treaty relationship between Israel and them (Josh. 9:15). Clearly the psalmist's enemies were breaching the terms of the treaty, and making false claims against those living in quietness in the land.

The enemies make the claim that they have seen something which broke the requirements of the covenant they had made *(verse 21)*. The cry 'Aha!' is an exclamation of joy over the fact that they have discovered something with which they can accuse the psalmist. But someone else had seen the situation. God had been witness to the treaty, and the psalmist appeals to him to intervene *(verse 22)*. 'Do not be silent' and 'do not be far from me' are simply ways of asking for God's immediate help to rectify the situation.

Legal terminology is used to show the action which is needed by the LORD *(verses 23-24)*. The request for God to contend for him with which the psalm opened, is now repeated. God is asked to 'awake', i.e. to stir himself and to act on behalf of the psalmist, for he seemed so distant. He longs for deliverance, and the phrase 'vindicate me in your righteousness' may refer to victory in battle as much as to legal vindication. The final clause of verse 24 is the same as the first in verse 19.

If God does not intervene then these enemies would be able to think and say, 'We got our wish!' *(verse 25)*. Again the exclamation 'Aha!' denotes joy. With rejoicing they would be able to claim that the psalmist had been destroyed (cf. Ps. 124:3 for the idiom concerning being swallowed).

This section of the psalm closes with a contrast between two groups of people *(verses 26-27)*. For those who desire his ruin, the psalmist asks that they will be covered with shame and disgrace, as though they were wearing it like clothes. On the other hand he longs for his supporters to be able to rejoice in what the LORD has done for him. The covenant theme is continued here with reference to the well-being (lit. 'the peace') of the LORD's servant. Human treaties might promise peace, but it is only the LORD who can give it. True peace is a gift of the Saviour (John 14:27).

4. *A Word of Gratitude (verse 28)*
The response from the psalmist is praise for God's salvation. He will ever speak (the same word is used in Psalm 1:2 for murmuring or meditating) of his deliverance, and make mention of his praise. It is noticeable that God's praise is closely tied in here and elsewhere with God's acts of deliverance (see Exod. 15:11; Pss. 78:4; 106:47).

PSALM 36
For the director of music. Of David the servant of the LORD.

There are features in this psalm which resemble appeals to God, but there are also other features which are more like wisdom psalms such as Psalms 37 or 73. Perhaps it is best to compare it to the first psalm, though it deals with the subject matter in reverse order. In fact, there are four sections in the psalm. It starts with the wicked, progresses to God's covenant love *(chesed)*, prays for the continuation of that love, and then reverts to the fate of the wicked. This chiastic pattern is clearer in the Hebrew text, but it can be set out in this fashion:

1. *The character of the godless* (verses 1-4) Subject: the wicked [*rasha'*] (verse 1)
  2. *The covenant love of the LORD* (verses 5-9) Subject: covenant love [*chesed*] (verse 5)
  3. *Continuation of the LORD's love* (verse 10) Subject: covenant love [*chesed*] (verse 10)
4. *The fate of the wicked* (verses 11-12) Subject: the wicked [*rasha'*](verse 11)

1. *The Character of the Godless (verses 1-4)*
The opening verse is what J. A. Alexander called one of the most difficult verses in the whole book. The word translated 'oracle' is a

technical word, occurring again in Psalm 110:1, and used more commonly in the prophets to introduce a divine proclamation. Here it is either used of the psalmist, as the NIV takes it, or else it refers to the decision the wicked man has made: 'I have resolved in my heart to do evil.' The second part of the verse is the psalmist's comment on the character of the wicked man. He has none of the terror inspired by God, and hence God is excluded from the whole horizon of his life. Paul quotes these words in Romans 3:18 as the cause of all the manifestations of sin he has just listed.

The nature of sin is that it is self-deceptive *(verses 2-3)*. Without the fear of the LORD the transgressor does not view himself aright, and therefore is unable to acknowledge or come to hate his sin. His words reveal his true character, and being under the dominion of sin he has ceased acting wisely and doing good.

As part of his way of life, the evil man thinks that in the solitude of his own bedroom he can plot evil without God knowing *(verse 4)*. Instead of thinking about God's goodness while in bed (Ps. 63:6) he is deliberately setting himself to plot further evil for the next day.

2. *The Covenant Love of the LORD (verses 5-9)*

In stark contrast to these descriptions of the wicked is the covenant love *(chesed)* of the LORD *(verse 5)*. The idea of this verse is very similar to the opening of Psalm 89, which is proclaiming the wonder of God's grace shown in his covenant with David. Both 'love' and 'faithfulness' describe the unchanging commitment of God, his total dependability in keeping his pledged word. It is beyond human ability to grasp the full extent of this love (cf. Ps. 103:11 and Paul's words in Eph. 3:18-19).

Both 'righteousness' and 'justice' *(verse 6)* are terms which continue the idea of God's covenant commitment. They are compared to the great, unchanging parts of God's creation to demonstrate how unchangeable they are. He will continue to preserve both men and animals. The allusion is probably to the covenant with Noah, in which God pledged himself never again to cut off all life by means of a flood (Gen. 8:21-22; 9:9-17).

An exclamation or a doxology is a fitting response to what has just been said *(verse 7)*. The NIV takes the Hebrew word *'elohim* to stand for men of high station. It is better to take it in its normal meaning of 'God', and so render: 'How precious is your unfailing love, O God!

Men find refuge ...' An expression of God's covenant love is that men
can find shelter with him, just as Israel did of old (cf. Deut. 32:10-11;
Ps. 17:7-8).

God's grace is depicted as feasting or drinking *(verses 8-9)*. As
people came to the sanctuary they found that God provided richly for
them. The idea of feasting may come from the practice of participating
in the fellowship meals. Linked with this is the picture of drinking from
a cool fountain of water. It may be that 'house' here is God's creation
as a whole, from which men and animals alike receive the bounty. All
of life is traced back to God as its source, and then the psalmist changes
the imagery to light. This statement is similar to the opening verse of
Psalm 27 where God is said to be light and salvation. This idea
anticipates the gospel message of the New Testament that Jesus is
indeed the true light (John 1:4-9; 1 John 1:5-7).

3. *The Continuation of the LORD's Love (verse 10)*
The verb used at the outset of this verse conveys the idea of drawing
out or prolonging something. It forms a prayer here that the covenant
love of the LORD will be maintained to those in a close relationship with
him. 'To know the LORD' is an expression denoting close fellowship
with him, because strangers to him do not have this knowledge (cf. 1
Sam. 2:12; 3:7). The parallel phrase repeats the same idea in variant
language, continuing the close connection between covenant love and
righteousness (see verse 5).

4. *The Fate of the Wicked (verses 11-12)*
The thought of the wicked plotting evil ways against the righteous is
taken up again from the beginning of the psalm. The psalmist prays for
protection against the feet and hands of the wicked.

Whereas the earlier picture of the wicked in this psalm was one of
business in their own sinful ways, now their end is depicted with
startling brevity *(verse 12)*. 'There they lie!' exclaims the psalmist.
The place or time is not mentioned, making the statement an even
greater threat. The person who does not live in the fear of the LORD will
ultimately perish.

PSALM 37
Of David

None of the previous acrostic psalms (9-10, 25, and 34) are as elaborate as this one. Every letter of the Hebrew alphabet is included, and two verses are allocated to each letter. In its general theme the psalm is most closely related to Psalm 73, though it has many verses which have parallels in the Book of Proverbs. Many of the statements are in the form of proverbs, which are general assertions of a truth rather than promises to individuals. Its teaching centres on the source of true blessing, and it encourages its readers to follow the ways of the LORD. It concludes on the note of salvation for those who find refuge in him (verse 40). While the alphabetic pattern places constraints on the author, yet there do appear to be some divisions in the psalm.

1. *A Call to Trust in the LORD (verses 1-9)*
The opening and close of the psalm are marked by imperatives and prohibitions. The Hebrew word for 'fret' comes from a stem meaning 'to burn', and it is used here in a reflexive form: 'Do not let yourself burn [with envy]'. The problem here and in Psalm 73 is the seeming prosperity of the wicked. The psalmist says to his readers, 'Don't be jealous of the wicked, for they are just like grass, which seems to be flourishing and then is gone.' The comparison with the grass is used elsewhere in the Psalms to teach about the frailty of all human life (e.g. Ps. 103:15).

What was needed was not envy, but trust in the LORD! *(verses 3-4)*. This command has as its background the possession by Israel of the land of promise. What was needed was continuing commitment to the LORD and the appropriate obedience to his word which would result in them 'doing good'. The references to the land are reminiscent of passages such as Deuteronomy 11, in which 'the land' was a summary of all the blessings promised under the covenant. There was to be enjoyment in the LORD (the verb is a very rare one in the Old Testament), and the assurance is given that he would respond to the prayers of his people.

The theme of verses 3-4 is repeated in alternative language in *verses 5-6*. The call is to commit (lit. roll) their way on the LORD (cf. Ps. 22:9). When this expression is compared with Proverbs 16:3 – 'Commit to the LORD whatever you do, and your plans will succeed'

– it seems to suggest that heavy demands, like a great burden, are to be rolled onto the LORD. He is able to do whatever is demanded. The New Testament equivalent is to cast all our anxiety upon him because he cares for us (1 Pet. 5:7). The outcome of this trust will be that the cause entrusted to him will flourish just like the appearance of the sun in its glory. The NIV takes the Hebrew word *'or* (light) as dawn, but the parallelism suggests 'sun' is the better rendering.

The situation confronting the readers of this psalm was that the prosperity of wicked men was causing them problems *(verse 7)*. When they thought about it they were becoming angry and resentful. What they should have done was to be still before the LORD (cf. the use of the same verb in Ps. 62:1) and to wait patiently for him to deal with the situation. The command 'Do not fret' is taken up from the opening verse and is repeated in both this and the following verse. Present success of ungodly men is no true indication of God's favour or blessing.

Becoming angry about the situation is only to imitate the unrighteous ways of the wicked *(verses 8-9)*. Inward turmoil over it results in more evil, and places one in danger of God's judgement. 'To be cut off' is used here as in Exodus 30:33, 38 and 31:14 of being put to death. To remain in the good land and enjoy its benefits required true faith and hope in the LORD. This latter expression complements the other expressions already used such as 'trust', and 'commit your way to the LORD'. To hope in the LORD indicates long, patient endurance in waiting on him. The New Testament parallels to it are our LORD's experience in Gethsemane (Luke 22:44, 'in anguish') and the description of Epaphras' prayers (Col. 4:12, 'always wrestling in prayer').

2. The Ruin of the Wicked (verses 10-15)

The seeming prosperity of the wicked is only an illusion, for they are going to be cut off *(verse 10)*. When one looks to see where they are (lit. you perceive his place), they are gone. The contrast is that the meek shall abide in the land and enjoy (the same word as translated 'delight' in verse 4) abundant peace *(verse 11)*. The word 'meek' represents all those who are truly waiting on the LORD. It is often contrasted with the wicked as here in this verse, or with the scoffers (Prov. 16:19). They experience God as their deliverer (Ps. 10:17-18), receive grace from him (Prov. 3:34), and know that God is finally going to save them (Pss. 147:6; 149:4).

Those whose hearts are not right with God spend their time scheming against the righteous *(verse 12)*. In their bitterness they vent their rage by grinding their teeth as they display their anger. In Psalm 2:4 the LORD mocks the scheming of the hostile kings. Here he mocks the wicked in general *(verse 13)*. The reason for this is that he knows that 'his day' is coming. This could refer to the LORD's 'day', but in the context it seems to be the wicked man's day. In effect it amounts to the same thing, for his day will be the final day of judgement.

Hostility towards the righteous is the hallmark of the wicked *(verse 14)*. They plot to use weapons against them, and even to kill them. The verb 'to slay' is a very strong word, being used elsewhere normally of the slaughter of animals. However, what they will find is that their own schemes turn against themselves and they are destroyed by their own weapons *(verse 15)*. This theme of evil turning back on its practitioners is found in Psalm 7:14-16 (see commentary; for a similar idea see Jer. 2:19).

3. *The Blessing of the LORD (verses 16-26)*

Wealth may be part of a happy life but it is not its real basis. The righteous may be poor, but that is better than living thinking that wealth is what matters in life *(verse 16)*. Money in itself is not wrong. It is the love of it which the Bible condemns (1 Tim. 6:10). The wicked will find that their ability to acquire wealth will disappear *(verse 17)*. The word 'power' is literally 'arms', for often 'arm' is used as a symbol for power (see Pss. 77:15; 89:10). On the other hand, the sustenance of the righteous comes from the LORD. He is the constant provider for his people, and his role is emphasised in the Hebrew text (and all the ancient translations) by placing his name at the end of the verse.

The whole idea of Canaan as the land which God swore to give to Israel lies behind the words in *verses 18-19*. Canaan was the inheritance which the LORD provided (Exod. 15:17; Deut. 31:20), and his eyes were 'continually on it from the beginning of the year to the end' (Deut. 11:12). God knew each day of his people's lives, and he so met their needs that even in times of famine they enjoyed abundance. At times this was done by extraordinary means, as in the time of Elijah (1 Kings 17:1-6).

The stress in *verse 20* is on the passing nature of the wicked. Probably two illustrations are involved. The first one is that of the beauty of the grass, which then fades. The second is of things being consumed by fire. Both of them draw attention to how fleeting the existence of the wicked is.

In *verses 21-22* the contrast is between the wicked who borrow so extensively and are unable to pay when the crisis comes, and the righteous, who not only have sufficient for their own needs, but are also able to help others as well. The introduction of the reference to blessing and cursing recalls the sections in the covenant which list the appropriate blessings and cursings (Deut. 27:11ff.; 28:1ff.; 28:15ff.). The description of death as a 'cutting off' goes back to the language of instituting a covenant (lit. 'cutting a covenant') and the threat of being cut off because of failure to keep the provisions of the covenant (Gen. 17:14).

The general principle stated in *verses 23-24* is that the righteous may experience falls during life, but yet the LORD will uphold them so that they are lifted up again (see the similar teaching in Prov. 24:16). The LORD's pleasure is shown towards the righteous as they walk in his ways and as he establishes those ways. The righteous are not isolated from trouble, but when it comes, the LORD strengthens with his hand (the same verb 'uphold' occurs here as in verse 17).

The old psalmist reflects on his knowledge of life *(verses 25-26)*. While he has seen the righteous passing through difficult times (verses 7, 12, 14, 16, 19), yet he has never seen them completely forsaken by the LORD. Though they may have periods in life when it seems that the LORD has withdrawn his love, yet that is never final. The righteous are able to show compassion to others and share with them their resources. The lending is not in a commercial sense, for no interest was to be charged on such loans (Exod. 22:25). The final phrase of verse 26 points to the fact that not only will the righteous be provided for by the LORD, but their children in turn will receive from him.

4. The Marks of the Righteous (verses 27-33)

In the closing parts of the psalm there is a return to the style of the opening, with commands again evident. The theme of dwelling in the promised land continues.

Continuity of life in the promised land depended on obedience by the people (see Deut. 11:8-9, 'Observe therefore all the commands I am giving you today ... so that you may live long in the land that the LORD swore to your forefathers to give them and their descendants ...'). Following the LORD meant that they had to turn from evil and do good *(verse 27)*, which is a reference to living in a morally good way (1 Kings 8:36). The Hebrew text of *verse 28a* says that the LORD loves 'justice', but it seems best to take this as meaning 'the just' as in Proverbs 2:8. To those who are just and who are his loyal servants (*chasidim*, see on 4:3; 12:1; 18:25) there is given the promise that God will never forsake them (Deut. 31:6, quoted in Heb. 13:5).

In *verses 28b-29* the contrast is between the just and the wicked and their respective descendants. The seed (NIV 'children') of the righteous will be blessed (verse 26), whereas the seed (NIV 'offspring') of the wicked will be destroyed. This is a repetition in other words of what has already been said in verses 9 and 22. The psalmist builds here on the concept of the land being an inheritance for Israel. God's covenant people had to maintain their inheritance by obedience to his demands. The idea of this statement forms the background for Jesus' words in the Sermon on the Mount: 'Blessed are the meek, for they will inherit the earth' (Matt. 5:5).

In *verses 30-31* there is a another parallel with a saying in the Book of Proverbs (Prov. 10:31). The righteous person ponders over God's wisdom and speaks about it. The word 'utters' is translated as 'meditate' in Psalm 1:2, but it can also mean 'speak' (see Ps. 35:28). Here meditation and speech are linked together, for the righteous man has God's law in his heart, and thus he speaks of what is wise and just. His steps do not slip because he has God's instruction as his guide.

Verses 32-33 have the ring of the courthouse about them. Hence it may well be that 'seeking their very lives' (lit. 'seeking to kill him') refers to action in a court to secure a verdict of guilty. The 'lying in wait' would then be giving false evidence against the righteous. But while men may condemn, God will acquit. The righteous judgment of God is here contrasted (as in 1 Cor. 4:3) with human judgment. Tertullian, the early Church Father, said: 'If we are condemned by the world, we will be acquitted by God.' The righteous will not be forsaken at this time of trial, but rather find vindication from the LORD.

5. *Salvation from the LORD (verses 34-40)*

The final verses of the psalm sum up its message, repeating ideas already seen in verses 7, 9, and 11. The psalmist issues a call for patient and expectant waiting for the LORD, which is coupled with following his paths *(verse 34)*. 'The way of the LORD' is an expression which goes back to God's words concerning Abraham and his descendants (Gen.

18:19). David, at the end of his life, instructed his son Solomon to 'observe what the LORD your God requires: Walk in his ways, and keep his decrees and commands' (1 Kings 2:3). 'To exalt' in this context is practically equivalent to deliver (cf. Ps. 27:6). Once more the land of Canaan comes into focus here. When the wicked come to destruction, the righteous are going to be observers (for the same idea see Pss. 52:6; 91:8).

In the psalmist's own experience he had seen wicked and tyrannical men (*verses 35-36*). They seemed to be like indigenous trees, well rooted and luxuriant. But when he next looked they were gone, and no searching could locate them. This is using the same illustration as in Psalm 1, but in the opposite way.

Another imperative follows (*verse 37*). 'Consider' is the Hebrew verb 'to keep' or 'guard'. It is used here in the sense of 'regard', or 'pay attention to'. The object of this attention is the righteous man, called here 'the blameless' (see on Pss. 15:2; 18:23) and 'the upright'. His final end (NIV 'future') is one of well-being and prosperity. His character and his destiny stand in marked contrast to the man of violence (verse 35). All transgressors will be destroyed, for at the end they will be cut off by the LORD (*verse 38*).

The psalm ends with a summary of its entire message (*verses 39-40*). The source of salvation is the LORD, who is a refuge in time of trouble. He sustains and delivers. The verb 'deliver' used here (*palat*) is almost exclusively a Psalter word. It is often used as here in a word of testimony regarding God's deliverances, and also, as here, it frequently has as its parallel the verb 'help'. The final words are important because they explain the reason for God's deliverances. The righteous have taken refuge with him, and hence he saves them.

PSALM 38
A psalm of David. A petition.

The title of this psalm does not provide much help in trying to put it into an historical setting. The description 'a petition' is literally 'to bring to remembrance'. Some suggest a link with the memorial offering of Leviticus 2:2 and 24:7. The Aramaic Targum links the psalm with the daily memorial offering (Lev. 6:8-13), while the Greek Septuagint ties it in with the Sabbath memorial offering (Lev. 24:5-9). It is better to think of the title as a later description of a psalm used by sufferers to bring their plight to God's remembrance. It has many affinities with Psalm 6, except that here there is no recorded answer to the appeal for help.

1. *A Cry for Help (verse 1)*

The opening of the psalm is almost identical to Psalm 6:1 (different words are used for 'anger'). David knows that God will punish sin, but he asks God not to display his anger as he brings his case before him. He approaches the one who is 'the compassionate and gracious God, slow to anger, abounding in love and faithfulness' (Exod. 34:6).

2. *A Description of Illness (verses 2-10)*

It is hard to assess the nature of the illness described here. There are features which suggest a dermatological condition (see verses 5 and 7). It may have been a form of leprosy, which would also help to explain why the psalmist was so alienated from his friends and acquaintances (verse 11).

'Arrows' signify divine judgment, while the 'hand' is often a symbol of power in the Old Testament *(verse 2)*. This verse is an acknowledgment of the sovereign way in which God had dealt with him, penetrating deeply into his heart and life (the same Hebrew verb is represented by both 'pierced' and 'has come down'; cf. the use of the same verb in Proverbs 17:10: 'A rebuke impresses [penetrates deeply] a man of discernment more than a hundred lashes a fool').

There is not always a connection between sin and sickness, but here the psalmist confesses his sin *(verses 3-4)*, as he does again later in the psalm (verse 18). Throughout his whole body he is experiencing the consequences of God's judgement upon him. He feels that he is being engulfed by his sin and its consequences. The word 'burden' is a fitting term to use of sin and guilt, and its use recalls Cain's words: 'My punishment is more than I can bear' (Gen. 4:13).

The terms used here to describe the sickness denote the smell and the discharge of wounds *(verses 5-6)*, though they could be used as a figurative description of extreme suffering. 'Sinful folly' is a good translation of a Hebrew word which appears most commonly (22 out of 24 appearances) in the Book of Proverbs (cf. especially Prov. 24:9). Verse 6 picks up the idea of sin being a burden (verse 4), as the psalmist suggests he is bent over because of his sin. He goes about in mourning constantly. In later Judaism it was customary for someone coming for trial to appear as if mourning. If this was also an earlier custom, it would suggest that the psalmist was recognising his own guilt and that he stood accused before the LORD.

The psalmist's back is ulcerated and fevered *(verse 7)*, and he repeats his mournful cry of verse 3: 'There is no health in my body.' This was the way in which Isaiah later spoke of the condition of the nation (Isa. 1:6, 'from the sole of your foot to the top of your head there is no soundness ...'). Physically and psychologically the psalmist is enfeebled to an intense degree. He describes his anguished cries by using the verb *(sha'ag)* which is normally used of the roaring of a lion *(verse 8)*. The same verb is used of the LORD roaring (Amos 1:2; Jer. 25:30; Joel 3:16). But here it is the tortured psalmist who cries out in his grief and pain.

In his sickness and distress the psalmist knew that his whole life was open before the LORD *(verses 9-10)*. Nothing could be hidden from him, even his sighings. This is the real meaning of the word here, rather than 'longings.' When normal speech is impossible, sometimes only sighings can express emotional and physical anguish. God, who heard the groaning of his people in Egypt (Exod. 2:24), would understand his condition. His heart beats frantically, and all strength vanishes. The reference to the light going from the eyes probably means that his vitality had disappeared (cf. the note regarding Moses in Deut. 34:7: 'his eyes were not weak', for the positive use of the idiom).

3. *Forsaken by Friends (verses 11-20)*

The following verses go on to describe the sense of desolation which David was experiencing. First of all his friends left him, and then his enemies derided him *(verses 11-12)*. His friends (lit. 'those loving me') want to avoid contact with him. The affliction which he is undergoing was too much for them, and so they distance themselves from him. The word 'wounds' is literally 'affliction, smiting', a word which can be used for leprosy in the Old Testament (Lev. 13:2; Deut. 24:8). It is probably not just the repulsive nature of his illness which caused their alienation, but a realisation that it came from God. From a distance they plot how they can hurt him. All day long they are ready to plan things which will cause him even greater harm.

The psalmist rests his case with God, and he makes no attempt to justify himself to his accusers *(verses 13-14)*. He pretends to be both deaf and dumb, and he says it in emphatic fashion by repeating the main ideas in verse 14. He does not offer a response to the accusations of his friends and neighbours.

In the midst of the lament the psalmist shows where his hope really lies *(verse 15)*. He directs his prayer to the LORD, confident that God will answer. By the end of the psalm there is still no recorded answer, but it is part of the nature of true faith to continue in expectant waiting.

The Hebrew text of *verse 16* has simply: 'For I said, "Lest they rejoice over me ..."' Something needs to be understood, such as, 'I will take heed of my ways ...' This was probably a prayer which had been prayed earlier, asking for healing lest his condition give his enemies occasion to rejoice. Even when he stumbled they took the opportunity to exalt themselves, priding themselves that they were not in the same position.

It is hard to know what the 'falling' in *verse 17* refers to. It could be that in his heart he would come to a wrong conclusion about his present condition, and fail to see it in the light of God's word. He seems to even doubt the promise that God will not let the righteous fall (Pss. 15:5; 37:24; 112:6). Mental and physical distress were his constant companion. At the outset of the psalm he had acknowledged his sin (verse 3), and now he does so again *(verse 18)*. He was disturbed by it, and willingly makes known his condition before God.

While he seems near death, the psalmist's enemies are very much alive *(verses 19-20)*. One manuscript from Qumran reads 'my enemies without cause' (Hebrew *chinam* in place of *chayyim*), which is an emendation frequently suggested (cf. Ps. 35:19). However, this may well be a deliberate change, and it is preferable to stay with the Massoretic text. Without any justification the enemies repaid good with evil, and their hatred was inspired only by their own sinfulness.

4. *An Appeal for Help (verses 21-22)*
The psalm ends with a prayer for speedy help. At the centre of the psalmist's life there is still true faith. He fears abandonment by God, and asks for urgent help to be granted. The final verse is the equivalent of saying, 'Come and save me quickly'. The ideas in both verses are very similar to those in Psalm 22:1, 11, 19.

PSALM 39
For the director of music. For Jeduthun.
A psalm of David

There are aspects of this psalm which resemble some of those in the wisdom psalms (see the Introduction, pp. 52-54). This is especially so in relation to the teaching regarding the transitory nature of human life (verses 4-6). The psalm moves through two parallel phases, which can be set out as follows:

1. *Silence before the* LORD (verses 1-3)
2. *Prayer to the* LORD (verses 4-6)
3. *Appeal for Help* (verses 7-8)
4. *Silence before the* LORD (verse 9)
5. *Prayer to the* LORD (verses 10-11)
6. *Appeal for Help* (verses 12-13)

The name 'Jeduthun' in the title also occurs in the titles of Psalms 62 and 77. He was one of David's chief musicians (1 Chr. 9:16; 16:38, 41-42). It is unclear whether the use of the name is a reference to the musical director ('For the musical director, Jeduthun') or to a tune by this name.

1. *Silence before the* LORD *(verses 1-3)*
The psalm opens with the psalmist telling his readers what his thoughts had been. He had wanted to speak, but because of the presence of the wicked he had determined he would not. Perhaps he wanted to speak about the prosperity of the wicked or ask questions about their relative ease in life. Instead, he muzzled himself and prevented himself speaking hasty or angry words which would have been sinful.

His silence created other problems for him, for as he guarded his mouth his inner thoughts overwhelmed him *(verses 2-3)*. His anger is described by the terms 'grew hot' and 'burned'. From what follows in the next section it may be that the psalmist's concerns related to growing old and ultimately dying. He was like Jeremiah with a fire in his heart, which could not be contained (Jer. 20:9). Finally, he had to break his silence and speak, and the words 'then I spoke with my tongue' bring a dramatic end to the introductory verses.

2. *Prayer to the* LORD *(verses 4-6)*

This section starts with a prayer, includes a description of the fleeting nature of life, and then has three assertions, which all start in Hebrew with the word 'surely' (Hebrew *'ak*).

The word 'end' is never used of geographical limits but always of either God's judgments or, as here, of the end of life *(verse 4)*. The psalmist wants divine instruction regarding the nature of human life. It is only temporary, and short-lived, and he prays that he may understand this. This section is very similar in idea to Psalm 90:1-12.

God's understanding of our lifetime is quite different from our own, for our life span is insignificant before him *(verse 5)*. The word for 'span' occurs in a similar passage in Psalm 89:47. The first of the three assertions introduced by the Hebrew 'surely' comes at the end of the verse: 'surely, each man's life ... .'

The second and third assertions starting with 'surely' come in *verse 6*: 'Surely, like a shadow as man goes to and fro... . Surely, in vain he bustles about'. It is surprising that the word for 'mere phantom' is also the word for 'image' in Genesis 1:26, 27. But man is not God; he is only created in his image, and the image-bearer, because of sin, has a limited life span before death comes. All his activity is characterised as vanity, nothingness, and even his wealth will be enjoyed by others. The New Testament teaches that we should be content with God's provision, 'for we brought nothing into the world, and we can take nothing out of it' (1 Tim. 6:7).

3. *Appeal for Help (verses 7-8)*

The word 'now' *(verse 7)* is far stronger in Hebrew than in English, for it marks off a new stage in the psalm. It commences with a rhetorical question, to which the answer is given, 'I look expectantly to you.' Both question and answer suggest the very opposite of despondency and despair. The only hope for the psalmist was with God.

There is a confession implicit in *verse 8*. The psalmist prays for the forgiveness of his transgressions, including those already mentioned earlier in the psalm. They included his sinful thoughts and also wrong ideas concerning the meaning of life. Even a fool could note that he was taken up with his enemies and the passing matters of human existence. He prays that he will be delivered from their reproaches.

4. *Silence before the LORD (verse 9)*

The second phase of the psalm begins here, with the idea of silence in verses 1-3 being taken up again. David repeats from verse 2 the opening reference to his silence. However, there is a change here. Previously he had stopped himself from speaking, but now that he has seen what God has done, with his new insight he is content to stay silent.

5. *Prayer to the LORD (verses 10-11)*

David is conscious of the LORD's rebuke *(verse 10)*, using the word 'scourge' to describe it (see the same word in Ps. 38:11, 'affliction, smiting', and accompanying comment). It is a military figure, and this is continued in the following phrase, for the word 'blow' (used only here in the Old Testament) comes from a root associated with warfare. The distressing situation into which he has come is in fact the blow he has received.

The scourge from God is a form of rebuke to the psalmist *(verse 11)*. The biblical pattern is that 'the LORD disciplines those he loves, as a father the son he delights in' (Prov. 3:12, and cf. the use of these words in Heb. 12:6). David now knows that human wealth can vanish quickly, just as a moth can eat clothing. The final words of the verse are a repetition of those in verse 5.

6. *Appeal for Help (verses 12-13)*

As the psalm ends there is another cry to God. David pleads with God to receive his prayer, saying, 'Hear ... listen ...be not deaf.' But he feels that he is a stranger in God's presence, even though he addresses God using his covenant name, LORD. This is different from the idea that we are to live as strangers and pilgrims in this present world (1 Pet. 2:11). It takes its origin from the fact that the Israelites were themselves aliens in the promised land, for it belonged to the LORD (Lev. 25:23; 1 Chr. 29:15). Just as the strangers living among the Israelites depended upon their kindness, so the Israelites themselves depended upon God's mercy.

Normally the psalmists ask for God to look upon them. Here the request is that God will not look upon him *(verse 13)*. In the context it must be a plea that God will avert his judgment from him. He longs to know the joy of the LORD before death comes.

PSALM 40
For the director of music. Of David. A psalm.

There are unusual features about this psalm. It is most uncommon to have a song of thanksgiving (verses 1-10) followed by a lengthy complaint (verses 11-17). The psalm moves from a song of joy concerning the past actions of the LORD to a heartfelt cry from the depths of despair. It is also unusual because part of the psalm (verses 13-17) is substantially repeated as Psalm 70. There are a few other examples of this in the Psalter (14=53; 57:7-11=108:1-5; 60:5-12=108:6-13). The earlier experiences of the psalmist form the basis for his prayer in the present. He is pleading past mercies as the ground for his present trust in the LORD as his deliverer.

1. *A Testimony to Grace (verses 1-10)*
The psalmist is relating what happened to him in the past when he cried to the LORD *(verse 1)*. The rendering 'waited patiently' is probably too passive a rendering of the opening words. The verb means 'to wait expectantly' or 'to hope in the LORD' (see on Ps. 37:8-9), and the expression here is an emphatic one. Perhaps a rendering such as, 'I indeed waited expectantly for the LORD', captures something of the meaning. The cry was heard and the LORD answered.

David describes his experience as if it was like being in a pit *(verse 2)*, or in a cistern such as the one Jeremiah was put into, which had no water, only mud (Jer. 38:6). From his place of distress, with its desolation and danger, God had delivered him. He was rescued and set on a firm foundation.

With distress gone, there was a new song in his mouth *(verse 3)*. In later psalms such as Psalms 96 and 98, the phrase 'a new song' is linked with final, end-time events, as it is in Revelation 14:3. Here it denotes the salvation song which God gave him, as part of the sequence of actions by him ('he turned ... he heard ... he lifted ... he set ... he put'). His experiences will be a testimony to many others, who also will come and find refuge in this Saviour.

The contrast is now drawn between those who come to trust the LORD, and those who put their trust in idols *(verse 4)*. They are commended (for 'blessed', see on Ps. 1:1), for they have not followed the arrogant ones who deviate from the true God to trust in idols.

What had happened to the psalmist was another 'wonder' done by the LORD *(verse 5)*. A 'wonder' was a supernatural act of deliverance which God alone could perform (Ps. 72:18, 'who alone does marvellous deeds'). Just as the deliverance of Israel from Egypt was a 'wonder', so also was the recent deliverance of the psalmist. No-one could recount all the divine acts of salvation, for they were so numerous.

The section which follows (verses 6-10) has often been taken as Messianic because of its use in Hebrews 10:5-7. However, in the setting here in Psalm 40 the psalm is not primarily Messianic, for among other things David confesses his own sinfulness (verse 12). It is taken over and applied to Jesus, who as the greater David fulfils the spirit of these words. The New Testament quotation is from the Greek Septuagint, whose variations from the Hebrew text made its use easier in Hebrews 10.

Verse 6 should not be interpreted as if David was denying the validity of the Old Testament sacrificial system. Rather they are to be understood, as in 1 Samuel 15:22, as stressing that obedience was more essential than sacrifice. Four of the common sacrifices are designated. The first two are more general terms, while the last two are the terms for the offering completely consumed on the altar and the expiatory offering. The reference to the piercing of his ears is probably to his readiness to hear the word of the LORD and obey it, as the following verse makes plain.

The psalmist showed great readiness to respond in personal commitment to what God required *(verse 7)*. Like Isaiah (see Isa. 6:8) he puts himself totally at the disposal of God. If David is speaking as king he may well be referring to what was written about the king in the law of Deuteronomy (17:14-20). Otherwise, the scroll would refer to all the written demands of God upon him.

David longs to do God's will, for within his heart he has God's instruction *(verse 8)*. The idea of internal possession of the law is one which takes a significant place in the later Old Testament teaching regarding the new covenant (Jer. 31:33-34; Ezek. 36:26-27).

To the assembled worshipping community David proclaims (or the Hebrew could also be translated 'proclaimed', cf. verse 3) what God had done *(verse 9)*. Here 'righteousness' is probably not so much a characteristic of God but a term to describe his saving activity. It is virtually a synonym for 'salvation'. David puts the idea both positively and negatively: he proclaims the fact, and does not restrain his lips from taking part in such a proclamation.

Verse 10 continues the same ideas as in the previous verse. What is important is the accumulation of covenant terminology, with a cluster of words relating to God's character and works. 'Righteousness' is the key word, and 'faithfulness', 'salvation', 'love', and 'truth' are all ways of giving further explanation to it. Emphasis is placed on his public proclamation by the repetition of the phrase 'the great assembly'.

2. *A Prayer for Fresh Mercy (verses 11-17)*

Attention now focuses on the present situation. While there is no express reference to the earlier part of the psalm, yet it forms the foundation for the requests which are made.

The repetition of the phrase 'your love and your truth' *(verse 11)* from the previous verse makes the interconnection of the two parts of the psalm plain. God is the protector of his people, and the appeal is made to him to show his love and truth in this way. The appeal is even more direct than our English versions suggest, as the Hebrew text begins, 'You, O LORD, you do not ...' It is possible to render the verse as a statement, expressing confidence in God's mercy, or (like RSV and NIV) as a prayer.

The abundance of difficulties is overwhelming for the psalmist, and he feels as if his courage has forsaken him *(verse 12)*. The verb 'troubled' is used in 2 Samuel 22:5 and Jonah 2:5 of floodwaters. His sight is also affected and his vision has become dim because of the immensity of his troubles (cf. Ps. 69:3-4: 'my eyes fail', 'those who hate me without reason outnumber the hairs of my head').

The section from *verse 13* to the end of the psalm reappears in the Psalter as Psalm 70, with slight verbal alteration. David longs for a speedy resolution of his problem by the LORD, but that resolution has to be in accord with God's will. 'Be pleased' is an echo of the word 'will' in verse 8, and it is used in other prayers as well as this one (see Deut. 33:11, 24).

Verse 14 is very close in wording and meaning to Psalm 35:4 (see the comment). This verse makes it plain that it was not just his sins which troubled him, but the activities of his enemies. His very life was in danger from them.

The cry of 'Aha!' is one of human joy (Ps. 35:21, 25; Ezek. 25:3), and it is here said over the misery of another *(verse 15)*. The psalmist wants these enemies to be made desolate. As with other curses in the Psalter, the enemies are not just personal enemies, for David is speaking here as king. It may well be that the enemies were aggressive, neighbouring nations who were ready to attack Israel.

There is much similarity between *verse 16* and Psalm 35:27. In contrast to the shouts of the enemies, the psalmist wants the true worshippers of the LORD ('seek' is often used in this sense) to proclaim his greatness. Nothing can add to God's greatness, but praise is a way of drawing attention to it. Praise for God's salvation is to be a perpetual characteristic of his people.

The call to God to 'not delay' *(verse 17)* balances the call to 'come quickly' in verse 13. David pleads for urgent assistance, just as Daniel did using the same words (Dan. 9:19). The psalmist knows his own weakness and inability, and expresses the desire that God would think and plan for his salvation. To the God to whom he had looked expectantly in the past, he now looks again for help and rescue.

PSALM 41
For the director of music. A psalm of David

There are many similarities between this psalm and the ones immediately preceding (38-40). In them there is repeated mention of human frailty and sickness, though in each there is confident appeal to God for his mercy and deliverance. This psalm begins with a general assertion concerning God's character in relation to the righteous. Then follows a prayer for help, with a repeated cry for mercy (verses 4 and 10). The psalm ends with a doxology, which also concludes the first book of the Psalter.

1. *Confidence in the LORD (verses 1-3)*
The opening word 'blessed' recalls the use of the same word in the first verse of Psalm 1 (see comment). It is a word used only of men, whereas the expression 'praise to ...' which occurs in verse 13 is only applied to God. The person who looks with favour on the needs of the poor will himself be delivered by the LORD. The idea of this verse finds its fullest expression in the Sermon on the Mount: 'Blessed are the merciful, for they will be shown mercy' (Matt. 5:7).

The theme of the LORD *(verse 2)* as the keeper of Israel finds fuller development in Psalm 121:7-8. Part of the protection referred to here was preservation in time of serious illness. The phrase 'preserve his life' can also be rendered 'keep him alive'. There are difficulties with the following words. The Hebrew text has: 'he will be blessed in the land and do not you give him ...' The NIV follows the Septuagint, the Vulgate, and the Syriac in translating it as active ('he will bless'). That certainly represents the meaning in the context, while the change to 'he' is also in keeping with the context. In the good land he will be kept safe (see Psalm 37:22), and his enemies will not see their desire for him fulfilled.

During illness, strength will be provided by the LORD, with the promise of a radical change to take place *(verse 3)*. Restoration is possible for those who cry to the LORD for help so that their illness can be turned around. In the first three verses the idea of preservation comes to its climax here. The LORD can so intervene that the situation is totally changed.

2. *A Cry for Mercy (verses 4-9)*

The initial 'I said' *(verse 4)* may refer to past prayers, though it could also be translated 'I say'. Later in the psalm it becomes clear that David is still sick (verse 10). He makes his plea for mercy and for healing. God had promised through Moses that he was the healer (Exod. 15:26), and the psalmist claims that promise. With his request comes open confession of his sin. All sin is committed against God, as David acknowledges even more specifically in connection with his sin with Bathsheba (Ps. 51:4, 'against you, you only, have I sinned').

His enemies are just waiting for his death to take place, so that they can rejoice over it *(verses 5-6)*. To have one's name perish meant that there would be no descendants (Ps. 109:13). Even when they visit him in his sickness (and this was a normal practice, cf. 2 Kings 8:29), their intent is evil, and they do not speak truthfully. They gossip about him to others and spread false rumours.

The word used in *verse 7* for 'whisper' is always used of whispering in groups, such as when David's servants whispered about his son's death (2 Sam. 12:19). His enemies hope that his disease will be fatal, and that where he lies will become his deathbed. They seem to be thinking that his disease is a fitting judgment from God. Hence their actions show that they are not recipients of the ascription 'blessed' as in verse 1 (for the New Testament teaching concerning helping the needy, see James 1:27).

In this situation even the closest of friends (lit. 'a man of my peace', i.e. with whom I have the friendliest relationship) turns against David *(verse 9)*. The very friend who shared his food proves to be a traitor to him. The exact phrase, 'to lift up the heel', does not occur elsewhere, but it seems to mark out an aggressive or traitorous action. This is the meaning that is given to the verse when Jesus quotes it of Judas (John 13:18). What was true of David's experience was fulfilled to an even greater degree in Judas' betrayal of Jesus.

3. *A Renewed Request (verses 10-12)*

The prayer of verse 4 is now renewed in *verse 10*. What he had prayed in the past is fitting for the present, because it represents the urgent cry of a needy sinner. The enemies were saying that he would never get up (verse 8), but the psalmist knows that God is able to lift him up again. He seeks this, not for selfish vengeance upon them, but in order to see God's honour vindicated (see verses 2-3).

If the psalmist is raised up by the LORD, then the enemies would not be able to shout out in triumph *(verse 11)*. The word translated 'triumph' is often used in situations of great festive joy (cf. 1 Sam. 4:5). No such occasion could happen, since he can confidently look for God's support. The final phrase is best taken as referring to life in the promised land (verse 2) as God's servant. Just like Elijah, he shall stand before the LORD (1 Kings 17:1).

4. *Doxology (verse 13)*

This is the first of the doxologies with which all five books of the Psalter conclude. It is a fitting ascription of praise to the God of Israel. The ascription of 'praise' or 'blessed' to God cannot add to his person, but it tells that he is worthy of praise, and such praise directs attention again to his greatness. The double 'Amen' sets the seal to this declaration.

BOOK 2

PSALMS 42-43

For the director of music. A maskil of the Sons of Korah.

In many Hebrew manuscripts Psalms 42 and 43 are regarded as one psalm. This fact is supported by the observation that Psalm 43 has no title, which is surprising, for all the psalms in Book 2 of the Psalter (with the exception of Psalm 71) have one. Moreover, the two psalms share a common refrain, 'Why are you downcast, O my soul? Why so disturbed within me? Put your hope in God ...' (42:5, 11; 43:5). The transition from Book 1 to Book 2 of the Psalter is marked by the substitution of the word 'God' (*'elohim*) for the name 'Lord' (*yhwh*). While 'Lord' still occurs, it is vastly outnumbered by the occurrences of 'God'. The 'Sons of Korah' were Levites who had special respon-sibilities in the Temple (1 Chr. 6:22; 2 Chr. 20:19).

1. *Longing for God (verses 1-4)*
Intense longing fills the heart of the psalmist *(verse 1)*. For some unstated reason he is not able to go and enjoy communal worship. He likens himself, however, to a deer which longs for water. So, from the barrenness of his isolation he has a similar longing after God.

In *verse 2* he repeats his desire for God, and calls him 'the living God'. This phrase is unusual, and it may be connected with the idea that God was the 'living water' (cf. Jer. 2:13; 17:13). The psalmist voices his concern as to when he can go and see God's face (NIV 'meet with God'). 'To see the face of God' is the technical expression which the Old Testament uses of appearing before God at the sanctuary (Exod. 23:17; Ps. 84:7).

His enemies taunt him continually, for it seems as if God has deserted him *(verse 3)*. The doubts he had while absent from the sanctuary were aggravated by these unfeeling comments. In his grief his tears flood down his face and seem to become his food. His memory also recalls the happier times when he led the festive crowd going to the sanctuary *(verse 4)*. The annual pilgrimages like Passover, the Feast of Weeks and the Feast of Tabernacles, were meant to be happy occasions as the tribes went up 'to praise the name of the Lord' (Ps. 122:4).

2. *The Refrain (verses 5-6a)*
In the midst of his spiritual barrenness and longing for God, the psalmist encourages himself. Why should he be so troubled in spirit if

he has God as his Saviour? He calls upon himself to wait for God, and expresses the conviction that he is yet going to praise him.

3. *The Cry of a Troubled Heart (verses 6b-10)*

The geographical expressions in *verse 6b* suggest that the psalmist was far off from the sanctuary, perhaps even in exile. He seems to be speaking from the area in which the Jordan River rises, though Mount Mizar is otherwise unknown. The thought of the tumbling waters of the Jordan, such as can still be seen at the waterfall at Banyas in northern Israel, provides the idea of the waves which are presently coming over him. No longer is his mind on the 'living water' which God provides (verses 1-2), but on his own situation in which he has been engulfed *(verse 7)*.

In the midst of his distress he is still able to recall God's graciousness to him *(verse 8)*. In the day time God commands his love; at night time he gives a song, which is turned into a prayer. Many Hebrew manuscripts have 'the living God' instead of 'the God of my life'. There is only one letter different in the Hebrew, and certainly 'living God' matches well with the same expression in verse 2.

The psalmist feels forsaken, yet he is able to call God his 'Rock' (cf. for the use of this description of God, Pss. 18:2; 31:3; 71:3). No fuller explanation is given of the enemies, yet the use of the word 'oppressed' may well be significant *(verse 9)*. It is most often used of the enemies of the nation of Israel, who attacked and marauded the land.

Illness plagues him, and he has the added pain of opponents who constantly mock him *(verse 10)*. His present distress is deepened by the attitude and words of others, for they are suggesting that God is unable to help.

3. *Refrain (verse 11)*

The refrain of verses 5-6a is taken up again, as he expresses confidence in his God.

4. *A Prayer for Vindication (Psalm 43, verses 1-4)*

From the mountains of northern Palestine, the scene now moves to Mount Zion, and the joy of worship there.

Several factors here confirm the impression that the enemies were external ones *(verse 1)*. They are clearly 'ungodly', using an expression which suggests that they are strangers to covenant love (lit. 'not *chasid'*). His appeal for God to plead his cause is typical of covenantal passages in the prophets (see, e.g. Jer. 2:9; Mic. 6:1; 7:9). He wants deliverance from those who practise deceit and unrighteousness, qualities which must not be characteristic of God's followers (Ps. 119:3; Mal. 2:6).

The psalmist cannot reconcile the truth that God is his stronghold with the fact that he is passing through difficult times and enduring such trouble from his enemies *(verse 2)*. He wonders why God seems to have rejected him. The second part of the verse repeats a question already asked in 42:9b.

He now asks for God's light and God's truth to be his guide, and that they will bring him back to Zion *(verse 3)*. This in effect would be the answer to the question he had asked at the very outset (Ps. 42:2). He wants these two angels to lead him through the desert and bring him into God's presence.

He looks ahead and anticipates the joy with which he will worship his God on Zion *(verse 4)*. In place of sorrow and grief there will be a fresh realisation of who God is. He is the joy and delight of his children, worthy of praise from those who can say of him, 'God, my God'.

5. *Refrain (verse 5)*
The refrain comes in for the third time, but now the emphasis probably falls on the latter part. The thought of joyful worship at the sanctuary revitalises the psalmist.

PSALM 44
For the director of music. Of the Sons of Korah. A maskil.

It was customary in Israel for a song to be sung to the LORD after victory in battle (see Judg. 5). It was also customary for a song to be sung after defeat in battle, and Psalm 44 is such a song. In this psalm the people and the king cry out to God to arise and help them. The language alternates between singular and plural. The singular passages (verses 4, 6, 15-16) may well have been the words which the king used, while the remainder of the psalm is an appeal from the army or the nation as a whole. Because there is no reference to the destruction of the Temple, the psalm is probably from late in the history of Judah, in the time of Hezekiah or Josiah.

1. Confidence in God's Past Help (verses 1-8)

It was the responsibility of one generation to pass on to the next generation the knowledge of God's actions on behalf of his people *(verse 1)*. They had to 'tell the next generation the praiseworthy deeds of the LORD, his power, and the wonders he has done' (Ps. 78:4). Similarly for the Christian community, what we receive we are to pass on (1 Cor. 15:1-11; 2 Tim. 2:2).

Recognition is made of God's sovereign provision of the land of Canaan for his people *(verse 2)*. He transplanted Israel as a vine (see Ps. 80:8-16) and caused its branches to grow. The NIV rendering at the end of the verse captures the sense well, though it is somewhat free (lit. 'you sent them out', i.e. the branches).

Verse 3 is repeating what Moses had taught the people long before (see Deut. 4:34; 7:19; 9:4-6; 11:2; 26:8-9). The victory over the Canaanites was not achieved by human power. It had to be attributed solely to God's intervention on their behalf, based on his love for Israel (Deut. 7:7-9).

In *verse 4* the king speaks in the first person. He confesses that God is both his King and his God. Even the human leader of the people was subject to a higher power. He knew that God alone could bring victory. 'Jacob' became an honourable title for the nation from Numbers 23 onwards, and 'Jacob' is spoken of as the object of God's love (Ps. 47:4; Mal. 1:2).

The imagery of *verse 5* is taken from the actions of cattle. The victories of the past were like a bull butting its opponents, or trampling on its enemies. Through calling on God's name and seeing his power displayed, Israel's enemies had been subdued before them. This type of imagery was widely used in the Ancient Near East of military activities.

Having stated positively the fact that all victories came from the LORD, the psalmist now puts this truth negatively *(verses 6-7)*. Wielding of human weapons of war did not in itself bring salvation in battle. Horses and chariots, bows and swords, would never save. The nation had to know that they should look only to the Holy One of Israel (Isa. 31:1). To shame an adversary was to deprive him of success.

At the end of this historical reflection, the psalm rises to a note of joy *(verse 8)*. The Septuagint captures the sense when it renders: 'All day long God is praised.' Grateful thanks had always been the hallmark of a rescued people, and there would ever be acknowledgment of God's name.

2. *A Lament in the Face of Defeat (verses 9-16)*

A sudden change comes into the psalm at *verse 9*. 'But now', with which this verse opens, marks the transition to complaint. Defeat had taken place on the battlefield, and the people took this to be a sign of rejection by God. They had been shamed in battle, and sensed that God was no longer with them, as for example he had been with David when he went against the Philistines (2 Sam. 5:24).

They had been beaten in battle and robbed by their enemies *(verses 10-11)*. They accuse God of giving them up to be slaughtered, and of scattering them among the nations. The scattering among the nations could be a reference simply to captives taken in battle (cf. the case of Naaman's wife's Israelite slave, 2 Kgs. 5:2). However, captives were often sold off as slaves, further increasing the dispersion.

So worthless were the people, runs their argument, that God had sold them for nothing *(verse 12)*. He was willing to part with them for no sale price. The imagery of the sale of Israel to their enemies is common in the Old Testament, especially of defeats suffered during the period of the judges (cf. Deut. 32:30; Judg. 2:14; 3:8; 4:2; 10:7; 1 Sam. 12:9).

Among the surrounding nations Israel's name had become a laughing matter, and they had proverbial sayings making fun of her *(verses 13-14)*. They scornfully mimic her, and treat her as if she was nothing. Elsewhere shaking the head is also linked with a scornful attitude (Ps. 64:8).

The reproach was not just a national one. Individuals within Israel could feel it as deeply too, and now the psalm speaks in personal terms, 'my disgrace', 'my face' *(verses 15-16)*. The enemy wanted more than just the opportunity to make fun of Israel. Revenge was the ultimate aim, though the reason which lay behind this desire is not given.

3. *Questions in Perplexity (verses 17-22)*

Verses 17-18 bring us to the heart of the problem which the people faced. They knew God had said that if his people were disobedient he would bring judgment upon them, including defeat before their enemies (Deut. 28:15-68, and especially verses 25-26 and 49-52). But here they claim that they have not broken the covenant nor turned from the LORD's ways.

The people cannot understand why God has permitted them to be overwhelmed by the enemy, who had turned their land into a terrible wilderness (cf. 'haunt of jackals' with the almost identical expression in Jer. 10:22). They are in despair and feel as though deep darkness has descended upon them *(verse 19)*. The words 'deep darkness' translate the same Hebrew word which appears in Psalm 23:4: 'through the valley of the shadow of death'.

Again the people profess that they have been faithful to the covenant *(verses 20-21)*. Had they been unfaithful, God would have known that, for he is able to dig into the darkest recesses of the heart. The same verb for 'discover' occurs in Psalm 139:1, 23 and Jeremiah 17:10 of God's activity in searching the human heart. Nothing is hidden from his all-searching eye (see the whole of Psalm 139).

The current afflictions of the people are not the result of their turning from God. Rather, they are undergoing oppression because of their faithfulness to him *(verse 22)*. For his sake they face constant persecution, and in their enemies' minds they are reckoned simply as sheep destined for slaughter. These words are quoted by Paul after he has summed up the tribulations which are endured by the people of God (Rom. 8:36). The fact that terms which are used in this psalm of the Old Testament believing community are applied by Paul to the situation of the New Testament church shows the continuity in the experience of believers throughout history.

3. *A Prayer for Deliverance (verses 23-26)*
While this call to God is similar in some respects to that in Psalm 7:6 (see the commentary), yet there is a difference. Here the people suggest that God is so uncaring of them in their trouble that it is as if he is asleep *(verses 23-24)*. They feel rejected for ever. In situations like this the people felt that God's face was hidden from them (cf. Pss. 10:11; 27:9; 88:14; 143:7; Isa. 8:17).

Verse 25 is a description of their present distress, but the significance of the expressions are unclear. It seems to be a description either of their grief which brings them to a prostrate position in prayer, or else they feel so near to death that they are almost in the dust of the grave.

The people have already claimed that they are loyal to the covenant (verse 17). Now they ask for the continuance of covenant love (NIV 'unfailing love'), and for this to be expressed in redemption from their present distress *(verse 26)*. After Paul quotes from verse 22, he similarly goes on to assert the unfailing love of Christ Jesus our LORD (Rom. 8:33-39).

PSALM 45

For the director of music. To [the tune of] 'Lilies'.
Of the Sons of Korah. A maskil. A wedding song.

It was probably a royal wedding which inspired the composition of this psalm, and it may well have been used repeatedly at later weddings. The greatest difficulty this assessment has is that verses 6-7 appear to be a direct address to God, not to the human monarch who was his vice-regent. Some would consider the whole psalm as Messianic, in view of the use made of verses 6-7 in Hebrews 1:8-9. It is preferable to suggest that the eyes of the psalmist were lifted up to see the glory of the Davidic ruler as typifying the kingly rule of the Messiah. Accordingly, he addresses him directly, and while this may seem a sudden introduction of a Messianic element into the psalm, yet it is not without parallel elsewhere (cf. Isa. 9:6-7 and its preceding context).

1. *Introduction (verse 1)*

No other psalm starts in this fashion. The psalmist tells about the great subject matter with which his poem is concerned. His heart is bubbling over with the good things which his verses contain about a king (so the Hebrew text, which lacks the definite article 'the'). His tongue is like a skilled writer such as Ezra (cf. Ezra 7:6, which uses, in the Hebrew, the very same phrase as here).

2. *Address to the King (verses 2-9)*

The king is extolled for qualities which he possesses and for blessings which he has been given *(verse 2)*. In the Old Testament men are called 'excellent' or 'beautiful', such as the king here, or Absalom in 2 Samuel 14:25. This term refers to their general perfection. The word 'forever' does not mean 'for eternity' but 'for as long as you live' (cf. its use of a slave in Exod. 21:6).

The king is thought of as a mighty warrior who needs to buckle on his sword before battle *(verse 3)*. The second part of the verse is paraphrased by the NIV, as the Hebrew text says simply, 'your splendour, your majesty'. These terms may refer to the king's armour, and if this suggestion is correct they may also refer to glorious victories in the past.

The king is pictured as setting out for battle, riding upon his horse *(verse 4)*. He makes his way through the ranks of the enemy as the champion of truth and righteousness. The same imagery appears in the Book of Revelation of the rider Faithful and True who comes forth on a white horse (19:11). These victories will be seen as the victories of God and so inspire awe. Elsewhere, such as in Psalm 65:5, 'awesome deeds' refer to God's own actions.

In *verse 5* the NIV and many other translations take the phrase 'the hearts of the king's enemies' from the end of the verse (where it comes in the Hebrew text) and link it with the military success spoken of at the start of the verse. The whole verse is difficult to translate, but the essential message of it is clear. From carvings we know that battlefields were littered with slain bodies, shot by arrows. Victory is sure for the king. The fact that the Hebrew text ends with the word 'king' makes the transition to the next verse easier.

Suddenly the psalmist looks beyond the immediate occupant of the throne of David to the kingly glory of the Messianic ruler *(verse 6)*. This is similar to the way in which Isaiah inserts direct address to Immanuel into a passage which is dealing with the impending Assyrian invasion (Isa. 8:8). The divine ruler is not subject to the possibility that his kingdom will be taken from him. The 'sceptre' stands for the rule of the king, which is depicted as being one of which justice is the hallmark. In Hebrews 1:8 this verse is quoted in a context which points to the eternal glory of Christ. He is the one who has been given 'the throne of his father David, and he will reign over the house of Jacob for ever; his kingdom will never end' (Luke 1:32-33).

The person designated as 'God' in the previous verse is now marked off from him by the reference to 'your God' *(verse 7)*. This passage has to be considered along with other Messianic passages in the Old Testament. Also in the descriptions of the Angel of the LORD, the 'Angel' is represented as being God himself, and yet at the same time he is distinguished from God.

In verse 6 the king is God, while in this verse he has been given by God an exalted position over his companions. These companions are probably other kings. This king is distinguished from them by the fact that his character is different. He is noted for his love of righteousness and his punishment of evildoers, and consequently God has given him special blessings. The anointing with oil is probably a figurative way of saying that God has blessed him with happiness. It should not be equated with the anointing at a coronation.

The scene shifts back to the wedding *(verses 8-9)*, and to the robes with which the king is adorned. Myrrh was a fragrant resin and it could be used as a valuable gift (Matt. 2:11). Aloes and cassia are both aromatic resins from the bark of trees. Wealthy homes and royal palaces were decorated with ivory (1 Kgs. 10:18; 22:39), while ivory could also be used as inlay on furniture (Amos 6:4). Festive music sounds from the palace as the wedding preparations continued. The bride comes adorned in the best gold (cf. Isa. 13:12). Ophir has never been identified with certainty, but it was probably between Mecca and Medina. The bride is accompanied by women of the royal family as she takes her position at the king's right hand.

3. *Address to the Bride (verses 10-15)*

The bride is now addressed and she must give attention to the words of advice *(verse 10)*. The command to forget her people and her father's house may imply that she is a foreigner. In the Book of Ruth Naomi speaks of Orpah 'going back to her people and her gods'. Ruth, on the other hand, makes her profession: 'Your people will be my people and your God my God' (Ruth 1:15-16).

The king's attachment to his bride is due to her beauty *(verse 11)*. The expression 'he is your lord' may indicate that they were already married, as 'lord' is used in this way by Sarah of Abraham (Gen. 18:12; and cf. 1 Pet. 3:6, 'her master', lit. 'lord'). If so, the instruction of the previous verse comes after their marriage and reflects the new relationship with her husband's people.

The marriage brings a new relationship to surrounding nations, as gifts are brought by their peoples to the new queen *(verse 12)*. The word 'gift' can imply tribute (2 Sam. 8:2, 6). Hence the setting of this psalm may be in a period in which Israel exercised rule over surrounding nations. 'Daughter of Tyre' may indicate the people of Tyre, just as 'Daughter of Zion' and 'Daughter of Jerusalem' are used.

Address is made again directly to the king concerning his bride and her companions *(verses 13-15)*. It is clear from these two verses that it is not the inward beauty of the princess which is being described, but outward adornment in beautiful garments. She is brought to the king accompanied by her maids of honour. They are brought into the royal palace in a festive procession, something similar to a modern bridal party entering the church.

4. *Conclusion (verses 16-17)*
The speaker seems to be the psalmist, as he reflects on the enduring dynasty which the king will have. His sons will be given positions of great responsibility, for 'princes' are frequently mentioned as being connected with a royal house (see 2 Chr. 21:9; 31:8; Jer. 26:21). This enduring dynasty would be a matter of praise even among the Gentile nations. Behind the words of the psalmist here lies the promises of the Davidic covenant (2 Sam. 7).

PSALM 46

For the director of music. Of the Sons of Korah.
According to alamoth. A song.

The historical circumstances which lie behind the composition of this psalm cannot be established with absolute precision. Jerusalem has been attacked, but God has intervened on behalf of his people and shattered the enemy. The situation depicted in 2 Chronicles 20 seems to fit best, when the Moabites and Ammonites came against Je-hoshaphat. Jahaziel at that time encouraged the people: 'Do not be afraid or discouraged because of this vast army. For the battle is not yours, but God's' (verse 15). Here the psalmist sings of victory won by the LORD Almighty, and of that city in which God dwells. The psalm is divided by the threefold appearance of 'Selah' and the repeated refrain in verses 7 and 11.

1. *A Safe Stronghold (verses 1-3)*
A favourite theme of many of the psalms is the fact that God is the refuge of his people (e.g. 61:3; 62:7-8; 71:7; 142:5). The words 'refuge' and 'strength' are often used in conjunction to depict God's character and his actions on behalf of his people. The confession here is communal (the Hebrew text has 'for us' here and in verses 7 and 11), and the people acknowledge that when in trouble God is always near to help *(verse 1)*.

The troubles they had faced (including the most recent battles) are described as if there was a tremendous upheaval of nature *(verses 2-3)*. A mighty earthquake has taken place, but amidst everything the people can say: 'We will not fear.' This is based on what has been asserted about God in verse 1.

2. *God With Us (verses 4-7)*

While the term 'Zion' is not used, the psalmist now describes how secure the people are because God has his dwelling in Jerusalem *(verses 4-5)*. In other Old Testament passages we also have the picture of Jerusalem, with water streaming from her (cf. Isa. 33:21). God's sanctuary was in Jerusalem, and as long as the people were trusting his provision for them, then God's help would never fail. When they despised the softly flowing waters of Siloam, then God would abandon them. God 'had pity on his people and his dwelling place' until the people mocked his messengers, and ultimately the sanctuary itself was destroyed by the Babylonians (2 Chr. 36:15-19).

In the midst of turmoil among the nearby nations, God has spoken *(verse 6)*. When his voice is heard, the inhabitants of the earth tremble in fear. 'The earth melts' is simply a poetical way of saying that people are terrified. Kingdoms 'slip', says the psalmist, using a word he has already used of the mountains (NIV 'the mountains fall', verse 2). The contrast which is so clear is that God's city will not 'slip' or 'fall' (verse 5).

The confession which the people make is that they have God's presence *(verse 7)*. The form of the first clause is reminiscent of 'God is with us', 'Immanuel' (Isa. 7:14; 8:8, 10). Instead of 'God' the psalmist here uses the expression 'the LORD of hosts' (NIV 'the LORD Almighty'; see comment on Ps. 24:10). The covenant God of the patriarchs is with them as a 'fortress'. This word signified a fortified height to which one could flee for safety, so symbolising the security of believers in God.

3. *A Summons from the LORD (verses 8-11)*

The invitation goes out to take notice of how God has shattered the enemies which came against his people *(verses 8-9)*. The word 'desolations' is explained by what follows. He brought peace by destroying the enemy armies and their weapons. Their military power was broken as bows and spears were destroyed. In the final clause of verse 9 the NIV renders the Hebrew word 'chariots' by 'shields'. This is following three early translations – the Septuagint, the Targum, and the Vulgate. However, the word 'chariots' makes good sense, especially as we know that chariots were burnt after they were captured (Josh. 11:6, 9).

The call is addressed to the Gentile invaders to withdraw *(verse 10)*. 'Be still' conveys too much the idea of being quiet, whereas the

Hebrew verb means more 'to let alone', 'to abandon'. Because of his actions they should recognise that he is God and submit to his authority. The verb 'know' was used in secular treaties in this sense. He assures them that all nations are going to exalt him, even the whole earth.

The refrain from verse 7 is repeated to close the psalm. It is an appropriate way to sum up the gratitude of the people as they again profess their faith in their deliverer.

PSALM 47

For the director of music. Of the Sons of Korah. A psalm.

Psalms 46 and 47 seem to be positioned together in the Psalter because of their great similarity. Both celebrate God's victories on behalf of his people. This psalm has two calls to praise, followed by explanations. In each case there is a concluding statement. The first one points to God on his throne in Jerusalem (verse 5), while the second one praises him as the universal ruler (verse 9). These explanations are introduced in the Hebrew text in the manner typical of hymns by the presence of 'for' as the introductory word (see the Introduction, pp. 46-47). This is not so apparent from the NIV translation.

1. *Call to Praise (verse 1)*
Clapping hands was a sign of joy, and the call goes out to Gentile nations to share with Israel in praising God. At coronations it was apparently customary to clap the hands and shout, 'Long live the king!' (2 Kgs. 11:12). Reference to clapping also occurs in a later song of rejoicing over God's kingship in Psalm 98:8. The content of the shouting could be simply that God is King, or expressed in terms such as we have later in this psalm.

2. *God's Rule over Israel (verses 2-5)*
The nations are asked to rejoice concerning the LORD, for he is 'the great King' *(verse 2)*. This term was used by Near Eastern rulers (see 2 Kings 18:19 in reference to the King of Assyria), but here it is appropriated of the even greater King, the LORD Most High. His territory is not restricted as with earthly rulers, but rather it embraces the whole earth.

The song reflects upon the conquest of Canaan by Israel *(verses 3-*

4). It was God who acted sovereignly to dispossess other nations and to make them submissive to Israel's rule. Verse 4 is explaining the conquest and allocation of the land of Canaan in terms which echo statements in the Book of Deuteronomy (see especially 4:37-38). God's love for the patriarchs and for Jacob in particular (see Mal. 1:2) resulted in him giving them as their inheritance the land of Canaan, called here 'the pride of Jacob'.

The verb 'ascended' is used *(verse 5)* because God is thought of as having descended when he came to help his people. The same thought appears in Psalm 68:18: 'When you ascended on high, you led captives in your train ...' The LORD is pictured as returning to heaven amidst joyful acclaim from his people. Blowing of trumpets was specified for certain festive occasions including New Year (Lev. 23:24; Num. 29:1).

3. *Another Call to Praise (verse 6)*
The second call to praise is notable for its fourfold repetition of the verb 'to sing praises'. This adds both emphasis and urgency to the command. The people's relationship with God is defined in terms of his lordship over them. They sing to him as their God and as their King.

4. *God's Rule over the Nations (verses 7-9)*
The reason given for this second call to praise is that God's lordship is over all the earth *(verses 7-8)*, and this knowledge should result in another psalm of praise. This is the fifth call to praise in two verses. The Old Testament understands God's kingship to be from eternity (cf. Ps. 93:2). From his throne he exercises his rule and judgment over all nations.

The word rendered 'nobles' *(verse 9)* is literally 'willing ones', but the NIV has taken its cue from the parallel word 'kings'. The context gives a picture of princes of the Gentile nations coming voluntarily and uniting with Jews as 'the people of Abraham'. This is part of the universalistic vision of the psalmists for the ultimate future of God's kingdom (cf. Pss. 67:1-7; 72:8-11). Gentile rulers 'belong to God' in the sense that they have become his servants. The conclusion is that God is indeed 'exalted', using a verbal form connected with 'Most High' (verse 2) and 'has ascended' (verse 5).

PSALM 48
A song. A psalm of the Sons of Korah.

While there are similarities with Psalm 46, yet this psalm is much more specific in relation to Mount Zion (called simply 'the city of God' in Psalm 46:4). Whereas Psalm 46 speaks more of the LORD's victories, Psalm 48 is a song of rejoicing over Zion and the blessings associated with her. It is notable for the collection of phrases used, especially in verses 1-2, to describe Jerusalem.

1. *The God of Zion (verses 1-3)*
The initial emphasis is not on Zion, but on the God of Zion *(verse 1)*. The opening invocation sets the theme for the whole psalm as it directs attention to his greatness, and in particular as it is displayed in the symbolism of Mount Zion. The choice of Zion was the LORD's (Ps. 132:13-14), and from the time that David captured it (2 Sam. 5:6-7) it was central to the theology of the Old Testament. In the wider biblical picture Zion became the model for the New Jerusalem, and in Christian hymnology its imagery is taken over for the church (see John Newton's 'Glorious things of thee are spoken, Zion, city of our God').

Mount Zion is not actually the highest peak in the area, yet because of its religious significance it is extolled by the psalmist *(verse 2)*. He pictures it as a place of joy not just to those who live or worship there, but to the whole earth. Zaphon was a mountain in northern Syria known from Canaanite sources, and it was supposed to be the dwelling place of the god Baal. Zion, though like Zaphon, was distinguished by the fact that it is the dwelling place of 'the great King' (see Ps. 47:2).

God's presence in Zion was shown by the bringing of the ark of the covenant there, and then by the building of the Temple. He had taken up his abode in her palaces, and he had proved to be her defender *(verse 3)*. God's demonstration of his protection for Zion may have been shown just before this psalm was composed, perhaps in some battle situation such as spoken of in Psalm 46.

2. *The Glory of Zion (verses 4-8)*
In a manner similar to Psalm 2, this psalm describes a gathering together of foreign kings against the LORD and against his chosen dwelling place, Jerusalem *(verses 4-7)*. Coalitions could be formed, but they were soon shattered. What the attackers 'saw' is unclear. It

could have been the fortified Zion, or on the other hand it could have been some visible appearance of God, a theophany. 'There', where they had that vision, they were frightened and panic seized them. The idea of a woman in travail is a frequent Old Testament illustration of pain and anguish (cf. Isa. 21:3; Jer. 4:31; 49:24). Even if they are like the mighty ships which trade to Tarshish (see Jon. 1:3), they will be destroyed as easily as an east wind brings them to a watery grave.

These words of *verse 8* sum up the experience of the people. They had heard in the past of the wonderful things which the LORD had done for his people (cf. Ps. 44:1: 'we have heard with our ears, O God'). Now, however, their own eyes had seen his saving power right in the midst of Jerusalem. They thought that this experience would make her safe for ever, but God's presence was conditional on their continued obedience.

3. *The Words of the Worshippers (verses 9-11)*
After their deliverance the people address God directly *(verses 9-10)*. When the worshippers assemble in the sanctuary they recognise that it is due to covenant love that they have been saved. They now have fresh evidence of the LORD's steadfast love. What had happened was known far and wide, so that the praise of the LORD was co-extensive with knowledge of his actions. Wherever people heard about the events in Jerusalem they would praise the mighty actions of God in giving victory to his people.

On Mount Zion and throughout the villages of Judah there is gladness on account of the recent victory *(verse 11)*. That victory was called a filling of God's hand with righteousness in the previous verse, and now it is called his 'judgments'. The demonstrations of power shown in overthrowing Israel's enemies were expressions of God's judgments as he established his kingdom. This verse is very similar to Psalm 97:8.

4. *An Invitation to View Zion (verses 12-14)*
An invitation is given to view Jerusalem and to see her fortifications *(verses 12-13)*. Clearly this was not to take pride in her simply because of her good defences. She was 'the city of the LORD' (verse 8), and as such she was given divine protection. Passing on to the next generation this truth would continue the transmission of knowledge of the LORD. His praiseworthy deeds could not be hidden from the next generation

(Ps. 78:4). Each generation of believers has a responsibility to teach the following one.

The people make confession of the fact that this God who has saved them is indeed their God *(verse 14)*. They own him as their personal deliverer, and they know that he will shepherd them to the very end. This last clause continues the imagery of God as a shepherd of his people which is frequent in the Old Testament (cf. Pss. 23:1; 77:20; 80:1; Isa. 40:11; 49:9-10; Ezek. 34:11-12).

PSALM 49
For the director of music. Of the Sons of Korah. A psalm.

The first series of Korahite psalms (42-49) ends with a wisdom psalm (see the Introduction, pp. 52-54). In its general form it is like passages in the books of Job and Proverbs, even using the word 'proverb' (verse 4). Whereas in another wisdom psalm, Psalm 37, the solution to the problem of the prosperity of the wicked is that God providentially cares for his own, the solution given here is that there is life beyond the grave for those whom God redeems. After an introduction it provides two answers to the problem, each with its own refrain.

1. *Introduction (verses 1-4)*
The call is given to all to listen to the words of wisdom which are going to be spoken *(verses 1-3)*. An uncommon Hebrew word is used for 'world'. It not only denotes the physical environment but the whole sphere of transitory life. All classes of society are addressed, and the promise is that much (or possibly, profound) wisdom and great understanding will be bestowed. The issues of life and death to be addressed are of interest to all.

'Proverb' and 'riddle' occur together in *verse 4* as they do in Psalm 78:2, Proverbs 1:6, and Ezekiel 17:2. They tell of the ways in which wisdom and understanding are going to be conveyed. A 'proverb' could be much longer than the short saying we think of in English, while 'riddle' has a range of usage from the 'riddles' Samson set his Philistine guests (Judg. 14) to the 'hard questions' which the Queen of Sheba asked Solomon (1 Kgs. 10:1-3). The usage here is nearer the latter in meaning.

2. *Transitory Wealth (verses 5-12)*

The psalmist already knows the answer to his question, and it will be given later on (see verse 15). He is surrounded by evil men who have put their confidence in their wealth, and he wants to set the record straight concerning them, for no amount of money can buy off death *(verses 5-6)*.

The teaching of *verses 7-9* is that no-one can escape death by paying money. A rich person may live well, and in such a way as to give the impression that he is going to live forever. But there can be no ransom paid to God for him, for such a ransom is beyond the ability of men to achieve. Ultimately even the richest person will see decay (lit. 'see the pit'; cf. its use in Psalm 16:10, where it is used in parallelism with 'Sheol', 'the grave').

The common experience of life is that everyone dies, and whatever wealth they have acquired is left to others *(verses 10-11)*. The biblical teaching is that we bring nothing into this world and we can take nothing out of it. The real wealth consists of 'godliness with contentment', while storing up treasures is achieved by being rich in good deeds and being generous and willing to share (1 Tim. 6:6-7, 17-19). Rich people may build luxurious mansions, even naming them after themselves. Such buildings may last, but they themselves perish.

A concluding statement sums up this section of the psalm. Riches cannot bestow eternal life, for man is no different from the animals *(verse 12)*. The rich have tried to provide for themselves a lodging place, but they will find no permanent lodging there (the word translated 'endure' literally means 'to lodge the night'). The grave will receive both men and animals.

3. *Redemption by God (verses 13-20)*

The folly of the rich concerning death has been dispelled in the preceding section. Now the teacher goes on to show their folly in life, but he also points to the way in which God can redeem a soul from the grave.

Those who have a false confidence, namely in themselves or in their riches, follow a particular way of life (Hebrew text, lit. 'their path'). Their followers could either be their descendants or perhaps more likely those who imitate them (Exod. 23:2; 2 Sam. 2:10). They listen to their teachers and adopt their instruction as their own way of life *(verse 13)*.

The Hebrew text of *verse 14* is difficult to translate, as is shown by the variety in the English versions of it, and also by the footnote in the NIV. The proud rich are like sheep ready for the slaughter. The grave will swallow them, and the distance between their place of burial and their former mansions will be great. On the other hand, the righteous will come through their suffering and enter a new day.

One man cannot redeem another (see verse 7), but God is able to do that *(verse 15)*. Resurrection of the body will be God's ultimate redemption of his saints. The use of the verb 'take' is important for it is used of the translation of both Enoch (Gen. 5:24) and Elijah (2 Kgs. 2:5). Redemption and being brought into God's own presence are divine works. It is God alone who takes us to glory (Ps. 73:24).

A word of advice is now offered to all the readers of the psalm *(verses 16-17)*. After what has been said already about the position of the rich it is clear that they should not be envied nor feared. Their wealth may be real, but a time comes when they have to leave it behind.

Two characteristics mark out the unrighteous person *(verses 18-19)*. First of all, instead of praising God, he blesses himself. Then, secondly, he enjoys the flattery of other people. These experiences will not gain him any lasting benefits, for when he joins the dead there is no prospect of life with God. 'To see the light [of life]' implies resurrection from the dead (cf. Isa. 53:11 of the Servant of the LORD).

The refrain in *verse 20* is picked up from verse 12, with the change of 'does not endure' to 'without understanding'. That change is intentional to stress that riches, when spiritual understanding is absent, make a man no better than the animals which die.

PSALM 50
A psalm of Asaph.

The covenant relationship comes to the fore in this psalm, with the covenant being expressly mentioned in verses 5 and 16. It has strong resemblances to covenant law-suit passages such as Deuteronomy 32, Isaiah 1, Micah 6, and Jeremiah 2 in which heaven and earth are summoned to listen to God's judgment against his people. It also has strong affinities with Psalm 81, especially in the call to the people to listen, followed by the opening words of the Decalogue (cf. 50:7-8 with 81:8-10). The psalm may have been written for a ceremony renewing the covenant, such as was carried out every seven years at the

Feast of Tabernacles (Deut. 31:10-11). The opening of the psalm recalls the manner in which God revealed himself at Sinai to his people.

1. *God Comes to Judge (verses 1-6)*

God is not described by a single title, but by a cluster of them *(verse 1)*. The words 'the Mighty One' and 'God' seem to draw attention to the position of God as the judge over all, while 'LORD' identifies him as the covenant God of Israel. He summons the earth, not for judgment, but to witness his accusations against his own people. Because of God's choice of Zion it is regarded as a place of beauty (cf. Ps. 48:1-2), from which the LORD 'shines forth' *(verse 2)*. This term is used of his shining from Mount Paran (Deut. 33:2) and from between the cherubim (Ps. 80:1). In the Bible God is pictured as dwelling in light (cf. Exod. 13:21-22; Dan. 2:22; 1 Tim. 6:16).

The description of God's coming *(verse 3)* is borrowed from the account of the revelation he made of himself at Sinai. God, who is a consuming fire (Deut. 4:24; 9:3) revealed himself by fire at Sinai, where he spoke 'from out of the fire on the mountain' (Deut. 5:4). The people heard his voice 'while the mountain was ablaze with fire' (Deut. 5:22-23).

The heavens and the earth are summoned to listen to what God has to say to 'his people' *(verses 4-5)*. Those who belong to this category are then defined as God's 'consecrated ones' (*chasidim*; see on Ps. 31:23) and as those who are entering into a covenant by sacrifice. The reference seems to be to the ensuing ceremony which reaffirmed the covenant described in Exodus 24:5-8. The Hebrew text uses the technical term for making a covenant, 'to cut a covenant', which goes back to the common practice of including some cutting ritual as part of a covenant ceremony.

The very heavens seem as if they are announcing God's righteousness, as he comes to enter into judgment with his covenant people *(verse 6)*. What is left indefinite in verse 4 (namely, who is doing the judging) is now clarified. The judge of the people is none other than their covenant God himself.

2. *The True Sacrifices (verses 7-15)*

The opening words of the LORD *(verse 7)* echo the formula which appears frequently in the Book of Deuteronomy (4:1; 6:4; 9:1; 20:3;

27:9), while the words 'I am God, your God' recall the opening words of the Decalogue (Exod. 20:2; Deut. 5:6). God is now ready to provide the evidence against his people. The use of the word 'testify' provides a link with the prophetic ministry of warning the people of their sins (cf. 2 Chr. 24:19; Neh. 9:26). Psalm 81:8 is very similar to this verse.

There is no intended rejection of sacrifice in itself in the accusation of the LORD *(verse 8)*. The people were observing the law regarding the offering of sacrifices, and they were constantly coming to the place of sacrifice with the required offerings. What was wrong, as succeeding verses show, was that a wrong spirit motivated them.

God makes the declaration that he is the Creator of all things. Hence, he does not need the small offerings presented to him as sacrifices *(verses 9-11)*. All the animals in the world, both wild and domestic, are his possession, so he does not require a few more gifts to supplement his vast empire.

Even within Israel there were false views of God *(verses 12-13)*. Some thought that their sacrificial offerings were a form of food for him, as happened in other religions in the Near East (see Deut. 32:38). Here God disabuses them of these ideas, for he is already the owner of the whole world and everything in it (cf. Deut. 10:14; Ps. 24:1). He did not need food of this kind to be provided as his meat and drink.

What was needed were sacrifices offered in a true spirit of thanksgiving *(verse 14)*. Both 'thank offerings' and 'vows' were sacrifices in which the worshippers shared in a meal, partaking of what they themselves had brought (cf. Lev. 7:12; 22:29). The LORD did not need such sacrifices, but they were a means of expressing gratitude to him. A promise is added to the command *(verse 15)*. In difficult times prayer to God will result in deliverance. He does not need to be bribed by offerings, but will respond readily to the heartfelt cry of his servant.

3. *True Obedience to the Law (verses 16-23)*

The first part of God's speech was directed against those who were trusting in the formal offering of sacrifices. Now attention is paid to those who, though offering sacrifices, were offending against God's covenant standards.

There were those within the covenant community whose life was a lie *(verses 16-17)*. They were transgressors, yet outwardly professed their obedience to God's demands. They even recited the covenant regulations, but in reality they hated God's discipline (NIV 'instruction'). This word 'discipline' in its Old Testament usage suggests the fatherly correction which a son receives (cf. Deut. 11:2ff.; Jer. 31:18). The reference to God's 'words' may well be specifically to the Decalogue, which is called 'the Ten Words' elsewhere in the Hebrew text (Exod. 34:28; Deut. 4:13; 10:4). They were even prepared to reject the core of the covenant. Paul develops the ideas present here more fully in Romans 2:17-29.

The Seventh, Eighth, and Ninth Commandments were openly flouted *(verses 18-20)*. Theft and adultery were encouraged, while the sins of the tongue were very evident. The closeness of family relationships did not prevent slander and lying. The sins of the tongue, as compared with other breaches of the Ten Commandments, take up an important place in the warnings of the New Testament as well (Col. 3:9; Jas. 3:1-12).

God's silence was being misunderstood by the people *(verse 21)*. They were thinking that silence was acquiescence in their sin. This was not the only time in the Old Testament when this took place (see Mal. 2:17; 3:14-15). One of the greatest mistakes humans can make is to think that God is like themselves. Sinners constantly want to exchange 'the glory of the immortal God for images made to look like mortal man and birds and animals and reptiles' (Rom. 1:23). At last God speaks, and he now reproves his erring covenant children.

As many as God loves he rebukes and chastens (Rev. 3:19). Those who are forgetting God and despising his instruction are warned that God will come like a lion and tear them *(verse 22)*. Amos also uses the analogy of a lion to describe God's activities (Amos 3:8). Saying that there is 'none to rescue' is simply acknowledging that salvation was from God alone.

What God wants is heartfelt worship from his people *(verse 23)*. This was a way of honouring him, just as God requires of Christian people that they 'continually offer to God a sacrifice of praise – the fruit of lips that confess his name' (Heb. 13:15). As he thus prepares his way aright, he will know indeed that salvation is of God alone.

PSALM 51

For the director of music. A psalm of David.
When the prophet Nathan came to him after David
had committed adultery with Bathsheba.

This is the second of Luther's 'Pauline Psalms' (see Introduction, p. 37), which declares the same way of forgiveness proclaimed in the New Testament. It is a psalm of confession before the LORD and of assurance of his pardon. Redeemed sinners know the reality of God's pardon, and they also share with David in his desire to tell others of the way back to him (see verse 13). Traditionally, this psalm was one of the seven penitential psalms (Psalms 6, 32, 38, 51, 102, 130, 143), a collection known to Augustine, and mentioned by Cassiodorus (c.584 AD). It was often known by its opening word in Latin, *miserere*.

1. *A Cry for Mercy (verses 1-2)*

David cries for mercy out of the anguish of his heart (*verse 1*). Realising his own great need, he calls for God's gracious act of mercy towards him. This is a prayer which David uses on various other occasions at the beginning of psalms (see Psalms 56, 57, and 86:3). The basis for his cry is God's unfailing love (Hebrew, *chesed*). This word carries with it the idea of absolute commitment. God had revealed himself to Moses as: 'The LORD, the LORD, the compassionate and gracious God, slow to anger, abounding in love and faithfulness' (Exod. 34:6). He would not go back on that word, and David accordingly pleads for a fresh visitation of mercy for himself.

The second part of verse 1 parallels 'great compassion' with 'unfailing love', and 'blot out my transgressions' with 'have mercy'. Because he was conscious of his 'great' sin, he recognises that he needs 'great' compassion. The verb 'blot out' has the idea of wiping a dish clean, or removing something completely.

Verse 2 repeats the call for mercy but uses other terms. The verb 'wash' is preceded in Hebrew by a form of the verb 'to be many', which some think means that David is praying for repeated cleansings. This goes contrary to the context, which suggests a once-for-all act on God's part, and the verb 'wash' is used elsewhere in the Old Testament for the removal of sin (Isa. 1:16; Jer. 2:22; 4:14). Similarly, the word 'cleanse' is used of a declaration which the priest made over the cleansed leper (Lev. 13:6, 34). Only God can declare the sinner clean.

The cluster of words in these first two verses is remarkable. It contains a rich vocabulary of language relating to sin and forgiveness, which blends together. To describe his (and our) relationship to God, David uses:

transgression: rebellious actions against authority;
iniquity: what is crooked or bent;
sin: missing the mark;
have mercy: a request which speaks of graciousness beyond expectation;
unfailing love: the term of covenant commitment;
compassion: the word describing the tenderest love;
blot out: complete removal;
wash away: used of scrubbing clothes and removing all stain;
cleanse: a ritual term for pronouncing someone clean.

2. Confession of Sin (verses 3-6)

David cannot escape from his sin (*verse 3*; cf. Ps. 32:3, 4). Luther puts this truth in this way: 'My sin plagues me, gives me no rest, no peace; whether I eat or drink, sleep or wake, I am always in terror of God's wrath and judgement.' The psalmist is ready to acknowledge his wayward actions, and he is unable to escape from the consciousness of guilt. For no matter how much he has sinned against others (and specifically against Bathsheba and Uriah), yet the reality of the situation is that his sin was primarily against God (*verse 4a*). The NIV translation brings out well the force of the Hebrew word order here. The primary focus of sin is against God. Though men might have acquitted David, yet he knows that before God he is guilty of adultery and murder.

The words which follow, 'so that you are proved right when you speak and justified when you judge' (*verse 4b*), have created considerable discussion, because how can God be justified in his speaking? Probably, it is best to think of God being true to his pledged word (see comments on verse 1). He is 'justified' when he hears the cry for mercy and acts in accordance with his covenantal promise. These words are quoted by Paul in Romans 3:4.

David's sin, in this case, was not his first sin, for he has been a sinner from the very beginning (*verse 5*). He is referring to the inborn bias which affects all of us by nature. Sin inevitably appears in each new life because it is part of human nature as a result of Adam's sin ('sin entered the world through one man, and death through sin, and in this way death came to all men', Rom. 5:12).

Yet even as a sinner David knows the standard which God requires (*verse 6*). God demands integrity and uprightness, characteristics which David now knew that he lacked. The way of God's wisdom has been forsaken for the way which seems right to a man, but which in the end brings death (Prov. 14:12).

3. *Prayer for Forgiveness (verses 7-12)*

With deep intensity of heart David prays for cleansing and forgiveness (*verse 7*). Hyssop, a common plant, was used at the Passover (Exod. 12:22), and in various procedures carried out by the priests (see Lev. 14:4, 6, 49, 51, 52). Now David asks for God to sprinkle him so that he will become even whiter than snow. This analogy is taken up later in the Old Testament, seemingly in conscious dependence upon this verse. To the sinful people in Isaiah's day, whose hands were full of blood, the LORD says: 'Though your sins are like scarlet, they shall be as white as snow' (Isa. 1:18).

To his petition David adds: 'Let me hear joy and gladness; let the bones you have crushed rejoice' (*verse 8*). Under God's chastening hand, he feels crushed and bruised, and longs for festive joy to be given to him. This is part of God's forgiveness, as his children rejoice in his mercy and love to them. Jeremiah uses the phrase 'joy and gladness' five times (Jer. 7:34; 15:16; 16:9; 25:10; 33:11).

At other times in the Old Testament the people cry out to God because he has hidden his face from them (see e.g. Pss. 10:1; 44:24; 88:14; 104:29; Isa. 8:17). In *verse 9* David desires that God will not look on his sin, but rather blot it out completely.

He recognises that what is needed is a new creative act by God (*verse 10*). The Hebrew verb used for 'create' (*bara'*) is exclusively employed in the Old Testament with God as the subject, and here it is parallelled with 'renew'. It is also linked with the word 'steadfast', which comes from a Hebrew root which is often associated with God's creative activity (Ps. 24:2, 'established it upon the waters'; Isa. 45:18). Purification from sin is a work of God alone.

> Not the labours of my hands
> Can fulfil thy laws' demands;

Could my zeal no respite know,
Could my tears for ever flow,
All for sin could not atone;
Thou must save and thou alone.

(Augustus Toplady, 1740-1778)

When confronted with our sin, there is a feeling that we are to be
banished from God's presence. Hence David prays: 'Do not cast me
from your presence or take your Holy Spirit from me. Restore to me
the joy of your salvation and grant me a willing spirit, to sustain me'
(*verses 11-12*). The Holy Spirit was operative in the Old Testament
period, though a new phase of the Spirit's ministry began with the
death and resurrection of Jesus and the Day of Pentecost. Old Testament believers had the same indwelling Spirit as Christians today, and
David pleads that he will not experience the withdrawal of that Spirit.
The presence of sin also causes absence of joy, because peace has gone.
With the coming of forgiveness there can be a restoration of the joy of
salvation.

4. *A Thankful Heart* (verses 13-17)

The response of a purified sinner is to seek to make known the good
news of God's grace, just as Isaiah later offered himself so willingly
as the LORD's messenger (Isa. 6:8). The psalmist had a similar
experience (*verse 13*). An experience of redeeming grace creates an
urge to tell others of the LORD's forgiveness and a desire to teach them
his ways. The ultimate aim is to see other sinners coming back to God
in repentance and faith. The verb 'turn back' (Hebrew, *shubh*) is often
used of repentance and of a return to God (e.g. Isa. 44:22; Hos. 6:1).

David's sin weighs heavily upon him, and he seems to fear
especially the result of his murder of Uriah *(verse 14)*. The word
'bloodguilt' is literally 'bloods', and by comparison with Genesis 4:10
it denotes bloodshed, murder. Rather than thinking of protection for
David from vengeance by Uriah's family, it is preferable to see it as a
prayer for deliverance from the guilt of his crime, by the God who
saves him. In this way the ideas fit in best with the whole context in the
psalm.

A forgiven sinner also wants to praise God for what he has done
(*verses 14b-15*). Here David shows the spirit of thanksgiving which
filled him after God heard his cry. The word of pardon came through
the prophet Nathan who said to him: 'The LORD has taken away your

sin' (2 Sam. 12:13b). David's desire is that God will open his lips, and that his mouth will be filled with God's righteousness and God's praise. Under the Mosaic law various sacrifices were appointed, but there was none for premeditated murder. David's action came under the category of sins of a high hand (see Num. 15:30), for he had acted defiantly and in rebellion against God's law. But even if a sacrifice could be offered, yet David rightly recognises that the spirit, in which it is offered, is primarily important (*verses 16-17*). Mere formal ceremony could never result in forgiveness. Rather, there had to be a heart touched by the Holy Spirit who convicts of sin (John 16:8). Brokenness in this case is a sign of deep distress of heart over sin, and God will not turn his ear away from the cry of the needy (Ps. 102:17).

5. *Prayer for Zion* (*verses 18-19*)
David seems to have felt that his sin could have serious consequences for the whole nation. So he prays for Zion and Jerusalem (*verses 18-19*). These words show that the preceding reference to sacrifices was not to disparage the whole sacrificial system as such. God had set his choice upon Jerusalem, and David prays for his protection to continue over his people. Then the people will be able to continue with their sacrifices, and bring offerings which God would be pleased to accept.

PSALM 52
For the director of music. A maskil of David. When Doeg the Edomite had gone to Saul and told him: 'David has gone to the house of Ahimelech.'

The historical note contained in the title alludes to the incident in David's life when Doeg betrayed the priests who had helped David. When the king's officials were not prepared to kill the priests, Doeg carried out the executions (1 Sam. 22:6-19). The title is appended to this psalm because Doeg was typical of all the evildoers, who will ultimately be uprooted 'from the land of the living' (verse 5). While complaining about evildoers at the beginning of the psalm, by the end the psalmist is expressing confident trust in God.

1. *A Complaint against the Evildoer* (*verses 1-4*)
It is very unusual to find a psalm which does not begin by addressing God, but this one is first directed to an evil man. He is described as a

'mighty man' or 'noble', and because 'nobles' had the privilege of bearing arms for the king (cf. Ruth 2:1; 1 Sam. 9:1) the term then became applied to warriors or soldiers *(verse 1)*. The last part of the verse is difficult and the NIV translation follows the LXX. The Hebrew text says: 'covenant love *(chesed)* of God all the day'. It is best to take this as the meaning of the Hebrew word *chasid*, which denotes a loyal covenant servant. It would then be a description of the psalmist: 'Why do you boast all day long against God's loyal servant?'

The warrior is not described by exploits in battle, but by his ability to use his tongue as his weapon to cause harm *(verses 2-3)*. Deceit and destruction are his hallmarks, and they proceed from a heart which is set on evil ways. Falsehood takes the place of righteousness (NIV 'truth'). The words which bring destruction are what he treasures *(verse 4)*. A 'harmful word' is one which devours or swallows (cf. Jer. 51:44, which has the only other instance of this word in the Old Testament). It adds to the accusation when the psalmist speaks directly to the tongue itself (cf. a similar usage in Ps. 120:2).

2. God's Judgment Announced *(verse 5)*

The contrast is presented of God's righteous judgment, and the words used to describe it suggest the suddenness with which it comes: 'snatch', 'tear', 'uproot'. The reference to the 'tent' does not seem to be to the tabernacle, but rather to the individual dwelling of the unrighteous person. To be taken from the land of the living is synonymous with death (cf. the same phrase used of the Servant of the Lord in Isa. 53:8).

3. The Blessing of the Righteous *(verses 6-9)*

When the righteous see the judgment of God they stand in awe. They also understand that this judgment is meant to be an encouragement to them, and so they rejoice in it *(verses 6-7)*. Their laughter is not so much derision as joyful recognition of the just nature of God's actions. If a man fails to make God his refuge, and trusts in his own riches, isn't it right then if he is uprooted?

The same sort of contrast is drawn between the righteous and the wicked *(verse 8)* as is made in Psalm 1. Whereas the wicked are like trees which will be uprooted, the righteous are like a flourishing olive tree. The comparison with an olive tree is probably because of its long life, and its productive nature.

The psalmist expresses the constancy of his trust in God's covenant love (*verse 9*). God's actions on behalf of his people call forth praise, and this also involves offering praise in an assembly of God's people. His goodness has been displayed to the psalmist who now wants to acknowledge that fact. With the acknowledgment comes a further expression of confident trust in God's character ('your name'), which has been shown to be both good and loving.

PSALM 53
For the director of music. According to mahalath.
A maskil of David.

For comments on the comparison between this psalm and Psalm 14, see pp. 97-98. It has a longer title than Psalm 14, including two technical terms 'mahalath' and 'maskil'. The former means 'sickness' or 'suffering', and so may denote a mournful tune of that name (cf. also Ps. 88). 'Maskil' is probably a skilfully constructed song or tune. In the early part of the psalm, in addition to the alteration of the divine name ('God' replaces 'LORD'), 'iniquity' replaces 'deeds' in verse 1. The NIV appears to regard it as meaning 'ways'. Then in verse 3 there is a slight change concerning 'all', and in place of 'turned aside' in Psalm 14:3, the verb is 'turned back' (Hebrew, *sag* in place of *sar*).

The more important change is in connection with verses 5-6 in Psalm 14: 'There they are, overwhelmed with dread, for God is present in the company of the righteous. You evildoers frustrate the plans of the poor, but the LORD is their refuge.' In place of that, Psalm 53:5 has: 'There they were, overwhelmed with dread, where there was nothing to dread. God scattered the bones of those who attacked you; you put them to shame, for God despised them.' This verse seems to have been altered to this form to make specific reference to a great historical occasion. The most probable one would have been the destruction of Sennacherib's army by the angel of the LORD (2 Kgs. 19:35). The meaning would be that God's people were greatly afraid, when there was nothing to fear. The bones of the Assyrian army were scattered on the field, and God had shown how he despised those who were classed with the fools and those who did not know him. For comment on the other verses see the notes on Psalm 14.

PSALM 54

For the director of music. With stringed instruments.
A maskil of David. When the Ziphites had gone to Saul and said,
'Is not David hiding among us?'

The title of this psalm is similar to that of Psalm 52, in that an incident
from David's life, fleeing from Saul, forms its basis (cf. 1 Sam. 23:19;
26:1). The contents of the psalm do not explain how the psalm ties in
with that incident. Its scope is sufficiently wide to allow any persecuted believer to use it as a request for divine intervention.

1. *Petition for Deliverance* (verses 1-3)

The psalm starts with a reference to God's name, and it ends with
praise of it. The psalmist calls to God because he knows God's
character, and therefore he can confidently cry for help. He seeks
deliverance from his present distress, which went beyond the slanderous attacks being made on him. Murder was also part of the scheme
(verse 3). The call is to his Saviour and to his Judge. 'Vindicate' *(verse*
1) has practically the same meaning as 'judge'.

The opening words of *verse 2* seem to have been a standard way of
requesting help: 'Hear my prayer, listen to ...'(cf. Pss. 84:8; 143:1). At
times, though, customary expressions take on a new urgency, when
circumstances drive us to seek God's immediate help. This prayer is
a request for God to hear and answer.

The word 'strangers' (*verse 3*) is replaced by a very similar word
('proud') in many Hebrew manuscripts and in the Targum. This
explains the variation in some English translations here (cf. NEB
'insolent men'), and it fits the context well. When this verse reappears
in Psalm 86:14 the word is certainly 'arrogant'. These violent men are
coming against the psalmist with murderous intent. They do not give
God the pre-eminence in their lives, and consequently they do not live
by his commands.

2. *Confidence in God* (verses 4-5)

The psalmist turns to the one source of assistance. He knows that the
Lord is his only helper. The wish for judgment to come upon his
slanderers has to be understood in the light of the broader question of
cursing in the Psalms (see Introduction, pp. 60-62). Because the
slanderers are indeed opponents of God himself, the psalmist prays for

their destruction. The psalmist knows that God acts in accordance with his faithfulness.

3. Spontaneous Thanksgiving (verses 6-7)

The offer is made of a voluntary sacrifice. Such a sacrifice could be made at any time by a thankful Israelite (see Lev. 22:17-30; Num. 15:1-12). Praise is to be given to God because he has shown his goodness. The psalmist anticipates the LORD's deliverance from all his troubles, and his opportunity to see what has happened to his enemies. He acquiesces in God's judgment.

PSALM 55

For the director of music. With stringed instruments.
A maskil of David.

Older Jewish interpreters linked this psalm with the betrayal of David by his counsellor Ahithophel (2 Sam. 16:15-22; 1 Chr. 27:33). Modern writers have often drawn a comparison between the experience of the psalmist and that of the prophet Jeremiah. He too wished to be far off in a desert (verses 6-7, cf. Jer. 9:2), he suffered at the hands of his own family (Jer. 12:6), and a fellow priest, Pashur, had him beaten and placed in stocks (Jer. 20:2). There is an ancient tradition in the Latin church that the psalmist's experience points to the betrayal of Jesus by Judas. Certainly our LORD's betrayal gives us the highest example of the pattern of suffering described here by the psalmist. It is of great encouragement to us that because Jesus 'suffered when he was tempted, he is able to help those who are being tempted' (Heb. 2:18).

1. A Call for Help (verses 1-3)

The psalm opens with a despairing cry (verses 1-3). From his distress the psalmist appeals for help. His request, that God should not ignore his plea, recalls the passage in Deuteronomy 22:1-4 where the same verb is used. When a person saw a neighbour's ox or sheep in trouble, he was not to ignore it. Here the psalmist feels as if he is being ignored by God, as if he was unwilling to help. He not only has trouble from outside himself, but his own thoughts cause him distress. He is humiliated, and the sound of the approaching enemy overwhelms him. That enemy is not identified, except by the description of being 'wicked'. What the wicked does to him is the result of hatred.

2. *Anguish of Heart* (*verses 4-8*)

A succession of words descriptive of the deep trouble of his heart flow from the psalmist's mouth (*verses 4-5*). He is under intolerable strain as he faces the attacks of his enemy. He even compares himself to a woman in childbirth (NIV 'in anguish'). The fear he has is that death is near at hand, and the great anxiety he is experiencing produces physical symptoms of trembling and shuddering.

Another way of describing his despair is to wish that he was far off in some desert location (*verses 6-8*). He wants to fly like a dove and find a safe dwelling place (NIV 'be at rest'). Lodging in the desert would mean that there would be escape from his persecutors as he found a hiding place there. Jeremiah uses the same imagery of a place in the desert (Jer. 9:2) and of the dove finding a safe nest (Jer. 48:28). 'Tempest and storm' tell of the reality of his present distress.

3. *A Lament over Betrayal* (*verses 9-15*)

The psalmist lodges his complaint with the LORD (*verse 9*). 'Confuse' is literally 'swallow', and it is used to ask for the destruction of the oppressors. The idea of confounding the speech is probably intended to recall what happened at Babel, when God thwarted the sinful plans of men by confusing their language (Gen. 11:1-9). There is no way of identifying the city, as the Hebrew word (*'ir*) denotes a settlement with fortifications, irrespective of its size. It is a place where the psalmist had experienced violence and strife.

His expressions depict both the character of the city, and the constancy with which the forces of evil show themselves in it (*verses 10-11*). Rebels and terrorists control it, and associated evils like 'malice' and 'abuse' are evident everywhere. Its market area (NIV 'streets') is no longer a place for peaceful trading but is distinguished by deceitful practices.

We are not provided with enough information to enable identification of David's friend (*verses 12-14*). Someone within his own close circle of friends proved to be a traitor, and that makes the pain of the incident all the more intense. A friend of equal rank with himself, and with whom he had been associated in worship at the sanctuary, had turned against him. It is not 'an enemy' or 'a foe' who was insulting him, but one of his own companions. The tragedy of David's words here is that they apply to his own treachery against Uriah, who is reckoned among David's closest associates (2 Sam. 23:39). In applying the truth of God to others, it must also be applied relentlessly to one's own life.

David asks for God's sudden judgment to come on his enemies (*verse 15*). It is not just the one former friend who is spoken about, but a group of enemies ('let them ...'). The reference to going down alive into the grave seems to be an allusion to the incident concerning Korah, Dathan and Abiram (Num. 16:23-40). Just as those who had treated the LORD with contempt in Moses' day were destroyed, so David wants his enemies (who were also God's enemies) to have a similar fate.

4. *Justice with God* (*verses 16-21*)

As is typical in psalms of complaint, David tells of his approach to God in prayer, and his believing trust in him (*verses 16-17*). 'Evening, morning and noon' are probably not meant to be taken as the only times in the day when he prayed. Rather, these expressions speak of the constancy of his requests to God. His actions stand in sharp contrast to his former friend, this being marked out in the Hebrew text by an emphatic 'you' at the start of verse 13, and an emphatic 'I' at the commencement of this verse. He is assured that God both listens to his plea and acts upon it.

The confidence the psalmist has is that God is his deliverer (*verse 18*). 'Ransom' is used here in this general sense of deliverance from trouble. God is able to bring his people into a peaceful situation (NIV 'unharmed'), even when their opponents are so many and their attacks so hostile.

It is to the Creator God that the psalmist calls, for the NIV 'forever' is an attempt to translate a Hebrew word (*qedem*) which points backwards, not forwards (*verse 19*). It speaks of God as being enthroned from creation itself (cf. Deut. 33:15, 'the *ancient* mountains'). The eternal God is the one who hears not only his people, but who also takes notice of the wicked. They are described using a term which is normally used of changing a garment (cf. Gen. 45:22). Their characteristics are that they do not change from their ungodliness and they lack the fundamental mark of godliness, the fear of God. The position of *Selah* is most unusual, in that it comes in the middle of the verse.

Another aspect of the attack by his so-called friend comes out in *verses 20-21*. The psalmist is in a covenant bond with this person, as covenants were often made between people (cf. David and Jonathan, 1 Sam. 20:16). But this 'friend' has no regard for such solemn commitments. On the surface he speaks smoothly, but underneath he is plotting treachery. In stabbing his covenant allies in the back, he violates a sacred bond to which God is witness.

5. A Divine Burden-Bearer (verses 22-23)

The 'cares' are all that God gives to us, and the invitation is to throw them on the LORD (verse 22). The promise is not that he will carry them, but rather that 'he will sustain you'. The word 'sustain' is used of the action of Joseph in providing for his family in Egypt (Gen. 45:11), and especially of God's gracious provision for his people in the wilderness (Neh. 9:21). That sustaining mercy will be given to ensure that there is no final disaster awaiting the righteous. The first part of the verse is echoed in the New Testament in 1 Peter 5:7, while the general theme is amplified in Jesus' teaching (Matt. 6:25-34; 10:19; Luke 12:22-31).

The relationship between the psalmist and his God is what matters most (verse 23). The words 'But you, O God' and 'But as for me' highlight this. God may indeed deal with the wicked, bringing them to a premature death, though he does not always act in this way. However, the psalmist's trust is in his God. He clearly has cast his cares on the LORD; already he enjoys being sustained by him.

PSALM 56

For the director of music. To [the tune of] 'A Dove on Distant Oaks'. Of David. A miktam. When the Philistines had seized him in Gath.

The historical note in the title refers to an incident in David's life when he was seemingly held captive in Gath. The biblical text in 1 Samuel does not actually say he was captured, but the comment, in 1 Samuel 22:1, that he escaped to the cave of Adullam leaves no doubt about it. The Philistines came from, or via, Crete (referred to as Caphtor in Jer. 47:4; Amos 9:7), and they settled on the coast of Palestine. Their major cities were Ashdod, Ashkelon, Ekron, Gath, and Gaza. The psalm moves from appeal in the opening, through lament in the central part, to joyful thanksgiving at the conclusion.

1. A Plea for Mercy (verses 1-2)

This and the following psalm begin with the identical plea, though NIV varies the translation. It occurs frequently in the Psalter (cf. 4:1; 6:2;

27:7; 86:3; 123:3). The description of relentless pursuit certainly fits the experience of David. He cries to God because his enemies are breathing down his neck, and he has no relief from their oppression.

There is an emphasis in this psalm on the role of the enemies in using bitter words against the psalmist (see also verse 5), though he clearly felt in deadly peril (verse 6). The repetition of 'all day long' in successive verses speaks of the feeling that there was no let up in the attacks upon him (*verse 2*).

2. *Refrain: Trust in God (verses 3-4)*
There is no doubt that David knows fear, but he claims that trust in God robs it of terror. He is afraid, yet not afraid! At the time when he fears, he will trust in God, and at the moment of speaking he is confidently placing his reliance on God's word of promise. He can then throw out the challenge to mortal man (Hebrew is literally 'flesh'). Human power is nothing compared to God's might, as King Hezekiah said to his officers when Jerusalem was faced with an attack by King Sennacherib of Assyria (2 Chr. 32:8).

3. *Complaints against the Enemies (verses 5-9a)*
The evil designs of the enemies are now spelt out in greater detail *(verse 5)*. The words of David were distorted by his enemies, presumably Saul and his supporters. Another possible rendering is 'they injure my cause', as in Hebrew 'word' can have a wider connotation than is normal in English. All their endeavours are directed with evil intent.

In every possible way the enemies are seeking to harm the psalmist, even to the extent of taking his life *(verse 6)*. What they may have in mind is some kind of legal murder, such as happened in the case of Naboth (1 Kgs. 21:1-14). They treat him unjustly and are on the lookout for any opportunity to injure him.

The great variation in the English versions of *verse 7* points to difficulty in understanding the Hebrew text. Some have suggested that there was an early copying mistake because, with the change of one letter, the verb 'escape' could be 'requite'. However, leaving the Hebrew text unchanged can still provide the basis for a translation which forms a question: 'On account of their evil, will there be escape for them?' The answer is clearly 'No', for God will show his anger against the nations. The use of the plural 'nations' suggests that it is the Philistines who are in view. David set himself, after he became king, to subdue the power of the Philistines (2 Sam. 5:17ff.; 8:1).

David knows that God administers justice in his time, not ours. Hence he asks for a record to be kept of his grief *(verses 8-9a)*, and even that his tears be kept in a bottle or wineskin (following the footnote reading in the NIV). God does not need a written record to remember his people and their needs, but the idea is used in the Old Testament as a reassuring way of speaking about God's knowledge of, and care for, his people (Exod. 32:32; Pss. 69:28; 139:16; Mal. 3:16). With certainty the psalmist can speak about God's intervention when he calls to him, for then the enemies will be put to flight.

4. *Refrain: Trust in God (verses 9b-11)*

The essential parts of the refrain of verses 3-4 are repeated in *verses 9b-11*. Instead of the opening reference to trust in God when he is afraid, the psalmist expresses absolute certainty that God is for him. The introductory 'by this', as well as the verb 'know', draws attention to his conviction that God's actions are proof of his continuing care and justice. The New Testament passage which presents the same message is Romans 8:28-39, and it may be based on this refrain. Paul starts with the certainty of knowledge ('we know', verse 28), and ends with the ringing affirmation that nothing 'will be able to separate us from the love of God that is in Christ Jesus our LORD' (Rom. 8:39).

5. *A Vow of Thanksgiving (verses 12-13)*

Seemingly David had made special commitments to God which he now says he will pay. Both 'vows' and 'thankofferings' can refer to sacrificial offerings. He looks back on the reality of deliverance from the danger of death, and though his enemies had watched his every step (verse 6), yet God had also delivered his feet from stumbling. The final clause expresses the confidence of walking joyfully before God in his light (cf. Ps. 36:9). The Old Testament expressions relating to God as light come to fulfilment in the coming of Jesus (John 1:3-5). Jesus declared: 'I am the light of the world. Whoever follows me will never walk in darkness, but will have the light of life' (John 8:12). His subsequent debate with the Pharisees added weight to the declaration.

PSALM 57

For the director of music. [To the tune of] 'Do Not Destroy'.
Of David. A miktam. When he had fled from Saul into the cave.

There are close links between Psalms 56 and 57, and the titles locate both psalms in the period of David's flight from Saul. They are similar in style, each beginning with a cry for mercy and ending on a strong note of thanksgiving. Also, both contain a repeated refrain (56:3-4, 10-11; 57:5, 11). There are also links between Psalms 57, 58, and 59 in that part of their title is common to all three. Psalm 57:7-11 is repeated in Psalm 108:1-5. This may suggest that the two parts of this psalm were originally separate compositions. God's covenant love and faithfulness resound in both sections of the psalm, while the opening verse suggests David's presence at the central worship centre of the covenant, the tabernacle.

1. *Lament and Refrain* (*verses 1-5*)

The psalm begins with a call for God to be merciful, along with a repeated assertion of trust in him. The reference to taking refuge under the shadow of God's wings could be either a general allusion to God's protective care, or it could relate to presence at the tabernacle. In Exodus 25:20 the wings of the cherubim are said to overshadow the cover (the mercy-seat) of the ark of the covenant. Hence it is possible that 'your wings' is a way of saying that the psalmist will go to the tabernacle to meet with his God and to find refuge there until the present distress passes by.

The psalmist calls to 'God Most High' *(verses 2-3)*, using a double name for God which also occurs in Psalm 78:56 (cf. 'LORD Most High' in Ps. 7:17). The verb 'fulfils' is a rare one, only occurring five times in the whole of the Old Testament, all of them in the Psalms. Here, and in Psalm 138:8, it speaks of the way in which God brings to completion what he undertakes for his saints. The Most High God, the ruler over all, brings blessing to his people while visiting his enemies in judgment. He 'sends' salvation to those who are in deep distress, showing in this way his continuing covenant commitment. He is the God who is 'abounding in love and faithfulness' (Exod. 34:6).

The enemies are described as if they were wild animals *(verse 4)*. The expressions used ('in the midst of lions', 'I lie among ravenous beasts') suggest the constant hostility with which the enemies attacked, while use of the comparison with spears, arrows, and swords depict their cruelty and their venom.

The psalmist knows that God is not an idle onlooker. His words in *verse 5* are both a declaration concerning God's glory and an indirect appeal for his help. He longs for the full expression of God's rule to be manifest, because that would mean that deliverance would come for him. One way God gets glory is by displaying his power over his enemies (cf. Exod. 14:4, 17, 18).

2. Transition – The Wicked Trap Themselves (verse 6)
This verse serves as a bridge between the earlier section of the psalm, with its cry to a faithful God, and the later section with its confident praising of him. The truth is that the wicked often fall prey to their own schemes. They prepare a trap for the righteous, but God so overrules in his providence that they fall into it themselves. The song, which follows, rejoices in this event, which is not brought about simply by the folly of the wicked, but by the direct intervention of God.

3. Thanksgiving and Refrain (verses 7-11)
The Hebrew word rendered 'steadfast' *(verse 7)* is the same word translated as 'willing' in Psalm 51:12. It could also be rendered 'prepared' or 'set'. Its use here describes the fixed trust which the psalmist has in God, and the repetition emphasises that still further. No object is given for the verbs 'sing' and 'make music', but it is clear that praise is to be sung to God. Faith and praise are very closely linked together.

The psalmist calls on himself and his instruments to wake up and to prepare for praise *(verse 8)*. Praise often helps to dispel darkness and despair (cf. the experience of Paul and Silas in gaol, Acts 16:25). Harps and lyres refer to stringed instruments which were used in both formal and informal worship situations, and there is little information to make a distinction between them. Before the dawn signalled a new day, praise would be given to the LORD.

The gratitude of the psalmist is so great that he wants even the Gentile nations to hear his praise of God *(verses 9-10)*, in accordance with God's promise to Abraham (Gen. 12:3). The subject matter of David's praise relates to God's covenant love and faithfulness (see verse 3). God has sent his love and faithfulness, and the psalmist wants others to know their dimensions. They cannot be measured for they reach to the heavens.

The refrain – 'Be exalted, O God, above the heavens; let your glory be over all the earth' – which has already been used (verse 5) concludes the psalm *(verse 11)*. It fittingly continues the theme of verse 10 and again focuses on the prayer for the manifestation of God's glory.

PSALM 58
For the director of music. [To the tune of] 'Do Not Destroy'. Of David. A miktam.

This psalm is directed against prominent officials who misuse their office, and so fail to administer justice rightly. After they are charged and a description is given of their sin, a sevenfold curse is pronounced upon them. At the close of the psalm the righteous are depicted as rejoicing in the fact that God, the judge of all the earth, will avenge them.

1. *Leaders Charged (verses 1-2)*
The various English versions show great variety in *verse 1*. The problem is the Hebrew word rendered 'rulers' in the NIV. The Authorised Version took it as meaning 'congregation', but this has no real basis. The Hebrew word in question (*'elem*) is best taken as being the word 'gods', and having the meaning of 'judges' or 'rulers', just as a related Hebrew word (*'elohim*) has this meaning in Psalm 82:1 (cf. John 10:34-35). The charge is that the rulers neither speak justly nor judge uprightly. The very people who should have represented God's concern for justice, instead conjure up evil plans in their hearts and then act them out. The sequence of 'heart' and 'hands' is important, for this is the way in which sin works (cf. Jesus' words in Matt. 15:16-20).

2. *The Sins of the Leaders Described (verses 3-5)*
While the context is not dealing with universal sinfulness *(verse 3)*, yet the comparison with David's confession in Psalm 51:5 should be made. What was happening with the judges should not have been thought surprising, because the judges were only displaying their true character. From birth they have been estranged from God and his ways. This is the way in which the Bible constantly pictures sinful men and women. 'They are darkened in their understanding and separated from the life of God because of the ignorance that is in them due to the hardening of their hearts' (Eph. 4:18).

The wicked are compared to a poisonous snake which will not even obey its trainer *(verses 4-5)*. It will turn against the person who has carefully trained it and will not listen. The reason for this, as is now known, is that the cobra is deaf, and it only responds to its trainer's movements, not to the sound of the music. The point here is that wicked rulers are just as insensitive, and they do not hear the cry for justice from the poor and needy.

3. *Prayer for Judgment* (*verses 6-9*)

The cry goes out for God to intervene in the situation and bring judgment upon these ungodly people (for curses in the Psalms, see the Introduction, pp. 60-62). This sevenfold curse is very difficult in the Hebrew text, and this causes the great variety in the English translations of it. The prayer for judgment increases in intensity until it reaches its climax in verse 9.

Instead of being likened to a cobra, the wicked judges are now compared to lions *(verse 6)*. They are all ready to attack with their teeth, unless God intervenes and breaks them.

Two different comparisons are made to suggest taking away the power of the enemies *(verse 7)*. The psalmist wants them to become 'like water spilled on the ground, which cannot be recovered' (2 Sam. 14:14). This is symbolism for death. If they do persist in their attacks, then he wants their arrows to be blunted so that they cannot harm him.

The connection between the slug and the stillborn child is that neither sees the light of the sun *(verse 8)*. The slug leaves its trail behind, but it is gone when the sun rises. The stillborn child never sees the light of the sun. So the psalmist wishes his wicked enemies to become as if they had never existed.

Concerning *verse 9* – 'Before your pots can feel [the heat of] the thorns – whether they be green or dry – the wicked will be swept away' – the NIV footnote rightly says: 'The meaning of the Hebrew for this verse is uncertain.' However, the introductory word 'before' is sometimes used to introduce prophetic speech which is depicting something going to happen (cf. Isa. 7:16; 8:4), while the last clause gives the expectation that God's judgment is going to be final. This is the climax to the whole prayer.

4. *Assurance for the Righteous* (*verses 10-11*)

The righteous delight in justice, and when God vindicates his own people in victory, then they can rejoice all the more *(verse 10)*.

Vengeance belongs to God, and he vindicates them (Deut. 32:35-36; Ps. 94:1-2). Bathing feet in blood is a biblical imagery for victory (cf. Isa. 63:1-6; Rev. 14:19-20; 19:13-14). Men in general *(verse 11)* will ultimately make the declaration that the righteous receive the fruit of their lives from the God who judges the whole earth (cf. Ps. 94:2 where God is called 'Judge of the earth'). The psalmist is confident that a day is coming when even the heathen will acknowledge this fact. Believers know that God, the righteous Judge, is going to reward them at the last day (2 Tim. 4:8) and they must wait patiently for the day of reckoning (Jas. 5:1-11).

PSALM 59
For the director of music. [To the tune of] 'Do Not Destroy'.
Of David. A miktam. When Saul had sent men to
watch David's house in order to kill him.

Two sets of enemies seem to be in view in this psalm. On the one hand, there are wicked men within the nation who attack the psalmist like a pack of wild dogs (verses 6 and 14). On the other hand, surrounding nations are in view (verses 5-8). It seems, then, to be a psalm appealing for help from both local and foreign enemies. Within the psalm there are features which are unusual, in that there are repeated refrains (verses 6 and 14) and repeated affirmations of confident trust in the LORD (verses 9 and 17). There are some interesting word parallels between this psalm and the account in 1 Samuel 19 and 24 of David's flight from Saul (including the reference to wild dogs, cf. verses 6-7, 14-15, with 1 Sam. 24:14).

1. A Cry for Deliverance, and a Refrain (verses 1-10a)
From the psalmist's heart comes this cry of distress. He longs for the deliverance which comes only from God *(verse 1)*. The word 'protect' means 'to set on high' or 'defend'. God takes the afflicted and he lifts them up (Ps. 107:41). This is what David asks here, as he acknowledges the fierce opposition he is facing.

In *verses 2-3* David repeats his plea for deliverance, and in so doing uses two more terms to describe his opponents. These terms are all practically synonymous in this context. The people have planned their attacks with military precision, and they are busy stirring up strife against the psalmist. He protests that he has done them no hurt to cause such spite, and the words he uses recall his words in 1 Samuel 20:1 and 24:11. So strong is his protestation of innocence that he uses still another term ('no wrong') to speak of his lack of offence to either God or man *(verse 4)*.

To him it looks as if God is asleep, and therefore he calls on him to stir himself and come to his rescue *(verse 5)*. The combination of divine names, 'LORD God Almighty' recurs in Psalms 80:4, 19 and 84:8. This combination points to the power of God, while the addition of 'the God of Israel' is suggestive of his loving concern for his people. He appeals to God to deal with the nations around Israel and also with those within the nation who are disloyal to God's covenant (cf. Ps. 78:57 for the use of the same verb of covenant unfaithfulness).

In *verse 6* the opponents are compared with wild dogs, which hunt for their prey around the city at night. They habitually look for ways to attack and, if possible, to destroy him. They speak so sharply that their words are like swords *(verse 7)*. The expression is unusual, though other psalms speak of the cutting effect of the tongue (52:2; 57:4; 64:3). In their arrogance they claim that no one, including God, hears them, or will take any action to curtail their activities.

Verse 8 seems to be a standard way of describing God's derision of the ungodly (cf. the use of the same two verbs in Ps. 2:4). The contrast is very marked. Wicked men express their blasphemies, but God in heaven knows that his rule will be vindicated. His enemies will in the end become his footstool (Psalm 110:1; 1 Cor. 15:24-25).

While the enemies coming against David are strong (verse 3, 'fierce'), yet his trust is in even greater strength *(verses 9-10a)*. They watch for him (see the title), but he watches for God. He has asked that God will protect him (verse 1), and he now confesses that his place of protection is indeed God himself ('protect' and 'fortress' come from the same Hebrew root). He looks expectantly to his gracious God. In the expression 'my loving God', the word 'loving' represents the Hebrew word *chesed*, and another rendering could be 'my God of covenant love'.

2. A Description of the Enemies and a Refrain (verses 10b-17)

David prays for God's judgments to be made known, not immediately, but progressively, and he wants this to be a testimony to the surrounding nations. He knows that God will meet him (cf. the use of the same Hebrew verb in Ps. 21:3, NIV 'welcomed'), and he will allow him to gaze on the victory he is providing *(verse 10b)*. The demonstration of God's judgment will be satisfying to him as he sees God vindicated. In *verse 11* the request is that the judgment should not be a speedy one, lest it be over and done with so quickly that the lesson will not be learned by the people. Instead, the prayer is that the people will wander about aimlessly and thus be seen as a living example of God's judgments.

The sins of the enemies are again spelt out as involving vicious words of cursing and lying *(verses 12-13)*. The idea of being caught by their own pride is similar to that found in Psalm 57:6. The wicked are often too clever for themselves, and their own sin rebounds on them. The repeated cry of 'consume them' emphasises the prayer for utter destruction of the enemies. The end result will not only be satisfying to the psalmist (verse 10b) but glorifying to God as well. Judgment is a demonstration of his sovereign rule over his people, and this serves as a witness to the ends of the earth.

In *verse 14* the words of verse 6 are repeated in a fresh description of the characteristics of the enemies. The use of this refrain draws attention to the pack of roaming dogs which are always ready to attack. They are always on the lookout for food, and if they do not find it they whine *(verse 15)*. Some English versions take the verb translated in the NIV as 'howl' to be the verb 'to spend the night' (see Authorised Version margin and Revised Version), but it is best to assume that the verb means 'to murmur', and hence is descriptive of the whimpering of hungry dogs.

While the mention of singing is new *(verse 16)*, all the other ideas are already found earlier in the psalm (for 'strength' see verse 9; for 'love' see verse 10a; for 'fortress' see verse 9). These ideas form the subject matter of song and praise. The psalmist's approach to God in this way stands in marked contrast to the arrogance of his oppressors.

The words of verses 9-10a are picked up in *verse 17* as a concluding refrain. The main alteration is the replacement of 'I watch [for you]' with 'I sing [to you]'. In these two concluding verses there are three synonyms in the Hebrew text, all rendered by 'sing' in English. In spite of all his circumstances the psalmist ends on a note of praise, with the very last word in Hebrew being the word *chesed*, 'covenant love'.

PSALM 60

For the director of music. To [the tune of] 'The Lily of the Covenant'. A miktam of David. For teaching. When he fought Aram Naharaim and Aram Zobah, and when Joab returned and struck down twelve thousand Edomites in the Valley of Salt.

The title of the psalm links it with David's victories against Aram Naharaim, Aram Zobah and Edom (see 2 Sam. 8:1-4; 10:6-18; 1 Chr. 18:1-13; 19:6-19), but the psalm itself is not commemorating any victory. It is a lament of the people when they have been defeated and apparently lost some of the southern part of the land. Twice in the psalm they challenge God's rejection of them (see verses 1 and 10). The difficulty of reconciling God's sure promises to his people with the reality of military defeat and even loss of some of their territory is faced in other psalms as well (see 44:19-26 and 89:38-51). Part of this psalm (verses 5-12) is combined with Psalm 57:7-11 to make up Psalm 108.

1. A Complaint over Rejection (verses 1-3)

God's anger is spoken of as the primary cause of the present distress *(verse 1)*. The people complain that he has made a breach in their defences (NIV 'burst forth'), and they feel that this is a sign that God has rejected them. The same Hebrew verb for 'reject' occurs in other laments (cf. Pss. 44:9, 23; 74:1; 88:14; 89:38). What the people want is action by God to change the situation, for it is beyond their power to remedy it. A metaphorical description is given of the trouble as if it were an earthquake which had occurred *(verses 2-3)*. Deep fissures have appeared in the land and God is appealed to as the one who alone can heal and restore. The people are going through bitter experiences which have left them dazed as if they were drunk.

2. Confident of Victory (verse 4)

The banner mentioned here is not calling for a military campaign but rather to show where protection is to be found. Against the attacking armies (called here 'the bow'), God is providing a place of refuge for those who fear him. Jeremiah 4:6 illustrates this same use of the word for 'banner' (NIV 'signal').

3. *An Appeal for Salvation* (*verses 5-8*)
In spite of all the troubles, the psalmist still sees the nation as God's
people (NIV 'those you love'). He wants God's might to be shown in
saving them *(verse 5)*. The appeal is stated even more urgently than our
English versions suggest. He asks: 'Save by your right hand, and
answer us!'

The assurance which the psalmist has about ultimate victory comes
from a declaration which God has made *(verse 6)*. The word 'sanctuary' in the NIV could also be rendered 'holiness', which would make
the expression like that in Psalm 89:35: 'I have sworn by my holiness.'
The declaration refers to all the major areas of David's kingdom, both
on the west bank of the Jordan and in Transjordan. Occupation of these
areas is by the sovereign determination of God. Shechem is north of
Jerusalem, near the mountains Ebal and Gerizim. Succoth is east of the
Jordan near the brook Jabbok.

God's sovereignty embraces all the territory occupied by Israel, but
also that of the surrounding nations Moab, Edom and Philistia *(verses
7-8)*. Gilead and Manasseh represent the territory captured on the east
bank of the Jordan before the main conquest took place (Num. 32:33-
42; Deut. 3:12-13). Ephraim and Judah, in turn, represent the territory
on the west bank of the Jordan, and they are the Lord's helmet and the
commander's staff (for Judah, as the sceptre, see Gen. 49:10 and Num.
24:17). The references to Moab, Edom and Philistia imply that they are
totally subservient to God.

4. *A Further Complaint over Rejection* (*verses 9-11*)
In the midst of the seeming alienation from God, the psalmist still
knows that help only comes from him. He asks to be brought against
a fortified city (possibly an allusion to Tyre, see 2 Sam. 24:7), and for
leadership in battle against Edom. In spite of defeats which they had
endured, the people recognise that if victory is to come, it will only be
by God's leadership in battle. Hence they appeal to God to intervene
with divine help. They know that they cannot gain assistance from
other human sources, for the strength of man is a delusion (cf. 1 Sam.
17:47; Jer. 17:5).

5. *A Song of Victory* (*verse 12*)
The psalm began with God's rejection of his people. It ends with a note
of assurance. Strength for battle is the Lord's, and he is able to subdue

his enemies, who are also the enemies of his people. God, who had allocated the land to Israel (verses 6-7), and who controlled the destinies of the surrounding nations (verse 8), is able to bring deliverance to his people.

PSALM 61
For the director of music. With stringed instruments. Of David.

While the central plea for help contained in this psalm is typical of many other psalms, yet the prayer for the king (verses 5-7) raises various questions. Is this psalm composed *by* the king, or is it written by someone else who includes the petition *on behalf of* the king? While no definitive answer can be given to these questions, yet it is most probable that the prayer is on behalf of the king by some other Israelite. Abrupt prayers for the king occur in others psalms as well (cf. 63:11). The prayer for the king reached its fullest answer in the provision of Christ as the one to whom is given the throne of his father David and who will reign for ever and ever (Luke 1:32-33).

1. A Prayer for Protection (verses 1-5)
The nature of the distress is not spelled out, but the psalmist asks for God to pay attention to his cry *(verse 1)*. This word 'cry' is used in the Old Testament both of cries of joy (cf. Isa. 14:7, NIV 'singing') as well as of cries of sorrow (cf. 1 Kgs. 8:28). Here it is clearly used of sorrow, as the following verses show. The request is for God to hear, and by implication, to answer his call.

The opening of *verse 2* has suggested to some commentators that the psalm was composed when David was fleeing from Saul and therefore when he was literally far away. However, the expression need not be pressed in this geographical way. It may well be expressing the conviction that wherever he is, he will call on God. In his weakness he calls out, and desires to find a sure place of refuge with his God. In the Old Testament God is often called a rock (cf. 1 Sam. 2:2), and some personal names also reflect this concept (cf. Zuriel [Num. 3:35, 'my Rock is El']; Zurishaddai [Num. 1:6, 'my Rock is Shaddai']). The psalmist looks back at past deliverances, and he makes these the basis for confidence for the future. He had found in God a true shelter when he was attacked by enemies *(verse 3)*.

Refuge *(verse 4)* may well have been found at the Tabernacle in

Jerusalem (see, in addition to this verse, Isa. 14:32). This was an extension of the custom that in certain circumstances a fleeing criminal could find safety by seizing the horns of the altar (1 Kgs. 1:50). To take refuge under God's wings may be an allusion to the wings of the cherubim over the ark of the covenant, or else as a general allusion to the protective care of God which resembled a bird's care of its young.

In times of past distress the psalmist had made vows to God, and his prayers had been answered *(verse 5)*. The 'heritage' normally refers to the life in the promised land, which was a possession belonging to those who fear the Lord (Ps. 25:12ff.). In more general terms, 'heritage' refers to the benefits of covenant life. The idea is carried over in the New Testament in the words of Jesus: 'Blessed are the meek, for they will inherit the earth' (Matt. 5:5).

2. *A Prayer for the King* (verses 6-7)
The focus switches from personal petition to a prayer for the divinely established monarchy *(verses 6-7)*. To ask for 'days' for the king is equivalent to requesting prosperity for him, and this is strengthened by reference to 'years' and 'generations'. The psalmist wants the king to remain for ever, supported and upheld by God's love and faithfulness. The Davidic dynasty had been promised an enduring existence (cf. Ps. 89:36), and ultimately Christ would come of this line. The Aramaic Targum on this psalm (dating from the Christian era) refers to 'the King Messiah', showing how Jewish understanding of this psalm interpreted it after the seeming end of the Davidic line.

3. *A Vow to God* (verse 8)
The subject in the closing verse is again the psalmist himself. The psalm, which begins with an appeal for help, closes on a note of confidence. Praise shall constantly be made to God's name, and vows will be fulfilled as an expression of gratitude. The emphasis is on continual praise, rather than eternal praise. This is made clear by the parallelism between 'ever sing' and 'day after day' (Hebrew is literally 'day, day').

PSALM 62
For the director of music. For Jeduthun. A psalm of David.

This psalm is unusual in that it does not contain prayer or address to
God. However, it does contain repeated assertions concerning his
character, especially as Saviour and Defender. There is a refrain in
verses 1-2 and 5-6, though this comes at the beginning of sections,
rather than at the end of them as is more common. The term *Selah*
appears twice (verses 4 and 8), and in these cases it does seem to
designate an end of a specific division of the psalm. Six times in the
psalm the same Hebrew particle occurs (*'ach*), always at the beginning
of verses. It is very noticeable in the refrain, where in the NIV it is
rendered 'alone' in verses 1-2 and 5-6.

1. *Confidence in God (verses 1-4)*
The concept of rest in the Lord *(verse 1)* is found in other psalms as well
(see 37:7; 131:2; and cf. Lam. 3:26). It denotes a quiet waiting for
salvation which comes exclusively from him. The psalmist mounts up
expressions to point to his utter confidence in God *(verse 2)*. He is a
rock and fortress, able to give sure defence to those who trust in him.
The promise was given that God would never let the righteous be
shaken (Ps. 55:22; NIV 'never fall'). The psalmist appropriates that
promise for himself and rests in that knowledge.

From speaking of his refuge in God, the psalmist turns to the
enemies who have been coming against him and addresses them
directly *(verses 3-4)*. There is much similarity to the words and
situation in Psalm 4:2. The words 'how long' imply that they have been
opposing him for some time. They are attacking him as if he is a rickety
fence, which can be pushed over easily. Hypocrisy is involved, as
outwardly these people speak words of encouragement, but inwardly
they curse. They think that the psalmist is in a lofty place and are
endeavouring to bring him low.

2. *Salvation in God Alone (verses 5-8)*
In *verses 5-6* the refrain of verses 1-2 recurs with slight alterations.
'My soul finds rest' gives way to an imperative, 'Find rest', while
'salvation' in verse 1 is replaced by 'hope' in verse 5. The final word
of the Hebrew text in verse 2 is omitted in verse 6, and this accounts
for the variation in the NIV: 'I will *never* be shaken', compared with

'I shall not be shaken'. The new section starts with a familiar affirmation that salvation is found in God alone.

Verse 7 carries on the theme of the refrain, repeating some of the terms already used of God ('salvation', 'rock'). It is an assertion that the psalmist's whole hope is to be found in God alone, and the accumulation of so many expressions forms a tremendous climax to his reaffirmation of trust in his sure refuge.

An assurance of salvation for himself impels a call to others to share in the same experience of God *(verse 8)*. He wants the people as a whole to trust God at all times, for he is their refuge as well as his. The verb 'pour out', while a common verb, appears only rarely in this expression, 'pour out your hearts' (see Lam. 2:19, 'pour out your heart like water'). It seems to imply prayer to God, openly acknowledging all the needs of the heart and life.

3. A Call to Trust in God, not Man *(verses 9-12)*

The last division of this psalm is introduced by a statement which speaks of the futility of trusting in men, whether rich or poor *(verse 9)*. It follows the positive call to trust in God in verse 8 and the negative call of verse 10 not to trust in riches. The Hebrew text uses two different words for man (*'ish* and *'adam*), represented in the NIV by 'lowborn men' and 'the highborn'. It does not matter what status or wealth a person has, for he is nothing and he provides no lasting support.

In *verse 10* the sins of extortion and robbery are added to the ones mentioned in verse 4 (lies and cursing). Those who have enriched themselves in this way may think that they have acquired lasting wealth and power. However, the psalmist rightly instructs his readers not to trust in these things. 1 Timothy 6:17 could be a commentary on this section of the psalm: 'Command those who are rich in this present world not to be arrogant nor to put their hope in wealth, which is so uncertain, but to put their hope in God, who richly provides us with everything for our enjoyment.'

Verses 11-12 provide the basis for the disparagement of trusting in men given in the preceding verses. The affirmation of God's strength and his covenant love may have come through a recital of his great deeds for his people (cf. Ps. 136). The opening assertions of the psalm are now repeated in an alternative form. Rest and salvation are found alone with God who is both strong and loving. The concluding statement gives the subsidiary truth that God deals justly with his creatures, a truth reaffirmed several times in the New Testament (Rom. 2:6; 1 Cor. 3:8; 2 Tim. 4:14; Rev. 22:12).

PSALM 63
A psalm of David. When he was in the Desert of Judah.

The desire for God, which this psalm expresses, is similar to that in Psalms 42-43 and 84. While it contains some elements similar to the psalms of complaint, yet it is better seen as a song of rejoicing in God. Because of the reference to 'early' (verse 1; the AV, NKJV, and the NEB follow the Latin text in this regard) and to 'night' (verse 6), this psalm was used as a morning prayer from early Christian times. The title sets the psalm in a period when David was a fugitive, and because of the reference to 'the king' in verse 11, the period is probably that of Absalom's rebellion rather than that of Saul's persecution.

1. *Longing for God (verses 1-5)*
The psalm begins with a confession of absolute confidence in God. Faith always lays hold of the personal relationship with the living God. The verb rendered 'seek' comes in Hebrew from a noun meaning 'dawn', and because of this connection many versions have translated it by 'to seek early'. In the other usages of this verb in the Old Testament the idea of seeking God early is not present, and hence the NIV translation ('earnestly seek') seems close to the mark. As in Psalm 42:1-2, the psalmist compares himself to dry land which longs for water, and so does his soul long for his God. Gregory of Nazianzus (c.330-389) expressed it well: 'God thirsts, to be thirsted for' (*Deus sitit, sitiri*). He longs to see his people ardently desiring him.

Past experience of God vitalises his present relationship *(verses 2-3)*. He looks back to times when, at the tabernacle, he has had a vision of God. This could have been similar to Isaiah's vision (Isa. 6:1-3). The content of the vision is summed up in the words: 'your power', 'your glory', 'your love'. That love, in particular, is preferable to any kind of life without God's favour, and it causes the psalmist to sing his praise. The verb translated 'glorify' is normally used of praising God for his mighty acts of triumph (cf. Pss. 106:47; 117:1; 145:4; 147:12), and the NIV uses a variety of English verbs to convey the meaning ('glory', 'extol', 'commend').

Constant praise of the Lord is his pledge, as he directs his prayer to him *(verses 4-5)*. The lifting up of the hands was an outward expression of the uplifted heart (cf. Pss. 28:2; 141:2; 1 Tim. 2:8). The fact that it was the palms or open hands which are referred to may suggest waiting on God in order to receive his blessings. The psalmist has indeed received abundantly, being filled with 'the richest of foods' (lit. 'marrow and fat'). The language may be borrowed from the ritual of sacrifice, but the fat of sacrifices was never eaten (see Lev. 3:16-17). The idea is that God's presence is like the richest of foods, and a satisfied heart will overflow in praise. For Christians today the New Testament direction is that through Jesus we 'continually offer to God a sacrifice of praise – the fruit of lips that confess his name' (Heb. 13:15).

2. *Confidence in God's Protection* (*verses 6-10*)

The thought of verse 1 is expanded to describe a longing for God even during the hours of darkness *(verse 6)*. In Old Testament times, for civic and military purposes, the night was divided into three watches. The word 'remember' is used in the sense of 'meditate', as it parallels another Hebrew word (NIV 'think of') which is used elsewhere of meditation (see Psalm 1:2).

'Help' *(verse 7)* in the context means 'deliverance'. Assurance of divine protection gives ground for joyful songs. Many other believers have passed through similar experiences to the psalmist, including Paul and Silas (Acts 16:25). 'Shadow of your wings' refers in general to God's protective care of his servant (see comment on Ps. 57:1).

God had invited his covenant people to cling to him (see especially Deut. 10:20; 11:22; 13:4; 30:20; Josh. 22:5; 23:8), and the psalmist acknowledges that he is responding in this way *(verse 8)*. He is a loyal servant who is walking in God's way and fearing him. Consequently he is held in the sure grip of his God. The promise in the gospel is of a Saviour who holds his people so that no one can snatch them out of his hand (John 10:28).

Ultimate vindication lay ahead of the psalmist, when his enemies will come under divine judgment *(verses 9-10)*. Those who now seek his life will find that their own lives will be taken. The language of verse 10 describes a military battle and its aftermath, with dead bodies being left in the field as carrion for wild animals.

3. *Joy in God (verse 11)*

The psalm ends on a note of joyful confidence. David refers to himself as 'the king', for even when fleeing from Jerusalem he still knows that he is the divinely appointed king. In his rejoicing he will be joined by 'all who swear by God's name' (Hebrew, 'by him'). This is a reference to the practice of taking oaths in God's name (cf. Deut. 6:13; 10:20; 1 Kgs. 8:31). The liars are those enemies whose destruction has just been described (verses 8-9). Their voices will be stilled, while those of the faithful will rise in joyful song.

PSALM 64
For the director of music. A psalm of David.

Many of David's psalms of complaint are similar in tone to this one. They tell of enemies who wound with words, though these enemies are not named. There is a sharp contrast in this psalm between two kinds of attacks. On the one hand, the enemies attack with their deadly arrows (verse 3), but on the other hand God attacks them with his arrows (verse 7). The psalm rises to its climax in the final verse, with the thought of God's protective care of his people, and the resultant praise which the upright render to him.

1. *The Opening Call to God (verse 1)*

From a troubled heart the psalmist cries out to God. The more common form of request is 'Hear my prayer' (cf. 4:1; 39:12; 54:2; 84:8), though 'Hear my voice' also occurs elsewhere in the Psalms (cf. 27:7; 119:149), and the two expressions are practically synonymous. He prays for protection 'from the threat (lit. "fear") of the enemy', for he knows that God has the power to keep his people safe.

2. *The Description of the Enemies (verses 2-6)*

The battle is not fought with physical weapons but with sharp words which wound as if they are swords or arrows *(verses 2-3)*. These bitter words come after the wicked have taken counsel together, and from this noisy crowd there come attacks from which the psalmist needs God's protection. God is able to keep the psalmist and hide him from mortal enemies (see Ps. 17:8-9).

The enemies act in deceptive ways in that they wait in hiding places (NIV 'ambush'). From these they launch their attacks without warning, and they do so brazenly *(verse 4)*. The psalmist again protests his innocence, not in the sense of sinlessness, but in that he is clear in conscience before God (cf. the same word used to describe Job in Job 1:8; 2:3).

The threat of the enemy is further defined *(verses 5-6)*. Those who are plotting evil against the psalmist take mutual encouragement in their schemes. They also boast that this is hidden from others, and that they have devised the ideal plot. This displays the innate sinfulness of mankind. In addition, it betrays the pride which sinners take in their own wickedness. The statement, 'Surely the mind and heart of man are cunning', should be set beside that of Psalm 14:3, as a description of the depth of human sinfulness: 'All have turned aside, they have together become corrupt; there is no-one who does good, not even one.'

3. *God's Impending Judgment* (*verses 7-9*)
Earlier the psalmist has spoken of the suddenness with which the enemies shoot at him (verse 4). Now he says it is God who is going to shoot suddenly! *(verses 7-8)*. This is a presentation of the teaching given elsewhere in the Psalms that the sins of people often turn back against themselves (see 54:5; 59:12). God will bring judgment upon these wicked people, and this will be greeted with the recognition by others that this is indeed a just penalty for them. What form the judgment will take is not specified.

God's judgment will be seen by men in general and cause them to acknowledge the fitness of what has happened *(verse 9)*. Being an eyewitness of God's mighty hand at work should cause men to 'know that the LORD is God; besides him there is no other' (Deut. 4:35). True acknowledgment of God's actions should lead to proclamation to others of his actions, and meditation on the wonder of his works.

4. *A Call to Rejoice* (*verse 10*)
The righteous should take encouragement for the future from the promise of God's judgment. We are not to take revenge ourselves on enemies, but to 'leave room for God's wrath, for it is written: "It is mine to avenge; I will repay", says the Lord' (Rom. 12:19). Meanwhile, those who belong to the LORD take refuge in him and extol his name in praise and adoration. Quiet confidence in him has to replace fear of scheming enemies.

PSALM 65
For the director of music. A psalm of David. A song.

While the latter part of this psalm could easily be called simply a
harvest song, yet the clear framework of the psalm shows that it had
a much wider setting. Its structure is clear. It begins with a declaration
that God is the one who answers prayer, and then shows three ways in
which this prayer is answered. There is a meeting with God in his
temple (verse 4), there is a revelation of his power in the created world
(verses 5-8), and finally attention is drawn to the bounty of God in
providing so liberally for his creatures (verses 9-13). There are no
indications in the psalm of any specific setting for its use. Hence, it can
be assumed to be a thanksgiving song appropriate on many occasions
throughout the year.

1. A Prayer-Hearing God (verses 1-4)
The opening phrase is difficult, for literally it says, 'To you, praise is
silence' (cf. the AV margin which notes that lit. 'waiteth' is 'silent').
Most English versions follow the AV in suggesting the meaning is that
praise waits for God. The psalmist seems to be concentrating on
Jerusalem and the temple (see verse 4) as the places where praise is
specially dedicated to God, though the following verse shows that he
is not restricting it to these. The vows could have been made during
some trouble, or else may reflect a promise to God at the time of
planting of the crops.

The psalmist is confident that men everywhere will see evidences
of God's goodness, and they will turn to him *(verse 2)*. The words
imply that they will come to him as the prayer-hearing God, and make
their requests. 'All flesh' (NIV 'all men') elsewhere denotes all
mankind as here (see Ps. 145:21, NIV 'every creature').

In the past the psalmist and his people were in a position in which
there seemed to be no answer to the problem of their sin and guilt *(verse
3)*. But where sin abounded, grace abounded all the more (Rom. 5:20)!
God provided atonement for their sins, just as he did when he declared
to Isaiah: 'Your guilt is taken away and your sin atoned for' (Isa. 6:7).
How blessed is the person on whom God sets his love (cf. the use of
the verb 'choose' of Israel in Deut. 7:7), and whom he invites into his
sanctuary! Spiritual blessings are given in full measure to forgiven
sinners *(verse 4)*.

2. *A Creator God* (*verses 5-8*)

The great Creator God answers the prayers of his people by deeds which inspire awe *(verse 5)*. The phrase 'awesome deeds' can refer to the events of the Exodus (see Exod. 34:10; Deut. 10:21; Ps. 106:21f.), but here it refers to some more recent demonstrations of God's saving power. Three things are then said about this Saviour. Firstly, he is the object of the hope of all the world. Even those of the farthest seas will come to trust in him. The Psalms show us that the missionary vision flowing from Genesis 12:3 was very real for some Old Testament believers (cf. Ps. 67 also). Secondly, he is the Creator of the mighty mountains, which stresses how powerful he is as Saviour *(verse 6)*. Thirdly, he is the controller of his world, in that he stills both the roaring of the mighty oceans and also the turmoils of human society *(verse 7)*.

The vision of the psalmist is still on the ends of the earth *(verse 8)*. Even to the remotest place, knowledge of God's wonders will reach, and there people will come to fear him. The word 'wonders' is literally 'signs', which most commonly points to miraculous acts of God's power such as the plagues at the time of the Exodus (Exod. 7:3; Deut. 4:34). 'Morning' and 'evening' are used here to denote 'east' and 'west'. All over the world God is going to call forth songs of joy as people come to know and acknowledge him.

3. *A Bountiful God* (*verses 9-13*)

The last section of the psalm turns to the bounty of God's provision for his world. While this part could be a harvest song, yet its use is far wider than that. One of the promises of God to the children of Israel was that the land of Canaan was going to be a land 'that drinks rain from heaven. It is a land the LORD your God cares for; the eyes of the LORD your God are continually on it from the beginning of the year to its end' (Deut. 11:11-12). Here that promise is put into poetic language *(verse 9)*. 'The streams of God' may be equivalent to the expression 'the floodgates of the heavens' (Gen. 7:11; 8:2). The preparation of the land (see NIV margin) is described in greater detail in *verse 10*. The early rains prepare the ground for sowing, while later rains in mid-winter soften it and allow the crops to grow.

The climax of the whole process is that God gives the harvest *(verse 11)*. He is pictured driving through the land in his chariots, which are so richly laden that they drop some of their abundance. In *verses 12-*

13 nature herself is personified (as in Pss. 96:11-12; 98:7-8; Isa. 44:23; 49:13). She sings for joy at the bountiful harvest which God has given. Grasslands, hills, meadows and valleys have all experienced his bountiful provision, and together they rejoice at such evidence of his love and care.

PSALM 66
For the director of music. A song. A psalm.

There are obvious links between Psalms 65 and 66. Both have the vision of all the earth praising the Lord (Pss. 65:2, 8; 66:1, 4), and specific reference to his awesome deeds in both is a further connecting idea (Pss. 65:5; 66:3). No precise historical setting can be given for Psalm 66. It seems to be a song of thanksgiving after some victory by the nation, such as when Sennacherib of Assyria was defeated (2 Kgs. 19:35-36). The sudden switch from the use of the first person plural in verses 1-12 to the first person singular in verses 13-20 has suggested to many that two earlier psalms were joined together. However, the 'I' of verses 13-20 could be the king speaking on behalf of the people, or a personification of the nation as an individual (cf. a similar situation in Lam. 1).

1. *Universal Praise of the King* (*verses 1-4*)
The opening call is repeated in Psalms 98:4 and 100:1 (with the substitution of 'LORD' for 'God'). A series of imperatives call for praise to be given in song to God. Because of his greatness, glory is to be ascribed to his name. His character surpasses all others, and while human praise does not add to his glory, it is rightful recognition of his majesty and kingly rule.

When the people look on God's actions, both those in the distant past and those more recently, they acknowledge that they are demonstrations of his great power. Onlookers stand in awe of them, and enemies will submit before him *(verse 3)*. The Hebrew word translated 'cringe' is not a common word. Basically it seems to mean 'deny', and this may well lie behind this and other similar passages in which 'cringe' or 'submit' seems best in English (cf. Deut. 33:29; Pss. 18:44; 81:15). This would suggest that the submission takes place, but without true belief on the part of the enemies.

In *verse 4* the thought is probably that *in the future* all the earth will worship the Lord, rather than that it is doing so now. It is a picture of universal adoration and praise as the nations bow in worship before him. Ultimately all God's enemies will bow in subjection to him (cf. Phil. 2:10-11; 1 Cor. 15:25).

2. *Praise for God's Deliverances* (*verses 5-12*)

The invitation goes out (presumably to 'all the earth') to take notice of God's works *(verse 5)*, with this expression being practically the same as that in Psalm 46:8. In particular, his awesome deeds, as he intervened on behalf of his people, are to be the object of admiration and awe.

The two following verses illustrate this by appealing to the events of the Exodus *(verses 6-7)*. Part of God's miraculous provision for his people was that he dried up the Red Sea. 'The waters' is 'river' in Hebrew, but nowhere is this particular word used of the Jordan. Hence, rather than seeing here a reference to the Red Sea *and* the Jordan, it is better to take it as alluding to the former only. The recollection of past divine actions is meant to form the basis of continuing praise. The psalmist invites others to join him in praise of God. The reference to God's kingly rule in verse 7 is interesting, because the account of the departure from Egypt in Exodus is followed by the Song of the Sea which concludes with the words: 'The LORD will reign for ever and ever' (Exod. 15:18). It is as if the psalmist is making a conscious allusion to the Book of Exodus. God's eyes are on all the nations, for he oversees all and yet overlooks none. The warning follows that the rebellious person should not vaunt himself against such a sovereign.

Attention switches to more recent displays of God's power, and the nations are again asked to participate in praise of what God has done *(verses 8-9)*. Whatever the precise details were of the recent events, it was a difficult time for the people, for their lives were in danger. God had preserved them, and he had been their keeper. When the verb 'slip' is used with 'foot' or 'feet', it denotes slipping in a time of trouble. The Lord is the one who is immovable (Pss. 30:6; 62:2; 112:6) and he holds his children so that their feet do not slip (Ps. 17:5).

The experiences the people had just undergone were intended by God to purify them *(verse 10)*. This may have meant refining the people so that the ungodly among the nation were removed (cf. Jer. 6:29), or that the people were better prepared for service. The idea of refining of metals is a common Old Testament metaphor for the testing and refining of God's people (Pss. 17:3; 26:2; Isa. 1:25; Zech. 13:9).

The word translated 'prison' *(verse 11)* may mean a net or a fortress, and it serves as a metaphor for imprisonment. The word 'burdens' only occurs here in the Old Testament, and seems to indicate the afflictions associated with prison. The imagery in *verse 12* is of conquered people being forced to lie down and to be trampled underfoot, a practice widely attested in the Ancient Near East. 'Fire and water' speak of the great dangers which the people endured (cf. Isa. 43:2), before they were finally brought through them and into God's generous provision. The ancient translations of the Old Testament (Septuagint, Latin Vulgate, and the Aramaic Targum) all render the last phrase 'place of liberty', which fits well with the picture of prison in verse 11.

3. *Personal Thanksgiving* (*verses 13-20*)

During times of troubles vows were made to God *(verses 13-14)*. Some of these could be like the sinful vow Jephthah made when he went to fight the Ammonites (Judg. 11:30-40; the same verb 'promised' is used in verses 35-36 as here in Ps. 66). What had been spoken to God as a promise by the king, is now to be paid. Usually thanksgiving offerings were partially consumed on the altar and the remainder was used in a communal meal. In this case the whole offering is dedicated to the Lord, which indicates a sombre mood on the part of the people as they reflect on the gravity of the danger through which they have come. The variety of animals offered in sacrifice helps to emphasise the spirit of thanksgiving *(verse 15)*. Not content with one kind, the psalmist pledges himself to present several kinds as a reflection of his total dedication to the Lord.

The final section of the psalm starts with a double command: 'Come; listen' *(verse 16)*. While it is conceivable that 'all you who fear God' is a reference to the God-fearing Gentiles (cf. the use of the term God-fearers in the New Testament, Acts 2:5), yet in the context it is more likely that devout believers within Israel are intended. The psalmist gives his own personal testimony concerning the things God has done for him. With his mouth he both called to God, and with it he extolled him. The same lips which prayed, were ready to praise (*verse 17*).

The verb 'listen' binds verses 16-19 together. 'Come, *listen*', says the psalmist, for 'God has surely *listened*' (*verse 19*). The psalmist proclaims his innocence before God, announcing the truth that if a person looks with satisfaction on his sin (the Hebrew text says 'if I had *looked* on'), then God will not hear him. It is to the godly man who does God's will that the Lord will listen (John 9:31; cf. 1 John 3:21).

The concluding verse is an expression of adoration of God. The form of the expression seems to go back to Exodus 18:10, when Jethro, on hearing of what had happened to Israel, said: 'Praise be to the LORD, who rescued you from the hand of the Egyptians and of Pharaoh ...' The psalmist praises him for answering prayer and for bestowing covenant love upon him. God has not proved false to his own declared character (Exod. 34:6-7).

PSALM 67
For the director of music. With stringed instruments.
A psalm. A song.

Psalms 65-67 are all linked together because of their universalism. The expression 'all [the ends of] the earth' occurs in each one (65:5; 66:4; 67:7). Psalm 67 includes a prayer for double blessing – first on Israel, and then on the Gentiles. The repetition of the refrain in verses 3 and 5 highlights the vision of the Gentiles sharing in the saving mercy of God.

1. *A Prayer for Blessing (verses 1-3)*
The opening verse is an echo of the priestly benediction of Numbers 6:24-26. This is one of six occurrences of this expression in the Psalms (the others are 31:16; 80:3, 7, 19; 119:135). The use of well-known words forms a link with the past history of Israel as the psalmist seeks a fresh demonstration of God's mercy upon the people. 'Selah' comes at a most unusual place, though it may well be positioned to emphasise the opening petition.

The following request longs for Israel's saving knowledge of God and his ways to be manifest to all nations *(verse 2)*. The thought may be similar to Isaiah 43:10-13, where Israel is declared to be a witness that the LORD is God, and that there is no saviour apart from him. After being blessed, Israel becomes a blessing to the nations. Knowledge of God should flow into praise of him. Hence, the psalmist prays that when the nations have come into knowledge of the one true God, they will lift their voices in thankful song *(verse 3)*.

2. *A Prayer for the Nations (verses 4-5)*

The thought of the preceding verses is taken a step further. God's saving power (verse 2) is also seen in his just rule. Though in operation now, this rule will come to full expression at the return of Christ, when he 'will judge the world in righteousness and the peoples with equity' (Ps. 98:9). The Christian's prayer is:

> Let Zion's time of favour come;
> O bring the tribes of Israel home;
> And let our wondering eyes behold
> Gentiles and Jews in Jesus' fold.
>
> Almighty God, Thy grace proclaim
> In every clime of every name;
> Let adverse powers before Thee fall,
> And crown the Saviour Lord of all.
>   (William Shrubsole, 1759-1829)

The use in *verse 5* of the recurring refrain serves to draw attention to the theme of universal praise which dominates throughout this psalm. The vision is of a world falling down in praise to God the Saviour. Ultimately the Lord Jesus will be the object of praise as depicted in Revelation 5:12:

> Worthy is the Lamb, who was slain,
> to receive power and wealth and wisdom and strength,
> and honour and glory and praise!

3. *A Prayer for Universal Blessing (verses 6-7)*

One of the opening petitions is made the focal point of these final verses. The psalmist is confident that God, whom faith claims as 'our God', will indeed bless his people with abundant harvest. Material and spiritual blessings seem to be joined together, for blessing of Israel is linked with the idea that the ends of the earth will come to fear the Lord. The opening and close of the psalm strike the same note. God's blessing of Israel brings his knowledge to the nations so that they reverence him. Through the fall of Israel riches indeed came to the nations, and how much greater riches will the ingathering of Israel bring (Rom. 11:11-12)?

PSALM 68

For the director of music. Of David. A psalm. A song.

There is no more triumphant song in the whole of the Psalter than
Psalm 68. It begins with an echo of Moses' prayer when the ark of the
covenant led the people in the wilderness (Num. 10:35). It moves on
to a description of the journey from Sinai to the promised land, with
the procession of the ark into Jerusalem in David's time. This was seen
as God's coming there. It closes with a song of praise to the Lord who
rules over all the kingdoms of the earth. There are many textual
difficulties in this psalm, including the fact that fifteen words or
expressions occur in it which occur nowhere else in the Old Testament.
At times there is a sudden change of ideas which is difficult to fit into
the overall unity of the psalm. The emphasis on God is maintained
throughout the psalm, and a great variety of names for God is
employed (*elohim*, 23 times; *adonai*, 6 times ; *el*, 2 times; and *shaddai*,
Yahweh, *Yah*, *Yahweh adonai*, and *Yahweh elohim* once each).

1. A Prayer for the Coming of the LORD *(verses 1-6)*
The call to God is given in the language which Moses used whenever
the ark set out: 'Rise up, O LORD! May your enemies be scattered; may
your foes flee before you' (Num. 10:35). This processional hymn starts
with the request for God's intervention on behalf of his people, just as
he intervened in times past *(verses 1-2)*. The enemies are compared to
smoke and to wax to illustrate how feeble they are to stand against the
power of the LORD.

Whereas the wicked flee before God (verse 1), the righteous are
joyful before him *(verse 3)*. Relationship with God determines conduct in his presence. At the final coming of the LORD, the wicked will
be shut out from his presence, while the righteous believers will glorify
him in that day (2 Thess. 1:9-10).

In *verse 4* the invitation is to sing to God, whose name is the LORD.
In the Hebrew text the word 'LORD' is an abbreviated form of the divine
name (*Yah*), and it occurs most commonly in poetic passages such as
this, in names like Elijah or Uzziah, and in the expression 'Hallelujah'
('Praise the LORD!'). The translation of the description of the LORD as
the one 'who rides on the clouds' is difficult. It is better to follow the
NIV footnote, 'who rides through the deserts', which then would agree
with verses 7-8.

Though God is so powerful, yet he has a concern for the needy *(verses 5-6)*. The three groups most likely to suffer injustice were the orphans, the widows and the strangers (see Deut. 10:18-19; 24:17). Here, and in Psalm 146:9, the fatherless and the widows are said to be the special objects of God's interest. It is unclear whether God's holy dwelling is heaven or the temple. The strangers and other lonely ones are brought under his protection, while even the foreign prisoners (the word usually means this, cf. Ps. 69:33; Isa. 14:17; Zech. 9:11) experience his redemption, and consequently his joy. The rebellious within Israel, however, have none of this joy, and they are depicted as if they live in a barren place.

2. From the Exodus to Jerusalem *(verses 7-18)*

A poetic description is now given of the way in which God led his people through the wilderness to Canaan (verses 7-10), his gift to them of the land (verses 11-14), and how he then took up his abode on Mount Zion (verses 15-18). There is a change from the use of the third person to direct address to God himself.

This account of the Exodus *(verses 7-8)* seems to draw upon the Song of Deborah (Judg. 5:4-5). God went ahead of his people (Exod. 13:21), after the events at the Red Sea had demonstrated his great power. Earthquake and storm were symbolic of his presence and power. This God was the one who had displayed his greatness at Sinai when he entered into a covenant with his people Israel. The use of 'Selah' here and in verses 19 and 32 in the middle of a stanza appears to give special emphasis to the preceding expression.

The land of Canaan was a gracious provision of God for his people *(verses 9-10)*. He gave them a land 'which drinks rain from heaven' (Deut. 11:11). While these verses draw attention to material blessings in Canaan, most probably they also speak of all the bountiful and varied ways in which God blessed Israel. The mention of the poor is significant, for this word (translated 'afflicted' in other places) describes the condition of Israel in Egypt (see Exod. 3:7, 17 [NIV 'misery']).

Comparison of various translations shows how difficult all translators have found *verses 11-13* and the following verses. There seem to be allusions to Deborah's Song (Judg. 5), but perhaps also to other songs not recorded in Scripture. The general picture is that God gave his message concerning the conquest of Canaan, and the women proclaimed it ('those who proclaimed it' is feminine in Hebrew).

Armies were forced to flee before Israel (the *RSV* stays close to the Hebrew, and depicts the vividness of the action, 'they flee, they flee'!), leaving their spoils behind them. Verse 13 appears to be describing some of those spoils, though the exact nature of the 'dove' is unclear. Similarly, *verse 14* is perplexing, because we cannot be sure of the location of Zalmon, nor of the nature of the snow. It could mean that God sent a snowstorm to rout the enemy forces at Zalmon (probably near Shechem, see Judg. 9:48), or, that the bleached bones of fallen warriors looked like snow on the hillside.

God did not choose the highest of mountains within the land of promise *(verses 15-16)*. Rather, he chose Zion (see Ps. 132:13-18). Bashan may well have been Mount Hermon, and it represented what was powerful and rich (cf. Deut. 32:14; Amos 4:1; Ps. 22:12). It is rebuked for being envious of Zion, which is the seat of God's kingdom. Zion was the mountain of God's inheritance, and from there the LORD would reign (Exod. 15:17-18).

On the march into Canaan God is accompanied by his mighty forces *(verses 17-18)*. These are his heavenly servants (Deut. 33:2; 2 Kgs. 6:15). Jesus could have called for such heavenly assistants and his Father would have sent more than twelve legions of angels (Matt. 26:53). The revelation at Sinai was a revelation of God's holiness (the Hebrew has 'in holiness', which the NIV interprets to mean 'the holy place', 'the sanctuary') which left the people fearful (Deut. 5:23-27). God's holiness was shown in so many incidents on the way to Canaan. When Zion was finally reached it was like a victory procession, with captives being led there, along with their tribute gifts (cf. 2 Sam. 8:11; 1 Kgs. 4:21). Verse 18 is quoted by Paul with some variation in Ephesians 4:8, and in particular he has 'he *gave* gifts to men' in place of 'he *took* gifts'. Paul's stress lies on the fact of Christ's ascension and his bestowal of gifts on his people, just as the psalm goes on to speak of the blessings which God dispenses (verses 19ff.)

3. *Praise for the Saviour* (*verses 19-23*)

The account of the triumphal procession is broken off until verse 24 for an ascription of praise to the Saviour. Recollection of God's great acts of deliverance and redemption call forth a song of praise. He is extolled as the Saviour and as the burden-bearer *(verse 19)*. The wonderful thing is that the mighty God stoops to his people, and daily carries their burdens (or possibly it could be rendered, 'who daily carries *us*', i.e.

like a shepherd). The New Testament still encourages us to cast all our anxiety on the Lord because he cares for us (1 Pet. 5:7).

A more literal translation of *verse 20* is 'Our God is a God of *deliverances*, to the Sovereign LORD belong *escapes* from death'. The plurals may be used deliberately, as Calvin suggested, to show that although numerous threats of death may come against us, yet God has innumerable ways of delivering us. The reverse is also certain *(verse 21)*. God is pledged to destroy those who oppose him. The same verb 'to crush' is used in Psalm 110:5-6 of God's activity in judging kings and rulers. 'The hairy crowns' seems to refer to the pride of the enemies as they go on in their sinful ways.

In the Hebrew text the object of the verb 'bring' in *verse 22* is not expressed. While it could be 'you', i.e. the people of Israel, yet the context suggests it is 'them', i.e. the enemies. No place is so remote that God's enemies can find a hiding place from him. The graphic imagery of battle *(verse 23)* may be too strong for modern Westerners, but it certainly is in agreement with other Old Testament descriptions, including the account of the deaths of Ahab and Jezebel (1 Kgs. 21:19; 22:38; 2 Kgs. 9:36).

4. *Praise of God in the Congregation* (*verses 24-27*)

Attention comes back to the procession after victory in battle. Whereas previously God was called 'our God', the psalmist now speaks in more personal terms still, calling him '*my* God and King' *(verse 24)*. True faith appropriates this type of language as it responds to the close relationship with God (cf. Thomas', '*My* Lord and *my* God', John 20:28, and Paul's, 'the Son of God, who loved *me* and gave himself for *me*', Gal. 2:20).

The scene described in *verse 25* recalls what happened after the deliverance of the Red Sea, when Miriam led the women in singing and dancing (Exod. 15:19-21). The singers and musicians are going before the main procession, rejoicing in the deliverances which resemble the Exodus. The words of *verse 26* ('Praise God in the great congregation; praise the Lord in the assembly of Israel') form either what the women said in praise, or else they are a call to everyone to extol him in the midst of the congregation of Israel. Israel was made up of many companies (NIV 'great congregation'), which all stemmed from the one source, 'the fountain of Israel' (following the Hebrew text). The four tribes mentioned in *verse 27* (Benjamin, Judah, Zebulun, Naphtali) seem to represent the whole of Israel. North and south are together, as they were at the time of the conquest. Even in the New Testament these tribes were important, as our Lord and some of his apostles came from Judah, while Paul, 'the least of the apostles' (1 Cor. 15:9), came from Benjamin. The remainder of the apostles were from the territory of Zebulun and Naphtali.

5. *Praise of God in all the World* (*verses 28-35*)

God is enthroned, and now he is asked for a fresh demonstration of his great power *(verse 28)*. The psalmist wants God to reveal anew his power, seen in the Exodus and in many later deliverances (verse 20). However, now the demonstration is to all the kingdoms of the earth, and foreign kings will come to do homage before the Lord in Jerusalem *(verse 21)*. The eschatological picture here is amplified in the Book of Revelation. Into the New Jerusalem, which has the Lord God Almighty and the Lamb as its temple, 'the kings of the earth will bring their splendour' (Rev. 21:24).

'The beast' in *verse 30* is probably an allusion to an historical enemy, most probably Egypt. Elsewhere Leviathan (apparently either the crocodile or the hippopotamus) stands for Egypt (Ps. 74:14; Isa. 27:1). The herd of bulls is probably intended as a reference to the leaders or kings, while the calves seem to be less powerful nations. Egypt will come and do homage to the Lord, which is part of the prophetical picture of the events on the great day of the Lord (Isa. 19:18-25). Even ancient foes of Israel such as Egypt will come in submission, while her tributary Cush (Ethiopia) will also display her allegiance (cf. Isa. 45:14).

A song of rejoicing is needed from all the kingdoms of the earth as a fitting acknowledgment of the universal sway of God *(verses 32-33)*. 'Selah', inserted in the middle of the stanza, stresses this call. The song itself is an expansion of verse 4. 'The ancient skies' recalls Moses' assertion that 'to the LORD your God belong the heavens, even the highest heavens' (Deut. 10:14). The God of eternity, who had already made his proclamation (see verse 12), now speaks in mighty power (cf. Ps. 29:3-5).

The wording in *verses 34-35* seems to be echoing Deuteronomy 33:26. God's majesty is displayed in two ways. Firstly, he shows his power in creation and providence, as he rules over the earth and skies. Secondly, his majesty is seen in a special way as it is revealed to his people Israel. He is there in the midst of them in the sanctuary or holy place, and from there he imparts strength. Earlier the psalmist has spoken a doxology on behalf of Israel (verse 19). Now he concludes with one spoken by the kingdoms of the world: 'Praise be to God!' The New Testament points to a day when the kingdoms of this world will become the kingdoms of our Lord and of his Christ (Rev. 11:15).

PSALM 69

For the director of music. To [the tune of] 'Lilies'. Of David.

This is one of the most quoted psalms in the New Testament. The following list shows how widely it is utilised: v. 4 (John 15:25); v. 9 (John 2:17); v. 21 (Matt. 27:34, 48); vss. 22-23 (Rom. 11:9-10); v. 24 (Rev. 16:1); v. 25 (Acts 1:20). The psalm deals with sin and its consequences, and the extended use of it in the New Testament shows that even Christians today cannot evade the issues it raises. There is no separation of sin from the sinner in the Bible, in the way in which people often wish to divorce a sinner (who is loved) from his sin (which is hated). This is another psalm which has many curses in it (see Introduction, pp. 58-62), but the very fact that Jesus takes part of it on his lips should cause us to look carefully at it. Originally it referred to the bitter experiences of David, and then typically it is applied to Christ.

1. *A Personal Cry (verses 1-4)*
The psalm commences with a general cry, and it is not until a few verses later that the nature of his need is specified. The psalmist compares himself to a drowning man, who is desperately trying to keep his head above the water *(verses 1-2)*. Sudden floods in Palestine made very realistic the idea of water reaching up to the neck (see Isa. 8:8).

The psalmist's distress has been going on for some time for he is wearied by his attempts to attract God's attention *(verses 3-4)*. His throat is sore and, as he waits for God to intervene, his eyes are like those of a sick person. He protests that he has done nothing to cause the persecution he is undergoing, nor is there any truth in the false accusation that he is stealing from others.

2. *An Explanation of His Suffering (verses 5-12)*
Before going on to describe further his suffering, the psalmist makes an open confession to God *(verse 5)*. He has done foolish things in

God's sight, and he knows that he cannot hold anything back from him. His very nature is under the scrutiny of God (Ps. 139:15).

The cluster of names for God in *verse 6* is highly appropriate in this setting. Appeal to him as LORD Almighty (i.e. over all things) is made, yet he is also the covenant God of Israel who is near his people to help them in times such as this. The thought of not being disgraced has already been presented in Psalm 25:3. He does not want those who are truly God's (lit. 'your hopers' and 'your seekers') to suffer because of anything he does.

It is not for his own sake that the psalmist suffers reproach *(verses 7-9)*. He is cut off from his closest family members for God's sake (cf. the communal acknowledgment of suffering for God's sake in Psalm 44:22). He is so identified with the temple, for which he has the deepest longing, that he becomes the object of taunting from God's enemies. The manner, in which the longing for the temple is displayed, is not stated. The first part of verse 9 is quoted in John 2:17 in reference to Jesus' cleansing of the temple.

The taunting is made more bitter by being directed at him when he is clearly in mourning *(verses 10-12)*. Instead of joining him in his expressions of grief, his enemies make fun of him. Just as people gather in a town mall today, in ancient Israel they gathered at the city gate (Ruth 4:1ff.; 1 Sam. 4:12-18). The assembled community, as they gossip together, talk disparagingly of the afflicted sufferer, while even the drunkards join in with rowdy songs. While he longs for the worship of the temple (verse 9), all he hears is a totally different kind of singing.

3. *A Prayer for Help* (verses 13-18)
Out of his pressing need, the psalmist makes his cry to God *(verse 13)*. He knows, that in God's good and favourable time, help will come for him. There seems to be an echo here and in the following verses of Exodus 34:6, where God declared his own character as 'abounding in love and faithfulness'. Because of God's revelation of himself, the psalmist can appeal for a sure answer.

The imagery of flood waters *(verses 14-15)* is still to the fore (cf. the opening verses). The picture is of grievous trouble surrounding him, possibly even death, for the word 'pit' seems to be a synonym for 'Sheol', 'the grave'.

The psalmist appeals with great intensity for God to intervene and save him *(verse 16)*. It is for covenant mercy that he prays, as he picks up the theme of verse 13 and rephrases it. The same expression, 'the goodness of your love', occurs in Psalm 109:21. He wants God to let his gaze be set on him, and so see his need and send deliverance. Someone in a covenant relationship with God, like the psalmist, could plead as a servant *(verse 17)*. The use of this term 'servant' recognises that relationship and uses it as a basis for prayer. Speedy help is needed, and divine assistance is the only way of escape from trouble.

In this psalm a great variety of expressions is used as the psalmist pleads with his God. He has already said 'answer', 'rescue', and 'deliver'. Now he adds 'come near', 'rescue me' (a different word from that in verse 14), and 'redeem' *(verse 18)*. The multiplicity of terms adds intensity to his requests, but there is little advantage in trying to distinguish sharply between them.

4. *The Psalmist's Enemies* (*verses 19-21*)
The psalmist makes his renewed appeal to God, repeating the account of his experience of derision and shame (see verse 7). Those whom he expected to provide comfort failed to stand by him, and he waited in vain for them to offer support. The addition here is the reference to gall and vinegar in *verse 21*. 'Gall' was derived from a poisonous herb. The idea is that the comforters went so far as to betray him by application of poison to his food. In his agony Jesus was offered wine mixed with gall, but he refused to drink it (Matt. 27:34), as it could have affected his self-control at this crucial stage of his suffering.

5. *A Call for God's Judgment* (*verses 22-28*)
The psalmist appeals for God's direct intervention in the situation, and for his judgment to be visited on his enemies (for the wider problem presented by these passages, see the Introduction, pp. 60-62). Those who had tried to poison him will find their own table will become a trap for them. The NIV marginal note on *verse 22* follows the Aramaic Targum, which suggests that instead of 'retribution' the Hebrew word should be read as meaning 'peace offerings'. This provides a good parallel with 'table' in the first part of the verse. *Verse 23* refers to physical changes which would be a sign of God's disfavour.

In *verses 24-25* the psalmist continues to ask for the reversal of all the good things of life. In place of mercy the request is for wrath; in place of joyful family life a deserted dwelling place. Peter quotes the words of verse 25 in reference to the reward which Judas Iscariot received for his wickedness (Acts 1:18-20). He illustrated the same antagonism which had been displayed by the psalmist's enemies, and he came under a similar judgment.

The psalmist was willing to accept God's chastisements, but when he was under the afflicting hand of God, enemies visited him with even greater hurts. The talking about him was clearly a form of mockery (cf. verse 12), as they rejoiced over his suffering. He asks that they be given what they deserve – punishment corresponding to their sins, and exclusion from God's saving activity *(verses 26-27)*. The idea of the book of life *(verse 28)* comes from Exodus 32:32, where Moses prays that if God does not forgive his people, then let his name be blotted out of God's book. For the wicked, the request of the psalmist is that they perish, and that their names not be written alongside those of the righteous. The same concept of a book appears also in Revelation 3:5; 13:8; 17:8; and 20:15.

6. *A Song of Praise (verses 29-33)*

In *verse 29* the focus now shifts back to the psalmist himself a little more emphatically than the NIV rendering suggests: '*But as for me*, I am afflicted ...' He is concerned, not only for the punishment of evil enemies, but for his own salvation. The verb 'to protect' has the idea of setting on high, and therefore of putting in a position of safety.

In anticipation of God's salvation the psalmist declares his intention of praising him in song *(verses 30-31)*. The 'thanksgiving' could be a sacrifice (cf. Lev. 7:12; 22:29) which formed a thankoffering, or a song of praise, which seems to be the meaning here. Such heartfelt praise is more acceptable to God than the mere offering of animal sacrifice, even if it was complete with horns and hoofs!

When the humble (defined further by the expression 'who seek God') see what is happening and hear this praise, they too will rejoice *(verse 32)*. In turn they will find reviving comes through this experience of seeing and acknowledging the salvation of the LORD. *Verse 33* ('The LORD hears the needy and does not despise his captive people') is an abiding truth. It is characteristic of God that he listens to the cry of the needy. The 'needy' are shown elsewhere in the Psalms to be those whose distress is caused by their enemies, but whose trust is in the LORD. 'His captive people' is a rendering of the Hebrew 'bound ones', which is either a reference to binding in sin before the LORD brings release, or else to those who are bound in service to him as devoted captives.

7. Universal Adoration (verses 34-36)
Even inanimate nature should praise the Lord, for he makes himself known as the Saviour of his people. Earlier in the psalm there has not been any mention of the need of the nation, or of distress which has come upon Zion and Judah. It is possible that the psalmist's great need was but a microcosm of the need of the nation as a whole. God is able to provide help for Zion, and to bring his people back to settle again in the land. The lesson is clear from this psalm that, even in times of great distress, the eye of faith has to look to the full demonstration of God's restoring mercy. There is 'a home of righteousness' awaiting the people of God (2 Pet. 3:13).

PSALM 70
For the director of music. Of David. A petition.

This sung prayer is almost the same as Psalm 40:13-17 (see comments on that psalm). There are, however, several variations. The title has the same first two terms as Psalm 40, but the word 'psalm' is replaced here by 'petition'. There are also changes in respect to the use of the divine name, but not in a uniform manner, for twice *'elohim* replaces *yhwh* (LORD), but then LORD is used in place of both *'adonai* and *'elohim* and retained in verse 1b. Other changes include the absence of 'be pleased' (verse 1), the absence of 'to take' (verse 2), the change of 'be appalled' to 'turn back' (verse 3), and the alteration of 'think on me' to 'come quickly to me' (verse 5). These verses may have been taken over from Psalm 40 and used at some time of great distress. The fact that the Aramaic Targum has 'Make haste to deliver us' in verse 1 points to a use of the psalm with an application to the nation as a whole.

PSALM 71
This is a psalm of old age (see verses 9 and 18), written by a believer who, even near the end of life, is still being tormented by enemies. There is no heading to help set the psalm in a particular historical setting, or to note any ascription of authorship. Persecution is a fact of life for committed believers (2 Tim. 3:12), and there is no stage of life when they are exempt from it. Here the psalmist blends together phrases from other psalms, which shows how deeply ingrained in his mind and heart were the words of other singers of Israel. Yet the psalm is a song of hope, as he looks expectantly to the LORD.

1. A Confident Prayer (verses 1-4)

Verses 1-4 are very similar to the start of Psalm 31 (see commentary on that psalm). They express the sure confidence that his abiding refuge ever since his youth (see verse 5) has been the LORD. He continues to appeal to God to be attentive to his cry and to save him in his present trouble. The word 'refuge' in verse 3 follows a few Hebrew manuscripts and makes this verse conform to Psalm 31:2. However, it is better to retain the reading in the majority of manuscripts, 'rock of *habitation*'. Clearly, from early times, Israel had thought of the LORD as being the dwelling place of his people (see Moses' words, Ps. 90:1). Even in his old age the psalmist is still surrounded by wicked men, from whose grip he seeks release. Words like 'rescue' and 'deliver' stress the urgency of the situation.

2. A Declaration of Praise (verses 5-8)

Several times Jeremiah calls God 'the hope of Israel' (Jer. 14:8; 17:13; 50:7), which is one reason why it has been suggested that he may be the author of this psalm. The words also seem to echo Psalm 22:9-10. The psalmist's confidence in the LORD is no newly-found trust, but one which goes back to the very commencement of his life *(verses 5-6)*. It is not his own faith which is the object of his praise, but the grace of God which he has known since childhood. Constant praise is a way of indicating his response to God's keeping power.

To many of his contemporaries the psalmist has become a sign or wonder *(verse 7)*. The word 'portent' is used in the section of Deuteronomy dealing with the curses which will come on Israel because of disobedience (Deut. 28:46). Here it seems to indicate that the psalmist feels himself to be the object of God's chastisement, yet he does not hesitate to commit himself to his sure place of refuge. God's splendour or glory was what he wanted to proclaim constantly *(verse 8)*.

3. Prayer in Old Age (verses 9-13)

From reflection upon his commitment to the LORD from his youth, the psalmist now turns to his present old age *(verse 9)*. In his increasing weakness he pleads that God will not cast him off (the same expression as David uses in Ps. 51:11). Even at this stage of his earthly pilgrimage there are those who plot against him, watching to see if they can take his life *(verse 10)*. Evil men combine together as they plan their attacks on believers (cf. Ps. 83:3). One of the hardest taunts for believers to face is the one that in their distress God has forsaken them *(verse 11)*. But the reality is that God will not forsake his faithful ones (Psalm 37:28), and so the taunt is a lie. *Verse 12* ('Be not far from me, O God; come quickly, O my God, to help me') seems to be an echo of Psalms 22:11, 19 and 38:21-22. It is a help in times of distress to use words which others have used before us in their urgent situations. Others have passed the same way and have made their plea for speedy help. The words of *verse 13* are close to Psalms 35:26 and 109:29. His appeal is for God to vindicate him and he awaits divine judgment upon his enemies.

4. *Confidence in Old Age* (*verses 14-18*)

The contrast is very clear between the fate of the enemies and the future of the psalmist. He is confident that even in his old age he will proclaim God's salvation, and do so to an increasing degree *(verses 14-15)*. The word 'measure' is connected to the Hebrew word for 'tell', and it only occurs here in the whole of the Old Testament. It probably means he is unable to count the 'number' of God's saving acts. Several words are used to describe these actions *(verses 16-17)*. In coming to the Temple the psalmist will make mention of those actions which are God's alone, his royal power which has been displayed in victories. He is also declared to be a God of faithfulness who does things which are beyond human capability ('marvellous deeds'; cf. its use in Pss. 72:18; 86:10). All that he has learned of the Lord's actions on behalf of his people forms part of his songs of praise. As he nears the end of life the psalmist still wants to declare to the coming generation the great things that God has done *(verse 18)*. Not only the nation but he himself has experienced the power (Hebrew, 'the arm') of God, and this forms a further testimony to God's saving might.

5. *A Confident Song* (*verses 19-24*)

The psalm moves to a conclusion with a strong note of confidence *(verse 19)*. The early part of this verse ('Your righteousness reaches to the skies, O God, you who have done great things') echoes Psalm 36:5-6, while the rhetorical question, 'Who is like you?', is parallelled in Psalm 89:8. The whole verse is an emphatic assertion of the fact that God's righteousness is beyond human comprehension, and that no one can be compared with the LORD.

Just as the psalmist has declared that God's righteousness extends to the heavens, he now speaks of his own experiences as though they had brought him down to the depths of the earth *(verses 20-21)*. He is sure though, that God will not forsake him, and this must always remain the believer's confidence.

> Though troubles assail and danger affright,
> Though friends should all fail and foes unite,
> Yet one thing secures us, whatever betide,
> The Scripture assures us the Lord will provide.
>
> No strength of our own or goodness we claim;
> Yet, since we have known the Saviour's great Name,
> In this our strong tower for safety we hide,
> The Lord is our power, the Lord will provide.
>
> (John Newton, 1725-1807)

God's faithfulness and holiness form the subject of praise *(verse 22)*. The expression 'Holy One of Israel' is most frequently used as a title for God in the prophecy of Isaiah (see e.g. Isa. 1:4; 5:19; 29:19; 47:4; 60:14). God's holiness is seen in the way in which he redeems his people *(verse 23)*, and it will always be mentioned in the songs of the redeemed (cf. Exod. 15:11; Rev. 15:3-4). The psalmist knows that God will not desert him. The judgment of God upon his enemies is a demonstration of his righteousness, and as such it forms the subject of his continuous song of praise *(verse 24)*.

PSALM 72
Of Solomon.

> Jesus shall reign where'er the sun
> Does his successive journeys run;
> His kingdom stretch from shore to shore,
> Till moons shall wax and wane no more.

With these words Isaac Watts (1674-1748) captured the spirit of this psalm. The promises which are given concerning the king go far beyond anything which could be promised to an ordinary descendant of David. *All* kings are going to bow before him (verse 11), and the extension of his kingdom is described in terms identical to the Messianic passage in Zechariah 9:9-13. Early Jewish thinking took the same viewpoint, as the Targum adds after the word 'king' in verse 1, 'Messiah'. The background of the psalm is the covenant with David in 2 Samuel 7, but the vision is of the ultimate Davidic ruler, Jesus Christ. The Hebrew title is ambiguous, as it can mean either 'by Solomon' or 'for Solomon'.

1. A Prayer for the King (verses 1-4)

In terms of the covenant with David, the Davidic king was adopted as God's son (2 Sam. 7:14; cf. also Psalm 89:26-27). Hence he can be called either 'the king' or 'the son of the king' (NIV 'the royal son'). The initial appeal here is for the gift of righteous rule to him, so that his administration will reflect the very character of God himself *(verse 1)*.

The idea expressed in verse 1 is carried over into *verses 2-3*. The endowment with justice and righteousness will enable the king to rule well. This is stated poetically in the thought that there will be a harvest of peace and righteousness, so that even the mountain ranges will produce the crops which denote prosperity (cf. a similar poetic usage in Joel 3:18).

None of the oppressed need to fear during the reign of this king, for they will be defended by him *(verse 4)*. He will bring vindication to them, and so the thought of verse 2 is enlarged to embody the promise that the defenceless are his special care. The oppressors will find that they are treated in the way in which they themselves treated others, a principle which the New Testament reasserts (Jas. 2:13).

2. An Enduring Kingship (verses 5-7)

In contrast to other dynasties the promise to David was that his kingdom was going to endure, expressed here in comparison with the sun and moon *(verse 5)*. The promise was repeated several times in the Old Testament (Pss. 89:28-29; 132:11-12; Isa. 9:7), and it was renewed in the words of Gabriel to Mary, as he announced the coming birth of Jesus (Luke 1:31-33). The opening of *verse 6* picks up an idea from David's last words in 2 Samuel 23:3-4: 'when one rules over men in righteousness, ... he is like ... the brightness after rain that brings the grass from the earth'. The prosperity, under the Davidic house, is likened to the effect of rain which stimulates further the growth of newly mown grass. The righteous will have conditions in which they will flourish (for the same expression see Ps. 92:12; Prov. 11:28), and this will continue until the end of time.

3. *A Universal Kingdom* (*verses 8-11*)

The extent of the kingdom of the Messianic ruler is stated in terms of the promise to Abraham *(verse 8)*. However, there is one notable change. The boundary does not extend up to the [Euphrates] River, but from it outwards! No longer will it be the restricted territory allotted as the promised land, but it will consist of a universal kingdom. From far-off places people will acknowledge the rule of Messiah, and his enemies will be brought to own his authority over them *(verses 9-10)*. 'To bow before' and 'to lick the dust' are synonymous expressions of submission (see Isa. 49:23). The places mentioned (Tarshish, Sheba, and Seba) represent the distant nations, with their rulers coming to present their tribute as a sign of allegiance to this universal king. The New Testament speaks of a day coming when Jesus will have destroyed all other dominions and powers, and all his enemies will be placed under his feet (1 Cor. 15:24-25). Though *verse 11* ('All kings will bow down to him and all nations will serve him') and the previous verses express the idea of submission in terms alluding to Solomon's kingdom, yet the final fulfilment of this promise will be when Jesus as the Lamb overcomes because he is Lord of lords and King of kings (Rev. 17:14; 19:16).

4. *Concern for Righteousness and Justice* (*verses 12-14*)

Earlier in verses 2-4 the psalmist spoke about the king's support for those who needed his special care. Now he returns to this theme, with the assurance that he will act in mercy to those who are oppressed *(verses 12-13)*. In contrast to other Near Eastern kingdoms, the Davidic throne was established in love, and the Davidic king was 'one who in judging seeks justice and speeds the cause of righteousness' (Isa. 16:5). When his subjects are faced with violence *(verse 14)*, he rescues them (the Hebrew is lit. 'redeems'). The word often denotes the action of a kinsman in redeeming his kin from difficulty or danger (cf. its use in Ruth 4, where it refers to the redeeming of the land which belonged to Naomi). In the king's sight, the life of even these afflicted ones is very special (cf. the almost identical phrase used of God in Psalm 116:15).

5. *Universal Blessing* (*verses 15-17*)

The prayer for the continuing existence of the dynasty is put in terms of the normal salutation of a new king (*verse 15,* cf. 1 Sam. 10:24; 2

Sam. 16:16; 1 Kgs. 1:25, 34). Just as the Queen of Sheba brought gifts
to Solomon, including gold (1 Kgs. 10:10), so the psalmist pictures
further tribute being presented to the Davidic king. In addition, prayer
is made for his welfare and praise given to him for the prosperity he
brings. The picture of prosperity is painted in terms of abundant crops
(verses 16-17), even to the very tops of the mountains! Just as Lebanon
was noted for its bountiful forests, so may the land yield an abundant
harvest. An enduring kingship was going to bring blessing to many
more countries than just Israel. In fact, the promise of the covenant
with Abraham (Gen. 12:2-3) was going to find its fulfilment through
the Messianic kingship of Jesus, when the nations would receive the
blessing of the Spirit (Gal. 3:14).

6. *Concluding Benediction* (*verses 18-20*)

Like all the five books of the Psalter, this second one concludes with
a doxology *(verses 18-19)*. The covenant God of Israel is indeed the
only one able to do 'marvellous' deeds (see the comment on Ps. 71:17).
His name is worthy of praise because of the glory of his actions in
redeeming and keeping his people. The desire for the whole earth to be
filled with God's glory is an echo of Numbers 14:21. To that desire the
people respond with a double 'Amen'. 'Amen' is frequently used after
prayers and hymns of praise (see 1 Chr. 16:36; Neh. 8:6; Pss. 41:13;
106:48).

The note in *verse 20* ('This concludes the prayers of David son of
Jesse') does not refer to the whole Psalter, for there are later Davidic
psalms (cf. 86, 108-110, 138-145). It appears to have been added to the
collection which precedes to mark it off from the psalms of Asaph
which follow (73-83).

BOOK 3

PSALM 73
A psalm of Asaph.

This third book of the Psalter starts with a group of psalms attributed
to Asaph (73-83). He was a descendant of Gershon, son of Levi (cf. 1
Chr. 6:39-43), and he was one of the leaders of music whom David
appointed (1 Chr. 15:16-17; 2 Chr. 5:12). This psalm is close in style
to Psalms 37 and 49, in that it struggles with the problem of why
wicked people seem to prosper as compared with the righteous. Only
when the psalmist went into the temple did he understand what was to
be the final destiny of the wicked (verses 16-17).

1. *Complaint to God (verses 1-3)*
The psalm opens with a declaration of God's relationship to his people.
He is in covenant friendship with them *(verse 1)*. There can be no doubt
about God's goodness to his people Israel, who are further defined as
the 'pure in heart'. Here and in Psalm 24:4 this phrase describes those
with a single mind towards God, though the same word can be used of
God's commands (Ps. 19:8, NIV 'radiant'). Though he knew that truth
well, the psalmist gave way to doubt *(verses 2-3)*. The opening
expression in verse 2, 'but as for me', is very emphatic (it occurs again
in the Hebrew text of verses 22, 23, and 28). Although the truth of
God's goodness was so real, yet when he saw the prosperity (lit.
'peace') of the wicked he began to be jealous of them. Along with
many other saints, his observation that the wicked seem to do so well
led him to doubt God's goodness.

2. *The Character of the Godless (verses 4-12)*
Appearances often deceive. It seems at first to the psalmist that the
wicked never suffer sickness, and that they are immune to the troubles
which often afflict others *(verses 4-5)*. The full reality of the situation
only dawns on him later in the psalm (see verses 16-20). He has yet to
learn that affliction is not necessarily a sign of God's disfavour (see
John 9:1-3; Heb. 12:7-11).

The arrogant deck themselves with their pride, as if it was jewellery
to be displayed around their necks *(verses 6-7)*. Their boastful attitudes
lead to violent actions, because they think that they can 'get away with
it'. It is from the heart that all evil springs (Matt. 12:34-35; 15:16-20),
and the schemes which sinful minds can think up, are endless. The

description of arrogance and pride in the wicked continues in *verses 8-9*. As proud boasters they threaten others. They daringly talk as if they are God himself, and thus the whole world is theirs. Here we recognise attitudes and outward expressions of minds which dismiss God. Paul amplified the theme in Romans 1:28-32 (see especially verse 30). Another Old Testament wisdom passage reminds us that God resists the proud (Prov. 3:34), a statement which is quoted twice in the New Testament (Jas. 4:6; 1 Pet. 5:5).

Verse 10 is difficult to translate and explain (see NIV footnote), but its meaning also determines the meaning of the following verses. The NIV text makes good sense. The people who are attracted to and who follow such proud boasters turn to them, and try and share in their success. They mock at the idea of a God who has knowledge of their activities, and they act as if they will never have to give an account of their actions. Like the rich fool of whom Jesus speaks in his parabolic teaching (Luke 12:13-21), they hoard wealth for themselves, little expecting ever having to answer to God. Taking life easy – eating, drinking, and merry-making – conflicts with our calling to trust in the Lord.

3. A Personal Response (verses 13-20)
The psalmist openly admits that he has been troubled before with doubts *(verse 13)*. He has tried to live uprightly and he has avoided the overtly sinful actions of the wicked which he has just described. But now doubt grips his heart. Has it all been for no real purpose? Compared with the wicked, the psalmist has known constant affliction *(verses 14-15)*. He has felt no respite, and so was tempted to express his doubts to the believing community. He knows that if he yielded then he would have caused other believers to stumble. What one believer does and says may have a profound effect upon the believing community as a whole.

Trying to work out life's problems without God's help is futile. It was a matter of grief and pain to the psalmist until he went to the Temple *(verses 16-17)*. There he suddenly came to a fresh understanding of the ultimate end facing the wicked. This could have been through some specific revelation, or through his purposeful meditation on God's great goodness (cf. verse 1). God often resolves our perplexities when we think deeply about his revealed character. Present experiences must always be evaluated in the light of God's final judgment (2 Cor. 5:10). Apparent security and prosperity cannot help in the day of judgment *(verses 18-20)*, because a house built on sand will fall with a great crash (Matt. 7:24-27). Spiritual cultivation of heart and life is needed lest the sudden coming of the Lord finds one unprepared (Mark 13:36). Quite frequently the sudden intervention of God in judgment is described in the Psalms as if he awakens from sleep (35:23; 44:23; 59:4; 78:65). Fantasies here means mere vanities, unrealities, like the image-gods so common in neighbouring cultures.

4. *A Confession* (*verses 21-22*)

As he looks back on his misunderstanding, the psalmist humbly acknowledges the huge mistake he had made. His wrong attitude had been an affront to God. He had nearly fallen into unbelief. He had shown no more spiritual knowledge of God's providential dealings than an animal. True understanding eluded him until he entered God's temple. Spiritual truths are imparted by a direct and gracious work of God (1 Cor. 2:13-16).

5. *An Affirmation of Faith* (*verses 23-28*)

The turning point in the psalm was reached earlier (verse 17), so now the profession of trust and confidence in the Lord duly follows. We read a powerful recognition of the relationship between the psalmist and his God. Despite his feelings in times of doubt, the truth remains that God has not deserted him *(verse 23)*. To be held by the right hand is a vivid way of expressing the help which God constantly gives his children (cf. Isa. 41:10, 13; 42:6).

In *verse 24* ('You guide me with your counsel, and afterward you will take me into glory'), what is affirmed is guidance in life, and presence with God after death, for in the context 'afterwards' refers back to the 'destiny' which is coming for the wicked (verse 17). While the thought of the individual believer's heavenly dwelling comes into clearer focus in the New Testament, yet passages such as this show that it was a reality for Old Testament saints as well.

The psalm draws to a close on the note of triumphant confidence in God *(verses 25-26)*. What other saviour and sustainer is there besides the Lord? Even though the psalmist's physical and mental powers fail, yet God remains his strength (Hebrew, 'rock'). He has seen that other earthly treasures fail, but that there is eternal blessing in God's presence.

> Fading is the worldling's pleasure,
> All his boasted pomp and show;
> Solid joys and lasting treasure
> None but Zion's children know.

(John Newton 1725-1807)

Unbelievers are far from God, and their continued unbelief keeps them there *(verse 27)*. It is only through the blood of Christ that those who are far away can be brought near (Eph. 2:13). The word rendered 'unfaithful' is the technical term for the prostitute, but it is used in this psalm and elsewhere (see, e.g. Lev. 20:6) to describe any form of departure from God and his standards. The final contrast of the Psalm is in the last verse. The psalmist returns to his opening theme (verse 1) and re-asserts in personal terms how wonderful it is to be within God's saving mercy. He has found his lasting refuge, greatly values it, and therefore desires to tell others of all that God has done.

PSALM 74
A maskil of Asaph.

The devastation caused by the destruction of Jerusalem by the Babylonians in 586 BC left a deep impression on the faithful believers. They mourned the loss of the Temple, the absence of prophets, and the seeming rejection of the covenant. This psalm, probably from a later member of the sons of Asaph, comes from some period after the destruction of the Temple, when it appeared that the distress had lasted 'for ever'. It has many similarities to the conclusion of Psalm 89 and to the Book of Lamentations. It should also be compared for its covenant orientation with Daniel's prayer (Dan. 9:4-19).

1. *An Appeal to God (verses 1-2)*
Even though the fall of Jerusalem may well have been but a comparatively short time before, yet to the psalmist it seems as if it has been forever. To feel 'rejected' is common in psalms of complaint (see Pss. 44:9, 23; 60:1, 10; 77:7; 88:14; 89:38), even for those who claim to be the flock of God. His plea is that God will remember the people he purchased long ago at the time of the Exodus. The two verbs 'purchase' and 'redeem' are used together in Exodus 15:13, 16, and in the same Song of the Sea there is reference to Israel being planted on the mountain of God's inheritance (Exod. 15:17).

2. *A Destroyed Temple* (*verses 3-8*)

Historical accounts of the destruction of Jerusalem and its Temple, by the Babylonians, are given in 2 Kings 25:8-17 and 2 Chronicles 36:17-19. The sanctuary was invaded and they marked their conquest by setting up their military standards there. At the very place where God met with his people *(verses 3-4)*, there the Babylonians committed atrocities including murder (2 Chr. 36:17).

The Most Holy Place had cedar panelling (1 Kgs. 6:16) and it was attacked as if it were a clump of trees to be felled (*verses 5-6*). That destruction was completed by the burning of the Temple (*verse 7*, see 2 Kgs. 25:9; 2 Chr. 36:19). This was an act of defilement of the place where God had recorded his Name. Isaiah explains that this was not only an act of the Babylonians but God himself defiled his own inheritance because his people broke his laws (Isa. 47:6, 'desecrated').

The Babylonians under Nebuzaradan were determined to crush rebellious Israel, and they did so with overwhelming force *(verse 8)*. It is hard to know if the reference to burning is meant to apply just to the Temple (the singular of the 'place where God was worshipped' is used in verse 4 of the Temple). More probably it refers to other worship centres such as had existed in Elijah's time (1 Kgs. 19:10, 14), and which had arisen again after Josiah's attempt to centralise the worship in Jerusalem.

3. *A Cry for Help* (*verses 9-11*)

The only 'signs' *(verse 9)* which the people see are the military standards of the Babylonians (verse 4; the same word is used in Hebrew for 'standards' and 'signs'). They are without the valuable ministry of prophets to teach and guide them (cf. Lam. 2:9, 'her prophets no longer find visions from the LORD'). If the people had listened to Jeremiah, they would not have to ask the question, 'How long?' (see Jer. 25:9-12).

The devastation of Jerusalem and the people (by exile) is viewed as an affront to God *(verses 10-11)*. The people still cannot understand why God does not intervene and alter the whole situation. This prayer should be compared with that of Daniel, who after confessing that God's righteous judgments had come on the people, pleads for God's favour on the desolate sanctuary, the city and the people: 'For your sake, O my God, do not delay' (Dan. 9:17-19).

4. *The Record of the Past* (*verses 12-17*)

Suddenly the psalmist recalls great events of the past, in which God's power had been displayed *(verses 12-14)*. Whereas in other Near Eastern religions, praise was reserved for what *men* had done for the gods, in Israel praise was given for what *God* had done for his people. He had secured their salvation from slavery, dividing the waters of the Red Sea, and crushing the power of the Egyptian forces, which are called here 'the monster' and 'Leviathan'. 'Monster' not only indicates various animals and sea creatures, but also (in a figurative sense) God's powerful enemies (for other uses regarding Egypt see Isa. 51:9; Ezek. 29:3; 32:2; and in reference to Babylon, see Jer. 51:34). 'Leviathan' was probably the crocodile, and therefore a natural symbol in this poetic passage to describe the Egyptian soldiers.

The first part of *verse 15* is a reference to the incident when water came from the rock at Massah (Exod. 17:6), while the second part recalls what happened to the Jordan River when Israel needed to cross into Canaan. The same verb 'dried up' is used twice in Joshua to describe what God did to the Jordan (Josh. 4:23; 5:1).

The same God had done even greater things when he created the world *(verses 16-17)*. Hence, it was not surprising that he was able to control the waters, the day and night, the heavenly bodies, the earth, and the seasons of the year. This expresses in poetic form the basic truth of Genesis 1 regarding creation, which is enlarged further in Psalm 104.

5. *A Covenant Plea* (*verses 18-23*)

In *verses 18-19* the psalmist returns to his immediate concerns after his recollection of the power of his God. He uses the same verbs ('mocked', 'reviled') as he already has in verse 10, as he asks God to remember how his holy name has been blasphemed. Wild beasts are near, and he does not want God's dove (Israel) handed over to them for final dispatch. He pleads with God to bear in mind his afflicted people – 'Don't leave us in this state forever.'

Appeal is made to the abiding covenant relationship *(verses 20-21)*. Israel in exile was not divorced, only separated temporarily from the Lord (see Isa. 50:1; 54:4-8). The psalmist wants God to look with favour upon the land, and ensure that the present injustices stop. When that happens, even those now most oppressed, ('the poor and needy'), will be able to rejoice in his praise.

In *verse 22* another term is used in asking for God's intervention ('rise up'; see the comment on Ps. 7:6, where the same expression is used). 'Defend your cause' is a technical covenant expression which is used by the prophets when they speak of God having a legal case against his people. Here it is used of God's cause, which is also the people's cause. The enemies are not just Israel's enemies – they are God's enemies! The final plea *(verse 23)* is for the turmoil and uproar caused by these enemies to be noted by God and to stir him to action. The people had yet to learn that only when sin was confessed and repentance followed, would God restore them. Nehemiah grasped the point (Neh. 9:31) – in his great mercy God did not put an end to them, or abandon them.

PSALM 75

For the director of music. [To the tune of] 'Do Not Destroy'. A psalm of Asaph. A song.

Psalms 74 and 75 are linked thematically by the thought of God's judgment. At the end of the previous psalm the appeal has been made for God to rise up and defend his own cause (Ps. 74:22-23). In this psalm the theme of judgment occurs especially in verses 2-8, where it is made plain that the scope of that judgment is universal. There is no certain indication within the psalm of the historical setting, though the use of 'Do Not Destroy' in the title suggests it was composed in a period of impending danger for God's people.

1. *Praise to the God who is Near* (*verse 1*)
The opening song of praise is related to both the sense of the immediate presence of God with the people and the knowledge that he has acted on their behalf in a mighty way in the past. 'Name' here is used in a way similar to Exodus 23:20-21, where the Lord declared that his Name was in the angel who was being sent before the children of Israel. 'The Name of the LORD' occurs as a title for God in Isaiah 30:27. Knowledge of God's past deeds on their behalf brings reassurance to the people in their present distress.

2. *God Speaks in Judgment* (*verses 2-5*)
God speaks decisively to his people of the fact that he will intervene at his chosen time *(verses 2-3)*. He waits until the very foundations of the earth shake, lest his people think that they have been able to save

themselves. 'It is I' is emphatic, drawing attention to God's intervention, not theirs. A different form of reassurance is given to the proud *(verses 4-5)*. They need to realise that they can try and exalt themselves against God, but all their pride and boasting will come to nothing. 'Horn' is often used in the Psalms to denote power or strength (cf. 18:2; 89:17, 24), while 'outstretched neck' speaks of pride or arrogance.

3. *The Psalmist Confirms God's Judgment (verses 6-8)*
The variety of translations, both ancient and modern, of *verse 6* show that there is a difficulty. It is possible to translate the last clause of the verse as: 'from the desert to the mountains.' This would then be an assertion that no one from north or south, east or west, can usurp the place of God. He alone is the Judge and Deliverer who either brings judgment or deliverance. 'Cup' *(verse 8)* stands for God's judgment (as in Ps. 60:3), and he is pictured as putting the cup to the lips of the wicked until they drink it to the last dregs. The prophets repeatedly use the same imagery for the concept of God's wrath (see Isa. 51:17-23; Jer. 25:27-29; 49:12; Hab. 2:15-16).

4. *A Final Song of Thanksgiving (verses 9-10)*
The song of praise which began the psalm is repeated at the close, though now it is not communal ('we') but personal ('I'). In contrast to the arrogant oppressors, the psalmist will constantly sing praise to his God. It is surprising the number of times in the Psalter that God is called 'the God of Jacob' (20:1; 24:6; 46:7; 76:6; 81:1, 4; 84:8; 94:7; 114:7; 132:2, 5; 146:5). This is either to recall the special relationship between God and Jacob, or else a reminder that he is still the God of Jacob's descendants. The psalmist thinks of himself as sharing in the execution of God's judgment on the wicked, but he knows that at the same time the righteous are going to be exalted. For us today the principle remains valid that 'whoever exalts himself will be humbled' (Matt. 23:12).

PSALM 76
For the director of music. With stringed instruments. A psalm of Asaph. A song.

Psalms 75 and 76 fit together as a unit, for while Psalm 75 looks forward to the coming of God's judgment, this psalm rejoices in the fact that it has come. The actual occasion is not mentioned in the psalm.

However, the Septuagint adds to the title, 'concerning the Assyrian', suggesting the defeat of Sennacherib and his forces as recorded in 2 Kings 19 and Isaiah 37. Verses 6-7 and 11-12 could relate to this unusual victory, but nothing allows definite identification.

1. *God and His People (verses 1-3)*

God and his people are linked in a special way. Among his own people he has revealed himself *(verses 1-2)*. 'Judah' and 'Israel' are used in parallel to describe the whole nation. Moreover, the ark of the covenant has been housed in Salem (short for 'Jerusalem'), so that Zion, where the temple stood, can be viewed as God's dwelling place. The use of 'Salem' may be deliberate in order to highlight its meaning of 'peace' (cf. 'Shalom'). It was at Jerusalem *(verse 3)* that the Lord brought peace to his people, by destroying the weapons of war which were formerly used against them. 'There', in Jerusalem, where his name is great, he showed his power by overcoming the attackers.

2. *God Victorious (verses 4-10)*

Verses 4-6 certainly match the idea that the victory was over the Assyrians. On the mountains where the Assyrians planned to make Jerusalem their prey, they became the prey themselves. God had appeared in his glory, and he had destroyed the attackers (cf. 2 Kgs. 19:35). The connection with that event is strengthened by the fact that God had made a promise concerning Assyria: 'I will crush the Assyrian in my land; on my mountains I will trample him down' (Isa. 14:25). The reference to 'the God of Jacob' links this psalm with the previous one (see Ps. 75:9). Before the Lord his people must stand in awe *(verse 7,* cf. Isa. 8:13). Human might fades into insignificance before his presence.

The victory is viewed as a heavenly judgment which brings silence to the earth *(verses 8-9)*. On the one hand, God's action is judgment, while on the other it is salvation. Such redemptive judgment comes to its greatest expression in the cross of Calvary, where God's judgment and his mercy meet. *Verse 10* is very condensed in the Hebrew text and various ways of understanding it are possible. A fairly literal rendering is probably best: *Surely the wrath of man brings you praise, and you will gird yourself with the remainder of wrath.* This means that in the end man's anger against God will bring praise to God. Even the final outburst of that anger will serve as a garment or ornament for God's glory.

3. A Final Act of Worship (verses 11-12)
Because of God's intervention on behalf of his people, the call goes out to Israel and the surrounding nations to pay homage to him. The expression 'bring gifts' is used elsewhere of offering homage to the LORD in a time of judgment, and doing so at the temple in Jerusalem (Ps. 68:29; Isa. 18:7). What happened to Israel was inevitably noted by surrounding nations (Deut. 4:6-8), and after God's deliverance of Hezekiah many did bring gifts to Jerusalem (2 Chr. 32:20-23).

PSALM 77
For the director of music. For Jeduthun. Of Asaph. A psalm.

This psalm is the heartfelt cry of an individual to God, though there is nothing in the text to link it with any specific incident or date. What is remarkable is the change in tone as the writer recalls the LORD's powerful deeds, especially those connected with redeeming his people from Egypt. The poet's own troubles recede into the background as he remembers this great redemption.

1. Appeal in Distress (verses 1-3)
The urgency of his request is shown by the repetition of his appeal *(verse 1)*. Literally it is simply, 'my voice to God ... my voice to God'. Instead of becoming preoccupied with his own feelings, the psalmist turns his attention to the only true source of help. Just how deep his distress was becomes clear later in the psalm (see especially verses 7-9).

'To seek the Lord' *(verse 2)* is a common Old Testament expression. Often it means 'to seek with care', and the end in view is to gain knowledge or insight into a particular problem. In distress the psalmist prayed with hands outstretched in typical Oriental fashion, and he had found no help in human comforters. He meditates on the past actions of God. Clearly this forms the basis of his comfort which becomes stronger as the psalm progresses. While he felt keenly his present position, this meditation was the beginning of encouragement for him, as it gave new hope.

2. Remembering God's Mercies (verses 4-9)
At night when he could not sleep, the psalmist's perplexity was so great that he could not even utter words; all he could do was to let thoughts and memories of long ago flood through his mind *(verses 4-5)*. The

same word 'thought' occurs when Malachi is commending those who feared the Lord and 'thought' on his name (Mal. 3:16). In the past the psalmist had sung songs in the night, which seemed to help him sleep; however, at present this is no longer the case *(verses 6-9)*. Rather, his mind is full of questions about God's present dealings with his people. In tone the many questions he asks are like those in Psalm 85:5-6. It is striking that he looks beyond his personal distress, and mourns for the community as a whole ('Will the Lord reject *us*?'). He asks why God's forgiving grace is not shown to the people, nor his covenant love ('unfailing love') maintained towards them. If God is true to his word ('promise', verse 8; cf. God's own declaration of his nature in Exod. 34:6-7), then why is he not again showing his mercy and grace?

3. *Recollection of God's Mercies* (*verses 10-12*)

These questions just asked, all require the answer, 'No!' In the midst of his sleeplessness, he suddenly realises that the past history of Israel should give him the answers to his present perplexities *(verse 10)*. In particular the use of the name 'Most High' recalls the use of this title for God by Abraham (Gen. 14:22) after a notable victory. The psalmist finds encouragement in the mighty acts of God for his people in the past *(verses 11-12)*. These wonderful acts were things which only God could do (see on Pss. 71:17; 72:18). Different synonyms (NIV 'deeds', 'miracles', 'works'; the Hebrew also uses a fourth synonym, 'mighty deeds') are used to describe God's actions and portray the variety of ways in which he has acted towards and on behalf of his people. Meditation on God's actions for his people (both in biblical history and since) should always be an encouragement for the believing community.

4. *Confidence from Great Redemptive Deeds* (*verses 13-20*).

The contemplation of God's past deeds brings out this declaration of the holy nature of his actions: 'Your ways, O God, are holy. What god is so great as our God? You are the God who performs miracles; you display your power among the peoples' (*verses 13-14*). The question, 'What god is so great as our God?', recalls the statements to the same effect in Exodus 15:11, Deuteronomy 7:21 and 10:17, and Psalm 95:3. God's wonders are a demonstration both of his power and his love (see Ps. 31:21, God performs 'marvels of love'). They were intended not only for his own people, but also as a display among the surrounding nations. Even the Gentiles would have to say: 'The LORD has done great things for them' (Ps. 126:2b).

God's 'arm' is a way of describing his power *(verse 15)*. It occurs frequently in Deuteronomy, either by itself, or along with the word 'hand', as a way of speaking of God's power in redeeming his people from Egypt. While the term 'Joseph' can be used only of the northern tribes, yet here it is a synonym for 'Israel', the whole nation (as in Obad. 18).

The psalmist expresses in poetic language what happened when God intervened to let his people cross the Red Sea *(verse 16)*. Frequently in the Old Testament similar heightened descriptions are given in poetry of the events of the Exodus (cf. Exod. 15:8; Ps. 114:3-5). Here, not only are the waters in turmoil, but they are in travail.

No mention is made in the Book of Exodus of a thunderstorm or an earthquake at the time the children of Israel crossed the Red Sea *(verses 17-18)*. When God showed his glory and majesty at that time, he displayed his control over creation so that the flashes of lightning seemed to be his arrows. For the Canaanites Baal was the storm god, but the Israelites knew that their Redeemer was the God of great power and wonders. Not surprisingly, when he came as Redeemer, the Lord Jesus showed his control of all creation (Mark 4:35-41).

God guided the children of Israel by a pillar of cloud by day and a pillar of fire by night (*verses 19-20*, Exod. 13:21-22). They did not *see* God himself, just as Moses did not see him when he revealed to him his glory (Exod. 33:18-34:9). Hence in poetic terms, God's 'footprints were not seen'. God was the great shepherd who guided his own flock (cf. Pss. 78:52; 80:1), using Moses and Aaron as the great leaders. Isaiah 63:11-14 also describes the role of Moses as the shepherd who brought God's flock out of Egypt. The psalm may seem to come to an abrupt end, but the implications of past history would be clear. The God who saved his people in such a wonderful way could do so yet again.

PSALM 78
A maskil of Asaph.

While the opening of this psalm resembles the wisdom psalms (49 and 73) and also has strong affinities in style with the opening chapters of the Book of Proverbs, its main purpose is really to give a recital of the great historical events in Israel's history. In particular, it concentrates on events which confirm God's covenant dealings with his people, and in so doing acts as a call to faithfulness on the part of its readers and hearers in later generations. Whereas other Near Eastern peoples praised their human leaders, Israel praised God who had done so many wonderful things for her. The mention of David (verses 70-72) links this psalm with the previous one, which ended with reference to Moses and Aaron, earlier leaders of God's people. The use of the term 'Ephraim' is used to designate 'Israel', as it was the dominant tribe of the northern kingdom. Hosea and Isaiah both do the same, and it is likely that this psalm comes from the same period as the one in which these prophets ministered.

The pattern of the psalm is quite symmetrical. It has an introduction which gives the purpose of the psalm. Then follows the major part of the psalm (verses 17-64), flanked at beginning and end by a stanza which highlights the sin of Ephraim (verses 9-16) and the final one (verses 65-72) which focuses on God's salvation and his choice of David and Jerusalem. The overall pattern can be shown in this way:

1. Introductory call to pass on this teaching (vss 1-8)
2. Accusations against Ephraim (vss. 9-16)
3. First Cycle (vss. 17-39)
    3.1 Recollection of wilderness experiences (vss. 17-31)
    3.2 Judgment and mercy (vss. 32-39)
4. Second Cycle (vss. 40-64)
    4.1 Recollection of wilderness experiences (vss 40-55)
    4.2 Judgment and mercy (vss. 56-64)
5. Promises to Judah and Jerusalem (vss. 65-72)

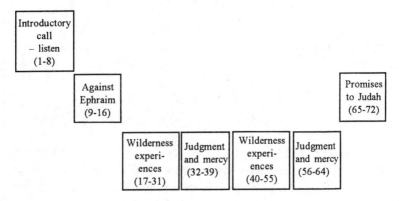

1. *Introductory Call to Pass on this Teaching (verses 1-8)*
One of the great responsibilities of parents and elders in Israel was to pass on the knowledge of the LORD to successive generations (see Deut. 6:4-9; 11:18-21; 29:29). The same responsibilities continue for Christians both in regard to children (Eph. 6:4) and adults (1 Tim. 4:11-14; Tit. 2:1-15). The Hebrew text places stress on the aspect of hearing: 'Give ear, my people, [to] my teaching; incline your ears to the words of my mouth' *(verse 1)*. Faith comes by hearing the message, and the message is heard through the word of Christ (Rom. 10:17).

The Hebrew word translated here by 'parables' *(verse 2)* has a somewhat different connotation than our English word 'parable'. It is used far more extensively than just for short sayings of general truth. It often appears either as a longer teaching passage (see Prov. 1:8-19) or as here, when the actions of an individual or a group are made a public example to others. The reader or hearer has to come to a judgment on himself or his situation, a principle which comes to fullest expression in the parables of Jesus. The word for 'hidden things' seems to have a similar meaning here. The lessons from Israel's history, which have been passed down from generation to generation, had to be passed on to children and grandchildren.

These object lessons from history were not to be concealed, but rather revealed! *(verse 4)*. Covenant history was a record of what God had done for his people, and the power and wonderful deeds which he had demonstrated were things requiring praise and adoration. The word 'hide' conveys the idea of refusing to make something known. The truth about the past had to be told to successive generations.

The basic demands of God expressed in the covenant responsibilities were to be taught generation after generation (Exod. 10:2; 12:26-27; Deut. 6:6-9, 20-22; 11:19-21). The process of educating later generations was specified by the LORD *(verses 5-6)*. The gap between the generations was to be bridged by instruction, so that there would be continuity in transmission of the statutes and laws of the LORD.

This transmission was intended to be something more than just knowledge of the past *(verses 7-8)*. It was to bring each generation to personal confidence in God, so that from the heart they would revere and obey him. In particular, this would avoid the problem which arose with the wilderness generation, which is often characterised, as here, as being stubborn and rebellious (Deut. 9:6-7, 13, 24; 31:27; 32:5, 20). There is the constant danger that a head knowledge of biblical history

will replace a heart relationship with God, and obedience which stems
from love to him.

2. *Accusations against Ephraim* (*verses 9-16*)

The central part of the psalm begins with reference to the northern
kingdom of Israel, here called Ephraim after its most dominant tribe.
The closing part of the psalm focuses by contrast on the southern
kingdom of Judah, for God 'did not choose the tribe of Ephraim; but he
chose the tribe of Judah, Mount Zion, which he loved' (verses 67-68).

There is no record of specific mention of the tribe of Ephraim being
cowardly in battle *(verses 9-10)*. The reference seems rather to be a
general one of disloyalty to God and the requirements of his covenant.
From its very beginning in approximately 931 BC the northern kingdom was marked by a rejection of covenant obligations, and the
alterations which Jeroboam I felt free to make in patterns of worship,
were evidence of this (1 Kgs. 12:25-33). Ultimately the northern
kingdom fell (in 720 BC) because its people rejected God's 'decrees
and the covenant he had made with their fathers and the warnings he
had given them' (2 Kgs. 17:15).

Before Israel even entered Canaan, God had warned about the
dangers of forgetfulness (see especially Deut. 8) and indicated the
covenant curses which would come upon a disobedient people (Lev.
26:14-35; Deut. 28:15-68). The psalmist recalls events which should
have reminded Ephraim of God's grace and power, and these memories should have helped to keep them faithful to the LORD *(verses 11-
12)*. He begins with the demonstration of divine power shown in the
miracles which took place in Egypt, mentioning specifically Zoan, a
city in the north-east of the Nile delta. Fuller details are given later of
the various plagues (see verses 44-51).

There were further miracles as Israel was led out of Egypt, and a
summary is given of the miraculous way in which God brought his
people through the Red Sea *(verses 13-14)*. Constant guidance was
provided by the cloud and by the fire (Exod. 13:21-22), so that Israel
was never without direction and protection from the Lord. One
impressive miracle was the provision of water from a rock *(verses 15-
16*, see Exodus 17:1-8). In addition to this passage other poets and
prophets celebrate the same provision which God made for his people
(see Pss. 105:41; 114:8; Isa. 48:21).

3. First Cycle: The Wilderness Experiences (1) (verses 17-31)
Mentioning the provision of water clearly recalled for the poet the way
in which Israel rebelled against the LORD, and doubtless he expected
his readers to bring the same episodes to mind *(verses 17-20)*. Even
redeemed Israel was noted for a spirit of constant grumbling against
the LORD and his provision for them. They 'rebelled' against their God,
the majestic and exalted God (cf. the use of the term 'the Most High'
in other psalms such as 18:13; 73:11; 77:10; 83:18). The contrast
between God's gracious provision and the sinful behaviour of Israel is
often brought out in this psalm by the use of 'he' and 'they'. To 'rebel'
against God is a technical term, used almost exclusively of the action
of Israel against God (forty out of forty-five times in the Old Testament). It is used particularly of what happened in the wilderness, and
it occurs four times in this psalm (verses 8, 17, 40, 56). At times the
rebellion was merely oral complaint (as at Massah), but here and at
other times the people were challenging God to provide special food
to meet their tastes. The psalmist seems to be combining the two
incidents of Exodus 16:2-3 and Numbers 11:4-6.

God's response was one of anger against his people *(verses 21-22)*,
and some of them died because of fire which he sent at Taberah (Num.
11:1-3). As a result of Moses' intercession the rest of the people were
spared. The reference to not believing in God seems to be an echo of
Exodus 14:31 ('the people feared the LORD and put their trust [lit.
'believed'] in him and in Moses his servant'). At the outset of their
wilderness wanderings they believed in the LORD, but soon they
reached the opposite position of distrust both in himself and his saving
power.

In spite of the unbelief of the people, God provided for them *(verses
23-25)*, sending down manna as if it was being poured out of the open
doors of heaven (for this expression, cf. Gen. 7:11; 2 Kgs. 7:2; Mal.
3:10). Elsewhere the manna is called 'bread of heaven' (Exod. 16:4;
Ps. 105:40; John 6:31-32) while Paul calls it 'spiritual food' (1 Cor.
10:3). The fact that it was divine provision is emphasised by calling it
'the bread of angels', and the provision was so liberal that their hunger
was completely satisfied.

The account in Numbers of the giving of the quail as a source of
meat supply does not specify the wind directions as here *(verses 26-
27)*. It simply says that the wind of the LORD brought them in from the
sea (Num. 11:31). If the quail were migrating at this time, then the

south wind would bring them north and the east wind would direct them across to where Israel was encamped. The quails were brought right to where Israel was encamped *(verses 28-29)*, inside the camp (Exod. 16:13) and round about it (Num. 11:31). What they lusted after, they received in abundance, even to the point where they loathed it. The use of the word 'craved' (Heb. *ta'avah*) alludes to the place name Kibroth Hattaavah, 'graves of craving' (Num. 11:34).

The psalmist returns to the theme of God's anger (see verse 21) and shows how that anger manifested itself *(verses 30-31)*. While they were still pleased with God's provision (Hebrew, 'they were not yet estranged from their desire') and had it in their mouths, God struck down the strongest of the young men, so that 'their bodies were scattered over the desert' (1 Cor. 10:5). This verse is clearly dependent on Numbers 11:33.

3. First Cycle: Judgment and Mercy (1) (verses 32-39)

Experience of God in both gracious provision and demonstration of wrath did not change the Israelites. The poet summarises the repeated acts of God in dealing with his people, as he showed both goodness and severity to them. In every generation the believing child of God can look back on life and say:

> With mercy and with judgment
>   My web of time He wove,
> And aye the dews of sorrow
>   Were lustred by His love;
> I'll bless the hand that guided,
>   I'll bless the heart that planned,
> When throned where glory dwelleth
>   In Immanuel's land.
>
> (Anne Ross Cousin 1824-1906)

In *verses 32-33* it is probably the rebellion of the people after the return of the spies that is chiefly in view (cf. verse 32b with Num. 14:11). Judgment was pronounced against all the men of twenty years of age and upward who had grumbled against the LORD (Num. 14:26-38). Those who had spread the disparaging report about the land of Canaan died of a plague (verse 37), so ending their days in futility and terror (terms descriptive of the brevity and uncertainty of life).

The cycle of events summarised in *verses 34-35* was typical of the period of the judges in particular (see the fuller description of the period in Judg. 2:6-23). God's judgment upon the people brought them to a realisation of their need of mercy, and so they sought him in their affliction. Temporary forgetfulness was replaced by memory of the fact that God was both their Refuge and their Redeemer. To call God 'their Rock' recalls an ancient title for the God of Israel (cf. Deut. 32:4, 15, 18, 31).

Verses 36-37 suggest that the people were deceitful, making promises which they had no intention of keeping, or else rash promises which they were unable to fulfil. Their turning to God was not from the heart, but only an expression with their lips (cf. Isa. 29:13; Jer. 12:2). Unfaithfulness to covenant commitments was characteristic of them, a point which has already been made earlier in the psalm (see verse 10).

In spite of all the repeated sin of Israel, yet God still displayed his character as the compassionate God (*verses 38-39*, cf. Exod. 34:6; Deut. 4:31; Num. 14:18). He made atonement for their sin by the provision of a substitute. Hence, he did not completely destroy them all, holding back his anger so that the people were not exposed to the full demonstration of his wrath. He knew the frailty of his people, and his understanding of their weakness awakened his compassion for them. The thought of verse 39 is developed more fully in Psalm 103:14-16.

4. *Second Cycle: The Wilderness Experiences (2) (verses 40-55)*

Rebellion against their covenant God was not just an isolated incident but something repeated over and over again *(verses 40-41)* (For the technical expression 'to rebel' see the comment on verse 17.) Isaiah uses the same language of Israel rebelling and grieving the Holy Spirit (Isa. 63:10). In spite of a clear instruction not to put God to the test as at Massah (Deut. 6:16) Israel did so, and this is emphasised in this historical song by mention of it three times (verses 18, 41, 56). The Hebrew word for 'vexed' occurs only here in the Old Testament, but there is no doubt as to its meaning in the context.

At times Israel could remember the LORD (see verse 35), but at other times the people were utterly forgetful of his great love and power shown to them *(verses 42-43)*. There may be the suggestion that this forgetfulness was a deliberate neglect of the LORD. He had promised to stretch out his hand against Egypt (Exod. 3:20), and did so, yet Israel forgot 'his power' (Hebrew, 'his hand'). The Redeemer of Israel had shown his 'signs' (cf. Exod. 4:9, 28, 30) and 'wonders' (cf. Deut. 29:3;

34:11), and even these miraculous demonstrations were not recalled.

Several of the plagues are mentioned, though not in chronological order *(verses 44-51)*.

first plague:	river of blood (verse 44)
fourth plague:	flies (verse 45a)
second plague:	frogs (verse 45b)
eighth plague:	locusts (verse 46)
seventh plague:	hail and lightning (verse 47)
fifth plague:	death of animals (verse 48)
tenth plague:	death of the firstborn (verses 50-51)

These plagues were to convince Pharaoh and his people to let the Israelites go. They culminated in the final plague, the death of the firstborn, and it is that final judgment which receives the emphasis here (verses 49-51). Four terms are used to describe God's attitude to the Egyptians ('hot anger', 'wrath', 'indignation', 'hostility'), and they are likened to a band of angels bringing calamities. God's anger was not restrained, and it resulted in the death of Egypt's firstborn. Elsewhere in the Psalms Egypt is called 'the land of Ham' (Pss. 105:23, 27; 106:22), and 'the tents of Ham' which occurs in verse 51 seems to be identical in meaning, even though this is its only occurrence in the Old Testament.

In describing the Exodus from Egypt *(verses 52-53)* the poet uses one of the terms which is often used in the Book of Exodus of the journeyings of Israel ('brought out', Exod. 15:22). He pictures Israel as a flock of sheep or goats (the Hebrew term refers to small animals) being led and cared for by God. The same imagery is also found in Psalms 74:1 and 80:1. Whereas the Egyptians were seized with panic, Israel had no reason to be afraid because God's saving power was shown in their deliverance (Exod. 14:13). Judgment came on the pursuing Egyptians and the sea covered them (NIV 'engulfed', the same word as in Exod. 15:10).

Some commentators have taken the reference to the territory in *verse 54* to be to the holy mountain, i.e. Zion, but the NIV translation makes excellent sense. God brought Israel to the eastern border of Canaan, the land of his choice and the land separated off for Israel's use, and hence 'holy land'. Then the hill country there was taken, and after entry into Canaan the other nations were driven out and the tribes were allotted their territory *(verse 55)*. The victory was the LORD's ('the nations *I* conquered', Josh. 23:4) and he allotted to them their inheritance (Ps. 105:11).

4. *Second Cycle: Judgment and Mercy (2)* (*verses 56-64*)

Once more the refrain of putting God to the test and rebelling against him is added (*verses 56-57*, cf. verses 8, 17, and 40). Possession of the 'holy land' did not change the character of the people, and they were no different from their forefathers. The Book of Judges and the early chapters of 1 Samuel provide many illustrations of disloyalty and faithlessness. The illustration of a faulty bow which disappoints the user is also used by Hosea of the waywardness of the northern kingdom (Hos. 7:16).

Often the people resorted to Canaanitish sites of sacrifice, or else built new local altars on hills. These led to the introduction of pagan practices into their worship, including idols. Because these challenged God's exclusive claims, his jealousy was provoked (*verses 58-59*). When he heard their prayers to such idols, he was angry and gave them over to their enemies. This must be the meaning of 'rejected completely' in this verse, as God never utterly abandoned his people, including the ten northern tribes.

What God did abandon was Shiloh (*verses 60-61*), the place where the ark was located from the time of Joshua (Josh. 18:1) until Shiloh was destroyed by the Philistines, seemingly at the time when God allowed them to capture the ark (1 Sam. 4:1-11; Jer. 7:12). In Psalm 132:8 the ark is called 'the ark of your might', while here 'might' and 'splendour' are used to describe it. The ark was a visible indication of God's strength and glory.

When the ark was captured, Israel was indeed put to the sword, losing 30,000 soldiers (*verses 62-64*, see 1 Sam. 4:10). The fact that God's anger was directed against 'his people', 'his inheritance', emphasises how greatly he was provoked by the sin of Israel. The young men in particular were killed in battle, and therefore many young women were unable to find husbands. The reference to priests dying is probably an allusion to what happened to the sons of the priest Eli, when the ark was taken (1 Sam. 4:11, 17). Likewise the reference to widows is especially to the wife of Phinehas who died in childbirth after hearing of the death of her husband and father-in-law (1 Sam. 4:19-22). As she was dying she named her son, 'Ichabod' ('no glory', or 'where is the glory?').

5. *Promises to Judah and Jerusalem* (*verses 65-72*)

The concluding section of the psalm balances the earlier one dealing with Ephraim (verses 9-16) by showing how God had chosen Judah (not Ephraim), Zion (not Shiloh), and David to fulfil his purposes. In comparison with previous periods, the time of David was a wonderful manifestation of God's action on behalf of his people. It was as if the sleeping warrior woke up and intervened on their behalf *(verse 65)*. It is possible to translate the second part of the verse, 'as a man shouts [or, 'is stimulated by'] wine', which would give a better parallel with 'wakes' (see RSV and NKJ).

While there are no details given of the victories referred to in *verse 66*, the context suggests that the reference is to those of David, and possibly also to those of Samuel and Saul. In addition, the word 'enemies' (lit. 'oppressors') points to the Philistines as intended, so that the victories would be those of 1 Samuel 5 onwards.

In *verses 67-69* the contrast is very pronounced: 'He *did not choose* ... but he *chose*'. God's choice was not the tribe of Ephraim (called here 'the tents of Joseph') but the tribe of Judah. Likewise, his choice was not Shiloh (cf. verse 60), but Mount Zion. To Zion the ark of the covenant was brought and there the temple was built. It seemed as secure as the earth itself. The description of it as being 'forever' has to be understood in the sense of lasting into the distant future, not lasting eternally. Because of the sins of the people Zion was to be captured and the sanctuary destroyed at the time of the Exile.

The historical narrative of the appointment of David draws attention to the fact that he was tending the sheep when the call came to him to be the shepherd of Israel (1 Sam. 16:11-13). When the elders of the northern tribes came to Hebron to anoint David king over Israel, they referred to God's promise to him: 'You will shepherd my people Israel' (2 Sam. 5:2). He was God's choice *(verses 70-72)*, and in that sense a man after God's own heart (1 Sam. 13:14). While the sanctuary in Jerusalem was important, yet the most important sign of God's presence with Israel was David, the chosen king. In general, he carried out his role with uprightness and knowledge, except in particular for the incident regarding Bathsheba and Uriah. David the shepherd of Israel became the hope of the Old Testament prophets (Ezek. 34:23; 37:24; Mic. 5:4), and in Jesus that hope was fulfilled (Matt. 2:6; Rev. 7:17).

PSALM 79
A psalm of Asaph.

The setting of this psalm seems to be the period just after the fall of
Jerusalem in 586 BC, and hence it shares many themes with Psalm 74.
The exiles, banished from the land, had seen so much destruction
wrought by the Babylonians. They now reflect on this, and particularly
on the underlying hatred towards the LORD and his people. The appeal
is to God for pardon and deliverance. They, as the flock of God (verse
13), want to be able to praise the LORD forever.

1. A National Lament (verses 1-4)
Even though the destruction of their cities was threatened long before
by Moses (Deut. 28:52), yet when it came the people were shattered by
it *(verse 1)*. The invaders had no thought that the land was God's
inheritance, nor that the temple was sacred. They came against Judah,
destroyed the temple (cf. the description in Ps. 74:4-7), and made
Jerusalem just a heap of stones. In spite of what had happened to
Jerusalem, the psalmist still knows that God has not completely cast
off his people. In his prayer he calls them 'your servants', 'your saints'
(verse 2). The historical accounts record the massive loss of life at the
time of the fall of Jerusalem (see especially 2 Chr. 36:17). The
reference to the bodies being left unburied as food for the birds of the
air may well be echoing Jeremiah's description of the death of the
covenant breakers *(verse 3*, see Jer. 34:17-20). *Verse 4* is almost
identical to Psalm 44:13. Instead of fulfilling a missionary function to
the surrounding nations, Israel had become a laughing stock. They cast
scorn on her, ridiculing her as her slain inhabitants lie unburied, and
others taken away into exile (cf. Dan. 9:16).

2. A Prayer for Forgiveness (verses 5-8)
The question 'How long?' *(verse 5)* marks the start of the prayer, and
it also suggests confidence in the LORD. The psalmist knew that he was
not going to leave them for ever in their present distress. The closest
parallel is Psalm 89:46. God was a jealous husband of Israel (Exod.
20:5), and the psalmist is appealing for an end to this period of anger.
    The threat of the covenant curse against unfaithful Israel also
involved turning that curse on the persecuting enemies (Deut. 30:7).
Of the prophets, Jeremiah and Ezekiel both speak of the way in which

God is going to turn his jealous wrath against the nations (cf. Jer. 50:9-16; Ezek. 36:5-7). The psalmist calls on God to honour his commitment *(verses 6-7)*, and he uses words taken almost exactly from Jeremiah 10:25. The prayer is an appeal for God's justice to be manifest.

The psalmist acknowledges that it was 'the sins of the fathers' which had caused the exile *(verse 8)*. This is a reference to the sins of those just prior to the exile (2 Kgs. 24:3 mentions particularly the sins of Manasseh). He beseeches God to show divine compassion to his afflicted people, not holding against them any longer the sins of a previous generation.

3. *A Prayer for Help* (verses 9-11)

While 'the fathers' had sinned, so also had those in exile *(verse 9)*. Hence the request for forgiveness, though the appeal is not for their sake. The only basis the psalmist could plead was that it would be for God's honour and for *his* name's sake (cf. Dan. 9:19). He knew that the only source of deliverance would be from the one he calls 'our Saviour'.

If God did not intervene, then the outcome would be that the heathen nations would make derisive comments about Israel's God *(verses 10-11)*. Instead of glory being given to him, his name would be a reproach. While the exile was a judgment on Israel, yet the psalmist wants to see those who carried out the massacres of the people punished. The exiles are called 'prisoners', though in fact they were not in prisons as such. They were compelled to stay in Babylonia, and any attempt on their part to return home would result in death.

4. *A Vow of Praise* (verses 12-13)

This appeal for judgment on the enemies of Israel does not stem from a sense of personal vindictiveness. The psalmist wants payment made in full measure to them (symbolised by the use of the number seven) because of what they had done *to God*. They had reviled him, and if the surrounding nations met their just reward, then Israel would in contrast praise the Lord's name for ever. Recovery of the prisoners would become a topic to be recounted from generation to generation. God's flock would rejoice in the memory of what their shepherd had done for them.

PSALM 80

*For the director of music. To [the tune of] 'The Lilies of the Cov-
enant.' Of Asaph. A psalm.*

The references in this song suggest that it came from the northern
kingdom of Israel, or else the author lived in the kingdom of Judah but
had a very deep interest in the north. It may be from about the time of
the attacks by Assyria which culminated in the fall of Samaria in 722
BC. The Septuagint version has the addition of the words 'concerning
the Assyrian' in the title, which lends some support to this suggestion.
It comes from a time of disaster for the nation, when foreign invaders
had trampled down the country. Appeal is made on the basis of God's
past help, and the assurance that Israel is a transplanted vine occupying
the land of God's appointment.

1. An Appeal for Help (verses 1-3)
The title used here for God – 'Shepherd of Israel' *(verse 1)* – goes back
to Genesis 48:15, where Jacob says: 'The God before whom my fathers
Abraham and Isaac walked, the God who has been my shepherd all my
life to this day.' 'Joseph' is used as a convenient designation of the ten
northern tribes which formed the nation of Israel, with the tribes named
after Joseph's sons (Ephraim and Manasseh) linked with the tribe of
Benjamin as a parallel expression in verse 2. The appeal is to the God
of power who sits enthroned between the cherubim (cf. 1 Sam. 4:4; 2
Sam. 6:2; 2 Kgs. 19:15). The idea is probably more than simply that
God is enthroned above the mercy seat. He is seated on his heavenly
throne. From there he is asked to come and execute judgment and lead
his people as of old, restoring them to their former position *(verse 2)*.

Verse 3 has the first occurrence of the threefold refrain used in the
psalm (see also verses 7 and 19). The prayer is expressed in terms of
the Aaronic blessing (Num. 6:25). God's face is pictured as being
hidden from them, and now fulfilment of the blessing is requested. If
that happens, then they will be delivered according to their request.

2. A Lament over Punishment (verses 4-7)
The psalmist recognises that the afflictions which the people are
undergoing have been caused by God's anger *(verses 4-5)*. The
historical account of the fall of the northern kingdom stresses this
aspect (2 Kgs. 17:17-18). The anger is said to be against the prayers of
the people because of the seeming lack of response on God's part to the

cries of the people. Their prayers were unavailing. Trouble and sorrow
are pictured as being their daily food, so that tears substitute for bread
and drink.

God was using the surrounding nations to bring judgment upon his
own people *(verses 6-7)*. Perhaps the mocking was in the form of the
question, 'Where is your God?' (cf. the similar theme in Ps. 42:3, 10).
In their situation of strife the people repeat the prayer which has
already been used (see verse 3). The only way that their condition can
change is for God to shine with favour on them.

3. *Prayer for the Transplanted Vine (verses 8-15)*
The Exodus from Egypt and the conquest of Canaan are described
poetically in terms of a vine being transplanted *(verses 8-11*, cf. Gen.
49:22; Isa. 5:1-7; Jer. 2:21; Hos. 14:7 for use of the imagery of the
vine). Verses 8-9 stress that the events were sovereign acts of God
('*you* brought ... *you* drove out ... *you* cleared the ground'). When the
vine was planted in Canaan, it then established itself and grew so that
it covered the territory which had been promised to Abraham (Gen.
15:18-21; 17:8; for later descriptions of the borders of Israel see Exod.
23:31; Josh. 1:3-4; 1 Kgs. 4:21, 24). The vine covered Canaan. It
reached north to the mountains [of Lebanon] and westward to the
[Mediterranean] Sea. On the north-east it reached as far as the
[Euphrates] River.

Continuing with the analogy of the vine, the psalmist speaks of the
way in which the defences of Israel have been broken down so that the
land has been exposed to the invaders *(verses 12-13)*. The fruit of the
vine is being taken by others who have no right to it. The boar was an
unclean animal (Deut. 14:8), and destructive, and therefore it was a
suitable description for Israel's enemies.

The appeal is for a visitation of God to remedy the situation *(verses
14-15)*. 'Watch over' translates a Hebrew verb which means 'to visit'.
Such a visitation can either be in judgment or (as here) to bring about
a beneficial result (cf. Ruth 1:6, 'come to the aid of'; Jer. 15:15, 'care
for'). While 'son' is a term used elsewhere of Israel (Exod. 4:22-23;
Hos. 11:1), yet it can also be used of a branch, which makes good sense
here especially seeing it is used in parallel to 'root'. The psalmist
pleads with the divine gardener to come and take care of his own
precious plant which he placed in the garden of Canaan. God had raised
it up for his own purposes and for his own glory.

4. *Restore Us, O Lord (verses 16-19)*

The psalm ends with a further plea for restoration, along with an assurance of renewed commitment to the LORD. The request is for judgment upon those who have devastated the vine, and at the same time help for the afflicted people *(verses 16-17)*. The NIV interprets verse 16b to be a reference to Israel ('your people'), but the Hebrew text does not specify the subject of the rebuke. Verse 16 can be translated, 'They burned it (i.e. the vine); it is burned with fire. May they perish at your rebuke.' This would then be an appeal to destroy the enemies who have burned the vine with fire. To have God's hand resting on Israel would be a sign of his favour. The language of the verse makes it clear that 'man' and 'son of man' are references to the 'root'/'son' of verse 15 (cf. also the use of the phrase 'you have raised up for yourself' in both verses).

The pledge is given on behalf of the people as a whole that they will never again turn away from God *(verse 18)*, i.e. become apostates and renounce their covenant obligations. The Hebrew word translated 'call' (*qara'*) can also mean to proclaim (see Exod. 33:19; 34:6; Deut. 32:3). If renewed life is given to Israel by God, then the people will proclaim his sovereign acts and gracious character.

For the third time the refrain comes in *(verse 19)*, this time to close the psalm. The amplifying use of divine names in the refrain seems to be deliberate, as the psalm mounts to a climax: 'God' (verse 3); 'God Almighty' (verse 14); 'LORD God Almighty' (verse 19). The characteristics of God as expressed in his names are used as a ground for the answer to this prayer.

PSALM 81
For the director of music. According to gittith. Of Asaph.

This psalm has much in common with Psalm 50, especially because of the covenant theme which pervades it. Likewise, it is a psalm of Asaph. It seems to depict a ritual ceremony in Israel which was kept by divine decree (verses 4-5), and which was connected with the covenant. It is unclear which festival is in view, but the use of the expression 'on the day of our Feast' suggests one of the pilgrimage festivals (Passover, Feast of Weeks, or Tabernacles).

1. *A Call to Praise* (*verses 1-2*)

The opening call is for all the people to sing a joyful song to the LORD (*verse 1*). The festivals were meant to be joyous occasions, and so the psalmist calls on the people to worship the LORD in a spirit of thanksgiving. The terms in which God is described are typical for the Psalter. God was the strength of his people (cf. Pss. 18:1; 28:7), and he was the God of Jacob (cf. Pss. 20:1; 46:7, 11; 132:2).

At the time of the institution of the Passover (Exod. 12), there is no mention of singing. However, the instruments mentioned in *verse 2* are also listed in later references to the worship at the temple (see 2 Chr. 5:12; 29:25). The musical accompaniment of the Passover in times of Hezekiah and Josiah was probably the regular practice for much of the Old Testament period (2 Chr. 30:21-22; 35:15).

2. *An Appointed Feast* (*verses 3-5*)

The call to the feast now goes out to the Levites to 'Sound the ram's horn at the New Moon, and when the moon is full, on the day of our Feast; this is a decree for Israel, an ordinance of the God of Jacob' (*verses 3-4*). The word translated 'New Moon' can also mean 'month', and it is probably better to assume that the psalmist mentions first the month, and then the specific part of it, 'when the moon is full'. The word 'feast' (Hebrew, *chag*, cf. Arabic *haj*) is used of various festival occasions (see Exod. 23:15-16; 34:18-22; Deut. 16:16; 2 Chr. 8:13), and specifically of the Passover (Exod. 12:14; Num. 28:17).

Reference is then made to the historical origins of this feast (*verse 5a*). The word rendered 'statute' or 'testimony' is used as a synonym for 'covenant' (cf. 'the tablets of the testimony', Exod. 31:18; 32:15; 34:29). If the subject of the whole sentence is 'God', then the reference will be to his actions against Egypt at the time of the Exodus. Should the subject of the sentence be taken as Israel, then the idea is simply that the Passover was established when Israel left Egypt (this is possible, but it requires taking a Hebrew preposition, *'al* in an unusual sense).

The words that follow, 'where we heard a language we did not understand' (*verse 5b*), are difficult. The NIV follows most English translations in taking the verbs as plurals, and making them refer to the past tense. However, the verbs in Hebrew are in the first person singular ('I hear a voice', 'I do not know'), and are best taken as referring to the present time. It is a statement of wonder at the LORD's words which are to come, and thus forms a transition between the opening verses and verses 6ff. The psalmist says: *I hear [something] unlike any language with which I am acquainted.*

3. *A Divine Word of Deliverance (verses 6-7)*

The divine word focuses first of all on the actual deliverance at the time of the Exodus. What is most interesting is the way that the people are addressed. While it is a much later generation of Israel, yet they are regarded as being part of the community at the time of the Exodus:

> *You called, and I rescued you;*
> *I answered you out of a thundercloud;*
> *I tested you at the waters of Meribah.*

This is carrying out the pattern which Moses set in Deuteronomy 5:2-3 where he identified all his hearers as being part of the covenant community at the time of the covenant making at Mount Sinai. So now the people stand in the same relation to God as their forefathers did long ago.

4. *The Decalogue Re-asserted (verses 8-10)*

The word of the LORD which comes to the people at this festival time is a reminder of the initial covenant relationship established at Sinai. The LORD's words to Israel in Deuteronomy 4:1 and 6:4 are echoed in this call to hear. God brings an accusation against his people and longs that they would heed him. The word which comes to Israel is put in terms of the opening of the Ten Commandments, reminding them in this way that it is the covenant God of Israel who is still speaking to his covenant people. The LORD re-asserts his own relationship as the Redeemer God of the Exodus and the one who claims from his people an exclusive worship. *Verse 9* is a paraphrase of the first two commandments. At this festival the people are invited to open their mouths and God will fill them. This will show their inability to meet their own needs, and accordingly that they are waiting for God's provision.

5. *A Rebellious People (verses 11-16)*

The festival is also a time to accuse the people as a whole of their erring ways (*verses 11-12*). The contrast between verse 8 and verse 11 is most marked. Israel was called to hear or listen carefully, but now comes the reminder that in the past Israel did not listen. There was a basic and enduring unwillingness to yield to the LORD. In turn, he gave them up (the word is used elsewhere of letting captives go, or giving over to sin) to their own stubborn desires. This is always the greatest of God's judgments against his people (cf. Ps. 78:29-31). However, the LORD's concern was still there for them.

Again the LORD repeats his strong appeal for his people to follow his ways *(verses 13-15)*. In the future he longs for them to be an obedient people, walking in his paths. If they respond, then he promises to deal speedily with the enemies who oppress them. This earnest desire of God is seen in its ultimate expression in the words of Jesus concerning Jerusalem (Matt. 23:37-39).

The final verse sets before them the prospect of rich blessing: 'But you would be fed with the finest of the wheat; with honey from the rock I would satisfy you.' The promise is given in terms which echo Deuteronomy 32:13, and in language which speaks of supernatural provision for their needs. The New Testament promise goes even further, and believers have the assurance that 'God will meet all your needs according to his glorious riches in Christ Jesus' (Phil. 4:19).

PSALM 82
A psalm of Asaph.

God always had deep interest in justice in Israel, and warnings were often given concerning its perversion at the hands of sinful rulers (see Exod. 22:22ff.; Deut. 10:17-18; Ps. 10:14, 18; Mal. 3:5). Psalm 82 is like other psalms of Asaph in which the judgment of the nation is in view (cf. Pss. 75, 81). This applies to the form of the psalm, the representation of God as judge, and the introduction of God as the speaker. Here 'gods' is a Hebrew term applied to human rulers, and Jesus' use of the passage supports this interpretation (John 10:34ff.). This is a much more satisfactory explanation than attempting to make it refer to angels.

1. *Judge of Judges (verse 1)*
The language is that of the courtroom. God takes his place as judge (cf. Isa. 3:13-14a) in the assembly of his people. The word 'assembly' is often used of the congregation of Israel. Alternately, the 'great assembly' could be just a gathering of judicial officials who are summoned before God.

2. *The Character of the Judges* (*verses 2-4*)

Perversion of justice is no new thing *(verse 2)*. The implication of the question is that it has been practised in the past, and how long is it to continue? Judges had the responsibility to see to it that the weak and downtrodden had justice administered fairly for them *(verses 3-4)*. The most vulnerable in the community should have been able to expect help (see the comments on Pss. 10:14 and 68:5-6, and cf. Isa. 1:16-17). Just as God was the one who rescued and delivered, so the judges are commanded to imitate him and to free the needy from the power of the wicked.

3. *The Frailty of Human Rulers* (*verses 5-7*)

God gives a description of these human judges *(verse 5)*. They lack the very qualities which should have been paramount in their work as rulers. Like Solomon, they should have asked for 'a discerning heart' and for the ability 'to distinguish between right and wrong' (1 Kgs. 3:9). Instead of walking in the light, they themselves were walking in darkness and ignorance. The conclusion of the verse sums up the consequences of all this – the whole moral order is rotten to its roots.

In *verses 6-7* God makes an emphatic declaration concerning the rulers. They are occupying an office in which they represent God and therefore are to administer his laws. Hence, they can be called 'gods' and 'sons of the Most High'. Jesus appeals to this verse in John 10:34ff. in his debate with the Jews over their accusation of blasphemy against him. Jesus' argument is of the 'how much more' variety. If the psalm applied this term 'god' to men, how much more may it be applied to one whom the Father set apart and sent into the world? (John 10:36). Verse 7 begins in Hebrew with a word which points to marked contrast – 'on the contrary!' Though called 'gods' the judges are mere men, and like all other rulers they will ultimately die.

4. *An Appeal to the Great Judge* (*verse 8*)

The conclusion of the psalm is an appeal by the psalmist for God himself to act as the judge. As in other psalms (see 94:1-3; 96:1-6; 98:9) there is a recognition that God is the supreme ruler, and when human rulers fail the prayer is that God will speedily deliver justice to all. The New Testament assurance is that God 'has set a day when he will judge the world with justice by the man [the Lord Jesus] whom he has appointed' (Acts 17:31). At the last great day, all will appear before the judgment seat of Christ (2 Cor. 5:10).

PSALM 83
A song. A psalm of Asaph.

Even with the explicit references to the enemies in verses 6-8 it is
difficult to find an event which matches exactly with the details given
in this psalm. The nearest identification appears to be the attack on
Judah during the reign of Jehoshaphat as recorded in 2 Chronicles 20.
The same nations are in view, with the Edomites, Moabites, and
Ammonites as the leaders. According to verses 4 and 12 the intention
of the enemies was to destroy Judah, which agrees with 2 Chronicles
20:11. When faced with a powerful coalition of armies, the psalmist
prays that the Most High will again demonstrate his saving power.

1. A Call for God's Help (verse 1)
As far as the people are concerned, their greatest danger does not lie
with the enemies. It is that God will remain a silent onlooker in this
time of danger and distress. While the appeal to God is put in negative
terms, yet the call is for him to speak and to be moved to help.

2. A Complaint about the Enemies (verses 2-8)
The psalmist calls on God to take notice of what the enemies are doing
(verses 2-3). 'Rearing the heads' may well be more a description of
pride and boldness rather than conveying the idea of readiness to
strike. The use of the word 'cunning' suggests a secret agreement was
reached by the enemies as they plotted their attack. The psalmist does
not regard them as Judah's enemies, but as God's enemies. Also, he
does not call Judah 'my people' but '*your* people', 'those *you* cherish'.
His prayer is governed by the Godward direction of his thinking.

The plan of the enemies is very simple. They just want Israel utterly
destroyed as a nation, so that in time to come people will not even
recollect that Israel had ever existed *(verse 4)*. Destruction of the
people and possession of their territory (see verse 12) was their aim.

There is unity between the enemies *(verses 5-8)*, and they confirm
this by entering into a treaty together (the same Hebrew word *berit* is
used of treaty as is used elsewhere of the covenant between God and
his people). The attack is coming from every quarter. Firstly, the
nations on the south and east are mentioned (Edom, Ishmaelites,
Moab, and the Hagrites). Then those on the north-west (Gebal),
followed by those on the east (Ammon and Amalek), the south-west

(the Philistines), and then again those on the north-west (Tyre). The Hagrites were a nomadic tribe living east of Gilead (1 Chr. 5:10). Gebal has often been taken to be the hill country in the north of Edom, but the NIV footnote, which identifies it with the modern Byblos in Lebanon, is more probable. Even distant Assyria, seemingly just emerging as a major power, has joined the alliance, linking up with distant relatives of Israel, the Moabites and Ammonites, Lot's descendants (see Gen. 19:36-38).

3. Prayer for God's Judgment on the Enemies (verses 9-18)
As he prays for God's judgment on the coalition of forces arrayed against Israel, the psalmist recalls God's great victories in the past, especially in the time of the judges. He selects two notables battles, that of the victory over the Canaanites recorded in Judges 4-5 and the victory of Gideon over the Midianites in Judges 7-8. The fact that only the enemy kings are named, not the judges, draws attention to the fact that God was the deliverer.

The prayer is for a similar victory of the Lord to come as when Sisera and Jabin were destroyed *(verses 9-10)*. In Judges 4 there is no mention of Endor, yet the location fits the mention of Mount Tabor in Judges 4, for Endor was situated at the foot of Mount Tabor.

The same appeal to the mighty victory of the Lord over Midian (Judges 7-8) is made elsewhere in the Old Testament (Isa. 9:4; Hab. 3:7). According to Judges 7:25, Oreb and Zeeb were the commanders of the Midianite army, while Zebah and Zalmunna were the kings. The aim of the Midianite attack was to dispossess the Israelites and seize the land of Canaan. The psalmist prays that the present attackers may suffer the same fate as the Midianite leaders long before *(verses 11-12)*.

In *verse 13* the picture is of the tumbleweed (so-called because of its wheel-shaped stem) being driven before the wind. The request is for the divine warrior to chase these enemies in a like manner.

The thought of God's fiery judgment being like a forest blaze *(verses 14-15)* is developed further in Isaiah 10:16-19. Here the psalmist joins to it the idea of God bringing the storm clouds of his wrath (see also Ps. 68:4). The word 'tempest' is used elsewhere in the Old Testament for a visible manifestation of God (cf. Job 38:1; 40:6). Here, as in Isaiah 29:6, it is used as a symbol of God's judgment. He relentlessly pursues the enemies and out of the thunderstorm he terrifies them.

The request in *verse 16* is for the enemies to be shown their true place and position in God's sight. This is not simply to degrade them before God and men. Rather, the aim is that they will then come to seek God for themselves. The shame and disgrace which the psalmist seeks for the enemies is not inward feelings but outward position and standing *(verses 17-18)*. The aim of this judicial dealing with the enemies is that they will be brought to an acknowledgement of the sovereignty of God over the whole world. This is parallel to Hezekiah's request that God would save Judah from the hand of Sennacherib: '... so that all kingdoms on earth may know that you, alone, O LORD, are God' (Isa. 37:16-20). In the midst of a call to judgment, the psalmist is thinking of the enemies being constrained to 'know' God just as his people do. He wants the display of God's justice to end in conversion of Israel's (and God's) enemies.

PSALM 84
For the director of music. According to gittith. Of the Sons of
Korah. A psalm.

The general mood of this psalm is closest to the longing for God's presence expressed in Psalms 42-43. No exact date can be placed on it, but the reference to the king in verse 9 ('your anointed one') suggests a date prior to the exile. There is no reason to link it with David's life. It may well have been used by pilgrims to Jerusalem as they came to the entry of the Temple. There they would sing of their intense desire to be in the Lord's house, and of the blessing on those who make their dwelling there. This psalm is the first of the second group of psalms which are attributed to the sons of Korah (Pss. 84, 85, 87, 88).

1. *Longing for God's House (verses 1-4)*
The word 'lovely' normally means 'loved', but perhaps both ideas are involved: 'How loved and lovely is your dwelling place!' The term 'dwelling place' is commonly used of the Tabernacle, but here the plural is used (lit. 'your dwelling places'). In this psalm a variety of other terms are used to refer to the building in question: 'courts of the Lord' (verse 2); 'your house' (verse 4); 'your courts' and 'the house of my God' (verse 10). It is best to take the references as being to the Temple *(verse 1)*.

The psalmist is spiritually hungry for the presence of God, so that his intense desire makes him grow pale and it consumes him. His whole being ('heart' and 'flesh') sings for joy to the living God (cf. the same term in Ps. 42:2), who is also the mighty LORD of hosts *(verse 2)*.

The psalmist even envies the small birds which have been able to get so near to the altar *(verse 3)*. They have found a snug home for themselves in the sanctuary of God. This is where he longs to be also. The reference to the altar is followed by a cluster of terms which describe the great God whose altar it is, and the God with whom the psalmist is in such a personal relationship (*'my* King', *'my* God')

Those who spiritually make God's presence their dwelling place know his favour and blessing *(verse 4)*. 'Dwell' has the idea of constantly abiding somewhere (cf. its use in Pss. 15:1; 23:6; 61:4). Those who know what it is to abide with God, praise him for all the blessings he gives.

2. *Blessed Pilgrims* (*verses 5-7*)

How happy are those who have found that the LORD is their deliverer, and who want to go on a pilgrimage to Jerusalem! 'Set their hearts on' is literally 'in whose hearts are (the) highways', i.e. the pathways which led to Zion. The devout Israelites were always thinking about going up to the festive occasions *(verse 5)*.

The picture in *verses 6-7* is of a wilderness journey which becomes a place of springs (or, as in NIV footnote, 'blessings'). 'Baca' is unknown as a locality in Israel, so it may just be used to denote dry and difficult territory (it may possibly mean 'weeping'). The experiences of the pilgrims resemble the provision God made in the wilderness for his people as they journeyed to Canaan (see Deut. 8:1-20; Pss. 78:15-16; 114:8). In spite of the hardships on the way, the pilgrims find that God abundantly meets their needs until, with increasing strength, they reach their destination.

3. *A Prayer for the King* (*verses 8-9*)

No hint is given of the situation which calls forth this prayer. Some tragedy has struck the people and the psalmist addresses the great God who is able to deliver, just as he delivered Jacob of old. The expression 'God of Jacob' is common in the Psalms (see Pss. 20:1; 24:6 [in an abbreviated form]; 46:7, 11; 75:9; 76:6; 81:1).

God himself is the shield of his people (see verse 11), just as he proclaimed himself long before to Abraham (Gen. 15:1). The same expression is also applied to the king, who as the Lord's 'anointed one' is also the 'shield' (Hebrew, *magen*) or protector of the people. In Carthage in North Africa a related Semitic word was used of the generals (*magon*), translated into Latin as *imperator* (*leader, commander*). The king was to be to the people what God promised of himself.

4. *The Source of Blessing* (verses 10-11)

The psalmist traces the source of blessing to its true fountain *(verse 10)*. He considers *one* day spent in God's presence as better than *a thousand* elsewhere. The second part of the verse expands the thought and gives a variation on the same idea. The word 'doorkeeper' suggests too strongly the thought of being an official servant at the temple. The Hebrew word occurs only here in the Old Testament, and it merely indicates 'standing at the threshold'. To be on the very fringe of the temple was far better than any secure dwelling among the wicked.

The opening word ('for') in *verse 11* places emphasis on what follows ('*truly*, the LORD God ...'). Nowhere else in the Old Testament is God called directly a 'sun'. It seems to be similar to calling him a 'light' (Ps. 27:1). He is both the source of happiness and joy for his people, as well as being their protector ('shield'). Moreover, he gives abundantly to those who are upright in their lives, bestowing saving mercy on them (Hebrew, 'grace and glory'; NIV 'favour').

5. *Concluding Blessing* (verse 12)

The final blessing of the psalm (for the others see verses 4 and 5) announces the good news that anyone who trusts in the LORD will be blessed by him. A similar expression occurs in Psalm 40:4. With this concluding statement the psalm ties together its whole content, and it reinforces the point that true blessing belongs only to those who have committed themselves in believing trust to the LORD.

PSALM 85

For the director of music. Of the Sons of Korah. A psalm.

In this communal lament there is no precise indication of the occasion which prompted it. The absence of references to the king and temple suggest that it comes from the period after the return from exile. If that is so, then the reference in verse 12 may well be to the drought which God brought on his people in the time of Haggai (Hag. 1:5-11). The key ideas in the psalm are shown by the repetition of words which relate to the covenant relationship: *return/restore* (Hebrew verb *shuv* in verses 1, 3, 4, 6, 8); the covenant terms *peace, unfailing love, faithfulness,* and *righteousness* (verses 7, 8, 10, 11, 13); *land* (verses 1, 9, 11, 12); *saviour/salvation* (verses 4, 7, 9).

1. *A Confession of Faith (verses 1-3)*

The psalmist recalls God's graciousness to his people and land in the past *(verses 1-2)*. The expression 'restore the fortunes' can also be translated 'bring back from captivity' (see NIV text and notes at Jer. 29:14 and Ps. 126:1). God had heard and answered the urgent prayers of the people in exile, typified by Daniel's staccato pleas: 'O Lord, listen! O LORD, forgive! O LORD, hear and act! For your sake, O my God, do not delay, because your city and your people bear your Name' (Dan. 9:19). The psalmist uses common expressions (cf. the almost identical ones in Ps. 32:1) to describe the reality of forgiveness.

God had made it plain that he was angry with his people for all their sins, and so he sent them into exile (see 2 Kgs. 17:18; 2 Chr. 36:16-21). Now the psalmist rejoices in the fact that this righteous anger has been replaced by tender favour *(verse 3)*. Proof of God's forgiveness was seen in the return from exile, for Israel's sin has been paid for (Isa. 40:2).

2. *A Cry for Salvation (verses 4-7)*

It is the immediate situation which the psalmist now brings into focus. Since God was merciful before, he seeks a fresh demonstration of God's mercy towards the people in their present need *(verse 4)*. The way in which the prayer is expressed implies confession of sin as the psalmist pleads for a removal of God's wrath.

Similar requests to *verses 5-6* are found in other psalms (see Pss. 79:5; 80:4; 89:46) as the people long for the cessation of God's wrath. From the latter part of this psalm there is no doubt that the psalmist knew that this anger was not going to be displayed for ever against the people. A time was coming when God's favour would be upon them, and then the people would be glad in the LORD. The word 'revive' may have connotations for us which the Hebrew verb does not suggest. The meaning is close to 'preserve alive', 'maintain life'.

What the psalmist wants is a fresh display of covenant love (Hebrew, *chesed*), which is equated here with 'salvation' *(verse 7)*. His appeal in verse 4 is to the 'Saviour'. Now he looks for 'salvation' from him in the sense of deliverance from the present troubles.

3. *God's Word to His People* (*verses 8-13*)

The psalmist knows that God's word for his people is one of 'peace' *(verse 8)*, therefore there can be confidence for the future. Perhaps the Aaronic blessing is in mind (Num. 6:22-26). The promise of peace is renewed in a special way in the gospel, for Jesus, who is our peace (Eph. 2:14), is able to give his own lasting peace to his followers (John 14:27). It is in this way that peace and mercy flow to the Israel of God (Gal. 6:16). The accompanying warning given here is still applicable. Possession of God's peace is dependent upon not straying from his ways and returning to folly.

Verse 9 puts in another way what has just been said. The psalmist had earlier asked for God's salvation (verse 7), and now he affirms the truth that those who fear the Lord, 'his saints', indeed experience God's saving power. Through Isaiah God had promised that his salvation would draw near to his people (Isa. 46:13: 51:5). Just as the glory of the LORD had dwelt on Mount Sinai (Exod. 24:16-17), so it would take up abiding residence in the land.

The psalmist personifies God's favour to his people, and he presents a picture of 'love', 'faithfulness', 'righteousness' and 'peace' meeting and embracing one another *(verses 10-11)*. 'Faithfulness' springs up like a flourishing plant, while 'righteousness' oversees affairs among men (cf. similar ideas in Isa. 45:8). These four blessings are essential aspects of God's kingdom. Paul confirms this when he says that 'the kingdom of God is not a matter of eating and drinking, but of righteousness, peace, and joy in the Holy Spirit' (Rom. 14:17).

If the Lord brought an end to the drought, then the land would again produce bountiful crops *(verse 12)*. Renewed tokens of his favour would show the abiding nature of his love.

> All good gifts around us
>> are sent from heaven above;
> Then thank the Lord, O thank the Lord,
>> for all his love.

(Mathius Claudius 1740-1815)

Righteousness is regarded as a person who goes before the LORD and prepares for his intervention on behalf of his people *(verse 13)*. The coming of the LORD is often pictured as being preceded by preparation (see Isa. 40:3-5; Mal. 3:1; Matt. 3:1-12). Here the messenger going before him is his saving righteousness. The victory of the LORD will be followed by his coming in glory (see verse 9).

PSALM 86
A prayer of David.

In Book Three of the Psalter this is the only psalm attributed to David. The term 'servant', used both at the beginning (verse 2) and the end of the psalm (verse 16), points to the royal status of David who was called by God 'my servant' (2 Sam. 7:5; see also this description used of him in the title of Ps. 18). The nature of the distress which lies behind this plea is not stated. It could be the plotting of those within his kingdom, or else nations surrounding Israel who seek his downfall. The psalm is composed in a very symmetrical manner. It has five stanzas, with the first and last having four verses, and the others each having three verses. The other remarkable feature of Psalm 86 is that every verse is an echo of another part of the Old Testament. Well-known Scripture has been moulded into a new song. Memorised Bible passages should always be a basis for private and corporate prayer.

1. *A Servant's Prayer* (*verses 1-4*)
While the phrase 'poor and needy' is a common one (Pss. 35:10; 37:14; 109:16, 22), yet its use here stems from a sense of great urgency *(verse 1)*. He confesses his deep personal need (cf. the words of Pss. 40:17 and 70:5), and asks his sovereign LORD to listen to his plea.

The appeal is based on a relationship between the psalmist and his God; he is a servant who has a covenant commitment to his master *(verse 2)*. The phrase 'devoted to you' (Hebrew, *chasid*) is translated in the NIV by a variety of expressions: 'godly' (Pss. 4:3; 12:1); 'saints' (Pss. 30:4; 52:9; 79:2); 'consecrated ones' (Ps. 50:5); 'faithful people' (Ps. 89:19). The variety of expression is needed in English, but in all the contexts the focus is on devotion to the covenant God. The psalmist confesses that he is God's servant, and so appeals for protection.

In *verses 3-4* he pleads for mercy (cf. Ps. 57:1) and indicates how constantly his approach is being made to his God. The opposite of sorrow is joy, and so he asks that God will make his servant rejoice as his prayer is answered. 'To lift up the soul' is a synonym for praying to God (see Pss. 25:1; 143:8).

2. *A Gracious God (verses 5-7)*

In this next section, like so many other Old Testament passages, the language of Exodus 34:6-7 is clearly behind the words used by the psalmist. The verb translated 'forgiving' is only used in the Old Testament with God as the subject. He is able to blot out sin, and all who call upon him in their sinfulness and need find him 'abounding in love' (Hebrew, *rav chesed*; cf. verse 15; Exod. 34:6; Ps. 103:8).

With confidence the psalmist approaches a merciful God with his plea for mercy *(verse 5)*. Such a supplication is an expression of a loyal servant's trust in his Lord. The day of his trouble is the present distress he is experiencing, and he knows that in such a situation he must call for help. He is also assured that out of his love and mercy God will answer his prayer.

3. *The Only God (verses 8-10)*

The Old Testament repeatedly makes exclusive claims regarding God. *Verse 8* is an echo of passages such as Exodus 15:11, Deuteronomy 3:24, and Psalm 35:10. The living God is vastly different from the dead idols which the surrounding nations worshipped (Ps. 115:5-7). The New Testament reaffirms that people must turn from 'worthless things to the living God, who made heaven and earth and sea and everything in them' (Acts 14:15; see also 1 Thess. 1:9; Heb. 9:14).

From the preceding statement of the greatness of God, the psalmist draws the conclusion that all the nations will come and worship him *(verse 9)*. The closest parallel to this in the Bible is Revelation 15:4. In both passages the thought of the uniqueness of the living God leads on to a declaration that the nations are going to bow in submission before him.

Extolling the greatness of God is another way of stressing his uniqueness *(verse 10)*. Moreover, he does things which no-one else can do (cf. the comments on Pss. 71:17; 72:18), for he works wonders (NIV 'marvellous deeds'). This is because these acts are not within human power, they are demonstrations of divine power.

4. *A Prayer of Thanksgiving (verses 11-13)*

The psalmist wants further instruction from the LORD, and gives a commitment to continue to be guided by his truth *(verse 11)*. 'An undivided heart' indicates complete loyalty, and leads a person to revere God's character. As part of his commitment the psalmist pledges himself to praise God with singleness of heart *(verses 12-13)*. There is no apparent difference here between 'praise' and 'glorify'. The first part of verse 12 is practically the same as Psalm 9:1, while the opening part of verse 13 appears elsewhere in the Book of Psalms (cf. 57:10; 108:4). The psalmist has been brought to death's door, but God's deliverance of him becomes the subject of his praise.

5. *The Prayer Renewed* (*verses 14-17*)

The closing verses of the psalm return to the theme of its opening, and the petition is renewed for God's intervention in a dangerous situation. The only description of the enemies is that given in *verse 14*, and it is so general that they cannot be identified with any certainty. The word 'arrogant' is used of people who proudly go their rebellious and wilful ways. They are a group of men who cause terror and seek innocent lives, without giving thought to God and his demands.

Once more the declaration of Exodus 34:6 lies behind the psalmist's words *(verse 15)*. No greater appeal could be made in proclaiming the character of God than to use the very words which God used of himself. They seem to have had a place in the hearts and language of Old Testament believers as a kind of credal statement (see Num. 14:18; 2 Chr. 30:9; Neh. 9:17; Pss. 103:8; 111:4; 116:5; Joel 2:13; Jon. 4:2).

The urgent need of the psalmist is for God's compassion to be shown to him. He confesses his relationship with his God – he is a servant, the son of a female servant, and therefore bound in perpetual service to his master *(verse 16)*. The language of servanthood is used in both Old and New Testaments to denote the bond between a devout believer and the Lord (for the New Testament see the opening of Paul's letters [Rom. 1:1; Phil. 1:1; Tit. 1:1] and passages such as Eph. 6:6; 2 Tim. 2:24).

The final request is for the LORD to be victorious over his and the psalmist's enemies *(verse 17)*. The LORD's goodness would be shown by relieving his distress and bringing him deliverance. The contrast between the opening and the close of the psalm is most emphatic – 'I', 'I', 'I' (verses 1-2); 'you', 'you' (verses 15, 17). The plaintive repetition of 'I' gives way to declaration and appeal to God himself.

PSALM 87
Of the Sons of Korah. A psalm. A song.

While this psalm has much in common with other songs relating to
Zion (see Pss. 46; 48; 76), yet it goes beyond them in picturing
inhabitants of Gentile nations being incorporated among the citizens
of Zion. This could be understood as a widespread conversion of
people from the nations mentioned in the psalm, who were representative of those nations long hostile to Israel. However, it can also be
understood as a declaration of God to these nations (see NIV footnote,
verse 4) that he has recorded the names of all his people – 'those who
acknowledge me' – wherever they may be and he regards them as
belonging to Zion.

1. *Praise of Zion* (*verses 1-3*)
The Old Testament asserts that the choice of Zion (i.e. Jerusalem) was
made by God (Ps. 132:13; Isa. 14:32). That is why it was called 'the
city of the LORD Almighty' (Ps. 48:8). This choice of Jerusalem was
an expression of the LORD's love, and consequently Zion was preferred
more than any other town in Israel *(verses 1-2)*. 'Jacob' is used here as
a synonym for Israel, as it was the name by which the patriarch Israel
was earlier known (Gen. 32:28).

The psalmist has heard or read statements of others about Zion, and
in this psalm he summarises these 'glorious things' *(verse 3)*. The
expression 'of you' is ambiguous in Hebrew, as it could also be
translated 'in you'. If that rendering is preferred, the meaning will be
that in Zion itself prophecies concerning Zion are uttered. 'The city of
God' is the location as well as the theme of prophetic announcements.

2. *Enrolled in Zion* (*verses 4-6*)
It is probably best to take the places mentioned *(verse 4)* as being
directly addressed by God ('I will record [you] O Rahab, O Babylon').
God acknowledges that he has his own people in all the Gentile nations
near to Israel, with the nations mentioned being representative of the
wider Gentile world. 'Rahab' is a poetic name for Egypt (cf. Isa. 30:7;
51:9). The people of God among these nations are regarded as if they
were born in Zion.

No matter where true believers live, they are enrolled among the
citizens of Zion *(verses 5-6)*, the city which God sustains (cf. Ps. 48:8).

The idea of a register or book is simply a way of saying that God knows those who are his and not one of them will perish. These verses may well contain a note of warning to the nations too. If God has noted who his people truly are, then he will hold accountable those who harm them (cf. Isa. 14:28-32).

Finally, there is a description of this great crowd of enrolled citizens of Zion rejoicing in the fact that their source of salvation is in Zion and especially in Zion's God *(verse 7)*. The whole community of believers is looked on as a single group (*'my* fountains'). It has found that salvation flows from God's fountain (cf. Ps. 36:9; Isa. 12:3). When John Newton (1725-1807) wrote the hymn 'Glorious things of thee are spoken, Zion city of our God', he rightly saw the ingathering of Gentiles in gospel times foreshadowed in this psalm. Christians today can say with him:

> Saviour, if of Zion's city
> I through grace, a member am
> Let the world deride or pity,
> I will glory in Thy name.
> Fading is the worldling's pleasure,
> All his boasted pomp and show;
> Solid joys and lasting treasure
> None but Zion's children know.

PSALM 88
A song. A psalm of the Sons of Korah. For the director of music. According to mahalath leannoth. A maskil of Heman the Ezrahite.

This is probably the saddest song in the whole of the Psalter, even sadder in the Hebrew text than in English because it ends with the word 'darkness'. It could be an individual appeal for help, or else a communal one from the time of the exile. The Aramaic Targum and the Syriac version indicate that the latter is how they understood the content of the psalm. The title is unusual, for the first part is mirror of that prefixed to Psalm 87, while the second part seems to be the title of the tune (*mahalath leannoth*) with an ascription of it to 'Heman the Ezrahite'. The difficulty is that several men by the name of Heman are mentioned elsewhere in the Old Testament (see 1 Kgs. 4:31; 1 Chr. 15:17, 19). The term 'Ezrahite' is also ambiguous, for it could mean either 'of the family of Ezrah' or 'the native-born'.

1. *An Appeal for Help* (*verses 1-2*)

The opening of the psalm shows that even in the midst of his despair, the psalmist can turn to his Saviour. The personal problems of the psalmist become even more acute for him because of his trust in the covenant love of the LORD (verse 11).

Out of his sorrow and distress he cried to his covenant LORD, acknowledging that his salvation comes from him alone *(verses 1-2)*. Constantly he makes his prayer to him, and pleads for a ready hearing for his cry for help. A situation similar to the one in the psalm may be behind the words penned by Henry Francis Lyte (1793-1847):

> Abide with me: fast falls the eventide;
> The darkness deepens; Lord, with me abide;
> When other helpers fail, and comforts flee,
> Help of the helpless, O abide with me.

2. *Living on the Edge of the Grave* (*verses 3-5*)

There is no precise indication of what peril the psalmist is facing. It could be illness which brings him near to death, or some other situation which places him in serious danger *(verses 3-4)*. He is reckoned along with those whose bodies are placed in the grave, like a man whose strength has gone completely.

In *verse 5* the psalmist pictures himself lying in the grave, 'apart with the dead'. The Hebrew text has 'freed from the dead', which seems to mean released from the normal responsibilities of life. He is like those who are now in the grave, having been killed by battle wounds or dying from famine. He speaks from the standpoint of this life when he describes them as being outside God's care. This is not to be taken as denial of life after death or of God's eternal care of his children.

3. *God's Heavy Hand* (*verses 6-9a*)

The psalmist feels forsaken by man and by God *(verses 6-7)*. He accuses God directly of causing his present position ('*You* have put me', verse 6; '*you* have made me repulsive', verse 8). He cannot explain why it has happened, yet knows that God's hand has been at work. His distress is all the greater because his grief has been caused by the Saviour to whom he appeals (verse 1). The picture of waves breaking over him is used to describe the flood of troubles which have come upon him.

Isolation from his companions follows *(verses 8-9a)*. While he is not actually afflicted with leprosy, yet he reckons himself like a leper and feels hemmed in by the restrictions placed upon him. He is shunned by his former companions and constant weeping has affected his eyesight (cf. Ps. 6:7).

4. *A Cry of the Heart* (*verses 9b-12*)

The psalmist's prayer is the same day by day *(verse 9b)*. Even though he cannot explain his present distress, he makes his constant appeal to his covenant LORD. His gestures are those of someone imploring help, as he stretches out his hand. The expression used here is not a common one, but it may be similar in meaning to 'lifting up the hands' (see Ps. 28:2).

With a series of questions the psalmist draws attention to the condition of those who perish, and whom he considers he will soon be joining *(verses 10-12)*. He uses a variety of expressions to describe the state of the dead – 'the grave', 'Destruction', 'the place of darkness', and 'the land of oblivion'. 'Destruction' is *Abaddon* in Hebrew, and it is used in transliteration in Revelation 9:11 as a name for the devil. He also uses a variety of expressions to describe God's gracious acts on behalf of his people – 'wonders' (verses 10 and 12), 'love', 'faithfulness', and 'righteous deeds'. It is amongst the living that there is such divine manifestations of mercy and power.

5. *Another Call for Help* (*verses 13-14*)

One of the conventional times for prayer was in the morning. The Hebrew text emphasises the one praying and the one to whom he prays: 'But *I – to you* I cry for help.' While the afflicted psalmist cannot understand his present experiences, he still knows that his only possible source of help is with the LORD. He hangs on desperately to the truth that God alone can deal with his situation. Relief is not yet in sight, and he still feels rejected by his God.

6. *Lifelong Gloom* (*verses 15-18*)

The psalmist's experiences are not new. He confesses that he has lived with the shadow of death looming over him right from youthful days *(verse 15)*. He has had a difficult life, whether from sickness or some other reason. His condition brings him to the point of losing all hope.

Verses 16-18 do not introduce any new ideas, but re-iterate what

has already been announced (see in particular verses 6-9). The psalmist traces his troubles back to God himself, accusing him of separating
him from all his companions and loved ones. The only friend he has
is darkness itself. Yet we must balance this conclusion with the
opening of the psalm. Isolated from human help, he is still able to call
God his Saviour. That is where his true hope really lies. In days when
there is no light the believer has to walk, trusting the name of his God.
(Isa. 50:10), and say:

> When darkness seems to veil His face
> I rest on His unchanging grace;
> In every high and stormy gale,
> My anchor holds within the veil.
>
> His oath, His covenant, and blood,
> Support me in the whelming flood;
> When all around my soul gives way,
> He then is all my hope and stay.

(Edward Mote 1797-1874)

PSALM 89
A maskil of Ethan the Ezrahite.

The central theme of this psalm is the covenant God made with David,
promising a throne for his dynasty for ever. While David initially
wanted to build a house (i.e. a temple) for God, it was God who built
a house (i.e. a dynasty) for him. It is very clear that this covenant had
a great impact on the thought of God's people, and it is expounded in
various other psalms as well (see 18:24-27; 21; 61; 72; 132).

1. *Great is the Lord's Faithfulness* (*verses 1-4*)
The dominant theme of the first part of this psalm is the love and
faithfulness of the Lord. The words 'love' and 'faithfulness' each
occur seven times (allowing for an alternate word for 'faithfulness' in
verse 14). When used together they form a compound expression –
'love-and-faithfulness'. This is the foundation of the covenant relationship which is described in the following verses. It is the subject of
the psalmist's song as he declares his intention of continuing to
proclaim the covenant mercies of the LORD *(verse 1)*.

There is difficulty in linking up *verse 2* with the opening verse. It is best to take the commencement of verse 2 as referring to past time ('For I have said', AV, NKJ, NASB), indicating that the psalmist had earlier made a declaration concerning God's love-and-faithfulness. That declaration was to the effect that God had settled the matter of his covenant mercy in heaven itself, and its endurance did not therefore depend upon action of men. It would 'stand firm' (the Hebrew is literally, 'be built', a word very important in the covenant passage in 2 Sam. 7).

The words, 'You said' *(verse 3)*, are not in the Hebrew text, but their insertion makes clear that the words which follow are God's words. God had entered into a covenant bond with David, even though the word 'covenant' does not occur in 2 Samuel 7. However, the ingredients of covenant are there, and this is confirmed by passages such as this as well as 2 Samuel 23:5 and Psalm 132:11-12. David was indeed the LORD's servant (2 Sam. 7:5, 8, 26; Ps. 132:10) and chosen one (Ps. 78:70). An essential part of the covenant was the choice of David's family to form the continuing royal line *(verse 4)*. Accordingly, the Davidic throne was to last throughout all generations (see 2 Sam. 7:16; Isa. 9:7), and ultimately it found its fulfilment in the person of Jesus (Luke 1:32). There is no mention in 2 Samuel 7 of God's oath, but the reference to it here and Psalm 132:11 confirm that the arrangement was indeed a covenant.

2. *The Majesty of God* (verses 5-18)

At first glance it may seem that this section is a digression from the main theme of the psalm. What it does, however, is to emphasise the character of God which certifies that the covenant will be maintained.

God's glories are manifest in all the heavens, and his angels join together in a gathering to praise his faithfulness *(verse 5)*. The word 'wonders' (here the Hebrew has the singular) is used elsewhere of the miraculous acts of God in creation and especially in redemption. It is a term used to describe his sovereign lordship over events (cf. Ps. 78:11-12). *Verses 6-8* draw attention to the uniqueness of God. The questions which are asked find their answer in the response. 'You are mighty, O LORD'. There is no one else who can be compared with him, for his awesome character sets him apart from all of his creation, including his holy ones. The phrase 'heavenly beings' is literally 'sons of God', an expression used also in Psalm 29:1 (NIV, 'mighty ones') of the angelic host. His character separates him from his creatures, for he is more to be feared than any of them. Perhaps there are echoes here from the great song of redemption in Exodus 15 (see especially verse 11).

God's mighty power as seen in the creation is described as though it was a battle against other great forces *(verses 9-10)*. The sea is personified as 'Rahab' (cf. Job 26:12; Isa. 51:9), and here it may be the same as Leviathan (Ps. 74:14). All the powers of creation are under God's control, and he orders the seas in accordance with his will. Like slain warriors the waters are subdued before him.

The whole of creation came into being by God's command *(verses 11-13)*, and so 'the earth is the LORD's, and everything in it' (Ps. 24:1; cf. also Ps. 50:12). The mighty mountains give praise to God's greatness and help to proclaim his character. The fact that 'north' and 'south' are used in parallel to 'Tabor' and 'Hermon' suggest that two other mountains may be intended, though no clear identification can be given for them. Mount Tabor was the site of Deborah's victory, while Mount Hermon was symbolic of physical majesty. All of nature sings for joy, and as a testimony to the fact that it has been made by God's power.

God's rule is marked out by righteousness and justice *(verse 14)*. These form the basis on which his kingship operates (cf. Ps. 97:2b for an almost identical expression). The twin pair of love-and-faithfulness appear to precede all of God's works. They are like angels which go before him to proclaim his coming.

The psalmist now moves on to describe the kind of God upon whose promises Israel depends *(verses 15-16)*. Those who trust in the LORD are able to proclaim their knowledge of him, and they do so with a joyful or festive shout. Their daily lives are lived in the knowledge of God's favour to them (for 'the light of your presence', cf. the Aaronic blessing, Num. 6:24-26, and Pss. 4:6; 44:3). God's self-revelation of himself (his 'name') becomes a ground of unceasing joy for his people, and the demonstration of his saving power an object of their praise.

God is the ornament or glory of his people, just as Israel is said to be God's 'glory' (the Hebrew text of Isa. 46:13; 62:3; Jer. 13:11; 33:9). Moreover, he is their strength, which he renews according to his gracious will *(verses 17-18)*. Rather than understanding this strength as being the support God gives to each individual believer, 'horn' may be parallel to 'shield' and 'king'. Elsewhere the term 'shield' is used to describe kings in general (Ps. 47:9) and specifically the king of

Israel (Ps. 84:9, and see comment on that verse). Israel's king is regarded as a vice-regent of God himself, who is called here 'the Holy One of Israel'. This term for God becomes a favourite with Isaiah, who uses it twenty-six times, while it is only used six times elsewhere in the Old Testament.

3. The Covenant with David (verses 19-37)

This section of the psalm is a long poetic description of the covenant which God made with David (see 2 Sam. 7). It details God's choice of David and the promises given to him, as well as affirming the enduring love which was expressed in this covenant.

The opening word 'once' (verse 19) refers back to the occasion when the covenant was proclaimed. The narrative in 2 Samuel 7 refers to this vision (2 Sam. 7:17), though it does not say expressly that the revelation was for the faithful people (Hebrew, the chasidim, cf. the comment on Ps. 31:23). It becomes clear in David's response that the message has implications for Israel as a whole and the non-Jewish world as well (2 Sam. 7:18-29). The psalmist looks back to the earlier choice of David by God and his anointing by Samuel (1 Sam. 16:1-13). That God's hand was in the matter was demonstrated by the fact that after his anointing the Spirit of the Lord came upon him with power (1 Sam. 16:13).

The divine promise is that support will be given to David, so that his kingdom will be secure (verses 21-23). This is a poetic description of what is stated in 2 Samuel 7:10-11. David is to be given victory over his enemies, and hence the rest which the land already had will be assured for the future.

The assurance regarding God's love-and-faithfulness given earlier in the psalm (see especially verses 1-3) is now stated as God's own declaration to David (verses 24-25). Constant support for David comes from the LORD, and his strength will be maintained by him. The promise of verse 25 could be to the borders of the promised land as they were reached under the empire of David and Solomon, or more probably to the extent of the Messianic kingdom, without even the definiteness of Psalm 72:8. There is no need to try and specify which rivers are intended. The ultimate Messianic kingdom ruled over by Christ, the greater son of David, will be universal in extent.

In verses 26-27 the promise to David puts in individual terms what was the core of God's covenant with his people: 'I am your God, and you shall be my people.' This is now expressed in the affectionate language of a child speaking to his father. David will call out to God, 'My Father', and designate him as his God, Rock, and Saviour. The highest of privileges will be given to David, for as the firstborn he has royal honours, and no other earthly king could rise to his position. The language here is taken over and used of Jesus in Revelation 1:5.

The enduring nature of God's covenant with David is an expression of mercy and grace *(verses 28-29)*. Repeatedly the Old Testament reminds readers that God will not go back on his covenant word to David (see Ps. 132:11-18). Part of the promise is that his family will continue, and that possession of the throne by them is just as certain as the enduring nature of the heavens (for fuller expression of this idea, see verse 36-37). David's dynasty did reign for centuries, but the eternal fulfilment of the promise is to be found in Jesus Christ (cf. Rom. 1:2-4; Rev. 22:16).

Verses 30-34 are a paraphrase of 2 Samuel 7:14. Nathan indicated to David that the sins of individual kings are going to be punished, even though he promises that the whole family will not fail. God is going to act as a father in chastising his sons, and so punishment will follow breach of his laws. Chastisement is part of the father/son relationship (Heb. 12:7-11). However, a wonderful contrast is brought out by the repetition of the word 'violate' in verse 31 and 34. Individual kings might violate God's laws, but God will never violate his covenant! He will never go back on his word (Num. 23:19). Though the English rendering does not make it clear, the combination of love-and-faithfulness comes in again in verses 33-34. The security of the covenant is dependent on God's own gracious character.

In *verses 35-37* the psalmist returns to the theme of God's oath (see comment on verse 3). God's promise to David was: 'Your house and your kingdom will endure forever before me; your throne will be established for ever' (2 Sam. 7:16). Because there is no one greater than God, he swears by his own character (cf. the same thing in reference to his oath to Abraham, Heb. 6:13). The thought of verses 36-37 is an expansion of verse 29. The enduring Davidic family and its royal position is as sure as the sun and moon.

4. *Faith in a Time of Trial (verses 38-51)*
There is a sudden shift in the psalm at this point. The psalmist takes up the present position of the people and of the Davidic family, and pleads

for them on the basis of God's covenant promises. How is it possible that God could seemingly renounce his covenant? The setting seems to be the time of the Babylonian attack on Jerusalem in 597 BC, when the youthful king Jehoiachin was taken away captive to Babylon (*verses 38-39*, see 2 Kings 24:8-17). The emphasis is on what God has done, for the psalmist rightly sees his hand in the events surrounding the Babylonian invasion. The shift from the stress on the covenant to the present distress of the people is marked by the emphatic opening to this section: 'But *you*.' The psalmist rightly sees God's hand in the events which have happened, and the capture of Jerusalem and of the king as an expression of his wrath. The covenant seems to be broken, though the Old Testament points to a continuity of the covenant in spite of a temporary separation between God and his people (see, for example, Isa. 50:1-2; 54:4-8). The rejection of the Davidic king is as if the crown had been thrown away into the dust (cf. a similar expression in Lam. 5:16).

The language used in *verses 40-41* gives a picture of the overthrow of Judah by the Babylonians. The defences have been breached, and neighbouring countries have been able to take what they wanted (cf. the similar language of Ps. 80:12-13). God's people have become an object of derision because they seem to have been abandoned by their God (cf. also Ps. 44:13-14). Victory over Judah was granted by God to the nation's enemies *(verses 42-43)*, and so they rejoice in their success. The warriors of Judah might as well have been fighting with blunt swords, and there was no divine aid when the final assault came against Jerusalem. God's help had been withheld from his people, just as he had earlier prophesied through Isaiah to Hezekiah concerning the Babylonian invasion (2 Kgs. 20:16-18).

The king has been humiliated by being removed from his place of authority *(verses 44-45)*. Casting the throne to the ground is synonymous with defiling the crown in the dust (verse 39). The reference to 'the days of his youth' support the interpretation that the psalm comes from the period of Jehoiachin's captivity in Babylon. He was eighteen years old when he became king, and he only reigned for three months (2 Kgs. 24:8). It was a disgrace for a king to be taken away with all his family and attendants.

In *verses 46-48* the psalmist questions God regarding the length of time his favour is going to be turned away from his people. When God is angry with his people he is said to hide himself (cf. Pss. 27:9; 30:7;

Isa. 8:17; 45:15). The question, 'How long will your wrath burn like fire?', is a repetition, with slight variation, of Psalm 79:5. The psalmist speaks as the representative of his community, and wonders how short is his life-span. He and all men must die, but will God's wrath against his people be displayed *for ever*? No one is able to escape from death, not even a man at the height of his powers (the Hebrew word for 'man' in verse 48 is not the usual word for 'man', but a special word denoting man in his strength).

In the final verses of the psalm the argument alters. Whereas the psalmist has been pleading on the basis of the shortness of human life, he now pleads that what is happening is bringing dishonour on God himself *(verse 49)*. He bases his cry on God's covenant oath which had been made to David (see verses 3, 35), which was a demonstration of love-and-faithfulness. The psalmist goes right back to the note on which the psalm commenced.

Verses 50-51 may well reflect the shouting of the crowds as Jehoiachin and others were taken away into captivity (the Hebrew text has the plural 'servants'). The land may well have been full of strangers from 'all the nations', or else the psalmist is thinking of the way the surrounding nations are mocking the Jews. A defeated and captive king did not escape the jeers of enemies as he was led off to Babylon.

5. *Concluding Doxology* (*verse 52*)

This doxology, while it comes at the end of this psalm, is really placed here to conclude the third book of the Psalter. This is the shortest of all the concluding doxologies, but it contains the essential thrust of them all – an ascription of praise to the covenant LORD, with the affirmation of a double 'Amen'.

BOOK 4

PSALM 90
A prayer of Moses, the man of God.

This is the oldest psalm in the whole collection, and the only one attributed to Moses. In language it has many resemblances to the books attributed to Moses (the Pentateuch), especially to the Book of Deuteronomy. It is a solemn statement of the eternity of God in contrast to the brevity of human life. The main point of the psalm is reached in verse 12: 'Teach us to number our days aright, that we may gain a heart of wisdom.' Wisdom in the Old Testament is not just theoretical knowledge and understanding, but rather the ability to apply such God-given knowledge to the practical affairs of life. With the passing of days and years, Moses prays for himself and the people as a whole that they will understand the brevity of life and set their hearts on true wisdom. The paraphrase of this psalm by Isaac Watts (1674-1748) has been widely used and greatly loved.

> O God, our help is ages past,
> Our hope for years to come,
> Our shelter from the stormy blast,
> And our eternal home!

1. *An Eternal Refuge (verses 1-2)*
Moses reflects on the past, and recognises that the Lord has been his people's dwelling place. He begins by making a direct affirmation to the Lord. God is called the 'dwelling place', a Hebrew word applied elsewhere to God's heavenly dwelling place (Deut. 26:15). The idea of refuge seems heightened here and in Psalm 91:9 by the idea of God being our home, with all the comfort and personal security that a mere refuge might lack. The Greek translation (LXX) was probably para-phrasing when it used the word 'refuge', and some Hebrew manu-scripts also follow this reading (in Hebrew, having *ma'oz* for *ma'on*). Moses uses the general word for 'Lord' (Hebrew, *'adonai*), whereas in verse 13 he uses the covenant name 'LORD' (*yahweh*). Because he is eternal, God does not change from human generation to generation. Before the mountains came into existence, or the earth and the world were formed, God was there.

2. *Man's Mortality* (*verses 3-6*)

Man's very nature is such that he came from the earth and returns to it (Gen. 3:19). The NIV has inserted the second occurrence of 'to dust', and this is probably a correct interpretation of the meaning of God's words *(verse 3)*. In verse 8 is a reference to sin, which makes an allusion to the curse on man, pronounced after the Fall, all the more likely. As human beings work with the soil it is a reminder to them of their origin and their destiny.

The point of this *verse 4* is to contrast the Lord's unchanging presence with the fleeting time which man spends on this earth. The reference to a thousand years seems to be to those like Methuselah who lived almost that long. In God's sight this is like a day, or even just like a watch in the night (a third part of the night). 2 Peter 3:8 quotes and amplifies this verse when it says: 'With the Lord a day is like a thousand years, and a thousand years are like a day.'

How short is man's life on the earth! *(verses 5-6)*. It is only like grass, which springs up in the morning but by nighttime it has changed (twice the Hebrew verb for 'change', *chalaf*, is used in the verse; cf. its use in Isa. 40:31, where it indicates exchanging weakness for strength). Similar imagery for man's life is found in Psalm 103:15-16 where again grass is used as the illustration, along with reference to God remembering that we are dust. The reference to sleep should not be pressed to mean that there is no conscious existence after death.

3. *God's Wrath* (*verses 7-10*)

There were many demonstrations of God's wrath against his people in Moses' day, and against Moses himself (Deut. 1:37; 4:21). His testimony is: 'We are consumed by your anger and terrified by your indignation' (*verse 7*). Even against his own people, God shows his wrath, for he cannot bear to see sin in their lives. Nor can the secret sins be hidden from his sight (*verse 8*). Everything stands open in the eyes of the Lord, so that no sin is hidden from him. Elsewhere 'the light of your face' denotes God's favour (Ps. 89:15), but here a similar expression denotes the all-searching eye of God.

> Eastward, westward, still you guide me,
>   From your grip I cannot stray;
> Nor will darkness hide me from you:
>   Night to you is clear as day.
>
> (*The Book of Praises*, Ps. 139)

In *verses 9-10* Moses expresses his overall view on the waywardness of the people, who had experienced God's anger against them, so that even at the end there is just the expression of a moan or a sigh (the word is connected with 'meditate' in Ps. 1:2). A life span is seventy or eighty years, but however long it is, it is full of trouble and sorrow. Those years speed by so quickly, and are soon gone. Behind the words of these verses is the realisation that in life we make so many mistakes and achieve so little.

4. *True Wisdom* (*verses 11-12*)

The form of the question ('Who knows the power of your anger?') is one which is used especially in the Book of Ecclesiastes (see 2:19; 3:21; 6:12; 8:1), and it serves to highlight the subject about which it asks. It is the equivalent of 'no one knows'. The answer is expressed in a very condensed way in Hebrew (lit. 'like your fear [is] your wrath'). The only way to prevent ourselves from offending against God is to acknowledge his anger against sin and to seek his forgiving grace offered now in Jesus. The prayer of Moses is that he and the people as a whole would be able to assess their days and their use of them aright. The only way to true knowledge is to have God as our instructor. Here, 'to number' means something far more than mere arithmetic. It is a spiritual approach to our human life, and especially to our fleeting earthly existence. The end result of such numbering is that we are able to bring to God as an offering, a heart of wisdom (the same verb translated 'gain' is used of Cain and Abel's offerings, Gen. 4:3-4).

5. *Prayer for Blessing* (*verses 13-17*)

Just as God so often asked his people to repent, so now Moses prays the Lord will do so himself *(verses 13-14)*. He pleads for unmerited love to be shown to God's covenant servants. He asks that each morning God will give them a reminder of his steadfast love (*chesed*), so that joy and gladness may abound. In comparison to the years of trouble, he now wants to have as many years of joy in turn *(verse 15)*.

The final prayers of this psalm relate to the demonstration of God's power, not just in the present, but for future generations as well ('to their children'). In our prayers we need similarly to focus on future needs, and to think of a succession of believing generations *(verses 16-17)*. If God's favour rests on the people, then their work will see lasting results – they will have counted their days aright. So intense is his request that the psalm finishes with this repeated prayer.

PSALM 91

There are links between this psalm and both Psalms 90 and 92, suggesting that its position here in the Psalter is deliberate. It follows the request for God's favour with which Psalm 90 ends. Psalm 91 contains a multifaceted promise of God to believers in verses 14-16, and then it is followed by their response in Psalm 92. The major part of Psalm 91 is similar in style to the wisdom literature, and therefore it is best classified as a wisdom psalm (see the Introduction, pp. 52-54). The general statements of the psalm find dramatic confirmation in the LORD's word with which the psalm closes.

1. *Sure Refuge with the LORD (verses 1-8)*
The opening verse of Psalm 91 uses descriptive titles of God which go back to the patriarchs, and this may be one reason why the Psalm of Moses (Ps. 90) is immediately followed by this psalm. 'The Most High' as a title for God is first used in Genesis 14:18-20, while 'the Almighty' was a title by which God was known by Abraham, Isaac, and Jacob (Gen. 17:1; 28:3; 35:11). The psalm opens with a statement (possibly by one of the priests in Temple worship) concerning the sure place of refuge to be found with God. He is a hiding place (NIV 'shelter'), and under the shadow of the wings of the cherubim there is safety (see the comments on Ps. 61:4).

The words with which *verse 2* begins – 'I will say of the LORD' – may well be pointing back to the one who has found shelter with the Lord, and so be translated 'He says' (see NIV margin). He boldly claims the great blessing that he has indeed found security with his God.

The unseen danger from enemies is described by language referring to the bird catcher *(verse 3)*, imagery which is used elsewhere in the psalms in a similar way (see Ps. 124:7). Likewise, deadly pestilence was an occurrence which for Solomon called forth prayer to God for safety (1 Kgs. 8:37). In such situations the protective care of God would be given, and believers would be hidden (speaking metaphorically) under his wings (cf. Ps. 17:8; Matt. 23:37). God's faithfulness to his covenant promises would serve like a shield to protect them *(verse 4)*.

Verses 5-6 take up the ideas of verse 3 and enlarge on them. Attacks from enemies, either by day or night, are not to be feared if the LORD is protecting his people. Similarly, sudden plagues of disease should not cause terror, even though they reach epidemic proportions. However, not all believers enjoy this assurance of God's protective care in times of danger. His word is their stay and on it they must rest, rather than on their own emotions. The use of a thousand and ten thousand *(verse 7)* in parallel phrases is typical of Hebrew poetry (cf. Judg. 20:10; 1 Sam. 18:7; Ps. 144:13). No matter how many fall to enemy attacks or to disease, yet the speaker assures his listeners that God will keep them safe. They will be spectators of God's judgments on the wicked, rather than themselves being participants *(verse 8)*.

2. God's Gracious Care (verses 9-13)
Verses 9-10 form a parallel with verses 1-2, and in using 'dwelling' link up also with the opening verse of Psalm 90. Anyone who can truly say, 'The LORD is my refuge', has found a place of safety, and can rest in the thought that nothing happens outside his will. God knows all the circumstances of his children and directs them for their good.

Satan used the words of *verses 11-12* as he tempted Jesus, trying to get him to act rashly. However, Jesus responded by quoting Deuteronomy 6:16: 'Do not test the LORD your God' (Matt. 4:5-7; Luke 4:9-12). In the context here their connection with verse 9 is plain. Protecting care is promised to those who make the LORD their refuge. The metaphor concerning protection by the angels is probably taken from Exodus 23:20. The Lord, who carried Israel out of Egypt on eagles' wings (Exod. 19:4), is still able to ensure that his people do not stumble (Ps. 121:3). God will guard against all kinds of dangers *(verse 13)*, a promise which Jesus repeated as he sent out the disciples (Luke 10:19).

3. God's Word of Promise (verses 14-16)
The closing verses of the psalm are given in the form of a prophetic oracle, with God announcing through the speaker that he will keep safely those who acknowledge him *(verse 14)*. The verb to 'love' used here (Hebrew, *chashaq*) is not the most common Hebrew verb for 'love'. It denotes deep attachment, and is used of God's attitude to Israel (Deut. 7:7; 10:15). If anyone has a genuine love for God, then God promises to keep and guard him.

The main idea of *verses 15-16* is similar to Psalm 50:15, 23. The assurance is given in this prophetic word that there will be a ready response by the LORD whenever there is a call to him in troublesome times. He will intervene and bring deliverance. 'Honour' comes when others see how graciously the LORD has acted. In contrast to those visited by death (see verses 7-8), the person whose prayer is answered will be preserved alive. The Hebrew of verse 16 is a little less definite than the NIV makes it. The idea is that as long as he lives, God will provide food and so satisfy him (cf. Exod. 16:8; Ps. 132:15 for the use of the word 'satisfy'). God both preserves life and also provides daily spiritual and physical food.

PSALM 92
A psalm. A song. For the Sabbath day.

No other psalm shares this designation as a psalm intended for use on the Sabbath. We know from the Jewish Mishnah (*Tamid* 7:4), that this psalm was sung by the Levites in the Temple. The Greek (LXX) translation allots other psalms so that there is one for each consecutive day of the week. The schedule was: first day, Psalm 24; then, (2) Psalm 48; (3) Psalm 82; (4) Psalm 94; (5) Psalm 81; (6) Psalm 93. Psalm 92 does not indicate why it was chosen for the Sabbath. It celebrates the righteous rule of God and also the prosperity of the righteous.

1. *Praise to the LORD (verses 1-3)*
The opening declaration concerning the nature of praise to the LORD is not so much that praise makes us feel 'good', but that it is delightful to praise God. 'Good' is what is in accordance with his will (cf. the use of 'good' in the creation account in Genesis 1), and rightly he calls for praise from his creatures. Praise is due especially for his love-and-faithfulness, because his character calls forth adoration. 'Harp' and the 'lyre' are frequently mentioned in the psalms, but it is difficult now to distinguish between these two stringed instruments, and possibly (because of their use in parallel expressions) the two words refer to the same instrument. The rippling sound of both can evoke joy.

2. *Joy in God's Actions (verses 4-5)*
The prayer of Psalm 90:14-16 has been answered, and now there can be joy over God's saving actions. The 'deeds' and 'works' of the LORD are his actions in delivering the psalmist from the evil designs of his enemies (see verses 9-11). Contemplation of what God has done calls

forth exclamations of wonder at his deeds, and at the depth of his thoughts. Both of these ideas feature elsewhere in the Scriptures (great deeds, Pss. 40:5; 77:11: 106:2; deep thoughts, Isa. 40:13, 28; 55:9; Rom. 11:33).

3. *God's Exaltation over His Enemies* (*verses 6-9*)

The 'enemies' who are going to be destroyed (see verse 9) are described as lacking in spiritual understanding and insight (*verses 6-7*, cf. Paul's words in 1 Cor. 2:6-16). They are like animals, in that they share the same inability to understand God's purposes and they refuse to accept his grace (for the other four Old Testament occurrences of 'senseless', see Pss. 49:10; 73:22; Prov. 12:1; 30:2; for 'fool' see the comment on Ps. 14:1). Such people do not realise that God's eye is on the wicked, and though they may seem to flourish, yet there is an inevitable end for them. By contrast, God is eternal and remains forever as the exalted king and ruler *(verses 8-9)*. This theme will be developed in the psalms which follow (Pss. 93-100). The contrast is marked by the opening words ('*But you ...*') and by the phrases 'forever destroyed' and 'exalted forever'. As eternal King, God rules over all, and therefore his enemies must ultimately be destroyed. Paul develops this in 1 Corinthians 15 as he speaks of Christ destroying all dominion, authority and power, and then delivering the kingdom to God the Father (1 Cor. 15:24-25).

4. *Great Blessing for the Psalmist* (*verses 10-11*)

As a result of the way in which God has dealt with his enemies, the psalmist realises that he has been blessed by God *(verse 10)*. He has received special favours from him. The idea of fine oils may not seem to be connected readily with the wild ox horns. Probably the connection is that horns were used to hold oil for anointing (cf. 1 Sam. 16:1, 13). The psalmist has seen for himself how God has overcome their joint enemies *(verse 11)*. He does not gloat over this, but it is a thing of joy for him. The news about their overthrow is a happy message which he has heard.

5. *The Prosperity of the Righteous* (*verses 12-15*)

The distinction between the wicked and the righteous is now made plain. Whereas the wicked are going to be destroyed or be scattered, the righteous person will have a sure future, planted by the LORD in his own house, and so will be eternally safe *(verses 12-13)*. The palm tree and the cedar of Lebanon are used here as the symbols of the righteous. The palm is one of the most stately trees of the Near East, being widely used, especially for shade and food. The cedar of Lebanon is a massive tree with a vigorous root system and strong timber, and hence it too can be used as a metaphor for a person's or a nation's character in God's sight. Such persons will last, and even in old age they will still be fruitful *(verses 14-15)*. They are God's planting and they know his tender care. Right to the end of their lives they will proclaim the character of their God. The content of the proclamation is an echo of Deuteronomy 32:4. The idea of God's sure strength is linked in both passages with the idea that there is no unrighteousness in him. He is the righteous rock who also brings judgment to the wicked, as the psalmist has already declared (see verses 7, 9, 11; and cf. Hab. 1:12).

PSALM 93

This is the first of a group of psalms (93-100) which speak of the reign of the heavenly King who is far superior to any earthly monarch, and rules supreme over the whole world. There is no power of nature or of men which can challenge him. The content of these psalms is very similar to Psalm 47, which is another song rejoicing in God's kingship. While it is often suggested that this group of psalms was composed for some special religious ceremony in which the kingship of the LORD featured prominently, there is no indication of this within the psalms. They form a united confession concerning God's lordship and the extent of his kingdom. Psalm 93 was used in later Jewish liturgy on the eve of the Sabbath.

1. *God's Rule over the World (verses 1-2)*
God's kingship pre-dates time. He is a majestic God, whose glory is visible *(verse 1)*. Just as ancient kings were robed in garments suitable to their position, so the LORD is regarded as being dressed in majesty and strength. Because the LORD is the world's Creator, it stands firm forever. These words ('The world ... cannot be moved') are repeated in Psalm 96:10. God did not need to assume kingship like an earthly ruler, for his throne has been established from all eternity *(verse 2)*. This basic fact is repeated throughout this group of psalms, as well as elsewhere in the Old Testament (see Zech. 14:9).

2. God's Rule over the Waters (verses 3-4)
It is a graphic picture which the psalmist draws. The mighty waves of
the sea are displaying their might, and the threefold repetition of 'the
seas have lifted up' highlights their power. But over them reigns the
LORD, who is vastly superior to them. He reigns from his throne 'on
high', and just as he was able to calm the waters by his word (Pss. 33:7;
104:7; Job 38:11), so he will subdue all enemies who rise against him.

3. God's Rule over His People (verse 5)
God's rule is also expressed in another way. He is the sovereign over
his covenant people, and he gave them statutes to govern their lives.
Those statutes are trustworthy (Ps. 19:7) and exceptionally firm (the
Hebrew text here has 'very firm'; see NKJV). The king is also
characterised by holiness, and yet he condescends to make his dwelling with his people. The tabernacle was a constant reminder to Israel
of God's presence which he had set among them (Deut. 12:5, 11). The
ultimate realisation of the principle of God's presence with his people
will be experienced in the heavenly dwelling. Into that holy city
nothing sinful or unclean shall ever enter, because it will be the full
expression of God's holiness (Rev. 21:22-27).

PSALM 94

Within the group of kingship psalms (93-100), this psalm is unique. It
is an appeal to the 'Judge of the earth' (verse 2) to deal with the wicked
and to recompense them for their actions. No indication is given of the
time or circumstances of its composition, and it blends national
interests (verses 1-15) with individual concerns (verses 16-23). The
Jewish Mishnah indicates that this psalm was sung on the fourth day
of the week (Wednesday), and this is confirmed in the titles added to
the Greek and Latin versions.

1. Appeal to the Judge (verses 1-3)
The strident plea of the psalmist centres on the repeated call to the 'God
who avenges' *(verses 1-2)*. This description of God compares with the
following phrase, 'the Judge of all the earth' (cf. Gen. 18:25). God
carries out his just punishment and puts right the wrongs which have
occurred. 'Shine forth' is used in other passages of the majesty of
God's presence being revealed (Deut. 33:2; Pss. 50:2; 80:1). 'The
proud' are those who arrogantly carry out their own plans at the

expense of others, exalting themselves above God and men. The repeated 'how long?' *(verse 3)* gives further urgency to the plea. These proud boasters gloat over their success, and seem so sure that their actions will never be challenged.

2. *Description of the Wicked* (*verses 4-7*)

This section of the psalm gives a more detailed description of the wicked than verses 1-3. They are more than doers of wrong actions; they boast constantly of themselves, letting these boasts gush forth *(verse 4)*. This shows their real character; they delight in their wrong doing and are proud of it. Their attitude to God's people also shows their attitude to God himself. Instead of honouring them, they inflict great pain *(verse 5)*. To 'crush' and 'oppress' are verbs which describe the actions taken against an enemy. The actions of the wicked go beyond oppression and persecution. They take the lives of some of God's people, especially those who are less able to defend themselves *(verses 6-7)*. Those who are powerless are the very ones God himself will defend (see Pss. 10:14; 68:5; 146:9). The mistake of the wicked is to think that God takes no notice of what they do, and that they can get away with all their evil.

3. *The Wicked Rebuked* (*verses 8-11*)

The wicked make a great mistake if they continue to think and act as they have done, and now a rebuke is given to them. The way in which the wicked are addressed ('senseless ones', 'fools', *verse 8*) suggests that their actions show that they are making wrong moral decisions in life. They are living like animals (the Hebrew word 'senseless' is connected with a word meaning 'animals'), and so a word of instruction is given to them. One thing the fool does not understand is that because God is the Creator he knows all that is taking place in his world *(verses 9-10)*. He gave men their ears and their eyes. He also controls nations by disciplining them by punishment, while, as the source of all knowledge, he gives instruction to his creatures. God sees through humans, and he understands that they themselves are only short-lived *(verse 11)*. 'Futile' is best taken here in this sense, as its use is similar to that in other Psalter passages and in Job where it refers to the brevity and uncertainty of human life (see Job 7:16; Pss. 39:5, 6; 62:9; 78:33). Its use stresses the contrast between the powerful Creator and his frail creatures.

4. *Justice for God's People (verses 12-15)*

The psalmist picks up the words 'discipline' and 'teach' which he has already used in verse 10. Now he applies them to the way in which God directs the lives of the righteous *(verses 12-13)*. He gives instruction which explains the meaning of life, and this teaching stands in good stead in the days of trouble. Those who receive this teaching are indeed 'blessed', and they are able to understand the final fate of the wicked. Even though the wicked crush God's inheritance (see verse 5), yet that inheritance is safe *(verse 14)*. As Samuel said to the covenant people in his day: 'For the sake of his great name the LORD will not reject his people, because the LORD was pleased to make you his own' (1 Sam. 12:22). God will never abandon his children, but will sustain them even in the midst of oppression. Paul may well be echoing this verse in Romans 11:1-2.

The powerful Creator (see verses 9-11) is also the righteous Judge *(verse 15)*, and those who trust in him will follow his righteous ways. Other interpretations of this verse have been suggested, but it seems best to understand 'follow *it*' as referring back to 'righteousness'.

5. *Confidence in the LORD (verses 16-19)*

In the face of opposition from the wicked the psalmist knows where his help really lies *(verses 16-17)*. 'Rise up' and 'take a stand' are equivalent to saying 'help'. It soon becomes clear that there is no other helper but the LORD (cf. Ps. 124:1-2). Without his aid the wicked will succeed in silencing the psalmist who will lie silent in the grave. The psalmist had thought at some stage that he was going to be put to death, and so slip into the grave *(verses 18-19)*. But at that very moment he knew the sustaining power of God's love, and his deep distress was turned into great joy. In his heart he experienced the reassurance of God's gracious presence.

6. *The Righteous Judge (verses 20-23)*

The final verses of the psalm acknowledges that the only source of true judgment is with God alone. There can be no alliance between corrupt rulers and God *(verses 20-21)*. Those who set up themselves in a seat of power in order to pursue their sinful ways need not think that they can work along with God. Their concern is to oppose the righteous and they bring death and destruction to the good and the innocent. The psalmist has found a sure refuge with the LORD, who alone is the righteous Judge *(verses 22-23)*. He calls God his 'fortress'. This is the same word which occurs in Psalm 46:7, 11, and as there it signifies a fortified height to which one could flee for safety. The addition of 'rock' and 'refuge' strengthen the idea of how safe he felt in God's care. The psalm opened with the call to God to avenge. It closes with the assurance that God will vindicate his people and ultimately the wicked will be destroyed. The Christian's hope remains the same. God will avenge the blood of his servants, and then his redeemed people will say: 'Hallelujah! For our Lord God Almighty reigns' (Rev. 19:6).

PSALM 95

There is no express mention of kingship in this psalm, yet it fits well with the group of kingship psalms (93-100) because of its themes of creation and redemption. It consists of two calls to God's people (verses 1 and 6), each call being followed by a section which amplifies it. The second of these uses God's judgment in the past to reinforce the call to obey him in the present. It is quoted in Hebrews 3:7-11 when the subject of unbelief is being considered. This great psalm has inspired many hymns for Christian worship.

1. *Come Sing for Joy (verses 1-5)*
The psalmist gives a strong call to the assembly of Israel for hearty praise to the LORD in song *(verses 1-2)*. The undated setting was worship in the Temple and the call was probably given by a priest or a Levite. In the preceding psalm God is also called 'the Rock' (Ps. 94:22; see also Pss. 18:2; 89:26). To 'come before the LORD' means to appear at the sanctuary, and there the people are to sing to him in praise and adoration.

Verse 3 – 'For the LORD is the great God, the great King above all gods' – is a compelling reason for praising the greatness of the LORD. It is the supreme motive for songs of adoration and is amplified in verses 3-7. The Lord is exalted above all things and all other beings. There is no god that can be compared with him. The expression, 'the great King above all gods', is very similar to 'the great King over all the earth' (Ps. 47:2). It is an expression of his superiority over all of his creation, even over the so-called gods of the nations. Mention of such gods does not assume their existence. They are only the figments of the imagination. *Verses 4-5* draw attention to some of the awesome features of the world in which we live – the depths of the earth, the mountain peaks, the sea, the dry land – in order to show the control that the LORD has over his creation.

> He's the King above the mountains high,
> the sea is His, the land and sky
> subterranean depths that man defy
> are in the hollow of His hand.
>
> (Michael Perry 1942-)

2. *Come Bow Down in Worship* (*verses 6-11*)

The consequent call to the worshippers is to acknowledge the LORD as their maker *(verses 6-7a)*. The call itself is defined further by the words which follow. In Hebrew there are three verbs: 'bow down', 'bow the knees', and 'kneel'. While the words may give some indication of the posture in prayer, the real emphasis is on the heart attitude towards the LORD. The call is to come in reverence before him, because of the relationship, initiated by God, between him and his people. He by grace is their God and they are his flock (cf. Ps. 100:3, 'we are his people, the sheep of his pasture'). Just as kings are called 'shepherds' of their people, so are their kingdoms called 'pastures' (cf. Jer. 25:36; 49:20).

At a ceremony the leader would speak the words of *verses 7b-9* to the worshippers and encourage them to fresh obedience to the LORD. The switch to first person speech ('tested and tried *me*') happens in other cases where the spokesman of God is actually speaking (cf. Isa. 3:1-4). The response which God desires from his flock is starkly different from that which the people gave at the incidents at Meribah and Massah (see Exod. 17:7; Num. 20:13). Despite knowing so much about God's power, the people then challenged him. The experiences of their fathers at the Red Sea and the miraculous food supply which they received should have convinced each generation to trust the LORD and to be obedient to him.

All the disobedience of Israel came to a climax when the people faithlessly refused to carry out the conquest of Canaan, and wanted to return to Egypt (Num. 14:1-4). Only after Moses pled with God on their behalf were the people forgiven (Num. 14:13-20), but they were condemned to stay in the wilderness for forty years (Num. 14:34). God's declaration about the people *(verse 10)* paraphrases his words in Numbers 14:11.

The oath *(verse 11)* is given in Numbers 14:28-35 where it is said that the people will never enter into *the land*. However, the promise was repeatedly given of *rest* in the land of Canaan (see especially Deut. 3:20; 12:9-10; 25:19), and so 'rest' could easily serve as a synonym for 'land [of Canaan]'. The writer to the Hebrews points out that Joshua was unable to give the people rest. It is only through Jesus that believers come into possession of rest and look forward to the ultimate Sabbath of rest in heaven (Heb. 4:8-10).

PSALM 96

Psalms 96-99 form a small group within the wider section of Psalms 93-100. They have many words and ideas in common, and they may well have been composed by the same author. This psalm appears in a slightly altered form in 1 Chronicles 16:23-33 in connection with the bringing of the ark of the covenant to Jerusalem. It is a call to all nations to praise the LORD, and forms part of the missionary outlook of the Old Testament. It is an anticipation of the worldwide mission of the Christian church (Matt. 28:16-20). Early Christians saw this significance of the psalm, and the old Latin version in verse 10 has: 'Say among the nations, the Lord reigns *from the cross.*'

1. A Call to Praise *(verses 1-3)*
Like adjacent psalms, this one opens with a call for all the world to sing the praises of the LORD. This, and many other expressions, are similar to parts of Isaiah 40-66 (see the opening words Isa. 42:10). There is often a close link between the psalmists and the prophets.

The call to praise is repeated three times *(verses 1-2)*: 'Sing ... sing ... sing', emphasising the exuberant feelings of the psalmist. The term 'a new song' can indicate simply the freshness of the song (see comment on Ps. 33:2-3), or, as here, it can indicate an eschatological or end-time song (see Rev. 5:9; 14:3). The whole tenor of the psalm points to the final reign of the LORD as King and Judge. Universal praise is to be made to him, and there is to be constant proclamation of his saving grace.

God's amazing salvation is to be proclaimed to people everywhere *(verse 3)*. His saving acts on behalf of his people are to be made known to Jew and Gentile alike. This anticipates the New Testament proclamation that 'salvation is found in no-one else, for there is no other name under heaven given to men by which we must be saved' (Acts 4:12).

2. *The Majesty of the* LORD *(verses 4-6)*

A fuller explanation is now given why God should be praised universally *(verses 4-5)*. The expression 'great is the Lord' was clearly a regular way of ascribing honour to God (see the same phrase in Pss. 48:1; 145:3). Belief in God is repeatedly linked with confession of him in praise, for faith and joyful acknowledgment belong together (cf. Rom. 10:8-11). While other 'gods' are referred to, their existence is denied in verse 5. The psalmist puns on the Hebrew word for God (*'elohim*), saying that the heathen gods are only worthless idols or nobodies (*'elilim*). They are put to shame before our sovereign God (Isa. 19:1; Ps. 97:7). They are not real, and therefore do not have power like the one who made the heavens.

'Splendour and majesty' *(verse 6)* commonly occur together in the Psalms in description of God (21:5; 45:3; 104:1), while 'strength and glory' occur in the Hebrew text of Psalm 78:61 in reference to the Ark (NIV 'might', 'splendour'). It is difficult to decide whether 'sanctuary' refers to God's heavenly dwelling or to the temple. The overall thought of the psalm suggests the former, though in the context of a temple song the latter can hardly be excluded.

3. *A Call to Worship (verses 7-9)*

In parallel with the opening verses, another call goes out to the nations to worship the LORD *(verses 7-8)*. The threefold use of 'ascribe' in these verses parallels the threefold 'sing' in verses 1-2. They form a command to everyone from all nations to acknowledge the LORD and to offer to him such ascription of praise that recognises and promotes the glory of his person. This praise must be more than mere words; suitable attitudes and actions are required as well. In the New Testament the call becomes: 'Repent, for the kingdom of heaven is near' (Matt. 3:2), while the allusion to the promise given to Abraham of blessing to the nations ('O families of nations', see Gen. 12:3; 22:18) finds fulfilment in the redeeming work of Jesus (Gal. 3:10-14).

In ascribing glory to the LORD, his creatures acknowledge his greatness by humbly bowing before him *(verse 9)*. If the footnote in the NIV is followed ('with the splendour of his holiness') it would imply coming before him with garments which are ritually clean (see Lev.

11:24-28). Today God requires the offering up of our bodies as living sacrifices, holy and pleasing to him (Rom. 12:1). Likewise the church at the end of time is to be presented to him without stain or blemish, but holy and blameless (Eph. 5:27).

4. *Joy to the World* (*verses 10-13*)

Just as verses 4-6 explained the reason for singing to the LORD a new song, so these verses explain the reason for ascribing glory to the LORD. The basic reason is that the LORD is the King over all since he is the Creator of the world *(verse 10)*. It stands firm because of his decree (Ps. 33:8-11), and from all eternity his throne has been established. All mankind is subject to his equitable judgment. The New Testament re-affirms this principle, making it explicit that God will judge the world through the Lord Jesus, raising him from the dead as proof of this (John 5:19-23; Acts 17:31). The whole of nature *(verses 11-13) will* sing for joy when it is 'liberated from its bondage to decay and brought into the glorious freedom of the children of God' (Rom. 8:21). The repetition of both the phrase 'he comes' and the fact that he is coming to judge emphasise the certainty and the nature of that coming. He comes to bring justice to the ungodly and deliverance to his saints. The prospect is that Gentiles will also be among those for whom he comes in righteousness and truth. The New Testament picture is of every creature in heaven and earth at the last day singing:

> To him who sits on the
> throne and to the Lamb
> be praise and honour and
> glory and power,
> for ever and ever! (Rev. 5:13)

PSALM 97

This psalm, like Psalms 93 and 99, commences with the declaration of the LORD's kingship. Verse 7 is pivotal; around it the whole psalm revolves. The opening section is a call to the distant nations (probably including those around the Mediterranean, the Red Sea and the Persian Gulf) to acknowledge the greatness of the LORD, while the closing section is a call to Zion to rejoice in the LORD and in his righteous rule. The message of verse 7 is that idol worshippers and even their idols must bow before his sovereignty. Israel and the Gentile nations are both to confess that they have seen and acknowledge the glory of the great King.

1. Let Distant Shores Rejoice (verses 1-6)

The opening declaration concerning the LORD's kingship is followed by a call for earth to be glad and the distant shores to rejoice *(verse 1)*. All the inhabitants of the world are to be joyful in the knowledge that the LORD reigns. A fitting response to the eternal reign of a holy God is worship and adoration (see Rev. 11:15; 15:4; 19:6). The word translated 'shores' is also used of islands, which explains the variation in other translations (see AV, NKJV). It serves to draw attention to the universal nature of God's kingship.

The description of God's rule in *verses 2-4* echoes language in other passages which speak of the majesty of God's appearance (cf. Exod. 20:18-21; Deut. 5:22-27). His glory is such that it is veiled from human sight lest it dazzle the eyes. When his glory is seen it is like lightning flashes which serve both as a source of light and terror. His enemies perish before his presence (cf. Ps. 68:1-2). Amidst this description there is also a reaffirmation of the foundations of God's kingly rule. His kingship is characterised by the fact that he does not reign like a human ruler in self-interest and with perversion of justice. Instead, his rule is noted for its righteousness and its fair administration.

Even the mighty mountains, which symbolise all that is stable and enduring, cannot stand before the LORD *(verses 5-6)*. The repetition of 'before the LORD' (cf. the repetition of 'he comes' in Ps. 96:13) probably occurs to highlight his majesty and kingly rule over the universe. Undergirding the whole moral order is the righteousness of God, and his general revelation declares this fact (cf. Ps. 19:1ff.). The world of creation and providence proclaims its dependence upon God's character for its continuing existence. All men have a knowledge of God because they still bear his image. Though they try and suppress this knowledge, they are left without excuse before him (Rom. 1:20).

2. A Call to Worship (verse 7)

The thought of this verse is the central aspect of the psalm. Idol worshippers are called upon to renounce their allegiance to their present 'gods' and to confess the true God and King as their master. No man-made idol has the power to save those who worship it (Isa. 44:17).

All who trust in what are nobodies (see the comment on Ps. 96:5) will ultimately realise their folly. The psalmist makes it clear that even these so-called 'gods' are really subject to the one true God. Before him they must prostrate themselves.

3. *Let Zion Rejoice* (*verses 8-12*)

God's own people hear again the declaration, 'The LORD reigns', and they are glad *(verses 8-9)*. The fact that God's judgments are acts of deliverance on behalf of his people brings joy in the settlements throughout the land. The people acknowledge again that God is so exalted above all his creation, and none of the idols can compete with his position.

God's people are called on to show both love and hatred – love for God himself, but hatred towards evil *(verse 10)*. The description of those who are in a close relationship with God as those who love him is also found concerning Abraham (Isa. 41:8, 'friend'; Hebrew, 'the one who loves me'). Protective care surrounds God's 'friends', and he vindicates and delivers them from those who conspire against himself as well as against them.

The rule of God is described here and elsewhere in terms of light and joy *(verses 11-12,* cf. the combination of light and joy in Isa. 60). 'Shed upon' is literally 'sown', which may indicate something strewn in the path of the righteous. The expression used to describe them ('the upright in heart') is common in the Book of Psalms. The call to 'rejoice' links both with the last word in the Hebrew text of verse 11 ('joy') and also with the call in verse 1 for the distant shores to 'rejoice'. 'Name' is literally 'memorial', but clearly, as in Exodus 3:15, it is a synonym for 'name', though twice in the Psalms (111:4; 145:7) it refers to the recitation of God's wonderful deeds. Here something of this meaning would be quite in keeping with the context.

PSALM 98
A psalm.

There is much similarity between Psalms 96 and 98, especially the manner in which they start and finish. Psalm 98 has a marked progression in the main theme. First, the gathered people are called upon to sing to the LORD, then all the peoples of the earth, and finally, all of creation. The reason for such universal praise is the salvation which God has made known. This may well be understood as an accumulation of various acts of deliverance wrought by him rather than just a single one such as the return from exile in Babylon. There is clearly a focus too on the final coming of the Lord, when the Lord Jesus will return to gather his people and to judge the whole world (Matt. 25:31-46). Isaac Watts (1674-1748) captured the spirit of Psalm 98 with his words:

> Joy to the world! The Lord is come;
> let earth receive her King.
> let ev'ry heart prepare him room,
> and heaven and nature sing.
> and heaven and nature sing.
> and heaven, and heaven and nature sing.

1. *Israel – Sing to the* LORD *(verses 1-3)*
In words identical to the opening of Psalm 96 (see the commentary), the call goes forth to the congregation of Israel to respond to the LORD's goodness with a new song *(verse 1)*. He has performed acts which are unmistakably divine ('marvellous things' often has this meaning; see the comment on Ps. 71:17), and which are explained in verses 2-3. 'Right hand' and 'holy arm' are indications of the LORD's might, so that he has brought about the salvation without anyone else's intervention (cf. Isa. 59:16; 63:5).

When God acts in salvation that is a demonstration of his righteousness, and it is done openly so that it forms a self-revelation to the nations *(verse 2)*. In this way God proclaims to them his essential character and his saving power. No mention is made here of the fact that when God does bring salvation it so often is accompanied by judgment to the nations.

God acted with covenant faithfulness towards Israel in that he took appropriate action to deliver his people *(verse 3)*. When he 'remembers' he saves his people (Exod. 2:24-25) or preserves them (Lev. 26:44-45). This had been done openly, and frequently, so this salvation was apparent to the world at large. In this way God had proclaimed his saving power.

2. *The Nations – Shout for Joy (verses 4-6)*
It is not only Israel who is called on to rejoice in the LORD, but the [Gentile] nations as well. The opening words of *verse 4* are the same

as Psalm 66:1 (cf. also Ps. 47:1). The Hebrew text uses a cluster of commands to the nations, and in so doing highlights the praise which is expected from them. They are to 'shout for joy' (twice), 'burst forth into song', and 'make music'. The NIV text renders them quite idiomatically into English, though the smoothness of the translation loses something of the forcefulness that the repeated commands have in Hebrew. The closing words of *verse 6* point to the motive which is to lie behind their praise. The nations are to acknowledge the covenant LORD of Israel as their God and King. This, then, is really a call for conversion of the nations, and a commitment to the living God.

3. The World – Sing for Joy (verses 7-9)

The final stage of the psalm brings the whole world in on the song of praise. The whole of creation is to be part of this chorus, as well as all the inhabitants (the second part of *verse 7* is identical with the second part of Ps. 24:1). Nature is personified, and rejoices in the coming of the LORD as Judge of the earth. The description of the Lord's coming is almost identical to Psalm 96:13. To 'judge' involves deliverance for his people and destruction of those who are hostile to his ways. At the last great appearing of the LORD he will deal with all in accordance with his righteousness and uprightness. When the redeemed in heaven sing the song of Moses and the song of the Lamb, they will confess:

> Great and marvellous are your deeds,
>   Lord God Almighty.
> Just and true are your ways,
>   King of the ages (Rev. 15:3).

PSALM 99

Along with Psalms 93 and 97, Psalm 99 commences with the explicit affirmation of the LORD's kingship. It is clear that the psalmist did not regard this kingship as of recent origin, for he appeals to the relationship which God had with his people in the times of Moses, Aaron and Samuel. The psalm shows signs of careful composition, with the word 'LORD' occurring seven times (symbolically pointing to completeness), as well as a sevenfold occurrence of Hebrew personal pronouns referring to him. There is also a threefold division in the psalm, marked out by the refrain 'he is holy' in verses 3 and 5, and expanded to the fuller expression 'for the LORD our God is holy' in the final verse.

1. *The Exalted LORD* (*verses 1-3*)

The LORD is the King over Israel (he is enthroned between the cherubim, and he is exalted in Zion). This is a reference to the fact that he met with his people at the mercy seat in the tabernacle *(verse 1)*. Yet he is far greater than that for he is King of the nations and they are urged to tremble in awe before him *(verse 2)*. This verb 'tremble' is used in the Old Testament both for trembling before the judgment of God (Isa. 64:2; Joel 2:1), and also of the response to God's gracious actions (Jer. 33:9). In this psalm both aspects are present. As the nations bow before the holy and righteous King, they are to be reminded of his gracious character in forgiving sin (verse 8).

The nations are not only to tremble but to praise *(verse 3)*. God is indeed great and holy (Deut. 7:21), and the nations should acknowledge that fact and bow before him in reverence. There is a sudden shift from second person ('*your* great and awesome name') to third person ('*he* is holy'). The expression, 'he is holy', seems to be one used in a worship situation, as a declaration stemming from God's own declaration, 'I am holy' (see Lev. 11:44; 19:2; 20:26; 21:8).

2. *The Righteous Lord* (*verses 4-5*)

Verse 4 begins with a declaration about God, and then addresses him directly in the second person. Though God is mighty, and shows that in his kingly rule, yet he always acts in accordance with his own character, and so does what is right and good. It is his rule which is in view, not that of the Davidic family. The period when this rule began for Israel as a nation (called here by the alternative name 'Jacob') was when the covenant was made at Sinai.

For the temple worshippers the call is to lift up the name of their God in praise and adoration *(verse 5)*. The place where this is to be done is at the LORD's 'footstool'. Most probably this means the cover of the ark of the covenant, 'the place of atonement' (see 1 Chr. 28:2, 11). The motive behind this worship is that God is holy, repeating the declaration of verse 3.

3. *The Forgiving LORD* (*verses 6-9*)

God provided priestly servants who interceded for the people (cf. Exod. 32:11-13), and who taught them the way of the LORD (Mal. 2:4-6). Moses carried out various priestly functions (see Exod. 24:6, 8; 40:22-27), while Samuel prayed mightily on behalf of Israel (1 Sam.

7:9; 12:18). Their prayers were effective, in that God responded to them *(verse 6)*.

A summary statement is given of the manner in which God answered their prayers *(verses 7-8)*. While the reference to 'the pillar of cloud' points directly to the experience of Moses and Aaron (see Exod. 33:9; Num. 12:5-6), yet that of Samuel may also be included, as he was called by God at the sanctuary, where God's ark was situated (1 Sam. 3:3-4, 19-21). However imperfectly the decrees which God gave were kept in Israel, yet it was to his people specifically that they were given. Israel did not escape punishment for their sins, but mercy was shown so often to a wayward people by a forgiving God. The one whom the poet calls 'our God' repeatedly forgave his people's sins (Ps. 103:11-13; Dan. 9:9).

The psalm closes with an expanded version of verse 5 *(verse 9)*. In place of worship at 'his footstool' the people are called to God's 'holy mountain' (i.e. Zion). Since the coming of Jesus true worship is offered wherever believers 'worship the Father in spirit and in truth' (John 4:23). The addition of the words 'the LORD our God', which come last in the Hebrew text, throws emphasis on the relationship which the worshippers had with the holy God. Though so different in character from his sinful people, yet he was indeed their God.

PSALM 100
A psalm. For giving thanks.

The final psalm in this section (93-100) is a triumphal song of praise to the LORD. The second part of the title has suggested to some that it was composed to accompany the presentation of a thankoffering to the LORD (see Lev. 7:11-15). However, there is no indication within the psalm that this was its specific purpose. In the early church Psalm 100 was used for morning prayer, while throughout the history of the Christian church it has often been used by the assembled people of God as they engage in communal worship before the LORD. It is commonly referred to as 'the Old Hundredth', after the name of the stately tune to which it is often sung. This tune was composed by Louis Bourgeois and first appeared in the French Genevan Psalter of 1551.

1. *A Call to Worship (verses 1-3)*
The opening words are identical to Psalm 98:4a. All the earth should respond to this call when they recognise what the LORD has done for

his people. It is, in effect, a missionary invitation, for the psalmist wants everyone, Jew and Gentile, to rejoice before the King.

The Hebrew word rendered 'worship' *(verse 2)* has a range of meanings, which extends from acting as a servant or slave (Jer. 34:14), or functioning as subjects of a ruler (Jer. 27:7; 28:14), to serving the LORD (Exod. 23:25). The Gentile nations are called to give their allegiance to the covenant God of Israel ('the LORD'), and to join in joyful worship of him.

To 'know' God *(verse 3)* is to confess him, making open acknowledgment that he is the only God. An alternative rendering would be, 'Acknowledge that the LORD alone is God.' The nations should know that it is the LORD who formed the Israelites into a nation for himself, and that nation belongs to him. In place of 'and we are his', there is an alternative translation, 'and not we ourselves'. It comes from an ambiguity in the Hebrew text because two Hebrew words share the same pronunciation but differ in meaning (Hebrew, *lo*; it can mean either 'not', or 'belonging to him'). The thought of Israel as the LORD's flock has already been presented in Psalm 95:7. This concept is developed further in the New Testament with the teaching concerning Jesus as the shepherd (John 10:11; Heb. 13:20; 1 Pet. 2:25), with a special people (Tit. 2:14) whom he has purchased as his servants (1 Cor. 6:20; 7:21-23; 1 Pet. 2:24-25).

2. *A Call to Thanksgiving* (verses 4-5)

Those entering the temple and presenting themselves in its courtyards are encouraged to come with joyful thanksgiving before the LORD *(verse 4)*. The mention of 'thanksgiving' ties in with the expression in the title, 'with thanksgiving' (it is the same word in Hebrew). The worshippers are to have the LORD himself as their focal point. Some church buildings have a brass plate in their foyer with the Latin inscription: 'Ad majorem Dei gloriam' ('To the greater glory of God'). This captures the central point in this call.

Verse 5 – 'For the LORD is good and his love endures forever; his faithfulness continues through all generations' – may well have been the confession which worshippers in Israel made when they came to the sanctuary. God's 'goodness' is a summary expression for the things promised in the covenant (see the comment on Ps. 34:8). His covenant love and faithfulness never fail, and they are praised generation after generation (cf. Pss. 89:1-2; 106:1; 107:1).

PSALM 101
Of David. A psalm.

Another minor collection of psalms within the whole book commences with Psalm 101 and extends as far as Psalm 110. It is arranged symmetrically with the first five psalms dealing with the king, an individual prayer, praise of the Lord's great love, creation, and Israel's redemption. The following five psalms deal with the same topics in reverse order. The following diagram shows the pattern:

Psalm 101		Psalm 110
Psalm 102		Psalm 109
Psalm 103		Psalm 108
Psalm 104		Psalm 107
Psalm 105	Psalm 106	

In this psalm the king sings of his commitment to the LORD, and of his desire to see all unrighteous people removed from the LORD's realm. The ideal king pictured here only found fulfilment in David's greater son, the Lord Jesus Christ.

1. The Standards for the King (verses 1-4)
The opening verse captures the theme of the whole psalm. What the king desired for the nation was merely an expression of the righteous rule of God himself. Hence he sings of two of the major qualities which characterise God's rule, love and justice.

The patriarch Abraham was called to walk with God and to be blameless (Gen. 17:1). Here the psalmist commits himself to live by God's standard of blamelessness (*verse 2a*, perhaps 'upright' is closer to the idea). His question, 'When will you come to me?', expresses his longing for God's help in keeping his resolve. The LORD's words to Solomon after the building of the Temple help us determine the meaning of walking with a blameless heart (1 Kgs. 9:4). It was doing all that the LORD commanded by observing his decrees and laws. Frequently the Old Testament links heart and eyes together in relation to conduct (cf. Ecc. 2:10; Jer. 22:17). Influences both from within ('heart') and from without ('eyes') determine actions (Matt. 5:27-29). The psalmist pledges himself to have nothing to do with those whose minds are *set* on evil. Such rebellious people will not be his companions *(verses 2b-4)*.

2. *Righteous Rule in the LORD's City* (*verses 5-8*)

Slander is treated so seriously because it involves false testimony which threatens the life and reputation of another person (*verse 5*, cf. Lev. 19:16). The expression for 'haughty eyes' occurs only here in the Old Testament, but there is a similar expression in Psalm 18:27. 'A proud heart' is literally 'broad of heart', but in the context this is a reference to arrogance. The king will not tolerate such people. He has an obligation to discipline those who live by their own rules and violate the rights of others.

A further pledge is given that the faithful will be encouraged as they support the king *(verses 6-7)*. Those who are blameless (see comment on verse 2) will act as the king's servants, while the treacherous will be excluded from his presence. The expressions and 'in my house' and 'in my presence' may well mean the royal court and even the whole land (see 'in the land' in verses 6 and 8).

It seems to have been the custom for the king to hear cases every morning (see 2 Sam. 15:2; Jer. 21:12). Here the king promises to remove the wicked from the land and from the city of the LORD *(verse 8)*. Elsewhere Jerusalem is called the city of God (see Pss. 46:4-5; 48:1-8; 87:1-3). This ideal of a purified land will ultimately come to fulfilment in the New Jerusalem, when no-one 'who does what is shameful or deceitful' will be allowed to enter in, 'but only those whose names are written in the Lamb's book of life' (Rev. 21:27).

PSALM 102

*A prayer of an afflicted man. When he is faint
and pours out his lament before the LORD.*

The title of this psalm is very unusual, and no other psalm has one like it. No author is named, and there is no link with any precise historical circumstance. We are not even told the details of the affliction, though from the content of the psalm they could relate both to individual and national troubles. Most probably the psalm comes from the time of the exile in Babylon (cf. the references to Zion in verses 13, 16, 21 with the way that Lamentations 5:17-18 refers to the desolate city). The general nature of the psalm is reflected in the title, and it is not surprising that it has been used as one of the traditional penitential psalms.

1. A Cry for Help (verses 1-2)
The psalmist's serious plight produces a spate of requests to the Lord. He uses expressions which occur in other psalms, which suggests that psalmists often employed well-known forms of prayer in appealing to God (for similar prayers see Pss. 13:1; 18:6; 56:9; 65:2; 69:17). It is not just formal prayer though, for the urgency and anguish of his requests breaks through here and throughout the psalm. He pleads for God to pay attention to his prayer and to answer it quickly.

2. A Miserable Situation (verses 3-11)
After the initial appeal the psalmist convincingly describes his distress. The sufferer uses a variety of metaphors to depict his condition *(verses 3-5)*. He compares his life to smoke and grass (see also verse 11), which both disappear so quickly. The bitterness of his soul might have physical causes. He may be describing burning fever which has him in its grip. On the other hand he may be comparing his sense of being forsaken by God to a physical illness. Food loses its priority in life as distress increases, and he is now only skin and bones.

The owls are unclean birds (Lev. 11:13-18; Deut. 14:11-17), and they often live in isolated places (other versions including the AV have 'pelican' for the first bird, but this is unlikely as the pelicans are water birds). The psalmist feels his isolation, just as if he is one of these birds perched on a rooftop *(verses 6-7)*.

In addition to physical suffering he is enduring the torment of verbal abuse *(verse 8)*. His enemies even use his name in cursing. There is a case in Genesis 48:20 of names used in blessing ('May God make you like Ephraim and Manasseh'). Here the psalmist's name and condition have become such that they are a byword, able to be used in connection with curses.

People sat in ashes or dust when in mourning *(verse 9,* cf. Job 2:8; Jon. 3:6), and to say that tears become drink is simply to emphasise how deep the grief really is (cf. Pss. 42:3; 80:5). There is also the recognition that God is dealing in his great wrath (the Hebrew has 'your wrath and your anger') with the psalmist and with the nation *(verse 10)*. The reversion to the ideas of verses 3-4 in *verse 11* shows turmoil of mind. He feels that his life is about to vanish completely.

3. Confidence in the LORD (verses 12-17)
But over against the frailty and brevity of human life stands God's eternal kingship *(verse 12)*. His fame is permanent, not temporary. The

vision of the destitute psalmist turns from his own condition to the reality that the LORD indeed reigns as King. The contrast is marked very strongly by the words, 'But you, ...'

From *verses 13-14* it is clear that the psalmist is not only mournful personally, but his concern is also for afflicted Zion. Possibly he has in mind some word from one of the prophets concerning a visitation of the Lord to Zion. This will be 'the time to show favour', 'the appointed time', when God comes to deliver his people. The argument of verse 14 is that if the people treasure Zion so much, how much more concern does God have for the city which bears his name (Dan. 9:18-19).

God's saving actions will result in universal recognition *(verse 15)*. This had been true of the Exodus from Egypt, and it was to be true again at the time of the return from exile in Babylon. God's greatest act of salvation is in Jesus Christ, and it is through his atoning life, death and resurrection that the most extensive acknowledgement is going to come. Every eye will see him, and every knee will bow to him (Rev. 1:7; Phil. 2:10-11).

In *verses 16-17* the psalmist declares his confidence that God will respond to the pleas of his people and come in majestic power to restore Jerusalem. When he rebuilds Zion, that will be a demonstration of his mighty power. What actually happened when Jerusalem was restored in the late 6th century BC was only a faint foreshadowing of the ultimate city of God. When the heavenly Jerusalem is revealed it will shine with the glory of God (Rev. 21:11).

4. The Sure Promises of God (verses 18-22)

The assurances which the psalmist has just uttered are to be recorded for the benefit of coming generations *(verse 18)*. This is the only reference in the Book of Psalms to the recording of God's great deeds in a scroll or book. Just as God heard the cry of his people in Egypt (Exod. 2:23-25), so he will hear again. The psalmist rests in the confidence that God will respond to the groans of the exiled people, who are called here 'the prisoners' (see the comment on Ps. 79:11) and 'those condemned to death' *(verses 19-20)*. They themselves clearly felt that they were condemned to die far from their own land. The great King is going to look down from his dwelling place and take action to release those in captivity (see Ezek. 37:1-14).

In *verses 21-22* the picture is of a great gathering in restored Jerusalem when those who are converted from the Gentiles will take part in praising the name of the LORD. This is what the prophets had declared would take place (see Isa. 2:2-4; Mic. 4:1-3), and it is part of the vision of the end times which the prophets and psalmists shared. The ingathering which started on the Day of Pentecost (Acts 2) will lead eventually to an assembly before the throne of God of those 'from every nation, tribe, people and language' (Rev. 7:9).

5. A Renewed Complaint (verses 23-28)

The thought of the psalmist reverts to the personal complaints he has brought earlier (*verse 23,* see verses 3-11). He sees God's hand at work, taking away his vigour and limiting the length of his earthly life, and he then recalls what he had said concerning this. He remembers his plea to God that his life would not be cut short *(verse 24)*. In his earlier lament he had compared his life to smoke and grass. Here he acknowledges that God's existence is very different from our own, for God is eternal (cf. verse 12). The eternal God created the heavens and the earth *(verses 25-27)*, but he is so different to his creation. The words 'But you' in verse 27 are very emphatic in Hebrew. While he remains the same throughout all time, the creation perishes. Just like old clothing, the heavens and the earth will pass away. In Hebrews 1:10-12 the words of verses 25-27, here spoken of the LORD himself, are taken over and in a powerful argument applied to Jesus.

God's eternal nature is the ultimate and immediate security for his people *(verse 28)*. The promise is that the descendants of present believers will continue in God's presence and care. While the initial reference of the phrase 'live in your presence' refers to life in the land of Palestine after the exile, yet the wider application of the principle is found in the New Testament. God who commences a work in the hearts and lives of his children, carries on that work until the day of Christ Jesus (Phil. 1:6). As the author of their salvation, the Lord Jesus is able to bring many sons to glory where they shall live in his presence (Heb. 2:10).

PSALM 103
Of David.

This psalm emphasises the love and compassion of Israel's covenant keeping God. It begins and ends on the note of praise, with a double call in verses 1-2, and a fourfold call in verses 20-22. The core of the psalm is a recital of personal benefits received (verses 3-5) and of the LORD's compassion to his people Israel (verses 6-19). With clarity almost comparable with the New Testament, this psalm proclaims the greatness of God's love for his people and his gracious removal of their sins – though the method of such removal remains unrevealed.

1. *My Soul, Praise the LORD!* (*verses 1-2*)

The psalmist puts his whole being into a powerful chorus of praise to his God. This praise reflects the vitality of his relationship with God, and shows the fervour of his spiritual life. The word translated 'praise' is literally 'bless', a word used in the Old Testament to express thanks and gratitude. It is commonly used, as here, of God, and calls attention to his loving and faithful character. Both Psalms 103 and 104 commence with this self-exhortation. The 'name' of God refers to his character, and especially those aspects which are going to be recited in the following verses.

2. *Praise for Personal Blessing* (*verses 3-5*)

The psalmist recites first the various blessings he has personally received from the LORD. The pronoun 'your' refers back to 'my soul', and therefore it is equivalent to speaking about 'my sins' and 'my diseases'. The word translated 'forgives' is never used of people forgiving one another, but is used exclusively of God in the Old Testament, for it describes his gracious action in pardoning sinners. Here its parallel is 'heal', which can be used in the figurative sense of healing spiritual diseases (Ps. 147:3; Isa. 53:5). However, in this context it refers to healing from illnesses which almost brought the psalmist down to the grave. God redeems from death, and restores to a royal position, crowning with expressions of love and compassion. So enlivened is the psalmist that he feels as though he has the fresh strength of an eagle (cf. the same figure in Isa. 40:31). Covenant life should be an experience of God who 'forgives', 'heals', 'redeems', 'crowns', and 'satisfies'. This cluster of terms highlights the graciousness of God.

3. *Praise for National Blessing* (*verses 6-19*)

This section of the psalm opens and closes with declarations concerning God's reign and its character. Turning away from his own situation and his own individual experiences, the psalmist sings of the way in which the LORD supports the oppressed. He performs righteous and saving deeds *(verse 6)*, which are often at the same time judgments upon the godless.

In *verse 7*, which follows a verse which speaks of God's righteousness and justice, it is most likely that the reference is to the revelation of God's personal qualities, character and manner of operating which he showed consistently to Moses. Particularly after the incident with the golden calf, God, in response to Moses' request to be taught his ways (Exod. 33:13), granted him a fresh revelation of his glory (Exod. 34:6-7). Those ways involved both maintaining his covenant love but also not letting the wicked go unpunished

Verse 8 is almost an exact quotation from Exodus 34:6. It summarises the character of the covenant God of Israel – deeply merciful, not quick to anger, abundant in steadfast love. These characteristics are spelt out in the following verses. 'To accuse' *(verse 9)* is a technical term which means to bring a charge against an erring covenant servant. In spite of the sins of his people, God stretches out his hands to them in mercy *(verse 10)*. In his grace he gives them what they do not deserve – unmerited favour! The gospel proclaims that God, who is rich in mercy, makes believers alive in Christ even when they are dead in transgressions (Eph. 2:4-5). God acts the same in both Testaments.

In *verses 11-12* two illustrations are given to demonstrate the greatness of God's mercy. The immeasurable distances between heaven and earth and between east and west are used to draw attention to the measureless nature of God's love for his people. His forgiving grace is infinite towards 'those who fear him', a term descriptive of true believers (see on Ps. 34:7). In the New Testament it becomes clear that forgiveness comes through the shed blood of Christ on the cross.

> Marvellous grace of our loving Lord,
> grace that exceeds our sin and our guilt!
> Yonder on Calvary's mount outpoured,
> there where the blood of the Lamb was spilt.
>
> (Julia H. Johnston)

God's love is not indiscriminate, for he has compassion on 'his children', who are further described as 'those who fear him' *(verse 13)*. At the time of the Exodus the people of Israel were adopted as God's children, becoming a holy nation. The New Testament takes over this language of the church (1 Pet. 2:9-10). In the fullness of time Jesus came to lay down his life for his sheep (John 10:11, 14-15), purchasing his church with his own blood (Acts 20:28). The frailty of human beings is also a cause for God's compassion, for he knows that we are but creatures, made from the dust *(verse 14)*.

Not only is man a creature, but he is also frail, and his time on earth is temporary *(verses 15-16)*. This imagery is used elsewhere in the Old Testament of the fleeting nature of human life (cf. Pss. 90:5-6; 92:7; Isa. 51:12), while at other times 'flower of the field' is a similar comparison (Job 14:2; Isa. 40:6-8). The contrast with *verses 17-18* is so marked. Man, like grass, perishes, whereas the eternal God's covenant love and righteousness last for ever. To those who fear him, his character is displayed in the same way generation after generation. The nature of 'those who fear him' is defined by obedience to their covenant obligations. Outward allegiance to the covenant was quite insufficient; obedience from the heart was required (Deut. 30:11-16; Rom. 2:25-29). 'Circumcision is nothing and uncircumcision is nothing. Keeping God's commands is what counts' (1 Cor. 7:19). The sign of belonging to the truth is love with action (1 John 3:18-20).

The declaration – 'The LORD has established his throne in heaven, and his kingdom rules over all' *(verse 19)* – concludes this section of the psalm. From his heavenly throne the LORD exercises his rule over all his creation. He has a kingdom which is everlasting, and his authority and power extend to all generations (Ps. 145:13). What was said of his activity in verse 6 is dependent on the nature of his kingly rule.

4. *Let All Creation Praise the* LORD *(verses 20-22)*

The psalm comes to a climax with a fourfold call to praise, ending with a repetition of the opening words. Angelic multitudes are called on to extol the LORD *(verse 20)*. The angels are his messengers, often sent to perform some specific task. They are his 'mighty ones' (cf. Rev. 10:1-3), obedient to his requests, faithful in fulfilling his commands. The word 'hosts' *(verse 21)* can have various meanings in the Old Testament. It is used of the heavenly bodies, as well as of the armies of Israel. In this context it is best to think of it as being another description of the innumerable angels, who as the LORD's servants, bring to completion whatever he pleases.

The call to praise is broadened further to include all of creation *(verse 22,* cf. Pss. 96:11; 148). Everything within his realm is to acknowledge the LORD and give him praise. The whole creation is to be a choir, joining in exaltation of its Maker. The psalmist comes back to a personal focus with the closing call. He takes us again to where he began in verse 1, and thus ties the whole psalm together with the repetition of his opening words.

PSALM 104

Nowhere else in the Psalter is there such a long hymn in praise of the Creator and creation. There is the short song in Psalm 8 and slightly longer ones in Psalms 33 and 145, but in this psalm there is an extensive poetic description which matches the narrative of Genesis 1. Parallels with the days of Genesis 1 can be shown in this way:

Day 1: verse 2a
Day 2: verses 2b-4
Day 3: verses 5-9
Day 4: verses 14-16
Day 5: verses 17, 25-26
Day 6: verses 18, 23

Verse 30 brings the account to a climax, with reference to the creative power of the Spirit of God. Then follows a concluding song of praise, exalting the God of creation. Some of the expressions used also suggest that Job 38-41 was being referred to as well as Genesis 1.

1. *A Call to Praise (verse 1)*
The creation song opens with the same call to praise which occurs at the beginning and end of Psalm 103. God's person and character are not changed or increased by praise, but attention is appropriately drawn to them. It is an expression of adoration, acknowledging the perfection and wonder of his person. Here God is addressed as a great king, whose creation surrounds him like royal robes.

2. *The Splendour of God (verses 2-4)*
The first two days of creation are described, with the focus being on the Creator rather than his creation. God not only commanded light to shine, but no-one has seen him who 'lives in unapproachable light' (1 Tim. 6:16). He is light, in whom there is no darkness at all (1 John 1:5). The heavens form a habitation for the King, being described as a

canopy or tent (cf. the similar description in Isa. 40:22). His palace is formed above the waters of the firmament, and being sovereign he controls the clouds, the winds, and the flames of fire (lightning). God not only has his created angelic messengers (see Ps. 103:20-21), but the natural elements like wind and lightning also do his bidding (see verse 4, 'messengers', NIV footnote 'angels').

3. *The Creator Forms the Earth* (*verses 5-9*)

Day three of creation is described in this section of the psalm, and it has strong parallels in Job 38:4-30 and Proverbs 8:22-31. All three mention the laying of the foundations of the earth and the decree of God by which the boundaries were set for the oceans. In *verses 5-6* the psalmist sings of creation as the foundation which God laid in his creative work. The building is secure because of the work of the almighty Creator, and hence it stands for ever (cf. Ps. 93:1). At that stage in creation the dry land had not yet appeared. In *verses 7-9* the poetic description continues to describe the separation of the waters from dry land (see Gen. 1:9-10). God had only to speak and the waters obeyed him (cf. Ps. 33:6-9). The waters are pictured as being some mighty foe, which by the word of the Lord is put to flight. The waters receded, revealing the dry land, and this happened by the decision and power of God. Everything which took place was under his complete control.

4. *The Creator's Provision of Food* (*verses 10-18*)

The sequence of creation is interrupted in *verses 10-13* by reference to God's providential care of his world. The thought of the waters in verses 7-9 continues in these verses, as the psalmist proceeds to draw attention to the Creator's way of sustaining his world. He gives the water which flows down mountain streams, so that all wild animals can find refreshment from it. Likewise, birds can nest by the waters and sing in the trees growing beside them. In addition to springs of water, God gives rain from heaven which descends upon the mountains and refreshes the earth. This description may well echo Moses' words concerning the land of Israel in Deuteronomy 11:11-12a: 'a land of mountains and valleys that drinks rain from heaven. It is a land the LORD your God cares for.'

The third day of creation involved the creation of plant life which was intended to sustain the life of cattle and of man *(verses 14-16)*. The psalmist concentrates on the bounty of God's provision, so that all the main needs of an eastern banquet (wine, oil, and bread) are mentioned as part of God's gifts for man. These products stem from the basic crops of grapes, olives, and wheat. Of the trees, the cedars of Lebanon are singled out because their majestic appearance points in a special way to their Creator, and since he planted them they are called 'the trees of the LORD'.

Provision has been made for the birds and wild animals as well *(verses 17-18)*. The birds nest in the trees, while the mountains form a natural home for wild goats and coneys (not a rabbit but a type of rock badger). These are only a selective sample of the whole range of animal and bird life sustained by God's care. Lebanon was famous for its trees and for the wealth of its bird and animal life, and so its riches are used to illustrate the bounty which God has provided in his world. Our response has to be:

> This is my Father's world,
> and to my list'ning ears
> all nature sings,
> and round me rings the music of the spheres.
> This is my Father's world;
> I rest me in the thought of rocks and trees,
> of skies and seas,
> His hand the wonders wrought.

(Maltbie D. Babcock)

5. *The Creator's Rule over the Seasons* (*verses 19-23*)

Now the fourth day of creation comes into focus (*verses 19-20*). The rhythmic flow of the seasons is a result of God's appointment of the sun, moon, and stars. They were set in the expanse of the sky to 'serve as signs to mark seasons and days and years' (Gen. 1:14). There is an orderliness about creation which is by God's design, and both men and animals regulate their activities according to the fluctuation of day and night and the various seasons of the year. The lion, the lord of the night, is used to represent the movements which take place in the animal world. They prowl by night, and return to their dens at dawn *(verses 21-22)*. Man, the lord of the day, then goes out to his work, fulfilling the divine pattern for human life (*verse 23,* see Gen. 2:15; Exod. 20:9). 'Work' and 'labour' are synonymous terms used to describe the task which man, God's servant, is called on to fulfil. Just as God worked, and then rested, so we are appointed to imitate him.

6. *The Creator's Rule over Earth and Sea* (*verses 24-26*)

Before going on further to speak of the sea, the psalmist pauses to praise God for his manifold works *(verse 24)*. The opening words are an exclamation, which, by drawing attention to God's works, in effect are a statement of praise of them. Several Old Testament passages in addition to this one draw attention to the manifestation of God's wisdom in creation (see Ps. 136:5; Prov. 3:19; Jer. 10:12).

On the fifth day of creation God formed the ocean life (see Gen. 1:20-21), including the large sea creatures such as dolphins and whales. The term 'leviathan' was known in the ancient Near East as a reference to a mythological monster of creation. Here, however, the psalmist refers to leviathan as God's pet, frolicking in the oceans and joining the ships as they travel *(verses 25-26)*.

7. *The Creator's Rule over Life* (*verses 27-30*)

The sixth day of creation comes into focus at this point *(verses 27-28)*, with emphasis being placed on God's gracious provision for mankind and for animals (see Gen. 1:28-30). The closest parallel to this passage is Psalm 145:15-16, in which there is similar reference to expectant waiting on God until he opens his hand and provides liberally for his creatures. His creation flourishes because he looks with favour upon it, and he gives bountifully in order to sustain it.

All of life is dependent on God *(verses 29-30)*. His Spirit is the source of that life, and by his sovereign act creation takes place. If that Spirit is withdrawn, then creatures die and return to the dust. Perhaps Job 34:14-15 was in the mind of the psalmist as he penned these words. Normally the 'hiding' of God's face describes anger (cf. Ps. 13:1), but here it refers to the withdrawal of his sustaining power.

8. *A Final Song of Adoration* (*verses 31-35*)

Clearly 'the glory of the LORD' here is the creation which displays his wisdom and power (cf. Ps. 19:1). Just as God looked over the initial creation and pronounced it 'very good', so he rejoices in all his providential care of the world *(verse 31)*. His relationship with creation is such that he is in complete control of it, so that even a look or a touch can alter it *(verse 32)*. Not only does God rejoice, but the psalmist does as well *(verses 33-34)*. He makes a vow that as long as his earthly life continues he will praise God, and rejoice in the work of his hands. The 'meditation' is what has already preceded in the psalm itself. Response to the display of God's mighty power should always be one of praise and adoration.

The presence of sin mars God's creation. So the psalmist prays for the removal of sinners *(verse 35)*, for they have no rightful place amidst the beauty and purity of God's creation. Even creation longs for its own liberation (Rom. 8:19-22), and in the new heavens and the new earth there will be no more sin (Rev. 21:27). This creation song ends on the same note of praise with which it began, to which is added a 'Hallelujah!' (NIV 'Praise the LORD').

PSALM 105

Two major historical psalms, 105 and 106, trace the history of Israel from God's covenant with Abraham through to later periods in Canaan. The unfaithfulness of the people (Ps. 106) is set over against the complete faithfulness of God (Ps. 105). This is a major teaching aspect of the historical psalms (see the Introduction, pp. 54-58). After an introductory call to worship, there is an historical statement in verses 7-11. This is followed by a long expansion of it in verses 12-41, then verse 42 resumes the theme of the covenant with Abraham, and the final verses form a balancing summary at the end of the psalm. The first fifteen verses of this psalm, along with Psalm 96 and Psalm 106:1, 47-48, make up 1 Chronicles 16:8-36, in the context of David's bringing the ark of the covenant to Jerusalem.

1. *Invitation to Praise (verses 1-7)*
The opening words set the tone for succeeding commands *(verse 1)*. They are a call to praise the LORD, and may well be an echo of Isaiah 12:4. From the context, 'to call on the name of the LORD' means here proclamation of God's name, rather than invoking his name in prayer. In praising the LORD, the psalmist wants his worshippers to recall the things which God has done (called in the following verses 'wonderful acts', 'wonders', and 'miracles').

The series of commands continues, with emphasis on making known how God saved his people *(verses 2-3)*. God's name (i.e. his character) is shown in what he has done. Therefore, praise is an appropriate response, and those who come to worship him should approach his presence with joyfulness.

The focus of worship is the LORD himself and his mighty power *(verses 4-6)*. Strength is an essential characteristic of God (Pss. 62:11; 63:2), and that strength is displayed in his benevolent actions on behalf of his people. The psalmist calls his listeners (described by a variety of terms in verse 6) to remember how that power has been shown, especially at the time of the Exodus from Egypt. God had performed actions which only he could do (for 'wonders', see Pss. 71:17; 72:18), and he had passed sentence on Pharaoh and his people (Exod. 6:6; 7:4; 12:12).

In *verse 7* the Exodus is further recalled by the use of the covenant name for God (the LORD) which was so closely linked with the whole experience of redemption from Egypt (Exod. 3:13-15). The confession is made that the covenant LORD is indeed the God of his people, and his judgments are open for all to see. What had happened in Egypt was well known to all the surrounding nations.

2. *The Sure Covenant (verses 8-11)*

Abraham and Jacob have already been mentioned (verse 6), and the foundational covenant bond made with them is re-asserted in this historical song *(verses 8-9)*. The people have to be encouraged to remember God's great deeds (verse 5), but God keeps his covenant pledge without the need for help in recalling it. The term 'oath' is used in the Old Testament in contexts such as this as virtually the equivalent of 'covenant'. Such an oath was not needed by God himself (who is unchangeable), but it was a blessing to his servants as a confirmation of his purposes (the oath to Abraham [Gen. 22:16] was repeated to Isaac [Gen. 26:3-5]). It was to last 'for a thousand generations', an expression meaning 'for ever' (see Deut. 5:10; 7:9).

Furthermore, the same covenant commitment was made to Jacob *(verses 10-11,* Gen. 28:13-15) and central to it was the promise of the land of Canaan as a dwelling place for God's people. From the descriptions given of the land, the promise of 'the land of Canaan' meant the whole of Palestine. It was a decree in the sense that it was an enduring provision which God made for his covenant people, but was conditional on their faithfulness nevertheless, as the exiles of both later kingdoms showed.

3. *Covenant History (verses 12-41)*

From here to the end of verse 41 there is a summary of the way in which God acted on behalf of his people, caring for them and redeeming them from slavery in Egypt. At the early stage of their history, God's people were only a small number and they were without any definite territory of their own. They migrated to and from Egypt, and even within Palestine they were only 'strangers', i.e. they did not have rights of permanent residents (verses 12-13). God's protective care was shown to the patriarchs (verses 14-15). He even rebuked kings such as Pharaoh (Gen. 12:17) and Abimelech of Gerar (Gen. 20:7). The term 'anointed ones' is synonymous with 'chosen ones' (verse 6), while 'prophets' is a general term applied here to Abraham, Isaac, and Jacob. Abraham is the only one of the three specifically named a 'prophet' in the Old Testament (Gen. 20:7), but all three were called by God and were recipients of his covenant revelation. As such their lives were to be regarded as sacred.

Verses 16-22 provide a summary of Genesis 37, 39-41, showing how God prepared the way for his people by bringing Joseph down to Egypt and having him appointed to a prominent position. He arrived in Egypt as a slave, sold by his own brothers (Gen. 37:28-36). The description which is given of his captivity is a poetic one, using the imagery of a later period ('his feet with shackles, his neck was put in irons'). In his dreams which he related to his brothers (Gen. 37:5-11) and in his interpretation of the dreams of his fellow prisoners (Gen. 40:4-23; 41:12) Joseph spoke prophetically. Ultimately this revelation from God was proved true when things came to pass as Joseph had said. He was released from prison and appointed as second-in-charge in Egypt (Gen. 41:41-46), having Pharaoh's princes under his control.

Verse 23 picks up the theme of the famine, introduced in verse 16, but interrupted by the account of Joseph's slavery. Jacob was stunned when he heard that Joseph was the ruler of Egypt, but agreed to go and live in Egypt with all his family (Gen. 45:25–46:7; from the statement in Genesis 10:6, Egypt is called 'the land of Ham' here and in verse 27, and also in Psalm 106:22; in Psalm 78:51 the expression 'the tents of Ham' is used). During some centuries stay there, Israel increased in numbers and consequently became a problem for the Egyptians (verses 24-25, Exod. 1:7-14). God's hand directed the Egyptians' actions so that ultimately even their sinful acts against Israel served his sovereign purposes.

Calling Moses God's servant is an echo of Exodus 14:31, while the appointment of Aaron as Moses' prophet and as God's 'chosen' one is given in Exodus 7:1 (verse 26). As in Psalm 78, the plagues are not

mentioned in chronological order. Rather, the poet highlights the final
two plagues (darkness and death of the firstborn) by placing the other
plagues between them. Also, two of them (the plague on livestock and
the plague of boils) are omitted. These verses are a summary of Exodus
7:14 - 11:10. They serve as a reminder of how important were the signs
and wonders which God performed at the time of the Exodus. They
were demonstrations of divine power which Israel never forgot, for
Israel was God's firstborn son (Exod. 4:22) who was redeemed from
slavery in Egypt by his mighty arm *(verses 27-36)*.

After the preceding description of Israel's time in Egypt, the poet
summarises the actual Exodus experience *(verses 37-41)*. He uses one
of the standard Old Testament expressions ('brought out') to describe
how it happened. God intervened on behalf of his people and he led
them out, and this intervention included making the Egyptians favour-
ably disposed towards Israel (Exod. 12:33-36). Initially the Egyptians
were glad to see Israel go, but they then realised that they had lost their
work force and so pursued them (Exod. 14:5-9). God sustained and
protected his people, so that during the daytime they had the cloud as
a covering, and at night they had fire. He also provided food and drink
for them in the wilderness. All these experiences confirmed the
supernatural nature of the Exodus and God's gracious care of them.

4. *The Blessing of the LORD (verses 42-45)*

The psalm concludes with reference again to the covenant with
Abraham. The Exodus was a fulfilment of what God had promised him
long before (Gen. 15:13-14), and Israel entered into possession of a
land complete with houses, wells, and vineyards that others had
laboured to provide (Deut. 6:10-12). The response of the people had
to be shown by more than joy. They were instructed to obey all the
decrees of the LORD and to fear him (Deut. 6:24-25). The covenant
carried responsibilities which the people were expected to honour, as
they conformed their lives to God's commands and thus learned the
holiness of his ways. The psalm which begins with a call to praise ends
with a 'Hallelujah'.

PSALM 106

Psalm 106 fittingly follows but contrasts with Psalm 105. Both are historical in approach, but Psalm 106 concentrates on the sins of Israel rather than on divine deliverance. In this regard it is closer to Psalm 78 in its treatment of Israel's history. Whereas Psalm 105 ends on the note of obedience to God's laws, Psalm 106 shows how often the people had rebelled against him and failed to observe his precepts. Its language is similar to the confessional prayers found in Nehemiah 9 and Daniel 9. Paul, in describing the universal sinfulness of mankind (Rom. 1:18-31), draws on the language of Psalm 106.

1. Praise and Prayer (verses 1-5)
It is appropriate that the further recital of the mighty acts of the LORD should start with the call, 'Praise the LORD' (Hebrew, *Halleluyah*). For Israel, recollection of past history was closely connected with praise, for the people were remembering what God had done for them. Here the call is to extol (a strong word) the goodness of their covenant God, and recognise yet again how enduring is his mercy *(verse 1)*. The question in *verse 2* suggests that no-one is able fully to make known all the deeds of the great warrior King. Human achievements pale into insignificance beside his mighty acts.

Those who serve this great King should show the same character-istics as he displays when it comes to matters of justice in the land *(verse 3)*. The pronouncement of a blessing upon them (for 'blessed' see the comment on Ps. 1:1) is really an encouragement for all to act in this way.

The appeal for God to 'remember' has the idea of paying special attention to needs *(verses 4-5)*. The psalmist requests that he may share in the communal blessings of God's people when the LORD visits them in bringing deliverance. He knows he is part of the covenant family, and he wants to share with all God's 'chosen ones' in the joyful acknowledgement of his saving power.

2. The Rebellion of Israel (verses 6-43)
As with other recitals of history, there is a confession of sin at the outset *(verses 6-7,* cf. Dan. 9:4-6). The psalmist links those of his day with those who sinned in Egypt (the Hebrew text says, 'We sinned *with* our fathers'). He and others of his generation are regarded as sharing in the

rebellion of Israel of old, and as continuing that rebellion. The three verbs ('sinned', 'done wrong', and 'acted wickedly') are all used in 1 Kings 8:47, and probably formed part of the regular vocabulary of confession of sin. Two important points are made here about Israel at the time of the Exodus. Firstly, the nation was rebellious from its very foundation, even despising God's miracles and rebelling by the Red Sea soon after the crossing. Secondly, the wonder of God's grace is displayed in that he redeemed such a sinful, rebellious people.

In biblical thought salvation is always an initiative of God and it is for his name's sake (*verse 8*, cf. Daniel's prayer, Dan. 9:19). It was in spite of their sins that the Israelites were delivered from Egypt, in order that God's promise to Abraham would be fulfilled (Gen. 15:13-15). Salvation from bondage and sin is always a demonstration of God's great power.

Verses 9-11 summarise in song Exodus 13:17-14:29. What God did for Israel ('*he* rebuked ... *he* led them ... *he* saved them ... *he* redeemed') is the subject of continuous praise. He controlled the forces of nature to deliver his people and to bring judgment on the Egyptians. Israel came through the Red Sea on dry land, but the pursuing Egyptians were engulfed by returning water.

Verse 12 summarises Exodus 14:30-15:21. The display of the LORD's power convinced the Israelites to trust him and Moses his servant (Exod. 14:31). The song with which Moses and the Israelites praised God (Exod. 15:1-18) was a hymn of triumph, celebrating *his* victory over the Egyptians. The LORD, the mighty warrior, had vanquished the enemy and therefore the people sang, 'Who is like you – majestic in holiness, awesome in glory, working wonders?' (Exod. 15:11).

The cyclic experiences of Israel continued soon after the deliverance at the Red Sea (*verses 13-15*). Sin in Egypt, salvation at the Red Sea, and then sin again in the desert! The psalmist links together some of the experiences of the people soon after the crossing of the Red Sea (Exod. 15:22-25; 16:1-17:7) with the later incident when, because they ate food without due preparation, they were punished with a severe plague (Num. 11:31-34; Ps. 78:28-29). Each incident illustrated the people's unbelief and their desire to go their own sinful way.

Many envied the special relationship which Moses had with the LORD (*verses 16-18*). Miriam and Aaron spoke against him (Num. 12:1-15), and then Korah, Dathan, and Abiram led another 250 prominent leaders in challenging the exclusive roles to which Moses and Aaron had been called by God (Num. 16:1-50). The earth opened and Korah, Dathan, and Abiram were swallowed up, and the 250 men were consumed by fire sent by the LORD. As in Deuteronomy 11:6 there is no mention of Korah here.

While Moses was still on Mount Sinai, the people sinned by making a golden calf *(verses 19-23)*. Their sin was an attempt to replace God with an idol, and it almost led to the destruction of the infant nation of Israel (see Exod. 32:9-10). God is called 'their Glory', i.e. their glorious one, and Paul echoes this language in Romans 1:23. They had soon forgotten all the miracles in Egypt (called by its poetic name, 'the land of Ham', cf. Ps. 105:23) and at the Red Sea. Moses acted as a mediator and his intercession resulted in the substitution of a plague for total destruction (Exod. 32:31-35). 'To stand in the breach' is military language, used of a soldier willing to give his life for others by defending the gap in the wall (see Ezek. 22:30).

Verses 24-27: One of the great promises to Abraham was of a land for his descendants (Gen. 15:18-21; 17:8). But when, a little over a year after leaving Egypt, they reached the southernmost portion of Canaan, and heard the report of the spies who went to survey it, the people rebelled and wanted to return to Egypt (Num. 13:1-14:9). They rejected God's promise of 'the pleasant land' (described by same Heb. phrase in Jer. 3:19; 12:10; Zech. 7:14; cf. Dan. 8:9, 'the Beautiful Land'). The penalty was an oath by God that that generation would die in the wilderness (Num. 14:28-32), and likewise that the generation of the Exile would be scattered among the nations (part of the covenant curse, Lev. 26:33-35; Deut. 28:64-68).

The incident at Shittim to which the poet refers in *verses 28-31* is recorded in Numbers 25. Not only was there sexual immorality with Moabite women, but, as is also made plain here, a breach of the covenant with the LORD by worshipping other gods (see Num. 25:2-3). Phinehas, the grandson of Aaron, killed an Israelite, who had brought to his family a Midianite woman. By Phinehas' action the plague which God had sent stopped. What he did was in marked contrast with the wickedness of his uncles, Nadab and Abihu (see Lev. 10:1-5). Just as Abraham's faith was credited to him as righteousness (Gen. 15:6), so this act was credited to Phinehas. God entered into a covenant of peace with him by which he and his descendants were given a lasting priesthood (Num. 25:10-13; Mal. 2:4-6).

Verses 32-33: Two incidents involving provision of water, in both of which the people tested God, seem to be joined together here (Exod. 17:1-7; Num. 20:1-13). The Hebrew text of verse 33 literally says: 'for they rebelled against his spirit, and rash words came from his lips' (see NIV footnote). However, comparison with Isaiah 63:10 ('Yet they rebelled and grieved his Holy Spirit') confirms the interpretation embodied in the NIV rendering. Moses' rash words were those recorded in Numbers 20:10. He spoke out of his anger and years of frustration with the people.

Verses 34-39 give a concise picture of the long years of rebellion which the people showed after they came into Canaan. What actually happened was in direct contradiction to the instructions which had been given (see especially Deut. 7:1-6; 12:1-9, 29-32). The Israelites intermarried with those outside the covenant, and soon they became ensnared in their practices – idolatry, human sacrifice, murder. Both the people and the land were rendered unclean by these actions. The language of prostitution is used in the Old Testament to describe both Israel's departure from God's moral standards (Isa. 1:21) and the nation forsaking the LORD by entering into marriage with other gods (Ezek. 16:32-36).

In *verses 40-43* the poet gives a shortened account of God's reaction to the sins of his people over centuries of life in the promised land (for a longer description, see 2 Kgs. 17:7-23). He showed his anger with his people, by allowing surrounding nations to invade and oppress them. Repeated divine deliverances did not alter the sinful bent of the people. They persisted in their rebellion, and the end result was predictable humiliation for them. Right through from the days of the judges to the Babylonian exile the curses of the covenant were applied to sinful Israel.

3. The Blessings of the Covenant (verses 44-47)

At times of great distress for his people, God is said to note (Hebrew, *see*) their condition (cf. Exod. 3:7; 1 Sam. 9:16). Just as God had pledged sanctions against his erring inheritance, so he had promised that he would remember his covenant (Lev. 26:42, 45; cf. also Ps. 105:8, 42). 'To remember his covenant' means to implement it, which he did by showing abundant covenant mercy *(verses 44-45)*.

In *verses 46-47* the use of language relating to 'pity' draws attention to the promises made in similar terms of what would happen when the people repented of their sins (see 1 Kgs. 8:50; 2 Chr. 30:9; Jer. 42:12). Therefore this reference to captivity means specifically the Babylonian exile, because of no other captivity is this language used. Recalling those promises, the dispersed community prays for God to gather them from among the Gentile nations where they have been scattered. Such restoration will result in triumphant praise of God's mercy.

4. Concluding Doxology (verse 48)
The psalm, and also Book 4 of the Psalter, ends with this doxology. The first part of it ('Praise be to the LORD, the God of Israel, from everlasting to everlasting') was most probably original to the psalm, while the second part ('Let all the people say, "Amen!" Praise the LORD') is an adaptation of the statement of 1 Chronicles 16:36.

BOOK 5

PSALM 107

There are strong links between Psalms 105, 106, and 107. They all
include the words, 'Give thanks to the LORD', in their introductions,
and they share a similar historical perspective. From one aspect, Psalm
107 gives the LORD's response to the prayer of Psalm 106:47, 'Save us,
O LORD our God, and gather us from the nations'. It recounts how in
four kinds of adversity, the LORD had delivered those who cried to him:
from hunger and thirst (verses 4-9), from prison (verses 10-16), from
sickness (verses 17-22), and from storm at sea (verses 23-32). Each of
these stanzas has the same basic form: an account of the distress, a cry
to the LORD and his deliverance, and then a summons to praise him for
his covenant love (Hebrew, *chesed*; see on 36:5). The two stanzas
which follow these are more general, showing how the LORD delivered
in more general ways (verses 33-42). The introductory call to praise
and the concluding words of admonition and exultation tie together the
whole structure of the psalm into a memorable testimony to the
redeeming grace of the LORD. This psalm comes from after the return
from the Babylonian captivity (see verses 2-3; and compare verse 1
with Jer. 33:11), and though it has strong links with Psalms 105 and
106, yet it was chosen to commence the final section of the Psalter.

1. *Invitation to Praise* (*verses 1-3*)
The words of *verse 1*, which have already been used at the beginning
of Psalm 106, form the command to the assembled community of
Israel (for the identical words, see also Ps. 136:1). They, and especially
those who have come back from captivity, are called to extol the
goodness and love of the LORD (cf. the combination of 'goodness' and
'love' in Ps. 23:6). The return from captivity was clearly an act of God
(verses 2-3). He delivered his people and gathered many of the
dispersed of Israel from all points of the compass. However, large
numbers remained in Babylon and contributed greatly to later Judaism. Instead of 'south' the Hebrew text has 'the sea' (i.e. the Mediterranean), but as 'west' has already been mentioned, the NIV is probably
correct in taking the Hebrew word to mean 'south' (one letter in the
Hebrew makes the difference).

2. *Deliverance from Hunger and Thirst* (*verses 4-9*)
The first description of distress is the hunger and thirst of those
travelling through the desert *(verses 4-5)*. Those who came out of

Egypt experienced first hand the problems of life in the desert, and while living in Palestine the people knew the reality of major deserts to the south and east. These had to be crossed by traders, as well as by all of the returning exiles. The standardised account of their prayer to God and of his response (cf. for almost the same words, verses 13, 19, and 28) is followed by a fuller description of God's special provision for them in their need *(verses 6-7)*. The wanderers, who could not find a dwelling place (verse 4), were led to a place, where in addition to shelter, there was food and drink, thus giving security to human existence. The Hebrew word used for the expression 'where they could settle' has become the modern Hebrew word, *moshav*, a smallholder's settlement. The psalmist bids the congregation (or readers) to praise the LORD for his love (Hebrew, *chesed*) and for his wonderful deeds *(verses 8-9,* see on Ps. 72:18). Such a supply of food and drink was a divine provision for the hungry and thirsty. The same refrain occurs again in verses 15, 21, and 31, in each case being followed by the appropriate reason for praise.

3. *Deliverance from Prison* (*verses 10-16*)

Hunger and thirst was not the only situation of distress which the people faced. There were others, including imprisonment (*verses 10-12*). One of the punishments which God inflicted on the people because of their rebellion was imprisonment in foreign countries. Instead of cherishing the words of the Most High, they treated them lightly, even the threats of exile and imprisonment (Lev. 26:33; Deut. 28:47-48). They landed in situations where there was no human help in their predicament. The expressions used here could include other distressing situations in addition to imprisonment.

The amazing thing about *verses 13-14* is that they are describing God's deliverance from a situation which was a result of the people's own sin. He sent them into bondage, but, in accordance with his promise (Lev. 26:40-45), when they humbled themselves and cried to him, God answered in mercy. The refrain calls again for praise *(verses 15-16)*, this time for the wonderful deliverance from captivity, especially that in Babylon. Part of the work of Cyrus as God's appointed deliverer of his people was to 'break down gates of bronze and cut through bars of iron' (Isa. 45:2). The language of verse 16 echoes that description in praising God for his release of the prisoners in Babylon.

4. *Deliverance from Sickness* (*verses 17-22*)

The sins of the people also caused physical illnesses, and from them God also delivered (*verses 17-18*). Another of the covenant curses was the threat of divinely imposed illness (Lev. 26:16, 25; Deut. 28:20-22, 35, 58-61). Those who suffered these illnesses are called 'fools', not because they were mentally stupid, but because their life was marked by insolence towards God (cf. the contrast between those who have the fear of the Lord and the fool who despises instruction, Prov. 1:7). Their illnesses were so serious that they lost all appetite and waited for death. *Verses 19-20* introduce the recovery which God commanded. He spoke the word, and they were restored, so being rescued from death. The refrain (*verses 21-22*) calls for praise for this further evidence of God's unfailing love and for tangible acts to show how deep their gratitude was. This call and the next one (verse 31) both specify the form which the praise is to take. Jeremiah 33:11 depicts the joy which was characteristic of the return from exile.

5. *Deliverance from Perils at Sea* (*verses 23-32*)

The fourth situation of distress is danger at sea (*verses 23-27*). While Israel was not noted for being a seafaring nation, yet she had traders who ventured far in search of precious goods. In Solomon's time particularly there was a very active sea-going trade (see 1 Kgs. 9:26-28; 10:22). Those who sailed on the seas acknowledged that the mighty storms were brought about by the word of the Lord. They came to a place where their own skills could aid them no more ('were at their wits' end', Hebrew literally, 'and all their wisdom was swallowed up').

For the fourth time the same description is given of prayer to God and subsequent deliverance (*verses 28-30*). In this case the deliverance took the form of calming of the stormy seas so that they were able at last to reach the harbour for which they were heading. The Lord of nature had the power to control the wild storm, just as the Lord Jesus was able to still the storm on the Sea of Galilee (Mark 4:35-41). The final occurrence of the refrain (*verses 31-32*) calls on the people in public assembly and before their leaders to acknowledge what God has done for them. Their praise had to have a communal aspect to it, as they testified to this demonstration of the Lord's wonderful love.

6. *Preservation in the Land* (*verses 33-38*)

A general description follows of periods of devastation for the land and then renewed blessings as God again gave them abundant harvests *(verses 33-34)*. As a consequence of the sins of the people, God sent reversal of fortunes to the land of Palestine. Instead of it being a land of milk and honey, it was visited by drought and famine, becoming a salt waste almost like Sodom and Gomorrah (Gen. 19:1-29). The point is again that God has complete control over nature, and his power extends to 'rivers', 'springs' and 'fruitful land'. The opposite reversal could take place just as surely *(verses 35-38)*, and the language used is similar to Isaiah 35:6-7; 41:18, and 43:19-20. 'The desert' and 'the parched ground' could become respectively 'flowing springs' and 'a city'. The hungry now had abundance, and they themselves and the cattle increased abundantly. This was a result of the LORD's blessing, part of the promises made to the exiles (see Isa. 49:19-20; 54:1-3).

7. *Protection in Calamity (verses 39-42)*

The final section of historical recollection deals with the devastation caused by invasion. Part of God's punishment of his people's sins was to allow invasion of their land *(verses 39-40)*. They had to face attacks from powerful armies such as those of the Syrians (2 Kgs. 6:24-25), the Assyrians (2 Kgs. 17:3-5; 18:13-15), and the Babylonians (2 Kgs. 25:1-26). Such attacks brought great devastation to the land, and they were particularly humbling to the nation's leaders. It is probably the last two kings of Judah – Jehoiachin and Zedekiah – who are particularly in mind (see 2 Kings 24:8–25:7). Even such disasters were reversed by God when he heard the cry of the people and freed them from their distress *(verses 41-42)*. Again the numbers of the population increased, and both good and evil within the land knew what had happened. The good saw it, and were glad. The evil saw it and, recognising God's hand in the matter, were silenced.

8. *A Call to the Wise (verse 43)*

The poet ends his composition in a manner reminiscent of the end of the prophecy of Hosea (Hos. 14:9). Both finish with the question, 'Who is wise?', directing attention to the teaching function of what has just preceded. 'These things' could refer to verses 33-42, or more probably to the whole of verses 4-42. The psalm, which commenced with an assertion of the covenant mercy of the LORD (verse 1), ends with a call to contemplate his great deeds and to reflect upon that mercy.

PSALM 108
A song. A psalm of David.

This psalm is composed of parts of two other psalms. Psalm 57:7-11 and Psalm 60:5-12 are combined, and there is no indication in the biblical text why this was done. There are some slight variations as compared with the original psalms, but none of major significance. For commentary, see those on Psalms 57 and 60.

PSALM 109
For the director of music. Of David. A psalm.

This is a prayer by one who calls himself the Lord's servant (verse 28). He appeals to his sovereign for intervention since he is under attack by his accusers. In verses 6-19 the accuser is referred to as a single person, but elsewhere in the psalm the accusers are plural. Perhaps it is best to think of a band of accusers, with the leader being singled out for special attention. There are three main petitions in the psalm (verses 1-5, 21, and 26-29), along with a long section involving curses against the [main] accuser (verses 6-20). A description of the poor and needy suppliant (verses 22-25), and a final song of praise to the Lord, complete the psalm. For the wider issues raised by the curses in this psalm of David, see the Introduction, pp. 60-62.

1. An Urgent Cry (verses 1-5)
The psalmist's prayer is directed to the divine Judge, from whom he wants a ready response *(verses 1-2)*. 'Praise' in this context has the idea of public acknowledgment that God is his defender. To remain silent would show an attitude of unconcern for his welfare (for the use of the same expression, cf. Ps. 35:22). The accusers had been spreading false reports about David, acting with malicious intent towards him. The fuller description of the accusations being made against the psalmist provide a contrast between his character and that of his enemies *(verses 3-5)*. He is devoted to prayer (the Hebrew simply says, 'but I am prayer'), while they attack without due reason and even repay good with evil. He maintains his innocence in the situation, trying to hold friendly relationships with others who only respond with hatred and bitterness.

2. *Appeal for Divine Justice* (*verses 6-15*)

His first call is for someone to be appointed to bring his enemy to the bar of God's justice *(verse 6)*. He calls him an accuser (Hebrew, *satan*), a meaning which the Hebrew word uniformly has in the Old Testament. To stand at the right hand was apparently the position which the accuser took in court trials (cf. Zech. 3:1).

For his enemy the psalmist seeks the judicial death penalty *(verses 7-10)*. The one who has been causing him so much trouble was a leader either in the nation or the leader of a band of men seeking his destruction. Even if such a one pleads for a different verdict, his prayers must go unanswered. The ultimate verdict will not only affect the enemy, but his wife and children will also suffer. This is an expression of the principle stated in the Second Commandment whereby God punishes the children to the third and fourth generation of those who hate him (Exod. 20:5). The words of verse 8 are quoted in Acts 1:20 in reference to the replacement of Judas by another apostle.

The family survivors will also be deprived of any wealth which might otherwise be available for them *(verses 11-13)*. Those from outside the family will profit from the work which has been put into business or property. Creditors had extensive powers (see 2 Kings 4:1) and they will take their share of the estate. Pity would normally have been expected for orphan children, but the psalmist asks that it be withheld in this case. To have no descendants was regarded as a disgrace in Israel, and so to have names blotted out will mean the extinction of the family line.

The whole family of the enemy is regarded as being involved in his sins, and therefore they are to share in his punishment *(verses 14-15)*. The use of the verb 'cut off' in verses 13 and 15 echoes language of the covenant (see Gen. 17:14), and suggests that the enemy has to be seen as a covenant rebel upon whom God's curse is due. With covenant disobedience the promises of long and prosperous life in the land of promise are reversed (Lev. 26:9; Deut. 6:2, 18, 24; 7:12-15).

3. *The Character of the Enemy* (*verses 16-20*)

The enemy has been notorious for ill-treating the destitute and even bringing about the death of those who should have been protected and nourished *(verse 16)*. Towards them he showed no commitment of love and mercy, denying even the basic responsibilities of protection and care.

In place of kindness the enemy substituted evil desires, which he expressed in terms of a cursing procedure *(verses 17-19)*. The words of verse 18 may reflect some practice in which there was a ritual involving water and oil. Perhaps they were poured over the body to demonstrate the way in which the curse was supposed to enter right to the bones. The curse was thought to so surround the person that it was like a garment held tight around the body by a belt.

Instead of reading *verse 20* as a continuation of the curse, it should be translated as a statement concerning God's judgment upon the enemy: 'This is my accusers' reward from the LORD'. The psalmist is innocent, and he is sure that God is going to redirect the curses back on the accuser himself.

4. *An Urgent Prayer for Help* (*verses 21-29*)

The opening words of the prayer ('But you') are very emphatic, contrasting the evil character of the accuser with the gracious character of the prayer-hearing God. David wants action from the LORD, not for his own sake, but for God's sake. He regards God's character as being on trial, and knows that the righteous Judge is his only source of deliverance. He will act in accordance with his own character.

In *verses 22-25* David claims that he is 'poor and needy', an expression which has already been used (see verse 16) and which denotes his depth of need at this time (cf. the use of the same phrase in Pss. 70:5; 86:1). His strength is gone and he is about to fade away. He uses a variety of expressions to convey the idea that he has no power of his own, with his body so weak and helpless. His accusers know the reality of his position, and so they mock him in his weakness and frailty. They think that the end is in sight for him.

To the previous cries of 'deal well' and 'deliver' (verse 21), the psalmist now adds, 'help me' and 'save me' *(verses 26-27)*. All of these point to his consciousness that only with the LORD is there any hope of relief from his distress. When his deliverance comes he wants his accusers to know that it is solely the LORD's action. Salvation is always of the LORD.

As this section of the psalm concludes *(verses 28-29)*, many of the ideas which have already been introduced are reinforced. David is confident that though the enemies may curse, yet God will bless. The outcome will be that he, as God's devoted servant, will be joyful while his opponents will suffer disgrace.

5. *A Vow of Praise* (*verses 30-31*)

As with many other songs of complaint, this particular one, though starting with the grave situation of the psalmist, ends on a note of praise. When gathered with the worshipping assembly of Israel, David pledges that he will sing praise to the LORD. The reason for this praise is that the LORD is at his right hand as his defender, not as his accuser (cf. verse 6). At the judgment, he will have one to stand there and deliver him from his accusers.

PSALM 110
Of David. A psalm.

No psalm is more frequently quoted in the New Testament than this one. Jesus used it (Matt. 22:43-45; Mark 12:36-37; Luke 20:42-44) and Peter appealed to it on the Day of Pentecost (Acts 2:34-36). The author of the Book of Hebrews also draws heavily upon it (Heb. 1:13; 5:6-10; 7:11-28). There is no indication of the setting or time of the psalm. It may have had its origin at the time of Solomon's enthronement, but David is looking prophetically (see 2 Sam. 23:2) to his greater future son, the Messiah. Even in pre-Christian times it was regarded as Messianic by the Jews, and Jesus, by his use of it, silenced his critics: 'No one could say a word in reply, and from that day on no one dared to ask him any more questions' (Matt. 22:46).

The psalm is structured around two prophetic oracles (verses 1 and 4), and these are the verses from the psalm which are quoted in the New Testament. A prophet speaks, and makes declarations concerning the Messianic priest-king. The psalm has this pattern:

1. A Divine Promise: 'Sit at my right hand' (verse 1)
   Explanation: A sceptre from Zion (verse 2a)
                     Rule over enemies (verse 2b)
                     A willing people (verse 3)

2. A Divine Oath: 'You are a priest for ever' (verse 4)
   Explanation: God's ready help (verse 5a)
                     Victory over the nations (verses 5b,6)
                     Confidence in the LORD (verse 7)

1. *A Divine Promise* (*verses 1-3*)

There are three persons involved in *verse 1* – the Lord God, the psalmist/prophet, and the one he calls 'my Lord'. The manner of introducing this statement ('says', Hebrew *ne'um*) resembles that of the prophets. It occurs only here in the Psalms, but it is very common in Jeremiah (175 times), Ezekiel (85 times), Isaiah (24 times), and Amos (21 times). The prophetic word points to the exaltation of God's Messiah to his right hand (the position of honour beside the king, see Ps. 45:9; 1 Kgs. 2:19). He is to take his seat there until his enemies are in subjection to him. As Peter points out in his Pentecost sermon, this refers to Jesus, who is 'exalted to the right hand of God' (Acts 2:33).

Verses 2-3 contain three explanatory comments. Firstly, his rule is going to extend outwards from Zion, which was not only David's city but the Lord's dwelling place (Ps. 132:13). Secondly, though his enemies will take their stand against him, yet he will exercise his kingly rule over them. Thirdly, his people, the covenant people, will show willingness to serve him, and especially covenant youth will follow him. They are likened to the refreshing dew which comes at dawn (see NIV footnote).

2. *A Divine Oath* (*verses 4-7*)

In *verse 4* there is a divine pledge by way of an oath. The Lord binds himself absolutely as he addresses the priest/king. He declares that the king is also an eternal priest (see also Zech. 6:13: 'he will be clothed with majesty and will sit and rule on his throne. And he will be a priest on his throne'). This could not be said of any human priest or king. It is given added emphasis by the reference to him being of the order of Melchizedek, who was king of Salem and priest of the Most High God (Gen. 14:18-20). Just as Melchizedek, who lived long before Levi and Aaron, was a priest/king, having his priesthood directly from God, so Jesus received a permanent priesthood through this oath by God (see the full New Testament explanation in Heb. 7:1-28).

Just as three points of explanation are given of the Messiah's kingship (verses 2-3), so now three points of explanation follow about his priesthood *(verses 5-7)*. Firstly, he is assured of God's ready help (verse 5a). Secondly, he will be victorious over his enemies in the day when God's wrath is shown against the rebellious nations (verses 5b-6; cf. Ps. 2:5). Thirdly, he will have such confidence that the victory is secure that he will stop to refresh himself at the brook before pressing on to final victory (verse 7). The writer to the Hebrews draws the practical implications from this teaching concerning Jesus' priesthood, that he is able to give eternal salvation to all who obey him (Heb. 5:9) and to save completely all who come to God through him (Heb. 7:25).

PSALM 111

Psalms 111-118 consist of a group of Hallelujah psalms, so-called because they emphasise praise, as is shown by the Hebrew word 'halleluyah' occurring so frequently. Psalms 111-112 form a pair to commence the group. They are similar in structure, in that the main body of the song expounds the opening idea, and then the closing verse brings that central focus to a fitting conclusion. They are also similar, being acrostic poems, which (contrary to the normal pattern) start *each short half-verse* with the consecutive letters of the Hebrew alphabet. The initial 'Praise the Lord' (Hebrew, *halleluyah*) stands outside the acrostic pattern. The main theme of Psalm 111 is praising the Lord's works by those who fear him, with the credal statement of Exodus 34:6 providing the main basis.

1. *Public Praise of the Lord (verse 1)*
An exclamation of spontaneous praise forms the opening and the closing of this psalm. The unnamed composer pledges himself, with fullest devotion, to confess the Lord both in the general assembly of the people and also in a smaller group. This latter group, called here 'the council of the upright', was probably a band of trusted friends who shared the same reverence of the Lord.

2. *Praise for the Redeemer (verses 2-9)*
The works of the Lord are great because they demonstrate his intrinsic power. They display his magnificence and manifest his unique character, especially as the Redeemer of his people *(verses 2-3)*. The word 'righteousness' in the Old Testament often means more than just uprightness. As here, it often denotes God's saving activity on behalf of his people and in accordance with his covenant promises (see verse 5). Those who are redeemed by him reflect deeply upon his actions, as they carefully consider those things which are to them a delight (cf. the use of the same word in Ps. 1:2). Just as Psalm 104:1 declares that creation is a display of God's 'splendour and majesty', so likewise are

God's actions in redemption 'glorious and majestic' (in Hebrew the words are the same in both psalms).

In various ways, but especially in the appointment of the annual Passover celebration, God provided for recollecting and pondering on the great facts of the redemption from Egypt *(verses 4-5)*. The people were always to realise and assert from the credal declaration in Exodus 34:6 that the LORD is 'gracious and compassionate' (the fact that these adjectives occur in the reverse order here is because the poet needed this order to fit his acrostic pattern). The LORD is also praised because he provides food for his people, so fulfilling covenant promises. The word 'covenant' (as distinct from the concept) is not common in the Psalms, yet it occurs twice in this psalm.

God did not act in secret. He made promises concerning his future actions, and then after the events themselves had happened, he provided explanations of what had occurred *(verses 6-8)*. This was so in relation to the gift of the land of Canaan to Israel; and not one of all God's good promises ever failed (Josh. 23:14). There is certainty about God's actions because, according to the Exodus 34:6 declaration, he is a God 'abounding in love and faithfulness'. All his requirements for his people ('precepts', a word used most commonly in Ps. 119) are sure and reliable. God's precepts reflect himself as the God of truth and uprightness.

Verse 9: Part of the commitment of God's covenant with Abraham was the promise of redemption from Egypt (Gen. 15:13-16), a promise reaffirmed to Moses (Exod. 3:7-10, 16-17). In later Old Testament prophecy (Isa. 42:6-7; 49:8-9; 55:3-5; Jer. 31:31-34) and in New Testament fulfilment (Matt. 26:28; Luke 22:20) redemption remained central to the covenant idea. The covenant God, the Redeemer of his people, also showed his character in what he did in providing redemption. He was seen as holy (Exod. 3:5-6; Deut. 5:23-27) and awesome (Deut. 10:17).

3. *A Summary of True Wisdom (verse 10)*
The conclusion drawn from all the wonderful works of the LORD is that reverence for him is fundamental for wise living. The God who is *awesome* (verse 9) is to be *feared* (the Hebrew for these two words comes from the same root). This special fear is practical. It is related to sensible everyday living, and in particular, it is shown by obedience to God's precepts (see commentary on 34:8-14).

PSALM 112

Psalm 111 praises God for his work and character and Psalm 112 complements it by recognising the work and character of the godly man. It takes up the idea of the fear of the LORD (Ps. 111:10) and develops it by describing the way of life of the righteous man. The content of the psalm shows great similarity with that of Psalm 1, though the contrast with the wicked is not developed as much. The structure of this psalm is the same as the previous one, and it shares the same acrostic pattern. Moreover, eleven terms or phrases used in Psalm 111 are also used in it, seven of them having been used of God in Psalm 111 are now used of the righteous person. The following table sets these out (in each case the Hebrew word used is the same, though the NIV translation varies).

Psalm 111 The Lord's Qualities	Psalm 112 The Qualities of the Godly Man
gracious and compassionate (4)	*gracious and compassionate (4)*
just (7)	*justice (5)*
remembers (5)	*remembered (6)*
steadfast (8)	*secure (8)*
provides (Hebrew, *gave*, 5)	*gifts* (Hebrew *he gave*, 9)
for ever (5, 8, 9)	*for ever (6)*

1. The Blessing of Fearing the Lord (verse 1)
The familiar 'Hallelujah' commences the psalm and sets the tone before a description is given of the true God-fearer. The language is reminiscent of Psalm 1:1-2. Fear of the LORD calls forth the proclamation of a blessing on such a person, whose main distinction is his delight in God's requirements. Reverence for God and joy in him flows into willing obedience.

2. The Description of the Righteous (verses 2-9)
The children of the righteous also enjoy blessings *(verses 2-3)*. In general, they will be privileged (the Hebrew word 'mighty' indicates nobility, i.e. those who had the right of carrying arms for the king), and so long as they maintain the character of the 'upright' they will be pronounced 'blessed'. 'Wealth and riches' stand for prosperity, while

what was said of God's righteousness in Psalm 111:3 is now said of the God-fearer. God's faithfulness to his covenant ensures that there is continuity in his care for his people. This is true notwithstanding acknowledgment in the Bible that adversity often comes upon them.

The language of *verse 4* may well be drawn from Isaiah 60:2. It means that in times of trouble ('in darkness'), God sends his salvation, called here by the figure of speech, 'light'. Those who are godly share in the very characteristics of God himself, and as they receive God's mercy, they show similar compassion to others.

'Good' *(verse 5)* in a statement such as this is equivalent to 'blessed' (in the Hebrew the phrases are parallel: *blessed is the man ... good is the man*). To be 'generous' is willingly to offer assistance when others need what one has available. The same phrase, 'generous and lends freely', is used in Psalm 37:26 (cf. the use of similar phrase, 'give generously', in verse 21 of the same psalm). The type of person described takes initiative to act justly, and in this is an imitator of God (see Ps. 111:7).

During his lifetime the righteous man will remain immovable *(verses 6-8)*, while in death he will be remembered and his memory will be a blessing (Prov. 10:7). He will not be perturbed if there is bad news or threats, because his confidence has been placed in the LORD. Such news may sadden, but he maintains his godly composure in the face of adversity. As for the wicked, he is sure that he will see them receiving their rightful punishment (cf. vs. 4 and Ps. 91:8). *Verse 9* reinforces verse 5. The righteous man scatters his gifts abroad, just as freely as someone sowing seed, and so meets the needs of the poor. This is a practical demonstration of his righteous character. Such behaviour does not go unnoticed by God, who lifts a person like this into a position of honour.

3. *The Contrast with the Wicked* (verse 10)

The closing verse offers the reverse picture. The wicked person is the very opposite of the righteous. He knows neither graciousness nor compassion, and his attitude to life is totally different. He will be angry, yet as is common with unrighteous anger, his hatred will not lead to any good result. Whatever his longings are, and especially if they include the destruction of the righteous, they will be futile. Lacking the blessing of God, he will utterly perish.

PSALM 113

With psalms 114 to 118, this psalm formed part of the so-called 'Egyptian Hallel' ('Egyptian Praise'), which in Jewish usage was sung at the time of the major religious festivals (Passover, Feast of Weeks, Tabernacles). The reference to 'Egyptian' stems from the fact that the first Passover was celebrated in Egypt (Exod. 12:21-30). At the commencement of the Passover service Psalms 113-114 were sung, while Psalms 115-118 were used at the conclusion (cf. Matt. 26:30; Mark 14:26). While on the one hand Psalm 113 is a hymn of praise to God, it is also a declaration concerning his care for the lowly. God manifests his power and grace in stooping to choose the foolish, weak, and lowly things of the world (1 Cor. 1:26-29), taking those who were alienated from him by their sins and exalting them to be seated with Christ in the heavenly realms (Eph. 2:1-7).

1. A Call to Universal Praise (verses 1-3)
This hymn opens and closes with a 'Hallelujah'. The use of the expression 'servants' *(verse 1)* appears to have become a standard description of the whole worshipping community in the period following the return from exile (cf. its use in Ezra 5:11; Neh. 1:10). Those servants are now asked to join in communal praise as the LORD's name is extolled.

In *verses 2-3* the call is for such praise to be perpetual and universal. The repetition of the phrase 'the name of the LORD' is typical of this kind of call to praise (cf. Ps. 96:1-2). The phrase 'from the rising of the sun to the place where it sets' also occurs in Psalm 50:1, with a similar phrase occurring twice in Isaiah (45:6; 59:19) and in Malachi 1:11. Its use points to the union of Israelite and Gentile in worship of the one true God, for it can hardly refer only to dispersed Jews. The fuller realisation of this vision only came with the ministry of Jesus and the proclamation of the gospel throughout the world.

2. The Universal LORD (verses 4-6)
Verse 4 ('The LORD is exalted over all the nations, his glory above the heavens') explains the call to universal worship in the preceding verse. The LORD is sovereign over all the nations, not just over Israel his special people. His infinite kingship is also displayed by the fact that his glory is above the heavens, drawing attention to his rule over the

whole of creation. In *verses 5-6* the psalmist uses a rhetorical question to highlight the main point. The gracious condescension of God is a thing which amazes, but it is taught in both Old (Ps. 138:6) and New Testaments (Phil. 2:5-8). The exalted God stoops to meet his created order with mercy.

3. *Practical Illustrations* (*verses 7-9*)

The psalmist illustrates the general truth which he has just stated by pointing to ways in which God shows his concern for the lowly. *Verses 7-8* are taken almost word for word from Hannah's song (1 Sam. 2:8). One of the greatest tragedies for a married woman in Israel was to be childless, because this meant that she could be desolate in old age, without anyone to help her. God was able to answer Hannah's prayer for a child, and when her son was born she named him 'Samuel', saying, 'Because I asked the LORD for him' (1 Sam. 1:20). The concluding 'Hallelujah' provides a fitting conclusion to a triumphal hymn in praise of the majestic and gracious God.

PSALM 114

In the midst of a group of psalms linked by usage with the Passover, there occurs this one with specific reference to the Exodus and the conquest of Canaan. The previous psalm extolled the majesty of God, and now that is illustrated in the control he had over his creation at the time of the Exodus. The psalm gives a very condensed account and telescopes events together which happened many years apart. It uses vivid poetic imagery to show how the Creator used the forces of nature to achieve his purposes, and it is constructed from four equally balanced stanzas.

1. *The Significance of the Exodus* (*verses 1-2*)

This simple opening description states the fact of the Exodus. Israel/Jacob had lived in Egypt among a people of 'foreign tongue'. This phrase occurs nowhere else in the Old Testament, but it appears to mean that the Egyptians spoke a language which was unintelligible to the Israelites. They heard what was for them a stammering tongue. Presumably the Israelites learned sufficient Egyptian so that there was communication between them and their masters. From that foreign environment God delivered them, and the whole nation of twelve tribes (Judah/Israel) became his sanctuary. That could mean that the sanctuary was the promised land itself (see Exod. 15:17), or else the tabernacle/temple situated in the midst of the people. In view of the use of the word 'dominion' the former is more probable, as Israel was God's special treasure, his kingdom of priests (Exod. 19:6).

2. A Poetic Description of the Exodus (verses 3-4)

The crossing of the Red Sea and of the Jordan River are brought together as if they were a single event. The events themselves are described in prose in Exodus 14:21-22 and Joshua 3:14-17. The rivers are personified, and so are described as seeing the approach of God and running away. Likewise the mountains (especially Mount Sinai) trembled before God's presence. The whole imagery is intended to bring to mind the formidable events of the Exodus (cf. Exod. 19:18) and conquest which were due to God's invincible power.

3. Questions Needing No Answer (verses 5-6)

Four rhetorical questions emphasise the point which has just been made in the previous stanza and prepare for the call to the earth which is to follow in verses 7-8. While they echo the words already used in verses 3-4, yet they also anticipate the climax in the closing verses.

4. The God of Present Blessing (verses 7-8)

The climax is reached in this stanza. 'The Lord' who controls nature is also 'the God of Jacob', the covenant God of his people. The repetition of 'at the presence of' reminds the reader that before this God the earth can only quake as his power is shown. Two experiences of great power are recalled (Exod. 17:6; Num. 20:11), one soon after leaving Egypt, the other when coming close to the promised land. That God is still one who 'turns' (so the Hebrew) rocks into water, is a reassurance of his continuing protective care of his people. It is no wonder that the earth is called on to respond to his divine power.

PSALM 115

Many of the ancient translations of the Psalms (Greek, Latin, Syriac, Arabic and Ethiopic) and a few Hebrew manuscripts join Psalms 114 and 115 together. However, there is no good reason for this, as the contents of the two psalms are quite different. This psalm is a song, probably prepared and used in the temple worship after the return from

Exile, which extols the person and character of the God of Israel in contrast to the worthless idols of the Gentile nations. Verses 3-8 appear in very similar form in Psalm 135:6, 15-18. Within the psalm there is alternation between second and third persons, which suggests that it was intended for antiphonal voices, with congregation and priest(s) sharing in the song or recitation. Repetition throughout the psalm is also typical of liturgical use (cf. Pss. 96:1; 103:20-22; 118:2-4; 135:1; 136:1-3).

1. *An Ascription of Exclusive Praise* (verse 1)
The opening statement is both an affirmation and a denial. It denies that any glory is due to the community of Israel because such glory belongs to the LORD alone. If the psalm comes from the post-Exilic period, as is most probable, the expressions here would fit in well with statements of both Ezekiel and Daniel (Ezek. 20:9; 36:21-23; Dan. 9:18-19). God had fulfilled his words of promise to his people, and shown yet again his love and faithfulness in restoring them to Palestine.

2. *The Futility of Idol Worship* (verses 2-8)
At various times in her history Israel was challenged regarding the reality of her God (see, e.g. 2 Kgs. 18:32-35; Pss. 42:3; 79:10). At the time of the Exile the Gentile nations were mocking the Israelites regarding God's ability to help his people (*verse 2*). The nations' question seemed to God's people to highlight the predicament of the Israelites, yet it failed to reckon with the fact that the God of Israel was the only living and true God.

In reply the people assert again the existence of their God in heaven who fulfils his sovereign will (*verses 3-7*).

> Not unto us, O Lord of heav'n,
> but unto Your Name be glory given;
> in love and truth Lord, You fulfil
> the counsels of Your sovereign will.
> Though nations fail Your pow'r to own,
> yet Lord, You reign, and You alone.
>
> (Trinity Hymnal, 1961)

Over against this God, the idols of the Gentiles are impotent and lifeless. They might have all the visible parts similar to a human body, but they have no ability to respond to human needs. They are simply the work of men's hands. Isaiah in even fuller fashion mocks the folly of those who think they can create their own gods (Isa. 44:9-20). The people who create and worship such idols of silver and gold will be just as ineffective as those gods themselves *(verse 8)*. They may mock worshippers of the true God, yet they are trusting in their own futile creations which can offer no help at all.

3. A Call to Trust in the LORD (verses 9-11)

The use of the three phrases 'house of Israel', 'house of Aaron', and 'you who fear him', also occurs in Psalms 118:2-4 and 135:19-20 (with the addition of 'house of Levi'). The involvement of the 'house of Aaron' is particularly fitting for the period after the Exile, when the priests had to assume a very prominent role in government and were the principal teachers of the people (Mal. 2:1-9). 'You who fear him' could be a reference to the whole worshipping community, or else it could refer to the proselytes who had come to trust in the God of Israel (cf. the New Testament use of the term 'God-fearers' for Gentiles who had become adherents to Judaism: Acts 10:2; 16:14; 17:4, 17). The call is for all these groups to renounce any allegiance to idols and to trust in the LORD. The expression 'help and shield' is used also in Psalm 33:20 (see comment there).

4. A Confession of Trust (verses 12-13)

In response to the call to trust, the people now give a fresh commitment to the LORD. The recurring 'he will bless' offers assurance of the continuity of God's love and faithfulness to all the groups already mentioned in verses 9-11. Added assurance is given by saying that God 'remembers' them. This means that God recalls his promises and acts upon them to all who trust in him. Social class or wealth make no difference when it comes to God's blessing. 'Small and great alike' are only distinguished by the presence (or lack) of faith in God.

5. The Priestly Blessing (verses 14-15)

After return from Exile Israel's numbers were very small. Part of the blessing of God for obedience was the increase in children (Deut. 28:4). The words used here may well echo the prayer which Moses uttered just before Israel crossed the Jordan into the land of Canaan: 'May the LORD, the God of your fathers, increase you a thousand times and bless you as he has promised!' (Deut. 1:11). They can be confident that the blessing will be realised because the one to whom the prayer is addressed is indeed 'the Maker of heaven and earth'. This is a standard description, used repeatedly of the living God (see Pss. 121:2; 124:8; 134:3; 146:6).

6. The Congregational Confession (verses 16-18)

The community of Israel join in a response which magnifies the God they worship. While he is the God of heaven, yet he has allocated the earth to humanity (verse 16). 'He did not create it to be empty, but formed it to be inhabited' (Isa. 45:18). Man has been given special responsibility for the earth, over which he rules as God's vice-regent (Gen. 1:28-30).

Part of the responsibility of living people is to praise the LORD (verses 17-18). Those in the grave do not engage in praise. It is not corpses but living bodies which render thanksgiving to the LORD. Hence the community encourage themselves to do this continually, and they immediately do so with the exclamation: 'Hallelujah!' The New Testament gives fuller teaching on the state after death and prior to the final resurrection. Believers at death are immediately present with the Lord.

PSALM 116

An unnamed psalmist cries out here in thanksgiving for his personal deliverance. The exact circumstances of his trouble are not indicated, but it is clear that he had been through deep waters, and he now wishes to express his heartfelt praise to God his Saviour. There are many ways in which this psalm is reminiscent of King Hezekiah's thanksgiving after his recovery from his illness (Isa. 38). The psalm appears to come from late in the period of the monarchy, as it uses phrases which we know from other psalms (especially 18, 27, 31, and 56).

1. A Cry Heard (verses 1-4)

The translation of verse 1 in the NIV is possible, but the position of the word 'LORD' is debatable. The preferred and more literal rendering is, 'I love, for the LORD heard the voice of my supplications'. Twice more in the psalm verbs are used without an object ('call' in verse 2; 'believed' in verse 10). This unusual expression may well call attention to the intensity of the love which he felt for the LORD, just as John the apostle says, '*We love* because he first loved us' (1 John 4:19). All through this psalm the covenant title for God (Hebrew, *yhwh*, 'LORD') is used, and later the psalmist declares that he is a true covenant servant (see verse 16).

'To turn the ear' *(verse 2)* is a common Old Testament expression for giving heed to what is said, or listening to a prayer. Because the LORD had responded to his prayer the psalmist pledges lifelong appeal to him as his deliverer. The pattern is set here for other believers to follow:

> I love the Lord; he heard my cries
> And pitied every groan.
> Long as I live, when troubles rise
> I'll hasten to his throne.

Some great sickness or danger had confronted the psalmist and he felt near to the grave *(verses 3-4)*. The combination of various expressions for the danger emphasise how pressing a danger it was. However, he tells how at that time he cried to the LORD, asking for deliverance. The verb translated 'save me', is literally, 'cause me to escape', which directs attention again to the pressing nature of his grief and trouble. He was entangled in death's cords.

2. God's Character Re-affirmed (verses 5-7)

The psalmist does not say that God answered him, but instead fixes attention on his God *(verse 5)*. A fresh experience of God's mercy calls for a fresh declaration regarding his character. By the word of Scripture and now again through personal experience the psalmist knows that God is merciful and righteous. He has already spoken of his earlier cry for mercy (verse 1) and now says that God is indeed merciful for having listened and answered! The linking together of God's attributes of grace and compassion is frequent in the Old Testament (see Exod. 34:6-7; 2 Chr. 30:9; Neh. 9:17, 31; Ps. 103:8).

The expression 'simple-hearted' *(verse 6)* does not imply lack of understanding but that these people are resting on the LORD and his promises. The psalmist was a simple-hearted person when he called on the LORD, and he was saved. The Hebrew word used here (*yehoshi'a*) reminds us of the name *Joshua*, which means 'saviour'. With the trouble behind him, the psalmist can encourage himself to take his rest *(verse 7)*, for the LORD has dealt with him as one of his children. The needy child has met with gracious, parental care, and there is abundant rest for the soul trusting in him (this is brought out in the Hebrew by the use of the plural noun, 'be at *rests*').

3. *Thanks for God's Mercy* (verses 8-19)

Now the psalmist returns to his past need *(verses 8-9)*. He had been looking death in the face, but God had delivered him. He uses yet another synonym to describe his release (cf. 'cause to escape', verse 4, 'save', verse 6). The outcome of his experience was that he was still alive, and living his life in the presence of his God. These verses seem to be a deliberate echo of Psalm 56:13, and this would also explain the change here to the second person singular ('*you*, O LORD').

Verses 10-11: At this point the Greek (LXX) translation starts a new psalm, probably as part of the need to restore the 150 psalms (see the Introduction, p. 25). While the words 'I believed' correspond to 'I love' in verse 1, yet there is no reason to break the psalm into two. Even in the depths of despair, the psalmist never lost hope in God. Men may well have been giving him false advice, and he knew them well enough to declare them to be liars. But God was ever faithful and worthy of trust.

Recalling his deliverance, the psalmist asks what would be a fitting acknowledgment to the LORD *(verses 12-14)*. The use of the word 'goodness' links the question directly with the latter part of verse 7. 'The cup of salvation' could be a general reference to experiencing the saving blessings which God gives his children, or it could refer to some specific festival occasion. The latter may well be in view, because of the reference to vows, and to the fact that the psalmist was going to be in the house of the LORD in Jerusalem (see verse 19). Some have seen the expression 'the cup of salvation' as a reference to one of the cups used in the Passover (cf. 1 Cor. 10:16). There is perhaps support for this idea, since this is one of the psalms used by the Jews at the time of the Passover celebration, and it was probably one of the psalms which Jesus and his disciples sang after the institution of the Lord's Supper (Matt. 26:30).

Verse 15 ('Precious in the sight of the LORD is the death of his saints') can hardly mean that God is pleased when his people die. In the context it means more that God will never be uncaring when his people come near to death. Their blood is precious in his sight (Ps. 72:14).

In *verse 16* the psalmist expresses himself in covenant language. To say, 'I am your servant', was a statement of submission and loyalty (cf. Ahaz' words, 2 Kings 16:7). He makes this statement to the covenant LORD, and repeats it in asserting that he is the son of a woman who was likewise devoted to her LORD. Yet this servant knows freedom.

Verses 17-19: The regulations regarding offering of sacrifices of thanksgiving and also sacrifices to fulfil vows are set out in Leviticus 7:11-21. The psalmist will not only make the offering, but he will also call on the name of the LORD. This could mean that he will pray, but 'call' in Hebrew can also mean, 'call out', 'proclaim'. The latter meaning fits best here, as it agrees also with Psalm 22:25 in that public proclamation or confession was part of thanksgiving. The vows he had made would be fulfilled in the courts of the temple in Jerusalem, when he would have the opportunity of sitting with others to eat of the cakes which would be presented. A communal meal was a fitting way to rejoice before the LORD. The final 'Hallelujah', 'Praise the LORD', is not at all surprising.

PSALM 117

This shortest of all psalms is a missionary call. Stemming from experience of God's steadfast love the psalmist looks to the Gentile nations to come and rejoice in God with Israel. Luther said that this psalm was short so that everyone could grasp its meaning. It speaks of abundant mercy. In response to it a loud 'Hallelujah' is needed. The psalm is an excellent example of a hymn of praise (see Introduction, pp. 46-48).

1. *A Missionary Call (verse 1)*
The psalmist issues a call to the Gentile nations to join in the LORD's praise. In effect this is a call to experience the saving power of God, and to know him just as believing Israel did. Paul uses this verse along with other Old Testament quotations to show that it was God's intention that the gospel would result in the Gentiles glorifying God for his mercy (Rom. 15:8-12).

2. *An Explanation (verse 2a-b)*
A double explanation is provided for the reason behind the call to praise. First, the psalmist says God's covenant love has been great to us. Secondly, he knows that God's complete faithfulness is an endur-

ing characteristic. These two, covenant love and faithfulness, go hand in hand, as they do in Psalm 89:1-2.

3. *Another Hallelujah* (verse 2c)

The psalmist practises what he preaches. Having called on the Gentiles to 'praise the LORD' he does so himself. That initial call is now put into direct address, an ascription of praise to the one who is worthy of all honour. The chorus of 'Hallelujah' will sound out fully in heaven: 'Hallelujah! Salvation and glory and power belong to our God' (Rev. 19:1).

PSALM 118

Various interpretations have been given of this psalm. The different approaches stem from the fact that it combines personal and communal elements, and its content involves both imagery of battle and of the temple. The most satisfactory background for the psalm is a time when the LORD had given victory to his people, such as when Jehoshaphat and his army defeated the combined forces of Moab and Ammon (see 2 Chr. 20:1-30, especially 20-23, 27-28). After the opening praise, the victorious warrior rejoices in God's salvation, while in the latter part of the psalm the people as a whole join in the praise. The use of this psalm as part of the praise at the end of the Passover was most fitting (see the introduction to Ps. 113). It has connections in language with the Song of Moses (Exod. 15), and it most probably formed part of the hymn which Jesus and his disciples used after the institution of the Lord's Supper (Matt. 26:30).

1. *Enduring Love* (verses 1-4)

The opening and closing verses of the psalm are part of the terminology of praise which appears in almost identical form in Psalms 105-107, 136; 1 Chronicles 16:8, 34; and 2 Chronicles 20:21. At a time of personal and national rejoicing, the use of the covenant title of God ('LORD') and the theme of covenant love direct attention to the object of praise. Once more the mercy of God has been experienced by king and people.

In *verses 2-4* the triple repetition of 'Israel', 'house of Aaron', and 'those who fear the LORD' recalls the same usage in Psalm 115:9-11, 12-13. These comprehensive titles are used so that no-one in the covenant nation is excluded from the call to affirm yet again the wonder of God's grace to them.

2. A Song of Deliverance (verses 5-21)

In verses 5-7 the poet reflects upon what happened when he was in distress. The terms he uses suggest some military situation, probably being besieged by opposing armies (see verses 10-12). Out of that position he was delivered, and therefore he can declare that because the LORD is with him, his fear is banished. The repetition of 'The LORD is with me' is one of many such repetitions throughout the psalm. They serve to enhance the poetic effect and to draw attention to the thought being expressed. To claim that the LORD is his helper also points to a battle situation, as 'helper' often has a military connotation. Since he has such divine assistance the psalmist knows that he can look in triumph on his enemies. Psalm 54 forms a fitting parallel, containing both the idea of God as the helper (54:4) and looking in triumph on enemies (54:7). Verse 6 is quoted in Hebrews 13:6 as an encouragement to contentment.

Verses 8-9 are identical apart from the final phrase in each. Both prophets and psalmists warn of the folly of looking to the strength of man for help, instead of looking to the LORD (Ps. 33:16-19; Isa. 30:1-5). The combined expression is a forceful way of emphasising how good it is to put one's trust in the living God.

When Israel was surrounded by neighbouring nations who were attacking like bees (for the use of bees to depict an attacking army, see Deut. 1:44; Isa. 7:18-19), the king was able to overcome them in the name of the LORD (verses 10-12). 'The name of the LORD' stands for his character, which was displayed in the victories he gave his people over their enemies. The king recognises that victory only came through trusting the LORD and his power. The language of verse 12 suggests a sharp attack by the enemies, but swift victory for Israel.

In verses 13-14 the king recounts how he was retreating and about to fall (i.e. be killed in battle) when the LORD intervened. Verse 14 is drawn from Exodus 15:2, which appears to have become a song of praise used in situations such as this (see also Isa. 12:2). Each new act of God's salvation can bring forth the same response as the people made to the salvation from Egypt.

Communal joy marks the victory which the LORD has brought (verses 15-16). By 'the tents' is most probably meant the permanent dwellings of the righteous, though it has also been suggested that it means the temporary accommodation erected in Jerusalem for the great festival occasions. The godly part of the nation extol the actions of the LORD's right hand. Again, the triumph song after the Exodus provides the language used by the people many centuries later (see Exod. 15:6). 'Right hand' points to the LORD's might, for he has brought about the victory. The divine warrior has conquered! (for similar use of this expression, see Pss. 89:13; 98:1).

The king has survived the battle *(verses 17-18)*, and now pledges to declare to others what the LORD has done. It is the living who praise him, not those who go down to the grave (Ps. 115:17-18). Even fatherly acts of discipline are praiseworthy. God disciplines with justice (Jer. 30:11), and the New Testament develops the idea to say that the purpose of discipline is that we may share in God's holiness (Heb. 12:10). The psalmist was spared death, and lives to testify to God's mercy.

The victorious procession arrives back at Jerusalem, and the king calls for the city gates to be thrown wide open to receive the grateful worshippers *(verses 19-21)*. They come with joyfulness to celebrate at the sanctuary and to give thanks for answered prayer. In time of battle God heard the cries of his people, and he answered by giving deliverance or salvation. The righteous person will enter the presence of God knowing his requirements (see Pss. 15:2-5; 24:3-6), and realising that on his appearance there 'he will receive blessing from the LORD and vindication from God his Saviour' (Ps. 24:5).

3. *Communal Praise of God's Mercy* (verses 22-27)

As the people sing of God's mercy, they use words which may well have been a proverbial saying *(verses 22-23)*. A stone which was spurned by builders, turns out to be the main stone over a doorway. The initial reference here is to the king, who was despised by the leaders of the invading armies. However, the words have been taken over in several places in the New Testament. Jesus uses them following his parable of the tenants to reinforce the point that the kingdom is being taken away from the Jewish people (Matt. 21:42; Mark 12:10; Luke 20:17). It is also applied to the rejection of Jesus (Acts 4:11) and to the fact that he has become the foundation stone of God's new building, the church (Eph. 2:20; 1 Pet. 2:7). Coupled with it in this psalm is an affirmation that the victory achieved has been the work of the LORD alone, and that is a thing of wonder in the eyes of the people. The day of the LORD's victory becomes a day of rejoicing for the people *(verse 24)*. This verse continues the theme which has already been noted in verses 15-17.

Verses 25-26: The rejoicing prompts the people to cry out, 'Save us' (Hebrew, *hôshi 'ah na'*, cf. *Hosanna* in Matt. 21:9; Mark 11:9-10, when the crowds in Jerusalem greet Jesus with the words of these verses). Originally this was a cry for help (Ps. 28:9) or for mercy (2 Sam. 14:4), but was later used in praise as a declaration that the LORD has saved. The great Jewish commentary on the Old Testament from around 200 AD (the Mishnah) records that these words were used by the priests after the offering of sacrifices at the time of the Feast of Tabernacles. Blessing is pronounced on the king who has won the victory in the name of the LORD (see verses 10-12). It is unclear if the king is also the one being blessed from the house of the LORD. This is because the *you* is plural (see NIV footnote). The plural may have been used as a mark of respect for the king (the royal *we*), or it could refer to the army collectively on return with him from battle.

Verse 27: The people again acknowledge that their Saviour, the LORD, is indeed their God. He has brought light from the midst of their darkness in a time of national distress. 'To make light shine' is an allusion to the words of the Aaronic blessing (Num. 6:25). The following expression is difficult to translate (cf. the NIV text and footnote), though the general meaning is clear enough. In addition to songs of joy, the people also came with appropriate outward manifestations of their response to God's mercy, probably bringing sacrificial thank offerings to the altar.

4. A Renewed Confession (verse 28)
As the individual speaker earlier in the psalm is the king, it is best to assume that he now reaffirms his relationship with his God. Trust in him inevitably leads to praise and adoration. Whenever there is a declaration that 'Salvation belongs to our God', there is also reverence and worship.

5. Enduring Love (verse 29)
The final words of the psalm are identical with the opening words, so that the whole response of king and people is framed by this declaration of the enduring nature of God's goodness and love.

PSALM 119

This psalm stands out in the whole collection of psalms for several striking reasons.

1. It is an acrostic poem, based on all the letters of the Hebrew alphabet in consecutive order and so is divided into twenty-two stanzas. All the verses of each stanza begin with the same letter of the Hebrew alphabet. The fact that it has eight verses in each stanza makes it the longest psalm of all. The effect of the acrostic is striking both to the eye when read and to the ear when heard.

2. It is a poem which rejoices in the fact that God has revealed himself to his people. He has spoken, and the unnamed psalmist shows intense devotion to the word of God. The focus of attention throughout is on God, either by direct address or by the use of the pronoun 'your': '*your* righteous laws', '*your* word', '*your* commands'. The acrostic pattern and the repetitiveness of the main ideas may seem quite foreign to modern Western readers, but the poet uses the features of Hebrew poetry with great skill to express his utter devotion to the word of God. That word provides his hope, but it also forms his guide to life.

3. A range of Hebrew terms is used to describe God's revelation: law, statutes, precepts, commandments, laws, decrees, word, promise. Their use is distributed throughout the twenty-two stanzas, so that all these eight terms appear in six stanzas, and never less than six in any one stanza. There are just a few variant expressions, such as 'ways' in verses 3 and 15 (different words in Hebrew) and 'faithfulness' in verse 90. It is only in verses 84 and 121-122 that no synonym occurs at all. There is no regular pattern to their use, either in regard to the number of times they occur in a stanza or the order in which they appear.

4. The psalm does not fit neatly into any particular category, because it embraces distinctive features of many types. It contains hymnic elements, but at the same time there are many verses which deal with sorrow and grief. It conveys confident trust in the LORD, but also appeals for help in times of danger and distress.

5. The two other psalms which are closest to this one are Psalms 1 and 19. The first of these shows the commitment of a believer to the law

of the LORD, while the second in praising God's revelation, uses six of the same synonyms which appear in Psalm 119. While those two earlier psalms contain the same theme, they cannot match the development of it in all its breadth and fullness in this psalm.

6. There is a strong affinity between this psalm and earlier portions of the Old Testament, with many expressions closely following passages in books such as Deuteronomy. For example, in the opening section of the psalm the words of verse 2 echo those of Deuteronomy 4:29, while the command of Moses in Deuteronomy 6:6-9 regarding the word of God is fulfilled in the psalmist's experience. For him the word of God is a living reality in his life.

7. While there does not seem to be any progressive development of the theme in the psalm, yet in most stanzas a major aspect is in focus. The choice of the acrostic structure, while itself striking, limits the development of ideas in a structural way leading to a climax.

Aleph (*verses 1-8*)

Verses 1-3 set the scene for the whole psalm. They resemble closely both the content and form of Psalm 1. They employ terms which are used time after time, yet without defining them. The word used for 'law' (Hebrew, *torah*) has a broad meaning, pointing to any instruction which God has given his people, while 'statutes' points to covenant stipulations. Just as Psalm 1 speaks of the blessedness of those who meditate on the law of the LORD, so Psalm 119 commences with an ascription of blessedness to those whose life follows the paths set out by the LORD in his word. The psalmist is not asserting sinless perfection for believers (as the following verses make plain), but a commitment to the revealed truth of God, and an obedient submission to his demands.

Verse 4: The first words of direct address to God in the psalm are a declaration that God has spoken and that his precepts relate to practice. The way to life is the way of obedience (see Deut. 30:15-16). The call to discipleship under the gospel remains a call to implicit obedience (John 14:23-24; 15:10, 14).

Verses 5-6: The psalmist's desire is that his life will be dedicated to the covenant directives which God has given his people (for the use of the term 'decrees', see Deut. 6:2; 28:15, 45; 30:10, 16). This may in fact echo the wish which God himself had expressed concerning his people: 'Oh, that their hearts would be inclined to fear me and keep all my commands always' (Deut. 5:29). 'To consider commands' means to pay attention to them. If that is done, then the outcome will be that the psalmist's hopes will not be disappointed and he will suffer no shame because of his commitment to God's directives.

Verses 7-8: God's laws are righteous, something which Psalm 19:9 has already asserted, and which this psalm repeatedly claims (verses 62, 75, 106, 123, 138, 144, 160, 164, 172). Just as God himself is righteous (Ps. 119:137), so are his laws. The confidence already expressed that obedience results in lack of shame leads to praise of God by those whose hearts are set on him and his ways. The final verse in the section is really an appeal for help. It is a confession that without God's presence and aid, his decrees cannot be kept.

Beth (*verses 9-16*)

Verse 9: The content of the question does not necessarily mean that the psalmist was himself a young man. He is speaking in a manner used by wisdom teachers in the Psalms and in Proverbs in particular (Ps. 34:11-14; Prov. chaps. 1-7). This must have been a regular teaching device. He answers his question by directing attention to the role God's word plays in restraining one from sin.

Verses 10-11: The psalmist identifies himself with those upon whom he has already pronounced a blessing in verse 2. His commitment is whole-hearted, and he has treasured up God's word in his heart in order to be kept in the ways of righteousness . 'Word' in this instance is a Hebrew word (*'imrah*) which, on many other occurrences, is often rightly translated as 'promise'. To hide God's word in the heart is much more than just being able to recite from memory. It is living in accord with the directives which he has given. To stop listening to that instruction causes one to 'stray from the words of knowledge' (Prov. 19:27). Hence he appeals to God to keep him faithful.

Verses 12-13: Before asking for further teaching the psalmist extols his God (Hebrew, *Blessed are you, O LORD*), which is a prelude to the joy he expresses in the final verses of this section. Recounting the laws could mean simply meditating on them, and in that way saying them over and over, one after another. However, it may point to something more formal, when there was recitation of the covenant stipulations (cf. Ps. 50:16). When the priests were reading the law as appointed by God (Deut. 31:9-13), the people may well have joined in the recitation, just as they do in Christian churches when the Ten Commandments or Apostle's Creed are being said.

Verses 14-16: The spiritual response to God's law is one of joy, just as when a great treasure has been found (cf. Matt. 13:44). God's ordinances are more precious than 'much pure gold' (Ps. 19:10), 'than thousands of pieces of silver and gold' (Ps. 119:72) or 'great spoil' (Ps. 119:162). The idea of meditating on God's precepts is quite frequent throughout this psalm, and the verb used here also occurs in verses 23, 27, 48, 78, and 148. It refers to rehearsing aloud things relating to God – his works, his precepts, his wonders, his promises. Such delight in God leads the psalmist to pledge that he will not become forgetful in relation to what God has spoken.

Gimel (*verses 17-24*)

Verse 17: A plea for gracious dealing from God opens this section. The expression 'do good' has a wide range of meaning in the Old Testament, but it is used in connection with weaning of children and (as here) of acting generously to someone (cf. its use in Pss. 13:6; 116:7). God's care will ensure life and as a grateful response the psalmist promises obedience.

Verses 18-19: God's law contains many precious things which require spiritual illumination. Without it, these wonderful things remain hidden, and cannot form part of meditation (see verse 27, where the same Hebrew word is translated 'wonders'). Confessing he is a 'stranger on earth' does two things. Firstly, it identifies the psalmist with his people, who experienced being strangers and exiles in both Egypt and Babylon. Secondly, it suggests that he has not a real home here on earth. He is not a citizen who feels he belongs to the kingdoms of this world. The New Testament develops this further with the reminder that we are strangers and pilgrims on this earth (1 Pet. 2:11), whose real citizenship is in heaven (Phil. 3:20).

Verses 20-21: The contrast between the righteous and the unrighteous is brought out in these verses. The one loves God's laws with deep and intense longing. The other despises them, refusing to obey their demands. God uses strong admonitions against the disobedient, who as rebels are cursed, and so deprived of his blessing.

Verses 22-24: For the first time in this psalm there is reference to the troubles which have come to the psalmist because of his attitude to God's word. His relationship to God is that of a servant (verses 17 and

23), who takes great pleasure in what God has revealed, making it his meditation and his guide. However, that also brings conflict with others who pour reproach on him and who misrepresent him. While appealing to God to change his circumstances, he shows no movement away from his devotion to his statutes. Like Asaph, he is guided by the counsel of the Lord (Ps. 73:24).

Daleth (*verses 25-32*)

The problems involved in composing a poem using an acrostic pattern come out in this section in Hebrew. Four of the verses start with the same Hebrew noun (*derek*, 'the way of ...'), one starts with the plural of this word, while two start with the same verb (*davaq*, 'to cling to').

Verses 25-26: The psalmist concentrates on his difficulties in this section, and he prays for the strength and consolation which come from God's word. His situation is desperate, almost bringing him to the grave. However, he knows 'that man does not live on bread alone but on every word which comes from the mouth of the Lord' (Deut. 8:3). Hence his appeal to God to keep him alive, for he knows that he has answered him in the past, and he also wants further instruction from him.

Verse 27: There is a contrast between the psalmist's ways and God's ways (Hebrew 'my ways', verse 26; 'the way of your precepts', verse 27). He previously recounted his ways, and now he wants to understand the path which God's precepts set out for him. Fuller knowledge of them will lead to thoughtful appreciation of the wonders they contain.

Verses 28-30: God's word ministers to those in grief, not only when there is a loss of a family member, but when difficult circumstances cause pain and vexation. Deceit on the part of others should not lead to similar behaviour on the part of a believer. Strength and comfort from God through his word confirm the resolve to shun the evil ways of the tormenters and to follow single-mindedly 'the way of truth' (Hebrew, 'the way of faithfulness').

Verses 31-32: The expressions of dedication to the Lord continue, seeing that his heart has been enlarged to give increased understanding (NIV 'set free'). He clings to God's statutes, and sets himself to follow the way set out in them. 'Run' does not appear to have any idea here of urgent action but rather of resolute adherence to the set path (cf. Prov. 4:10-12). The thought of being put to shame, first introduced in verse 6, is taken up again. Hopes will not be disappointed if there is such confident trust in the Lord and his word.

He (*verses 33-40*)

In these eight verses the main plea is for further instruction from the LORD, and preservation in his pathways.

Verse 33: The request is modelled closely on the prayer, 'Teach me your way', which occurs in Psalms 27:11 and 86:11. The translation 'to the end' is taken from the early Greek and Aramaic renderings of this verse. However, in Hebrew the final word of the verse is one which often indicates the consequence of something, or a reward, and it is best to preserve this interpretation (see also verse 112). What pleases the LORD is regarded by the psalmist as in itself a satisfying reward.

Verses 34-35: The thought of the previous verse is continued, with the psalmist confessing the pleasure he has in following the demands of God's law. He recognises that he needs spiritual understanding which comes from God alone, using the identical Hebrew expression already used in verse 27 (NIV 'Let me understand'). When that spiritual teaching takes place, he promises to act upon it and to give ready obedience to the law.

Verses 36-37: The combination of heart and eyes is common in the Old Testament (see Num. 15:39; Job 31:7; Jer. 22:17; Ps. 101:2-5). The heart is regarded as controlling the whole direction of life, while the mention of eyes suggests the external influences which affect behaviour. The psalmist wants a heart motivated by devotion to God's statutes, not by the thought of getting material rewards. He knows that looking at such things can tempt, but asks for God's word to be fulfilled towards him.

Verses 38-40: As so often throughout this psalm, mention is made of God's gracious promises which provide the basis of confidence. Each fulfilment of a promise brings further encouragement, and directs attention back to God himself. Action taken in accordance with his word gives new reason to revere and adore the living God. Devotion to God and his word often brings reproach, and the psalmist prays for release from such attitudes from his enemies. His heart is set on God's precepts and he knows that God's saving power (his righteousness) is able to keep him. The New Testament amplifies this, pointing to the words of prophecy which have been fulfilled in the salvation which has come through Christ. This means that we can be kept 'by God's power until the coming of the salvation that is ready to be revealed in the last time' (1 Pet. 1:5).

Waw (*verses 41-48*)

Each verse in this section begins with the letter *waw*, which is used to form the conjunction 'and' in Hebrew. The Hebrew constructions used indicate that the verses are tied together so that a common theme runs through them all. They consist of a prayer that God's word will remain with the psalmist and then he will be able to answer those who mock him, and also testify before kings.

Verses 41-42: The psalmist is still concerned because of the persecution for the truth which he is enduring. He relies upon the sure word of promise which he has been given as his stay, and knows that God will deliver him in accordance with his covenant love (Hebrew, *chesed*). The answer to those who taunt him will take the form of God's intervention and salvation.

Verses 43-45: Having God's word in one's heart constantly is necessary for a believer (see verses 11-13). The psalmist is probably thinking of the quiet murmuring of this word during meditation and desires that it will never be removed from him. The connection with the preceding verses can be seen more clearly if the opening of verse 43 is rightly translated, 'so do not remove the word of truth'. There may seem to be some contradiction between obeying God's law and walking in freedom, but coming into wholehearted devotion and service to God does set one's heart free (verse 32) to give lifelong attention to his demands.

Verses 46-48: Once again the psalmist makes reference to his official role, for he has responsibility to speak before kings (as mentioned here) and rulers (verses 23 and 161). As the priests were teachers of the law (Mal. 2:4-9) it is probable that he himself occupied such a position in the post-exilic period. His attitude is one of constant pleasure in God's commands, reaching out for them with his hands. This expression is unusual, but as the lifting up of hands is mentioned in connection with praise (Pss. 28:2; 63:4; 134:2), it probably means that he praises the commands which he loves.

Zayin (*verses 49-56*)

Just as the letter *waw* does not commence many words in Hebrew, so also the letter *zayin*. Three of the verses of this section begin with the verb 'remember' (Hebrew, *zakar*) and two with the word 'this' (Hebrew, *z'ot*).

Verses 49-50: As he reflects upon his experiences, the psalmist knows that he rests upon the word which God has spoken. This is a recurrent theme throughout Psalm 119 (see verses 43, 81, 114, 147). His confidence does not rest on his own plans, but on God's revealed purposes (which remain the sure basis for believing hope, Rom. 8:28-30). In his present suffering (i.e. persecution) he is assured by God's promises.

Verses 51-52: The taunts of proud scoffers fail to make the psalmist deviate from adherence to God's law. He recalls that this law is not new revelation. God's law was given from creation onwards, and at Mount Sinai it was put into a special form when God entered into a covenant with the nation of Israel. Prophets and priests can appeal for remembrance of the decrees and laws which God gave for all Israel (Mal. 4:4). The expression 'find comfort' comes from a reflexive verb in Hebrew, which suggests that the psalmist comforts himself as he contemplates these ancient laws.

Verse 53 expresses another aspect of relationship to the law. Love to God and his commandments has as its complement very strong feelings against those who refuse to submit to his demands (cf. the way in which Paul was greatly distressed by the idolatry of the Athenians, Acts 17:16). 'The wicked' are not Gentiles, but those within Israel who, though knowing the law, have wilfully chosen to reject its claims.

Verses 54-56: After the business of daytime activities, the night brings opportunity for meditation and praise. Several other psalms refer to nighttime songs (42:8; 77:6; 92:1-3). The phrase 'wherever I lodge' links with the reference in verse 19 to being a pilgrim on the earth. Throughout his earthly life the psalmist is committed to doing what he has promised, keeping and guarding the stipulations of the LORD. He shows by his obedience that he belongs to him.

Heth (*verses 57-64*)

Verse 57: The word 'portion' could imply that the psalmist was himself a Levite. It is the word used of the share which the various tribes received of the land of Canaan. No territory was allotted to the Levites, and the special provision made for their maintenance meant that the LORD was their portion (Num. 18:20; Deut. 10:9). However, the word took on a wider meaning as it was used to describe the relationship between God and his people (Pss. 16:5; 73:26), and this is probably its sense here. Obedience is the response to God's gracious provision.

Verses 58-59: The intensity of feeling for the LORD is brought out, both by the verb used ('sought') and again by reference to the fact that his whole being is behind his entreaty. The plea for mercy is grounded on the promise which had been given. The NIV rendering of verse 59 suggests a past time of reflection and resolve. It might, though, refer to the constant attitude of the psalmist: 'Whenever I consider my ways, I turn my feet ...'. This is an assertion that the covenant directives are a constant guide to the psalmist, whose plans for life are guided by adherence to revealed truth.

Verses 60-61: The promised obedience is not deferred, but is yielded with immediate readiness. The verb 'hasten' is often used by psalmists pleading for God's immediate help (Pss. 22:19; 38:22; 40:13; 70:1, 5; 71:12; 141:1), but it can also be used to indicate readiness to act. All the scheming of enemies will not distract from giving attention to God's law. 'Binding with ropes' is not just literal oppression, but any form of scheming which restricts or impedes.

Verses 62-63: The thought of songs in the night (see comment on verse 55) is taken up again. The identical phrase, 'righteous laws', has already occurred in verse 7. Walking in the ways of the LORD means sharing companionship together, just like those in Malachi's day who 'talked with each other, and the LORD listened and heard' (Mal. 3:16). Common allegiance to the LORD brings with it a fellowship of joint devotion and service.

Verse 64: God's love extends in one sense to the whole of creation, made by his skill and maintained by his faithfulness. He has an everlasting covenant between himself and all living creatures (Gen. 9:16). For guidance and salvation much more is needed than merely the knowledge of God we obtain from the natural world. Instruction in God's personal revelation is often stated in this psalm, with the particular phrase used here ('teach me your decrees') appearing seven times (vss. 12, 26, 64, 68, 124, 135, 171).

Teth (*verses 65-72*)

The thought of what is good dominates this section. The Hebrew adjective (*tov*) occurs four times, a related noun once (*tuv*), and the verb 'to do good' (*metiv*) also appears once.

Verse 65 summarises the teaching of the section as a whole. The appeal is for God to act in fulfilment of his word and deal graciously with his servant. Solomon's words may be in mind, when he assured the people during the dedication of the temple that not one word had failed of all the good which the LORD had promised his people (1 Kgs. 8:56). God will continue to act in utter faithfulness to his word.

Verse 66: The request for teaching is given in a variant form from the one already noted (see comment on verse 64), though with practically identical meaning. The word 'judgment' translates a Hebrew word which can mean 'discernment' or 'behaviour' (cf. its use in 1 Sam. 21:14 of David's change of conduct before Achish). This meaning fits well here, for the psalmist is requesting instruction in knowledge and good behavioural patterns, while confessing that he agrees in his heart with God's commands. He has confident trust in them.

Verses 67-70: The psalmist acknowledges that previously he had known what it was to err, but coming through a period of affliction (most probably the persecution and oppression he had faced) he is acting as an obedient servant. Arising out of his experience of God he can praise him both for his character and for the way he displays that in his actions. He gives further details concerning his enemies, whose hearts are callous and unfeeling (Hebrew lit. 'plump as fat'). They slander him, but even that does not cause him to change his attitude to God's law, for in it he still takes great pleasure.

Verses 71-72: The period of affliction turned the heart of the psalmist more and more to God's law. His estimation continues to be that it is more valuable to him than large sums of money (see the similar references in verses 14, 127, 162). Spiritual values override worldly riches.

Yodh (*verses 73-80*)

Verse 73: The psalmist looks to his Creator for spiritual insight for learning his commands. Just as he came into existence by God's power, so he needs to rely on him for illumination. The same combination of the verbs 'made' and 'formed' occurs in the Song of Moses; 'Is he [the LORD] not your Father, your Creator, who *made* you and *formed* you?' (Deut. 32:6).

Verses 74-76: Those who fear the LORD have already been mentioned as the friends of the psalmist (verse 63). He longs for them to be encouraged by his example of trusting the LORD. Earlier he has noted that it was the LORD who brought him to that attitude of trust (see verse 49). He continues to speak of his afflictions, but without any accusations against God. On the contrary, he confesses that God's decisions (Hebrew, *mishpatim*) concerning him are righteous, and that God remains absolutely true to his promises. The Song of Moses may also be behind the thought of verse 75 (cf. Deut. 32:4). The psalmist rests on God's word to him, finding that in his affliction there is the assurance of covenant love which the promises contain. The way in which the prayer is formed in Hebrew (using the particle *nā'*) suggests that it follows on from what he has just said about the nature of God's laws in the previous verse.

Verse 77: The preceding prayer is reinforced by a further request for mercy. It is practically synonymous with the first petition in verse 17: 'Do good to your servant, and I will live.' The reference to delighting in the law is identical in Hebrew with that in verse 70, though NIV varies in translation.

Verses 78-80: The attitude of two groups in his society are so different towards the psalmist. On the one hand, the arrogant persecutors have no desire for God's ways and try to shame him. On the other hand, those who fear the LORD share in fellowship with him, joining in a common understanding of the covenant stipulations. To pray for a blameless heart is to ask for a God-given devotion to his statutes. If that is given, then the psalmist knows that he will suffer no shame because of his commitment to God's directives.

Kaph (*verses 81-88*)

The first half of the psalm concludes with this stanza, which like the final stanza of the psalm (*verses 169-176*), is more of a prayer for help rather than just a description of need. In tone, with questions like 'When will you ...?' and 'How long ...?', it resembles the appeals for help such as Psalm 13.

Verses 81-82: The felt weakness of the psalmist is depicted by the phrases 'my soul *faints*' and 'my eyes *fail*' (in Hebrew these two verbs are the same). He thinks he is near death, and his eyes fail because of weeping. However, as in many laments, his confidence is still in the promises God has given, and he can ask, 'When?'.

Verses 83-84: The effect of his trouble is that he feels like a wineskin, dried and shrivelled, because it has been hung over a fire. His afflictions have left their mark on him, and he feels that he is near the end of his life (see verse 87). He wonders how long it will be before his God intervenes (Hebrew lit. 'How many are the days of your servant?'). However, in spite of his circumstances he clings to God's word and will not let it slip from him.

Verses 85-86: His enemies fail to live according to God's law, and in their rebellion against its demands they try and bring the psalmist to his end. 'Pitfalls' could have the meaning of 'traps', 'snares', but it may have the stronger meaning of 'graves'. Total destruction was their aim. They persecute without any valid reason, but given their hostility to God's law, anyone loving it would become a natural target for them.

Verses 87-88: In spite of the persecution which almost took his life, the psalmist is still committed to God's precepts. 'Not forsaken' is just another way of expressing 'not forgotten' (see verse 83). In the midst of all his troubles God's covenant love stands firm, and if his life is continued, he owns that he will obey what God has spoken. He repeats the cry for preservation which has already been made several times earlier in the psalm (see verses 25, 37, 40), and which is going to appear several times later as well (see verses 107, 149, 154, 156, 159).

Lamedh (*verses 89-96*)

This stanza concentrates on the enduring nature of God's word.

Verses 89-90: Just as God is eternal, so is his revelation and his faithfulness (see Ps. 89:1-2, and cf. Jesus' words in Mark 13:31). It was by God's word that the heavens were created (Ps. 33:9), and they remain as a testimony to that fact, as well as to his faithfulness in sustaining them. Creation is a witness to the power of God's word, and generation after generation has a testimony to confirm God's steadfastness.

Verse 91: The laws which govern creation are inherent, for the whole of creation has God as its maker and he established the principles on which it operates. Creation is not to be worshipped as though it was divine, for all parts of creation are servants who do his bidding.

Verses 92-93: The psalmist reflects on the encouragement and support which came to him from God's laws. By God's word he has been preserved (cf. verse 88), and those statutes which he delighted in (cf. the same or similar expressions in verses 24, 77, 143, 174) have been his stay in times of affliction. The pledge never to forget them repeats one already given several times in this psalm (see verses 16, 61, 83).

Verses 94-95: In Hebrew the emphasis falls on the psalmist's relationship with God: '*I am yours*; save me.' As a consequence, he directs his prayer to *his* God, and asks for preservation in the midst of present dangers (cf. Ps. 54:1). His enemies are intent on his total destruction, but he trusts in his Saviour to deliver him. He knows what God's word promises, and he makes that his meditation.

Verse 96: As he looks around him, the psalmist sees the limitations of earthly things, as everything fits within the boundaries which God has allotted. On the other hand, God's commands are limitless, and there are riches in them which can never be exhausted.

Mem (*verses 97-104*)

Verse 97: The central theme of this psalm is summed up by this exclamation. Twice already the psalmist has declared his love for God's *commandments* (verses 47, 48) and he returns to this later on (verse 127). Now for the first time he says he loves God's *law*, a statement which is repeated (verses 113, 163), along with affirmation of love for God's *statutes* (verse 119) and *precepts* (verse 159). Constant meditation on God's revelation provides wisdom which cannot be found elsewhere, and this wisdom exceeds that of enemies, teachers and elders, as the following verses explain.

Verses 98-100: These verses make comparisons with other sources of wisdom. The enemies, though they show great skill in devising plots, lack access to the enduring word of God. Teachers may have considerable worldly wisdom, but they have not been instructed through meditation on God's statutes. Senior members of the community may have wealth of experience behind them, but still not have as much spiritual insight as someone who obeys God's precepts.

Verses 101-102: The source of the psalmist's wisdom is from God: '*You yourself* have taught me.' God's laws have instructed him according to his earlier request for teaching (see verse 33). Obedience keeps him from walking in sinful ways, and ensure that he does not turn aside from the pathway of obedience.

Verses 103-104: Just as God's words have been compared to great riches (see verse 72, and cf. verse 127), so now the comparison is made with the sweetest thing imaginable. As the mouth loves the taste of honey, so the psalmist expresses his delight in God's words. They are extremely pleasurable to him, providing him with instruction which gives him joy in truth and avoiding false ways.

Nun (*verses 105-112*)

Verse 105: The idea that God's word gives light appears elsewhere in the Old Testament (cf. Prov. 6:23). It acknowledges that without God's teaching and direction we walk in darkness. The highest expression of the idea comes in the words of Jesus in John 8:12: 'I am the light of the world. Whoever follows me will never walk in darkness, but will have the light of life.'

Verses 106-107: Because covenants normally involved a solemn oath, the expression 'to take an oath' could be identical with 'to make a covenant'. Thus, even when deceived by the Gibeonites into making a covenant with them, the Israelites refer to that covenant by saying: 'We have given them our oath by the LORD ...' (Hebrew, 'we have *sworn* to them', Josh. 9:19; cf. also Neh. 10:29). The psalmist had not only entered into covenant with the LORD, but he had confirmed it at some later stage, pledging obedience to God's righteous demands. Such attachment to the LORD brought intense suffering on him, and so he once more pleads for preservation in the midst of his trials (see on verse 88).

Verses 108-110: Even when under persecution the psalmist has learned to live joyfully, maintaining his adherence to God's precepts. Constant danger to his life, as he continues to confess the LORD, has not caused him to deviate into other pathways. He lives dangerously, avoiding traps laid for him by his enemies, yet desires more instruction to guide and strengthen him.

Verses 111-112: As part of his spiritual inheritance, the psalmist has received God's statutes. Outward troubles do not take away his inward joy, as he confirms his resolve to observe the directions for life he has received from God. The expression 'to the very end' renders a Hebrew word (*'eqev*) which often indicates the consequence of something, or a reward. As in verse 33 it is best to maintain this interpretation and so translate: 'My heart is set on keeping your decrees: the reward is lasting.' Hence, what the psalmist is saying is that there is constant spiritual delight or blessing in keeping God's decrees.

Samekh (*verses 113-120*)

Verses 113-115: In contrast to the evildoers, the psalmist reaffirms his own relationship to God. He has in him a sure hiding place, bringing together two terms to describe God which are favourites with the psalmists (for Hebrew *seter*, 'refuge' or 'shelter', see Pss. 27:5; 31:20; 32:7 [NIV 'hiding place']; 61:4; 91:1; for Hebrew *magen*, 'shield' see Pss. 3:3; 28:7; 33:20; 84:11). Towards God's law he shows continuous love and hope, and wants no influence of evildoers to distract him from obedience to the law's claims. The first two verses of the section are directed to God, drawing attention to the way in which he views with disfavour all who are double-minded, i.e. who are divided in their loyalties. Such double-mindedness indicates an unstable man, who 'should not think he will receive anything from the Lord' (Jas. 1:7-8). The third verse is directed to the evildoers, wanting them to remove themselves far from him.

Verses 116-117: To be kept by the power of God is a promise given in both Old and New Testaments. Hence the prayer for God's continued help and support in the midst of trials. Answer to these prayers will mean life and salvation, without any cause for hope in God to be disappointed. The Hebrew verb translated 'have regard' is usually used of looking expectantly to someone, or looking with approval and favour. It is an apt word for the attitude of the psalmist to God's decrees.

Verses 118-119; The language used here of the wicked is similar to that of Psalm 1:4-5. Rebellious sinners are going to be cast aside like dross is removed during the refining process. Deceit brings no security for them. The only way to ensure spiritual progress and absence of judgment is to love the Lord and to love his commands. Whoever has Jesus' commands and obeys them thereby shows that he loves him, and anyone who so loves Jesus will be loved by the Father also (John 14:21).

Verse 120: The concluding expressions in this stanza speak strongly of reverence towards God and his laws. It is not the fear of judgment, but the devout attitude and feelings towards God which dominate a believing heart. Where there is perfect love, there is absence of fear (1 John 4:18).

Ayin (*verses 121-128*)

In a stanza in which prayer for deliverance is most prominent, there is also a threefold reference to the fact that the psalmist is God's servant (see verses 122, 124, 125). He makes his appeal as a devoted member of the covenant community.

Verses 121-122: The psalmist asserts that his present troubles are not because of his own wilful desertion of God's ways. He has acted uprightly, and so he pleads for deliverance, and his attitude shows that this is not a statement stemming from self-righteousness. These and verse 84 are the only verses in the whole of Psalm 119 which do not have either a direct reference to God's word, or an indirect one (see verses 90, 132). The opening expression is noteworthy, because in Hebrew it has the idea of taking responsibility for someone else. For example, Judah assured his father that he would guarantee Benjamin's safety if he went down to Egypt (Gen. 43:9). Here the servant appeals to his sovereign master to protect him and take responsibility for his safety.

Verses 123-125: Faith clings to the promises of God, even when deliverance or intervention is delayed. It knows that God continues to act in accordance with his promise and his covenant commitments. In facing continued opposition and oppression, the psalmist requests further teaching and enlightenment in relation to God's decrees. A teachable spirit is a mark of godliness, and the psalmist over and over again asks both for instruction (verses 12, 26, 64, 66, 73, 108, 135, 171) and for spiritual illumination (verses 27, 34, 73, 144, 169).

Verses 126-128: The reference to the law 'being broken' is a technical term used for breaches of the covenant (see Isa. 24:5; 33:8; Jer. 11:10; 31:32). The oppression against the psalmist is done by covenant breakers, who have turned to paths which he abhors. He asks for speedy help so that God's honour will be upheld. On his part he again refers to the preciousness of God's commands (see the earlier references in verses 14, 57, 72, and 111, and the later one in verse 162), heightening the comparison by using the word for 'pure gold'. At the time of the psalmist it was the most valuable metal, and hence referring to it is a fitting way to describe the priceless worth of God's law.

Pe (*verses 129-136*)

Verses 129-131: Further praise of God's word begins with the use of the word 'wonderful'. It is a word exclusively used of God's actions or words, and marks out what cannot be produced by human effort (cf. the comments on Pss. 71:17; 72:18). Here its use extols both the origin and the glory of God's truth. Recognising the nature of God's revelation (brought about by the Holy Spirit's work) produces conviction as to truth's authority over our lives. When the meaning of God's word is opened to us, then it is like light shining on our way (cf. verse 105). All who lack spiritual knowledge are included in the class called 'the simple' (see Ps. 19:7). As he reflects on the nature of God's word, the psalmist expresses his intense desire for it, comparing himself to a panting animal longing for water.

Verses 132-133: Knowledge of how God habitually acts ('you *always* do', Hebrew, *mishpat*) brings this appeal for mercy. Because God's faithfulness is great, his compassions never fail (Lam. 3:22-23). 'Those who love your name' is a way to describe faithful believers (cf. Ps. 69:36; cf. 'those who love your salvation', Ps. 70:4). The psalmist wants his footsteps to be set surely according to God's word of promise, and in this way sin will not be able to tyrannise him. The verb 'rule' has this connotation of exercising dominion in a tyrannical way (cf. its use in Neh. 5:15).

Verses 134-135: Once more the oppression the psalmist faces presses in upon him, and he cries for deliverance from it. The pressures of that oppression constrain him, and militate against his freedom to keep God's laws. The prayer of verse 135 is given in terms of the Aaronic benediction (Num. 6:24-26; cf. also Pss. 31:16; 80:3, 7, 19).

Verse 136: Previously the psalmist has described his indignation when God's law is forsaken (verse 53). Now he expresses his depth of grief as he sees others abandoning God's demands. His tears become a flood, just like the anonymous author of Lamentations who grieved over the destruction of his people (Lam. 3:48).

Tsadhe (*verses 137-144*)

The important thought of God and his righteous laws dominate this section, with the Hebrew words for right/righteous occurring five times in eight verses.

Verses 137-138: God's character is reflected in the laws he gives. In contexts such as this, 'righteous' has the idea of utter faithfulness, for the synonyms used with it are 'trustworthy' and 'true'. The divine King has laid down his statutes, which accord both with his nature and his plans for the well-being of his creatures.

Verses 139-140: 'Zeal' is practically equivalent here to 'anger' (cf. 'indignation' in verse 53). Whereas the psalmist often prays that he will not forget God's law (see verses 16, 61, 83, 93, 109, 141, 153, 176), this is the very thing which occurs with his enemies ('ignore' is the Hebrew *shakach*, 'forget'). In all his troubles the psalmist has been able to rely on God's word, and he finds it absolutely trustworthy. It is like a precious metal which has come through the refining process unscathed. In verses 121-128 the psalmist has already confessed that he is in a servant/master relationship with God, and now he acknowledges that again, and confirms his love for God's word.

Verses 141-143: Though others may treat him as insignificant, the psalmist commits himself to maintain his adherence to God's laws. In the midst of difficulties, he takes pleasure in them, as he has already declared several times (the same verb, 'delight', is used in verses 16, 47, 70; its related noun occurs in verses 24, 77, 92, 143 and 174). The second part of verse 142 may lie behind Jesus' words in John 17:17: 'your word is truth.'

Verse 144: The thought of verse 138 is amplified by reference to the enduring nature of God's righteous statutes. They are not the fickle decrees of a human king, but the lasting ordinances of the eternal God. Spiritual insight into their meaning provides wisdom which guides through life.

Qoph (*verses 145-152*)

Verses 145-146: Prayerfulness is one of the marks of a believer. As this psalm moves towards its conclusion, the direct prayers to God increase. The opening of this stanza is very similar to the first verse of Psalm 4: 'Answer me when I call to you, O my righteous God.' Following a stanza extolling the righteousness of God, the psalmist cries to him, and he longs for an answer which will bring deliverance to him. The commitment made in the second part of both these verses has already been made repeatedly earlier in the psalm (for the use of Hebrew *natsar*, 'obey, keep,' see verses 22, 33, 34, 56, 69, 100, 115, 129: for Hebrew *shamar*, 'obey, keep,' see verses 5, 8, 17, 34, 44, 55, 57, 60, 67, 88, 101, 106, 134). It is prompted by devotion to God and it is the response of a heart dedicated to his service. Jesus reinforced the principle when he taught that love to him must be demonstrated by obedience to his commands (John 14:15, 21; 15:10, 12).

Verses 147-148: The psalmist pleads with such urgency that he either gets up early or stays awake in the night. The New Testament application of the principle comes in the parable of the persistent widow (Luke 18:1-8), when Jesus asks his disciples the questions: 'And will not God bring about justice for his chosen ones, who cry out to him day and night? Will he keep putting them off?' (verse 7). Meditation on, and trust in God's promises, are a necessary foundation of believing prayer.

Verse 149: Covenant mercy is promised, so the psalmist pleads for an attentive hearing to his prayer. 'Voice' is an abbreviated way of describing a voice used in prayer, for normally in the Psalms 'voice' occurs in phrases which indicate it is a voice raised in prayer or supplication. The plea for preservation appears, to be repeated in identical form in verse 156.

Verses 150-151: The contrasts drawn are most marked. While the enemies are near, yet they are far from God's law. While they are near, the LORD is nearer still, ready to help and to provide deliverance. The attitudes and actions of the enemies show that they are far removed from following the ways of the LORD. The testimony of the psalmist is that the God of truth is indeed near, as he is 'to all who call on him, to all who call on him in truth' (Ps. 145:18).

Verse 152: Recent experiences have not brought the psalmist into knowledge of God's statutes. That knowledge came to him long ago and he relies upon the statutes because he knows that they are part of God's enduring revelation. As Jesus expressed it: 'Until heaven and earth disappear, not the smallest letter, not the least stroke of a pen, will by any means disappear from the Law until everything is accomplished' (Matt. 5:18).

Resh (*verses 153-160*)

Verses 153-155: An afflicted but loyal servant prays for God to look with compassion on him. Unlike the wicked, who do not enquire into God's decrees, he has set his heart on them and has kept them in mind. The words 'Defend my cause and redeem me' constitute legal terminology, with God being represented as the advocate who comes to aid the accused. The verbs 'defend' (Hebrew, *riv*) and 'redeem' (Hebrew, *ga'al*) come together in other Old Testament passages (e.g. Jer. 50:34), and the translation could rightly be 'Defend ... and vindicate me'. No such deliverance will be given by God to those who wilfully transgress his laws.

Verse 156: What so often sustains believers is confidence in the abounding compassion of God (cf. David's words to Gad, 1 Chr. 21:13). That is seen in acts on their behalf which display his mercy. The psalmist knows that it is the never-failing compassion of the LORD which will keep him alive.

Verses 157-158: The contrast between the psalmist and his enemies is again emphasised. Unlike him, they are characterised by departure from God's laws and an unwillingness to be subject to them. 'The faithless' is a description of those who prove false to the LORD (cf. Jer. 9:2; Ps. 78:57), breaching their covenant obligations. Though faced with a multitude of such enemies, the psalmist does not deviate from the way of righteousness. His attitude towards their manner of life is one of revulsion.

Verses 159-160: The viewpoint put in a negative way in the preceding verses is now stated positively. There is heartfelt devotion to God's precepts (see similar expressions of love to God's commandments [verses 47, 48, 127], God's law [verses 97, 113, 163], and God's statutes [verse 167]). The totality of God's words (Hebrew, 'the head of your words', i.e. the sum of them, as in Ps. 139:17) is absolutely sure, for all his words are trustworthy (verses 86, 138), true (verses 142, 151, 160) and eternal (verses 89, 111, 142, 144, 152).

Sin and Shin (*verses 161-168*)

Verse 161: Earlier (verses 23 and 46), reference was made to the relationship which the psalmist had to rulers and kings (see comments on these verses). Even though they derided him, the psalmist is prepared to declare to them God's statutes. He does not stand in awe of them, for his heart is devoted to God's word. The idea of a trembling heart is probably explained by Proverbs 28:14, where fearing God is contrasted to hardening the heart.

Verses 162-163: The inestimable value of God's word compares with the taking of spoil in battle (Hebrew, *shalal*, cf. the name of Isaiah's second son, Maher-Shalal-Hash-Baz, 'quick to the spoil, hasting to the plunder', Isa. 8:1). This links with earlier references to the treasure found in God's law (see verses 14 and 72). Such devotion expresses itself again as love for his law (see the comment on verse 97).

Verses 164-166: 'Seven times' expresses completeness. The psalmist is asserting that he praises God's law all the day. Over and above showing mercy to those who love his law (verse 132), God gives them 'peace' (Hebrew, *shalom*). This is much more than mere absence of hostility or strife. It is a gift to those who are blessed, guarded, and treated graciously by the LORD (Num. 6:24-26). It signifies an unimpaired relationship with him, which comes now through the Prince of Peace (Isa. 9:6) who himself is our peace (Eph. 2:14).

Verses 167-168: The section concludes with a double declaration of obedience to God's laws and statutes. The final verse is unusual in that it contains two of the synonyms for God's word in the same verse. The concluding declaration confirms what the psalmist has just said. His daily conduct, which is well known to God, shows his love for, and obedience to, God's laws.

Taw (*verses 169-176*)

Just as the first half of the psalm concludes with a stanza crying for help (*verses 81-88*), so the second half of the psalm ends in a similar manner. All but one of the verses has direct appeal to God. The psalmist's great need and his confidence in the LORD's word dominate his thoughts.

Verses 169-170: The approach to God is defined as 'my cry' and 'my supplication'. The first of these terms describes a ringing cry of either joy (cf. Isa. 14:7) or sorrow (cf. 1 Kgs. 8:28). From the context it is clearly the latter here. The second term always means either mercy, or a cry for mercy. The psalmist desires God to hear his prayer, and respond in grace. He needs further help in appreciating God's word and the way it ministers to him in his need. He also renews his call for deliverance.

Verses 171-172: The fitting response to mercy is praise, and so the psalmist asks that joyful song will be given to him. He expects God to answer his cry, and so he can look forward to his own subsequent praise. In the midst of all his experiences he still knows that God's commands are just, and that he needs further instruction concerning them.

Verses 173-174: 'Hand' is a synonym for 'power' (as in Deut. 32:39 and Isa. 28:2). The appeal is for a demonstration of divine action in rescuing him from his trouble. Near the end of his life Moses put before Israel the alternatives of 'life and prosperity', encouraging the people to choose 'life'. This was defined in terms of loving the LORD, walking in his ways, and keeping his commands, decrees and laws (Deut. 30:15-16). Here the psalmist speaks of his commitment of choice. He is following the ways of the LORD and as the psalm closes he reaffirms his delight in the law (cf. for the use of the verb 'delight in' verses 16, 47, and 70, and the noun 'delight' used here, verses 24, 77, 92, and 143).

Verses 175-176: The theme of praise is continued. As God preserves, then the psalmist will extol him in praise and adoration. The final words of this psalm are highly significant. Though professing deep love and devotion to God's commands throughout, the psalm ends on a note of confession. The psalmist has wandered like a lost sheep, and hence can share in Isaiah's confession: 'We all, like sheep, have gone astray' (Isa. 53:6; the same Hebrew verb is used). He is still a servant, and therefore asks to be found by a good and gracious shepherd. The beautiful imagery of God as the shepherd (cf. Ps. 23; Isa. 40:11; Ezek. 34:11-16) is taken up by Jesus, who declares that he is the good shepherd (John 10:11, 14). He also uses the picture of wandering sheep to teach God's concern for the lost (Luke 15:4-7).

PSALM 120
A song of ascents.

This psalm begins a group (Pss. 120-134) which share an unusual title. It suggests pilgrims going up to Jerusalem, probably for the Passover. The tribes went *up* to Jerusalem (see Ps. 122:4), and this group of psalms probably had special use at such a time. Psalm 120 follows on from the idea of the wandering sheep mentioned in the final verse of Psalm 119. Here the psalmist is like a sheep among wolves in his own country, and this sets the scene for the pilgrimage from a hostile home environment to the joys and blessings of worship in Jerusalem.

1. *Remembrance of Past Experiences* (*verse 1*)
The psalm opens, not with the immediate situation confronting the psalmist, but with recollection of former help from the LORD. He had repeatedly gone to him in the past and his cry always brought a speedy response. The remembrance of former help is the encouragement to direct prayer to God again.

> His love in time past
> Forbids me to think
> He'll leave me at last
> In trouble to sink.   (John Newton)

2. *The Cry of Distress* (*verses 2-4*)
The opening words of this section specify the present need (*verse 2*). The actual circumstances are not recorded. If the psalm is from the post-exilic period, the situation may well have been like that faced by the returning exiles, who contended with the slander of the Samaritans (Ezra 4:12ff.; Neh. 4:1ff.; 6:5-14). Christians should follow the

example of our Lord. He was called a glutton and a drunkard (Matt. 11:19), and yet did not respond in like manner (1 Pet. 2:23).

Verse 3 is an indirect appeal for God to send judgment on the slanderer. It is phrased in terms similar to Hebrew oaths such as 'May God deal with you, be it ever so severely' (1 Sam. 3:17; 20:13). The appeal in those oaths is for God to deal with the situation, though naturally the actual penalty is not prescribed. Perhaps there was some accompanying action to suggest the nature of the penalty. Here the punishment is specified (*verse 4*). The answer seems to have in mind the descriptions given elsewhere of the lying tongue. In the Old Testament it is called a sharp sword (Ps. 57:4), and a deadly arrow (Jer. 9:8), while later the New Testament calls it a member set on fire by hell (Jas. 3:6). The expected punishment will be a fitting response, for it will match the offence. The broom tree had very hard wood and therefore produced coals which were long-lasting. The act of judgment will be more deadly than the slanderer's own words.

3. *A Foreigner in His Own Land* (*verses 5-7*)

Meshech and Kedar (*verse 5)* were not close to one another. Meshech was named after a son of Japheth (Gen. 10:2), and refers to Eastern Anatolia (modern day Turkey). Kedar was one of Ishmael's sons and father of the tribe which bore his name (Gen. 25:13). It refers to Bedouin Arabs who lived south-east of Damascus. So acute was the psalmist's distress that he felt that he was living among barbarians! He was a foreigner in his own land!

The contrast between the two groups in his society is illustrated by *verses 6-7*. Light and darkness are incompatible. The psalmist's words of peace are met by their words of war. The Hebrew says tersely, 'I [for] peace; they for war'. While the cry for help in verse 2 is not repeated again, it echoes to the end of the psalm. There is clearly an intense longing for deliverance to come from the LORD.

PSALM 121
A song of ascents.

This psalm's setting certainly seems to show the idea of ascent to Jerusalem, for it appears to be an occasion on the way up to Jerusalem. Of all the psalms in the group this is the only one which has in Hebrew the particular designation, 'a song *for* the ascents' (cf. NIV), perhaps marking it out especially for use on the journey. The words of the psalm, though, have brought comfort and inspiration to many as it has been sung by Christians throughout the centuries. The Scottish metrical version of this psalm has some powerful expressions and its use has brought widespread appreciation of it.

1. *The Psalmist's Help* (*verses 1-2*)

As the pilgrim comes within sight of his destination he sees the hills surrounding Jerusalem. To many these hills gave a feeling of confidence. But the psalmist then asks where his help *really* comes from? His answer is emphatic. It certainly does not come from the hills! Emphatically it comes from God. The covenant God of Israel is his keeper, whose creative power as Maker of heaven and earth is a guarantee of his ability to help his people. The Maker of all things is able to stoop down to meet their needs.

2. *The Psalmist's Safety* (*verses 3-4*)

Will the singing pilgrim now stumble at this stage of the journey? Assuredly not, for he has a guard who does not sleep, and with emphasis he says that his feet will not be allowed to slip (cf. Ps. 17:5). This expression probably encompasses the idea that God is alert to any of the dangers of the journey. 'Indeed' calls attention to the emphatic statement which follows, while 'slumber' and 'sleep' seem to be synonyms. How different the true God was from Baal! Elijah on Carmel could taunt Baal's prophets that he was asleep (1 Kgs. 18:27).

3. *The Psalmist's Protection* (*verses 5-6*)

The LORD is not just the keeper of all Israel, but he can be spoken of as 'your keeper'. Calling him 'shade' is probably a shortened form of the expression 'the shadow of your wings' (Pss. 17:8; 36:7; 57:1; 63:7). The 'right hand' suggests the position of the defender or protector (Pss. 73:23; 77:10; 110:5), and the psalmist knows that his God is as near to him as that. By day and night he will be kept safe from any harm. Sunstroke was familiar in Palestine, and while we might not perceive any threat from the moon, the Greek and Latin words for insanity come from the word for the moon, hence our English word 'lunatic'.

4. *The Psalmist's Preservation* (*verses 7-8*)

The song closes by picturing Jehovah as an eternal keeper, having progressed from the small things (steps) to the big things (the whole of life). In the midst of a sinful and dangerous world he is able to keep us from falling (Jude 24). God will guard amidst all the varied experiences of life, and ultimately he will bring his called ones to glory (Rom. 8:30). If we are serious present day pilgrims we will rejoice that Israel's keeper and ours is still the living and true God. He continues to fulfil this role towards his people. May our prayer then be:

> Through each perplexing path of life
> Our wand'ring footsteps guide;
> Give us each day our daily bread,
> And raiment fit provide.
>
> O spread thy cov'ring wings around,
> Till all our wand'rings cease,
> And at our Father's lov'd abode
> Our souls arrive in peace.
>
> (Philip Doddridge 1702-1751)

PSALM 122
A song of ascents. Of David.

Three of the pilgrim psalms are ascribed to David, this one and Psalms 124 and 131. David's connection with Jerusalem – his capture of it, his building programme, and bringing the ark of the covenant there – make these expressions all the more relevant if David is the author. Later generations could take up his refrain and use it for their joyful arrival in Jerusalem, and express their prayer for her prosperity.

1. *Joy in Jerusalem (verses 1-2)*
David recalls his heartfelt joy when neighbours gave the invitation – 'Come to God's house!' These two characteristics of love for the presence of God and for the fellowship of his people marked out the early church (Heb. 10:25), and should do so still. The second verse suggests that the pilgrims have at last arrived at Jerusalem. The trials of the journey are over, and there is great joy as they pass through the gates they have longed to see. The name 'Jerusalem' means foundation of peace (see the play on words later in the psalm in verse 6).

2. *Esteem for Jerusalem (verses 3-5)*
For those coming from distant parts of Israel, the sight of Jerusalem must have been emotional. It was not just a conglomeration of

buildings, but a compact, well-ordered city – the capital. It was a symbol of the unity of the nation, as all the tribes of the LORD went up there on special festive occasions. It was the place God had chosen as a dwelling for his name. The purpose was to praise corporately the name of the LORD; because the great feasts like Passover, the Feast of Weeks and the Feast of Tabernacles, were meant to be times of personal and national rejoicing in the presence of the LORD (Deut. 16:1-17).

Jerusalem was also the centre of civic life *(verse 5)*, to which people came to have the king adjudicate their complaints. The system did not always work perfectly, for Absalom, David's son, exploited it in order to gain a following for himself (2 Sam. 15:1-6).

3. *Concern for Jerusalem* (*verses 6-9*)
The call to prayer *(verses 6-7)* involves a play on the name Jerusalem. It uses a form of the Hebrew word 'shalom', meaning 'peace'. The word-play (and also the combination of the same sounds in Hebrew) can be brought out approximately by rendering, 'Ask for the shalom of Yerushaláyim' ('Ask for the peace of the foundation of peace'). The psalmist also wants the blessing of security for all the inhabitants of Jerusalem and pilgrims. From the time David captured Jerusalem (2 Sam. 5:6-10), this city occupied a central place in the thinking of the people of Israel. Thus in the exile Daniel pleads with God: 'Turn away your anger and your wrath from Jerusalem, *your city, your holy hill*' (Dan. 9:16).

Not only is the nation as a whole in view, but also the psalmist's close friends as well *(verses 8-9)*. He realises that blessing for them depends on the prosperity of Jerusalem. In particular the house of God is so important that he longs for the continued prosperity of the city itself. Even before the building of the Temple, the ark stood in semi-permanent buildings such as at Shiloh (see 1 Sam. 3:1-3, 21) and in Jerusalem. These buildings could easily be described as 'the house of the LORD'. The deep feelings of the people towards the temple are shown in the laments over its destruction (Ps. 74:3-8; Isa. 64:11; Lam. 2:6-7), and the joy with which the returned exiles greeted its rebuilding.

PSALM 123
A song of ascents.

This short psalm has many similarities with Psalm 120. Both start with
reference to the source of help and both speak of the reproach of
ungodly neighbours. Whereas Psalm 120 focuses on God's ability to
rescue, this one concentrates on his grace. The psalmist looks beyond
earthly things to the heavenly throne and makes his appeal for mercy.

1. *Our Attitude to God in Prayer (verse 1)*
Here is the attitude of reverence for God. Our unknown psalmist comes
in prayer. He lifts his eyes to the Lord, as real believers always do (Ps.
25:15). The difference between himself and his God is emphasised by
recognising that the Lord is enthroned in the heavens as the all-
powerful Creator of all other beings – but the writer is only a dependent
creature. Our Lord Jesus teaches us not only to address God as 'Father',
but also to say, 'who is in heaven' (Matt. 6:9). As we come to God we
must say with John Newton:

> Approach my soul the mercy-seat,
> where Jesus answers prayer,
> There humbly fall before his feet,
> for none can perish there.

2. *Our Expectancy (verse 2)*
In Eastern countries servants are often directed by hand signals. Hence
they have to be very attentive to their master's wishes. Similarly the
attitude of the believing individual and community has to be expectancy towards the LORD. God, who will not despise the cry of the
destitute (Ps. 102:17), will answer in grace to his children. Paul knew
that God will supply all the needs of his children 'according to his
glorious riches in Christ Jesus' (Phil. 4:19).

3. *Our Need (verses 3-4)*
The climax is this repeated call for mercy. The psalmist lives in an
hostile environment. He has been exposed to ridicule from the proud
and the arrogant whose bitter words must have wounded so deeply.
From people the psalmist cannot expect mercy, so he turns to his
trusted God who alone can show true mercy. Out of his deep need
comes this cry for help.

PSALM 124
A song of ascents. Of David.

Some early manuscripts omit the reference to David. If it is David's, it probably comes from near the beginning of his reign, and so reflects the severe pressure put on his kingdom by the Philistines. At Baal Perazim he said, 'The LORD has broken out against my enemies before me' (2 Sam. 5:20). However, the psalm may well be from after the exile as the people rejoice in God's preservation of them. This would explain why the ideas are expressed in communal terms: 'Israel', 'against *us*,' 'did not give *us*,' '*we* have escaped,' '*our* help'. For long Christians have taken over this triumphant song of praise when God's arm has been stretched out to deliver them.

1. The Affirmation of the LORD's Help (verses 1-2)
The double use of 'if' is only hypothetical, for there is no doubt at all that their covenant God has been with them. The call is for Israel to make a declaration concerning God's deliverance, but the words to be used are omitted. It is possible that verse 8 provides them: 'Let Israel say ... Our help is in the name of the LORD, the Maker of heaven and earth.' The fact that by God's grace they were rescued from the brink of ruin, now calls for praise from their hearts and lips.

2. Illustrations (verses 3-5)
In order to make much more graphic the sense of deliverance, the psalmist uses two illustrations. The first one (*verse 3*) deals with the way in which their enemies had sought the complete destruction of the nation. The extreme peril in which the nation was placed is made more vivid by suggesting that the attacking monster would only need one bite to consume them. The second illustration (*verses 4-5*) relates to sudden torrents which are a familiar feature of life in the Near East. A dry wadi can become a raging stream within minutes. The picture of destruction caused by a flash flood describes the attacks made on Israel by arrogant enemies. Both illustrations point to attacks intending total destruction of the nation.

3. Escape Provided (verses 6-7)
The failure of such sudden and severe attacks is the cause for a song of praise and thankfulness (*verse 6*). The right response to the experience through which they have passed is, 'Praise (or 'Blessed') be to the

LORD'. This expression often occurs in the psalms when there is remembrance of what God has done for his people (cf. Pss. 28:6; 31:21; 66:20; 144:1). The terrifying monster had not devoured them!

The metaphor changes, as Israel is compared to a bird escaping out of a trap *(verse 7)*. The climax is reached in the words, 'the snare has been broken'. God had destroyed the trap, no less terrifying than gaping jaws, set for his people (likened to a defenceless bird). They were able to escape. These words have been applicable in many situations in the course of church history, when God's grace and power have been shown to his people facing severe oppression and persecution.

4. A Profession of Trust (verse 8)

As suggested earlier, this may be the refrain which Israel is called on to sing (see verse 1). While the intervening verses have viewed the past (verses 2-7), now sight is set on the future, with a profession of confidence in the covenant God of Israel. God had revealed his 'name' or 'character', and this includes his power which is evident in his work as Creator. The Maker of heaven and earth has the ability and power to be the constant helper of his people. Our confidence in our own strength or achievement must be replaced by boasting in the name of our God (Ps. 20:7). Past, present, future – he remains the helper, and into the hands of a faithful Creator we must entrust our souls (1 Pet. 4:19). It is not surprising that the Reformed Churches, among others, have so often used the words of this verse as the opening confession in their worship services.

PSALM 125
A song of ascents.

The pilgrims now meditate on Jerusalem's position – surrounded by mountains – and draw a lesson of faith. They contrast the ways of the righteous with those of the wicked. The same contrast appears in prophetical passages such as Isaiah 3:10-11, and is repeated in the New Testament by the Lord Jesus himself (see Matthew 7:13-14 and 25:31ff.).

1. The Song of Confidence (verses 1-2)

The psalm opens by asserting the derived character of God's people *(verse 1)*. Faith is a major theme of the psalms, and here we have the description of the abiding characteristic of God's people. They are not only saved by faith, but they should live by faith! This trust marks out the individual believer, but it should also characterise the church as a whole. The Lord's believing saints are compared to Mount Zion, with the point of comparison being its immovability. The psalmist speaks of Jerusalem's natural ramparts *(verse 2)*, and he makes this an illustration of the protection which the LORD gives his people. Just as the mountains encircle Jerusalem, so the LORD encircles his people for all time. The reference to 'his people' clearly refers to their standing as the covenant people of God.

2. *The Promise (verse 3)*

This is a difficult verse, though the general import of it is clear. The sceptre refers to the rule which conquerors exercise over lands which they occupy. This may refer to the exile, when God allowed other peoples temporarily to take over Judaean territory. However, God had set a limit to their rule, and the foreign sceptre would not be permitted to stay indefinitely over it. As a fact of history, the post-exilic period had little of the glory of the Davidic/Solomonic empire. The second part of the verse could mean that if the rule of the wicked were to continue for any great length of time, then the righteous might begin to envy them and turn their own hands to evil.

3. *The Prayer (verse 4)*

Following a promise, now comes a prayer: 'Do good, O Lord, to those who are good, to those who are upright in heart.' God often gives or reaffirms a promise which then prompts his people to pray. This word 'good' has covenant overtones, for it is used of the things which were promised under God's covenant (see for example, 1 Sam. 25:30; 2 Sam. 7:28; Ps. 23:6). The psalmist pleads for covenanted mercies to God's people who are also described as the upright in heart. This is a prophetic declaration that God only truly blesses those who have this type of character.

4. *The Warning (verse 5)*

The psalmist now brings in the other side of the two ways *(verse 5a)*. Those who focus themselves on things which are opposed by God will ultimately find that they themselves are banished by God (see our Lord's words in Matt. 25:31-46). Evildoers will not dominate for ever, because a day is coming when God's power over them will prevail.

The final declaration concerns the Israel of God. 'Peace be upon Israel' (*verse 5b*). What a blessing it is to belong to Israel, especially when Israel enjoys the blessing of God! For the Hebrew people 'peace' denoted prosperity and health, the enjoyment of the richest of God's blessing (cf. the similar prayer in Gal. 6:16).

PSALM 126
A song of ascents.

There can be no doubt that the experience in exile was a bitter one for the Jewish people (cf. Psalm 137). But restoration to home brought intense joy. While the people could not sing in Babylon (Ps. 137:1-6), when they were brought back to Judah they sang 'songs of joy' (verse 2). This psalm expresses something of the wonder of what God had done for his people. There are many similarities between this psalm and Psalm 85, and the prophecy of Joel. As in Psalm 85 this has the same two aspects in view – past restoration and an appeal for further deliverance. It is 'a song of ascents' because Jerusalem/Zion is the focus.

1. The Joy of Restoration to Zion (verses 1-2a)
Following the decree of Cyrus in 537 BC, some of the exiles in Babylon returned to Palestine. The foundation of the second temple was laid with intermingled weeping and joy (Ezra 3:13). God had raised up Cyrus for this very purpose (see Isa. 44:24-45:7), and through him brought about the return. The reference to dreaming may describe the amazement of the people at what had happened, or, more probably, to their condition while still in Babylon. They dreamed of a return, stimulated by earlier prophecies regarding such a prospect, and by those of their fellow exile, Ezekiel (see Ezek. 36:24; 37:1-14). The effect was that the sorrow and gloom of exile was replaced by laughter and song. This is in agreement with prophetic descriptions of how the restoration would take place (see Isa. 49:8-13; 52:8-10).

2. Announcement to the Nations (verses 2b-3)
In addition to an effect on God's people, the return also had an effect on the surrounding nations. Isaiah had spoken of God's people being his witnesses (Isa. 43:10-13; 44:8). The nations were now proclaiming

what had happened. The explanation was: 'The LORD has dealt magnificently with them.' This same profession was made by those returning, who from personal experience testified to the redeeming power of God. The manifestation of God's saving power in the exodus from Egypt and the return from exile were preparatory of a far greater display in the coming and work of Jesus.

3. *The Prayer (verse 4)*
There seems to be a gap in time between the initial restoration and the situation in which the psalm is written. This could be the period following the partial restoration in 536 BC up to the completion of the new temple in 516, or the longer period before the reforms of Ezra and Nehemiah in the following century (458/444). The psalmist asks for the fuller restoration to take place for captive Israel, so that there will be a further ingathering of those still scattered in exile. The second half of the verse contains a reference to a well-known phenomenon – flash floods in the Negev (the southern part of Israel). This reference draws attention to the suddenness with which the further return could take place, and the resulting blessing, just like the wilderness blossoming after refreshing rains (cf. Isa. 35:1).

4. *The Assurance (verses 5-6)*
The psalmist speaks of the time of exile as sowing and of the restoration as harvest. He looks back on former tears which have been replaced by joy. These words have the ring of a proverbial saying about them, not dissimilar to Jesus' words in John 4:36-38, which may be an echo of this psalm. The period of sorrowful sowing is over, and the harvest has come. As the psalm began, so it ends with the note of joy.

PSALM 127
A song of ascents. Of Solomon.

From the opening words of this psalm in Latin, the city of Edinburgh, Scotland, has derived its motto (*Nisi Dominus frustra, without the Lord it is in vain*). That use of part of the psalm picks up its main point. No human activity or work for the kingdom of God will be fruitful, unless God blesses with his presence and help. The three main activities mentioned in the psalm are building, security, and raising a family. The ascription to Solomon is notable, for he failed in the very things which the psalm emphasises. Part of his building programme was unwise (1 Kgs. 9:10-19), his kingdom ended in division (1 Kgs. 11:11ff.), and his marriages denied the covenant God of Israel (1 Kgs. 11:1ff.).

1. *Building without the LORD (verses 1-2)*

The first two activities with which the phrase 'in vain' is used are building a house and guarding a town *(verse 1)*. Both were common activities requiring considerable effort, often done with self-confidence, but without the LORD's help work is pointless. The third illustration is that of a 'workaholic' *(verse 2)*. He gets up early and goes to bed late, but after all that effort he knows sorrow, not joy. When the LORD intervenes there is blessing, and sleep is his gift to mankind and a special mark of steadfast love to his people.

2. *Building a Family (verses 3-5)*

The focus now changes to another sort of house. This change is marked out in the Hebrew text by the use of a word (*hinneh*) at the start of the verse, which arrests attention: 'Take notice!' The building of a family is ultimately the gift of the LORD himself *(verse 3)*, as those Christians who adopt children know better than most. God is the Creator and Sustainer of life, and the coming of children is to be seen as something he bestows upon parents.

Children bring responsibilities upon the parents *(verses 4-5)*, but in turn they become active in the life of the family. Their gifts and abilities serve the needs of the whole family. The illustration here is from Near Eastern society, with the thought of the children providing protection in time of trouble and old age. A full quiver would help to defend the family when it was under attack.

PSALM 128
A song of ascents.

This is a wisdom psalm similar to the previous one, setting out particularly the blessings of the family. The way in which it commences ('Blessed are ...') is the same as Psalm 1, while the ending may have been composed for use by a priest as a blessing on families gathered in Jerusalem for the annual festivals. The repetition of fearing God (verses 1 and 4) shows that the focus is on godly living and divine blessing.

1. *The Blessing of Family Life* (*verses 1-4*)
The godly person can be described in various ways. Here two marks
are brought to the fore: reverential fear of the LORD, and walking in his
ways *(verse 1)*. Where there is true reverence towards the LORD there
will also be a life of obedient attention to his ways. Those who walk
according to the law of the LORD are indeed blessed (Ps. 119:1). Part
of that blessing is the enjoyment of eating the fruits of their labour
(verse 2).

Another aspect of the blessing is a happy home life *(verses 3-4)*. A
wife and children are also gifts of God. The use of vine and olive as
illustrations is probably because both were so central to daily life in
Israel, and both were well-known for the fact that they live for a long
time. The psalmist returns to his opening thought to conclude the
picture, drawing attention again to the inevitable connection between
blessing and fearing the LORD.

2. *The Benediction* (*verses 5-6*)
Verses 5-6 appear to be a benediction pronounced on a God-fearing
worshipper in Jerusalem. He has come on pilgrimage, and now the
priest prays for the LORD's blessings to flow to him from Zion. An
earlier Song of Ascent had spoken of the peace and prosperity of
Jerusalem (Ps. 122:6-9). Part of the joy of the devout Israelite was
seeing the continuing prosperity of Jerusalem, and also of living long
in the promised land. The prayer used at the end of Psalm 125 is again
employed to conclude this psalm. God's blessing extended from
individuals to families, and then to the whole nation of Israel. We
should not think these repetitions trite, but indicative of confidence in
basic aspects of the faith, both Hebrew and Christian.

PSALM 129
A song of ascents.

The tone of this psalm marks it off from the ones which immediately
precede (Pss. 124-128). While they speak of the many blessings which
God has given to Israel, this one asks for the withholding of blessing.
No precise setting is given for the psalm, but the reference to deliverance in verse 4 suggests that it comes from after the return from exile
in Babylon. There are strong resemblances between this psalm and
Psalm 124, not least in the repetition which occurs in the first two

verses of each, and the use of the phrase 'Let Israel say'. It is a song
of confidence, in which Israel as a nation sings of release from
oppression, and in which she prays for judgment on her enemies.

1. Freedom from Oppression (verses 1-4)
Israel is asked to think back over her past history, even to her 'youth'
in Egypt *(verses 1-2)*. Just as she was in slavery then, so she endured
many years of domination by enemies during the course of her 'adult'
years. However, it is a victory song which Israel is to sing, because
these enemies have not achieved their goals. She is still alive and free!

While harsh treatment of prisoners of war, including drawing
farming implements over their backs, may have taken place (cf. Amos
1:3), yet the expression in *verse 3* is best interpreted figuratively. The
imagery of farming is used to illustrate both the sufferings of Israel and
her eventual release from captivity. The 'ploughmen' are the soldiers
who have attacked her, and her 'back', scarred with long furrows, is the
whole period of history during which she was at the mercy of her
attackers. Freedom has come because the LORD has cut her free from
her cords *(verse 4)*, just as when a yoke is taken off the neck of an
animal. The last great yoke has been taken away, and a restored Israel
rejoices in God's deliverance.

2. Judgment on the Oppressors (verses 5-8)
It is characteristic of the enemies that they hate everything that Zion
represents – God's presence, the covenant blessings, the believing
community *(verse 5)*. The prayer is that they will come to a position
where their evil plans are thwarted and they are disgraced in the eyes
of others. Just as Israel knew the shame of exile, so will the enemies
know confusion and disillusionment.

The analogy of farming is maintained *(verses 6-7)*. Grass may grow
on a roof, but because of lack of soil it soon withers. No-one can reap
a harvest from crops self-grown in such a place. The psalmist wants to
see the lives of Zion's enemies as unproductive, and their end as
certain.

There cannot be simultaneous blessing and cursing *(verse 8)*. No-
one should invoke God's blessing on those whose hearts are so
opposed to him and his kingdom. While they continue to hate Zion, the
only course of action is to withhold pronouncing any blessing on them.

PSALM 130
A song of ascents.

This is a cry from the depths of despair, and it forms the sixth of the seven penitential psalms (Pss. 6, 32, 38, 51, 102, 130, 143). In the history of the Christian church it has often been known by its opening words in Latin, *De profundis*. It is far more than just a cry for help, for it also contains the assurance of the abundant mercy of God which is able to blot out our sins and iniquities. The closest parallels to the wording used here are found in Psalm 86. The background situation was very similar for both, though the closing verse of Psalm 130 goes beyond the thought of Psalm 86.

1. *The Psalmist's Condition (verses 1-2)*
The opening words set the tone. The expression 'out of the depths' is not common in the Psalms, but when it does occur it denotes a situation of deep distress. When in a situation of utter calamity, and conscious of the gulf between himself and God which his sin has caused, the psalmist appeals to the LORD for mercy. The urgency of his situation is shown by the repetition of his requests using a variety expressions (*I cry ... hear my voice ... Let your ears ...*).

2. *Assurance of Forgiveness (verses 3-4)*
The impossibility of a sinner such as himself standing his ground in the presence of a holy God causes the psalmist to ask the question in *verse 3*. He knows that none are righteous before God (cf. Ps. 143:2), and that includes himself. God forgives and remembers sin no more for his own name's sake (Isa. 43:25), and forgiven sinners are aware of the reverence due to him for his grace and mercy. Receiving mercy increases our sense of awe and reverence in God's holy presence.

3. *Patient Waiting (verses 5-6)*
Verse 5 is a declaration of certain trust in the LORD. The psalmist is not waiting in case God should be gracious. On the contrary, he has clearly received forgiveness, and now continues in the sure confidence that God, while remaining just, is able to blot out iniquities (cf. Rom. 3:26). Upon God's own word he places his complete reliance (cf. the similar language in Ps. 119:49). *Verse 6* is a powerful picture of eagerness, patience and confidence – the dawn always comes. The longing of the

city watchmen for the dawn is not as great as that of the psalmist whose trust is in the forgiving God.

4. God's Mercy to Israel (verses 7-8)

Having experienced God's forgiveness himself, the psalmist appeals to Israel as a whole to trust in the LORD *(verse 7)*. With the LORD, and with him alone, is steadfast love (Hebrew, *chesed*), and the full measure of redeeming grace is only found with him. While the Hebrew verb 'redeem' occurs over sixty times, *verse 8* is the only place in the Old Testament in which it is used along with 'sin'. 'Redemption' is understood in spiritual terms, and Paul rightly uses the language of this verse when describing the work which Jesus did for his people – 'who gave himself for us to redeem us from all wickedness' (Tit. 2:14). In New Testament terms redemption flows from God's free grace (Rom. 3:23-25; Eph. 1:7), and forgiveness is based on Jesus' atoning sacrifice for sin (1 John 2:2). Ultimately redemption depends upon belonging by faith to the true Israel of God, for 'neither circumcision nor uncircumcision means anything, what counts is a new creation' (Gal. 6:15).

PSALM 131
A song of ascents. Of David.

Following Psalm 130, this short song continues the idea of trust in the Lord, with which that psalm finished (cf. 130:7 with 131:3). It describes the character of the humble worshipper who does not seek illumination in matters which belong only to God, nor tries to exalt himself into a position which belongs to God alone. The psalmist also reveals a spirit of contentment with his position in life.

The psalmist denies that he is motivated by pride, arrogance or ambition as he comes before the Lord *(verse 1)*. When it comes to his manner of life, he does not concern himself (lit. 'I do not walk in ...') with matters which are beyond him, and his focus is not on seeking great things. As the Hebrew word translated 'things too wonderful' is often used of God's great deeds (see Pss. 71:17; 72:18), the idea may be that he does not attempt to elevate himself into a Godlike position.

In quiet confidence the psalmist rests on the Lord *(verse 2)*. The thought of a weaned child is ambiguous. It could mean a child who was prematurely weaned, and therefore was restless because of lack of milk. More probably, it refers to a weaned child who is still resting contentedly on the breast of its mother. In a similar way, the trusting soul is depicted as being quiet and submissive since it is in the presence of the Lord.

In *verse 3* the call to Israel in the preceding psalm is now repeated (Ps. 130:7), but with the addition of the phrase 'both now and for evermore'. Just as David is resting in the Lord, so should all Israel do at all times. Hoping in the Lord is not a momentary act, but an abiding experience.

PSALM 132
A song of ascents.

Two psalms, 89 and 132, put into poetic form the covenant God made with David (2 Sam. 7=1 Chr. 17). They expressly call the relationship a covenant (see Ps. 89:3, 28, 34; Ps. 132:12), even though the historical passages do not use this term. In this they are in agreement with 2 Samuel 23:5 and Isaiah 55:3. Verses 8-10 of this psalm are quoted in 2 Chronicles 6:41-42 in connection with the dedication of the Temple in Jerusalem. The psalm is a prayer for God to show his favour to the king who sits on David's throne. The language and ideas point to a date of composition early in the period of the monarchy.

1. *Remember!* (*verse 1*)
An individual or the congregation pray for the Davidic king, and especially ask that God will remember all the hardships which David endured as a result of his oath. The word 'remember' may be significant as it is used in covenant settings in which God 'pays attention to' his promises. For example, he remembered his covenant and delivered his people from Egypt (Exod. 2:24), and he later remembered it in preserving them (Lev. 26:44-45). This idea fits in well here.

2. *David's Oath* (*verses 2-5*)
In the historical narrative in Samuel and Chronicles there is no express mention of an oath on David's part, though it is implied. Now it is made explicit that there were reciprocal oaths made by David and God. When David saw the blessing which had come to Obed-Edom because of the presence of the Ark of the Covenant (2 Sam. 6:12), he set about bringing the Ark to Jerusalem and establishing a permanent

home for it there. Twice in these verses the phrase 'the Mighty One of Jacob' occurs. This goes back to Genesis 49:24, where Jacob used this expression in invoking a blessing on his son Joseph. It is clearly synonymous with 'the Mighty One of Israel' (Isa. 1:24). David made the solemn pledge that he would not rest until he found a suitable resting place for the Ark of his God.

3. An Invitation to Worship (verses 6-9)

Many translations and commentaries assume that the reference to what was heard *(verse 6)* is to the ark (see the second footnote on verse 6 in the NIV). However, the Hebrew pronoun 'it' is feminine, whereas the word 'ark' is masculine. More probably, therefore, the call to worship which follows is what was heard. Both placenames here need some explanation. The ark is said to have returned from the Philistines to stay for twenty years at Kiriath Jearim ('town of the woodlands', 1 Sam. 6:21–7:2). David took the ark from Baalah of Judah to bring it to Jerusalem (2 Sam. 6:2; see NIV footnote). Here 'Ephrathah' is used of the region around Bethlehem from which David came (Ruth 4:11; Mic. 5:2), while 'fields of Jaar' is just another way of describing Kiriath Jearim ('Jearim' represents the Hebrew plural of 'Jaar'). Ephrath was the second wife of Caleb (1 Chr. 2:19), and so gave her name to her descendants around the region of Bethlehem.

In *verses 7-9* the picture is presented of the people in David's home region encouraging one another to go to Jerusalem and worship. The location of the ark was God's 'dwelling place' (verse 7), God's 'resting place' (verse 8). After all its travels it had finally come to its permanent home, and there the ark formed a footstool for the Lord (cf. Ps. 99:5). It is called 'the ark of your might' because it represented the very presence of the God of power with his people. Both priests and people were to be united in worship and to reflect God's saving righteousness.

4. Don't Reject! (verse 10)

The first half of the psalm is completed with this further reference to David, which ties in with the opening verse. The appeal is made on the basis of David's covenant relationship with the Lord. Those kings following him were regarded as being the Lord's anointed ones. The parallel to 'remember' in verse 1 is now 'do not reject', which means 'continue to look with favour' (cf. Ps. 84:9). The divine promise was that God would never take away his covenant love from the Davidic dynasty (Ps. 89:33-37).

5. The Lord's Oath (verses 11-12)

While the first half of the psalm is devoted to David's oath, attention in the second half is on the Lord's oath. His relationship with David was confirmed by a divine oath. The words here are not quoted exactly from 2 Samuel 7 or 1 Chronicles 17, but they summarise the promises given to David, which were also repeated to Solomon after the building of the temple and the royal palace (1 Kgs. 9: 3-5; 2 Chr. 7:17-18). In speaking to Solomon, God says that he covenanted with his father David (2 Chr. 7:18), and Psalm 89 makes mention of the swearing of an oath (verses 3, 35). The relationship was a binding covenant on the Davidic family, but conditional upon obedience to the Lord's statutes.

6. Chosen Zion (verses 13-16)

Just as God chose Israel to be his people (Deut. 7:7), so he also chose Zion as the place where he would make his name dwell (Deut. 12:11; Ps. 2:6). The prayer of the people (verse 8) is followed by assurance that Zion is indeed God's choice *(verse 13)*. Miraculous signs marked out that choice (fire from heaven on the altar of burnt offering set up by David on Araunah's threshing floor [1 Chr. 21:26], and the fire from heaven and the glory cloud at the dedication of the temple [2 Chr. 7:1]). David's desire for a permanent habitation for the ark in Jerusalem and God's own desire coincided.

The Hebrew word for 'resting place' *(verse 14)* is used not only of the temporary resting place which God sought for his people (Num. 10:33), but also of the rest he provided for them in the land of Canaan and particularly in connection with Jerusalem (1 Kgs. 8:56).

As the Great King he is enthroned in Zion, and consequently he promises abundant provisions to his people *(verse 15)*, including bountiful blessings even for the poor (cf. Deut. 15:4).

The prayer of verse 9 is answered in even fuller terms than the request, as *verse 16* shows. The desire for 'righteousness' is answered by the promise of 'salvation', while the saints will not just 'sing for joy' but 'shout aloud for joy' (Hebrew, *rannen yerannenu*, using two parts of the same verb to provide emphasis: '*really* shout for joy'). Christians have even greater cause for such joyous expression.

7. *God's Reassurance to David (verses 17-18)*

Frequently in the Old Testament 'horn' is used to symbolise strength or vigour (cf. Pss. 18:2; 75:4-5; and see NIV footnote here), while in David's sons he would have a continually burning lamp never to be snuffed out (see David's prayer in Ps. 18:28, and the Lord's words to Jeroboam in 1 Kgs. 11:36). The promise to David was of a continuing succession of kings, with the Lord Jesus ultimately being given the throne of David (Luke 1:31-33). The final verse reiterates this idea by contrasting the clothing given to the priests (verses 9 and 16) with a different sort of clothing for the enemies of God's people. 'Shame' will take the place of 'salvation' for them, while the Davidic family will not only grow but blossom. In Jesus Christ the Lord it does that.

PSALM 133
A song of ascents. Of David.

A suitable setting for this psalm would be the period after David became king not only of Judah but also of Israel (see 2 Sam. 5:1-5). Its original application to the joyful unity of the twelve tribes comprising Israel and Judah would be further enhanced as it was used in the annual pilgrimage to Jerusalem. As the tribes went up to Jerusalem and the proclamation of peace was made concerning it (see Ps. 122), the use of this psalm would reinforce the sense of unity among the people and recall for them the blessings of the Lord here and in eternity.

1. *The Privilege of Unity (verse 1)*

The Hebrew verse begins with a word which draws attention to statement which follows (Hebrew, *hinneh*, 'behold', 'take notice'). This word serves to alert the reader to the exclamation which follows. Unity in the family is extolled as a very precious thing.

2. *Application (verses 2-3)*

Two illustrations follow the opening statement. The first is that the oil used in anointing the high priest runs down his head, on to his beard, and even on the collar of his robes. So symbolically the tribes are pervaded with one holy anointing of brotherly love. The second illustration concerns the dew of Hermon which is pictured as reaching even to Mount Zion. Probably the idea is that the same moisture affects Hermon in the north as touches Zion in the south. God provides the refreshing dew for the whole land. Mention of Zion leads to the thought that it is the place where God meets in a special way with his people and bestows his blessings, which are summed up in the idea of abiding life which is found with him. Similarly, believers today have a unity in Christ as they make their way to Mount Zion, the city of the living God (Heb. 12:22-24; 13:14-16).

PSALM 134
A song of ascents.

The fifteen pilgrim songs end on a note of blessing. They conclude with the pilgrims asking the Lord's ministers to bless him (verses 1-2), and then in turn asking for blessing from the Lord in Zion (verse 3). It is an 'Amen' to the whole group.

1. Praise to the Lord (verses 1-2).
The command to praise is directed to the Lord's servants, which is explained by the next phrase with its reference to priestly ministry in the Temple *(verse 1)*. Part of the work of the Levites was 'to carry the ark of the covenant of the Lord, to stand before the Lord to minister and to pronounce blessings in his name' (Deut. 10:8). There was clearly an evening ministry in the Temple, but details about it are uncertain. Lifting up of hands *(verse 2)* represented outwardly an inward attitude of prayer. The New Testament carries over this terminology when Paul says that he wants 'men everywhere to lift up holy hands in prayer, without anger or disputing' (1 Tim. 2:8). In the holy place of the Temple praise should ascend from the lips of the priests.

2. Blessing from the Lord (verse 3)
The use of the phrase 'the Maker of heaven and earth' is important. It recalls Genesis 1, where God blesses his creation. The prayer is that the Creator would continue to bless and to empower his servants. The expression 'bless you' is an echo of the Aaronic blessing (Num. 6:22-26), while 'bless you from Zion' has already occurred in Psalm 128:5. Now in the New Testament era the emphasis is not on the Temple but on Jesus. Our blessings come through him from the heavenly Jerusalem (Heb. 12:22-24).

PSALM 135

The anonymous author of this psalm was clearly very familiar with other parts of the Old Testament, and especially with other psalms. This psalm is an expansion of the preceding psalm, and is complemented by the following one. Much of the thought and language resembles Psalm 115, including the threefold call to the houses of Israel and Aaron and to those who fear the LORD, expanded here to include also the house of Levi. The praise, 'fear the LORD', fixes attention on the Lord's character (contrasted with the inability of idols to help their worshippers), and on his great acts of salvation for Israel. Redemption forms the central theme of the psalm.

1. *Israel's Praise* (*verses 1-4*)

The psalm opens and closes with a 'Hallelujah' (NIV, 'Praise the Lord'). The call is to those who minister at the sanctuary (the priests and Levites) to praise unstintingly the Lord's name *(verses 1-2)*. The setting seems to be in the time after the exile, which is also indicated by the mosaic of earlier Scripture portions integrated into this psalm. The main reason given for praise is simply the Lord's goodness *(verses 3-4)*. Later in the psalm mention is made of specific ways in which that goodness was demonstrated. The phrase 'for that is pleasant' is ambiguous, since in Hebrew the subject could be God: 'for he is pleasant' (i.e. beautiful; cf. RSV, 'sing to his name, for he is gracious!'). However, comparison with Psalms 54:6 and 147:1 supports the NIV interpretation. It was an act of grace for God to choose Israel (Deut. 7:7-8), and to take her to be his treasured possession (Exod. 19:5). The Hebrew word rendered 'treasured possession' (*segullah*) is a rare word, only occurring eight times in the Old Testament. It denotes how special and treasured God's people are in his sight. Titus 2:14 and 1 Peter 2:9 build on this Old Testament idea.

2. *Praise of the Creator* (*verses 5-7*)

Preceding a later description of the lifeless idols (verses 15-17) comes a declaration concerning the living God *(verse 5)*. He is beyond comparison with any man-made gods. The same declaration was made by David just after God made a covenant with him (2 Sam. 7:22). The Hebrew word 'great' (*gadol*) is combined at times with the divine name to form personal names (e.g. Gedaliah, 'the Lord is great').

God is sovereign in his universe, being able to do whatever he takes delight in *(verses 6-7)*. The expanse of the heavens or the depths of the seas are equally at his disposal, for he is their Creator. All the forces of nature are part of his plan, and he is able to use wind, rain and lightning to fulfil his purposes. They are servants, not powers in their own right, as many near Eastern religions believed.

> I know the Lord is high in state,
> above all gods our God is great;
> the Lord performs what He decrees,
> in heaven and earth, in depths and seas.
> He makes the moisture to ascend
> in clouds from earth's remotest end;
> the lightnings flash at His command;
> he holds the cyclone in His hand.
>
> *(The Psalter*, 1912)

3. *Redeeming Grace* (*verses 8-14*)

Whenever the psalmists and prophets start to speak of sovereign grace, they invariably point to the redemption from Egypt *(verses 8-9)*. Not only Israel, but Egypt is also reminded of what happened at the time of the Exodus. Both then and at the more recent return from exile, God 'was appalled that there was no-one to intervene, so his own arm worked salvation for him, and his own righteousness sustained him' (Isa. 59:16). Smiting the firstborn and sending plagues is a very brief summary of what is recorded in Exodus 7-14, but yet it highlights the way in which God sovereignly acted on his people's behalf.

Verses 10-12 summarise the accounts of the defeat of Sihon and Og (Num. 21:21-35) and the occupation of the land of Canaan (Joshua 1-20). It was only by God's power that strong enemies were overcome, and Israel's possession of the land was his gift. Even before the occupation of Canaan, Moses reminded Israel that their own efforts were not going to achieve possession of cities, houses, wells, and vineyards (Deut. 6:10-12). The land was an inheritance gift from the Lord (Deut. 4:21; 4:38; 12:9; and many other passages throughout Deuteronomy). Part of Israel's song was praise for fulfilment of the promise to Abraham of a land for his seed (cf. Pss. 78, 105, 106, 136).

God's 'name' is the character he displays in his actions *(verses 13-14)*. This is brought to remembrance (NIV, 'renown') by successive generations. The language of verse 13 goes back to God's declaration to Moses: 'This is my name forever, the name by which I am to be remembered from generation to generation' (Exod. 3:15). The psalmist here is either directly echoing that statement, or picking up the language from a passage such as Psalm 102:12. Over both Israel and the nations God exercises government, and he is able to uphold his own people and to maintain his own name in the face of hostile attacks. Verse 14 is drawn from Deuteronomy 32:36.

4. *The Futility of Idol Worship (verses 15-18)*
These verses are almost identical to Psalm 115:4-6, 8 (see the commentary on those verses). The differences are minor verbal ones (such as different verbs for hearing being used), the omission of reference to hands and feet, and the substitution of 'nor is there breath in their mouths' for 'noses, but they cannot smell'.

5. *A Renewed Call to Praise (verses 19-21)*
While the call to the houses of Israel and Aaron and to the God-fearers resembles Psalm 115:9-11 (see also the threefold call in Ps. 118:2-4), yet the form of the call in *verses 19-20* is closer to the conclusion of Psalm 103:20-22. In both Psalm 103 and Psalm 135, the call is to 'praise the LORD' (Hebrew, *barak*, 'bless'), which indicates that the worshippers are being encouraged to express thanksgiving and adoration. There is also mention of the 'house of Levi', probably because the psalm comes from a temple setting, where the Levites would be ministering (see verses 1-2). The assembled congregation and officiating priests are to give united praise to the Lord.

The Temple in Jerusalem was the visible token of God's presence with his people. From there he blessed them (see Ps. 128:5), and in turn they ascribe praise to him *(verse 21)*. Praise is to flow out from Jerusalem. The ultimate fulfilment of this was the spread of the gospel from Jerusalem, to Judea and Samaria, and then to the ends of the earth (Acts 1:8). The initial 'Hallelujah' finds its counterpart in the concluding phrase. After so much evidence of God's power and grace, it is fitting that there should be a final ascription of praise.

PSALM 136

There is no other psalm like this in the whole Psalter, with a refrain occurring in every verse. It is very probable that a Levitical song leader led the historical recital, and that the worshippers responded with the refrain (2 Chr. 7:3, 6; 20:21). The same refrain occurs in Psalms 106:1; 107:1; and 118:1, 29. This psalm continues the themes of God as Creator and Redeemer which occur in Psalm 135. Many of the themes it uses parallel those which occur in the previous psalm.

1. A Call to Praise (verses 1-3)
The opening verses have an identical call to praise, except that the object of the verb is varied: 'LORD', 'God of gods', 'Lord of lords'. The reason for praise is the Lord's goodness and covenant love. Both these terms ground the praise in the realm of covenant, for God's goodness is a way of expressing the blessings of the covenant (see on 34:8), while his love is the commitment of covenant faithfulness (see on 36:5). The varied terms for God seem to be used to draw attention to his uniqueness, and therefore to his claim for exclusive praise.

2. Praise for Creation (verses 4-9)
Creation forms the basis for the recounting of the great historical happenings for Israel, and it is the first of the many wonders which God performed. It is also a display of God's wisdom (cf. Prov. 3:19; Jer. 10:12). 'Spreading out the earth upon the waters' is an echo of Genesis 1:6-8, with the Hebrew word for 'firmament' coming from the same root as the word translated 'spreading out'. The English word 'firmament' is simply a borrowing from Latin to try and express the idea of the expanse of the sky. Isaiah 42:5 re-echoes the same language. The formation of the sun, moon and stars is summarised in verses 7-9, with direct links with Genesis 1:16.

3. Praise for the Exodus (verses 10-15)
The exact language of Exodus 12:12, 23, 27, 29 is used in verse 10 to describe the last of the plagues of Egypt, while verse 11 reminds that it was only by the power of God that Israel was brought out from bondage and slavery in Egypt. 'Brought out' is one of the most common expressions in Deuteronomy to describe the Exodus (cf. Deut. 1:27; 4:20; 4:37: 5:6; 16:1; 26:8; 29:25), and it is often linked with 'a mighty hand and an outstretched arm' (verse 12) to indicate the manner in which the Exodus took place (cf. Deut. 5:15; 7:8; 9:29; 26:8). The redemption of Israel from Egypt was solely a wonder of God's doing.

Verses 13-15 summarise Exodus 14:21-31. The crossing of the Red Sea was salvation for the Israelites, but judgment for the pursuing Egyptian army. The one action of God had two entirely different consequences. The waters were divided, and Israel went through on dry land, but the Lord swept the Egyptians into the sea. Such a demonstration of divine power caused the Israelites to fear and to put their trust in him and in Moses his servant (Exod. 14:31).

4. *Praise for the Wilderness Experiences (verse 16)*

It was not only at the time of the Exodus that God displayed his power. During the wilderness experiences he gave his people divine protection and divine sustenance. He was the great shepherd who led his people like a flock and guided them to safety (Ps. 78:52-53). The psalmists seem to have borrowed expressions from Deuteronomy (see Deut. 8:2; 8:15; 29:5), and the prophets describe the wilderness leading in similar terms (see Isa. 48:21; Jer. 2:6; Amos 2:10).

5. *Praise for the Conquest (verses 17-22)*

In coming towards Canaan the Israelites had to cross hostile territory east of the Dead Sea. Neither Sihon king of the Amorites nor Og king of Bashan would allow undisputed passage, and after defeat at the hand of the Israelites their lands were taken. The historical accounts are given in Numbers 21:21-35 and Deuteronomy 2:24-3:11. The territory of Sihon and Og provided land for two and a half of the tribes – Gad, Reuben, and half of Manasseh. The basic promise of the land of Canaan given to Abraham (Gen. 12:7), was reaffirmed at the time of the Exodus and called an inheritance for Israel (Exod. 32:13). When Israel occupied Canaan it was distributed as an inheritance by lot (Num. 33:54), so that God settled 'the tribes of Israel in their homes' (Ps. 78:55). Individual Israelites were God's servants, but the nation as a whole could also be called by God, 'my servant' (cf. also Isa. 41:8; 44:1-2).

6. *Renewed Call to Praise (verses 23-26)*

The concluding verses serve to summarise the psalm as a whole, and perhaps they express the repeated experience of Israel from the time of the conquest to the exile. God did not forsake his covenant commitments but remembered his people (*verse 23*, on the use of 'remember', see the comment on Ps. 132:1). 'Low estate' is an Old Testament term for 'abasement' or 'humiliation', and it could describe times like domination by surrounding peoples during the period of the judges or some of the later periods including the abject humiliation of the exile.

The twin themes of creation and redemption are brought together again in *verses 24-25*. God was the deliverer, but he was also the one who provided for all flesh in accordance with his promise to Noah (the use of the phrase 'all flesh' [NIV, 'every creature'] ties Gen. 9:11, 15-17 and Ps. 136:25 together).

The final verse picks up the opening song of praise (verses 1-3), and reiterates it with one slight alteration. The mode of address to God becomes 'the God of heaven'. Nowhere else in the psalms does this title occur, and it seems to be essentially a designation for God in the period after the exile (Ezra 1:2; Neh. 1:4; Dan. 2:18).

PSALM 137

The reality of the bitterness of exile in Babylon is recalled by a psalmist who has recently returned home. To have undergone the horrors of the destruction of Jerusalem at the hands of Babylonians and Edomites, and then the cruelties of deportation, were experiences which deeply affected the people. There was a concern not only for themselves but for Zion and all that it represented. Even in a prayer of confession such as Daniel's (Dan. 9:4-19), with its acknowledgment of the rightness of God's judgment, there is the request that God would look with favour on his ruined sanctuary and see the desolation of the city which bears his name (verses 17-18). In this psalm the singer reveals that same deep love of Zion as he recalls the distress of alienation from all that was dear to him.

1. *Sorrow in Babylon (verses 1-3)*

The Tigris and Euphrates rivers and a series of irrigation canals provided the source of life in Babylonia *(verse 1)*. Being in exile was not harsh or close imprisonment for the Jewish people, yet to be separated from Zion deeply affected the faithful believers. Sitting was not a sign of ease or comfort. It was the posture of mourners, and tears were shed as they thought about all that was lost in the destruction of Jerusalem.

The Babylonian captors wanted to hear them sing some of the songs for which the Jewish people were renowned *(verses 2-3)*. How could they sing joyful songs and entertain their tormentors 'there' – the place of captivity and mourning? At such times 'the joyful harp is silent' (Isa. 24:8), and the poplars were a convenient spot on which to hang the harps and so show their refusal to take part in entertainment.

2. *Commitment to Zion/Jerusalem (verses 4-6)*

The question in *verse 4* ('How can we sing the songs of the LORD while in a foreign land?') should not be taken to mean that the Jews never sang at all when away from their own land. In the context it clearly means that they could not take part in a concert to entertain their captors. The songs of Zion were not meant to be used in such settings.

The place of Jerusalem in the affection of the faithful exudes from *verses 5-6*. The same attitude is taken in the Book of Lamentations, as the author of that book weeps for the desolate Jerusalem (Lam. 1:16; 2:11). As God had chosen Zion (Pss. 78:68; 132:13), so then his believing people remembered it as the place of his dwelling with his people and longed passionately for return to it. The psalmist calls down a curse upon himself if he is ever unfaithful to the promises concerning Jerusalem. He would prefer his right hand to wither (and so prevent him playing the harp), and his tongue to stick to the roof of his mouth so that he can no longer sing if he is ever untrue to Jerusalem. It is his highest joy because of its association with God.

3. *God's Curse on Edom and Babylon (verses 7-9)*

The Edomites *(verse 7)* were descendants of Esau (see Deut. 2:4-5). Earlier in the Old Testament there is comparative friendliness between Israel and Edom, but later bitter hostility developed (see the curses expressed against Edom in Amos 1:11-12; Jer. 49:7-22; Obad. 1-21; Mal. 1:2-5). While Edom was only a minor power, it had aided Babylon at the time of Jerusalem's fall. The Edomites had looted the city and killed fugitives trying to escape (Obad. 11-14; Ezek. 25:12-14; 35:5-15). Not only did they want to see Jerusalem razed to the ground, but the very foundations of God's rule obliterated. The call for God's judgment on Edom is spelt out more fully in the book of Obadiah.

Two important facts help us in understanding the vengeful wish in *verses 8-9*. Firstly, the language here echoes that of Isaiah 13:16, and recalls the judicial sentence already pronounced by the prophets against Babylon, the great enemy of Zion (see similar judgment on Samaria described in Hosea 13:16). Secondly, many of the biblical and extra-biblical treaties contain curses relating to absence of off-spring or the cutting off of succeeding generations (cf. Ps. 55:23; 69:25; 109:8-9, 13). When these facts are combined, they suggest that the psalmist is echoing well-known prophecies already given against Babylon and (using the language of brutal warfare of that time) asking for the destruction of Babylon as a nation. If her children are cut off, then her days as a nation will be numbered. The final enemy of God's people is called 'Babylon' in the Book of Revelation, and with joy her overthrow is greeted (Rev. 18:1-19:4).

PSALM 138
Of David.

This psalm is the first of the final group of psalms (Pss. 139-145) ascribed to David. The difficulties mentioned in the psalm (see verses 3 and 7) seem to be more than personal incidents. They reflect some major national situation in which God intervened to rescue his own people Israel. Thus the psalm has features in common with David's song of thanksgiving (Ps. 18), though much shorter and more direct. It is both a song of praise and an expression of confident trust.

1. *Praise for Deliverance (verses 1-3)*
In *verse 1* the psalmist rejoices in what the Lord has done for him. The reference to 'all my heart' may well be a deliberate recollection of Deuteronomy 6:5. Here as elsewhere, 'gods' is a Hebrew term applied to human rulers (see Exod. 21:6; 22:8-9; Ps. 82:1), and therefore synonymous with 'kings' in verse 4.

The mention of the temple *(verse 2)* does not compel a dating of the psalm after the building of the first temple, far less after the building of the post-exilic temple. The Hebrew term for temple (*hekal*) is applied to the tent which was God's house before the temple was built (1 Sam. 1:9; 3:3), and in Psalm 27 it is used along with house (*bet*), booth (*sok*) and tent (*'ohel*) to describe the temporary dwelling place for the ark of the covenant. The king will prostrate himself in adoration before God, and in particular will praise him for his covenant love and faithfulness. In providing deliverance for him and for his people, God has demonstrated above all else his abiding character and his commitment to his promises.

On the day of deliverance, a cry for help was heard and answered *(verse 3)*. God responded to the need of his servant the king and of his people. In the face of attackers he was encouraged and helped. Elsewhere David claims God as his 'strength' (Ps. 28:7). Here he confesses that God has imparted strength to him (NIV, 'made me ... stout-hearted').

2. A Prayer for Gentile Rulers (verses 4-5)

David's prayer is for the conversion of the kings (and presumably their subjects) when they hear his testimony (cf. his desire to praise God among the nations in Ps. 18:49). What they will hear will be the promises which God has made to Israel, the disclosure of his gracious purposes for those who trust in him. The ways of the Lord are the instructions he has given to guide his children and so direct their steps (see Ps. 25:8-12). Gentile kings and nations will join in praise for these loving and faithful ways, which in themselves testify that God is righteous (Ps. 145:17) and which show his supreme glory.

3. Confidence in God's Keeping Power (verses 6-8)

The God of glory stoops to look with favour on the lowly, while at the same time he notes from afar (possibly meaning, 'from heaven') the character of the proud *(verse 6)*. The proud he mocks, but to the lowly he gives grace (Prov. 3:34). The psalmist knows that he has been protected by God in his dangers, with God's hand being turned towards him in saving power. However, that same hand is turned to oppose his hateful enemies *(verse 7)*.

The verb 'fulfil' (Hebrew, *gamar*) is a rare word *(verse 8)*, but as in Psalm 57:2 it seems to refer to God's purpose or will being completed, and hence the NIV addition of the words 'his purpose' brings out the meaning well. Part of that purpose is that covenant love is maintained for all time (see the refrain in Ps. 136, 'His love endures for ever'). The final prayer is that God's people will not be abandoned. This interpretation of 'the works of your hands' is supported by reference to Isaiah 60:21 and 64:8.

PSALM 139

For the director of music. Of David. A psalm.

This psalm is intensely personal. Its main theme is the way God knows all about his creatures. There is nowhere we can hide from him, and darkness itself is not able to cover us or our actions from his all-seeing eye. After the first eighteen verses, there is a sudden shift in the psalm, for then we are confronted with a section invoking curses on the psalmist's (and God's) enemies. This is clearly an integral part of the psalm, for the concluding prayer (verses 23-24) repeats the ideas and language of verses 1-3. If we want to join in that final prayer, we must understand the content of the psalm and pray in the same spirit as the psalmist.

1. *The All-Seeing God* (*verses 1-6*)

Every detail of human life is open before God *(verses 1-2)*. The language of human digging and searching is used to show how deep and personal is God's knowledge of each one of us. Irrespective of our immediate situation, he knows us absolutely, and even the inmost recesses of our minds are like an open book before him.

The whole of life, summarised by the expressions 'going out' and 'lying down', is open before God *(verses 3-4)*. Our very thoughts are perceived by God before we even speak a word. As becomes evident later in the psalm, the psalmist's enemies are clearly in his mind as he speaks about God's knowledge of his situation. He is addressing God as the Ruler of the world and the divine Judge.

There is no escape from God's presence *(verse 5)*. If the psalmist goes forward, God is there. If he goes backward, he still meets with him. His hand (the Hebrew has the plural, 'hands') reaches out to keep him within grasp. His God is not only all-knowing (omniscient) but also everywhere present (omnipresent). God's knowledge is beyond human comprehension *(verse 6)*. It is called here 'wonder' knowledge, using a Hebrew expression which regularly denotes actions which by their very nature are beyond human ability (cf. its use in Pss. 71:17; 72:18; 86:10; NIV, 'marvellous deeds'). We can truly know God because he reveals himself to us, but we cannot know him exhaustively. That type of knowledge is his alone, and that is what the psalmist means when he says according to the Hebrew text: 'I cannot [attain] to it.'

2. *The Inescapable God* (*verses 7-12*)

The rhetorical questions in *verse 7* ('Where can I go from your Spirit? Where can I flee from your presence?') introduce several possibilities of where the psalmist could seem to go to escape from God. The point is being made, as in Jeremiah 23:24, that there is nowhere one can go to evade God. Nowhere in all of creation provides a hiding place from God *(verses 8-9)*. The extremities are used to signify the totality of the universe (for similar language, see Job 11:7-9; Amos 9:1-4). Height and depth, east ('the wings of dawn') and west ('the sea', i.e. the Mediterranean), embrace all that exists. Wherever one may go, God's hand is able to reach and to control the unfolding of events *(verse 10)*. Another illustration is given in *verses 11-12*. If distance (height/depth, east/west) will not let one escape from God, perhaps darkness will provide a suitable cover. The answer comes that day and night are alike to God. The final sentence is very brief in Hebrew: 'like the darkness, like the light' (the idiom has come over into English, 'like father, like son'). Darkness lets no-one escape from God's superintendence.

3. *The Creator God (verses 13-18)*

In *verse 13*, in describing his creation, the psalmist uses an unusual verb for create (*qanah*). It only occurs six times in this sense in the Old Testament, rather than the more common verb (*bara'*) of Genesis 1:1 and many other places. Abram used it when speaking to Melchizedek and the king of Sodom, when he called God, '*Creator* of heaven and earth' (Gen. 14:19, 22). From our conception we are God's creation, with a body carefully constructed and woven together. Hence, when the psalmist considers himself, he stands amazed at this creative work *(verse 14)*. The use of the words 'wonderfully' and 'wonderful' draw attention to the divine activity which brought life into existence (cf. the comments on Pss. 71:17; 72:18 for the use of this Hebrew word).

His life was open before God even from before birth *(verses 15-16)*. The womb is called 'the secret place' and 'the depths of the earth' because it shares with those areas the idea of separation from the normal realm of life. It is dark and hidden from human vision, but quite open to God's sight. The length of life is sovereignly determined by God, and with foreknowledge he knows the life history as if it was written beforehand. God does not need a written record, but the idea of a book is used in the Old Testament as a reassuring way of speaking of God's knowledge of, and care for, his people (Exod. 32:32; Pss. 56:8; 69:28; Mal. 3:16). These thoughts are very comforting to a believer, who sings:

> Whate'er my God ordains is right;
> Here shall my stand be taken;

Though sorrow, need, or death be mine,
Yet I am not forsaken;
My Father's care is round me there:
He holds me that I shall not fall,
And so to Him I leave it all.

(Samuel Rodigast 1649-1708)

God's 'thoughts' are his interest in, and concern for, the psalmist *(verses 17-18)*. They are precious or valuable simply because they come from the immeasurable depths of God's wisdom. If the attempt is made to count them, then it is just like counting grains of sand. If such counting brings on sleep, then on waking the psalmist still finds his mind is preoccupied with his God. This is rich meditation.

4. *The Avenging God (verses 19-22)*

The psalm takes a sudden change at this point. From gratitude the tone changes to judgment and curse, as the situation of the psalmist's (and God's) enemies is addressed *(verses 19-20)*. The psalmist appeals to God to intervene and remove his enemies. The character of the wicked is noted as being bloodthirsty, and malicious and blasphemous in speech. The last clause is ambiguous, because the Hebrew text says: 'lifted up in vain – your cities'. The NIV (along with most English versions, including the AV) considers that 'cities' should be read as 'adversaries' (only one letter is different in Hebrew), and that 'lifted up in vain' is an echo of the Third Commandment. The adversaries misuse God's name, either by using it blasphemously, or by bringing reproach on it by their false way of life.

Verses 21-22 show clearly that the cry for vengeance on enemies is not out of personal vindictiveness. As in Psalm 5:8-10 (see comment) the enemies are God's enemies. Here the psalmist is pledging his loyalty to the Lord in a manner customary in the ancient Near East. In the international treaties of the Ancient Near East a party entering into an alliance was obliged to treat the other party's enemies as his enemies. The principle was, as an ancient Hittite treaty put it: 'With my friend you shall be friend, and with my enemy you shall be enemy.' God himself had promised in the Book of the Covenant: 'I will be an enemy to your enemies and will oppose those who oppose you' (Exod. 23:22). For the wider issues raised by cursing in the Psalms, see the Introduction, pp. 60-62.

5. *The Guiding God* (verses 23-24)
The concluding thoughts echo the opening of the psalm. The psalmist exposes himself to the all-seeing eye of God and is willing for his thoughts to be tested by him. He contrasts two ways – the offensive way, and the everlasting way. He shuns the former and prays for his footsteps to be guided in the latter. 'The way everlasting' may be a reference backward, as well as forward. It is in the old way, revealed to Abraham, Isaac and Jacob, and in which they walked, that the psalmist wants to be led. If he goes in that way, then he will be kept and continue in God's presence eternally.

PSALM 140
For the director of music.
A psalm of David.

While this appeal for help describes the attacks made on the psalmist, it shows how faith holds on to God in the hour of trial. The latter part of verse 3 is quoted by Paul in Romans 3:13 as part of the list of Old Testament quotations pointing to universal sinfulness. The use of *Selah* in this psalm is very balanced, occurring after each of the first three stanzas (see the note on *Selah* in the comment on Ps. 3:2). The translation and interpretation of the psalm is made particularly difficult because it contains several words found nowhere else in the Old Testament. Comparison with Psalms 54 and 64 is helpful, because they are generally similar in content, and all three psalms end on the same note.

1. *A Plea for Help* (verses 1-3)
The psalmist uses the verb 'rescue' *(verse 1)*, which occurs quite often describing God's rescue of his people from distress (see e.g. Pss. 6:4; 18:19; 34:7; 50:15; 81:7). The wicked act in secret to make their plans, and then carry out their premeditated evil. With hostile intent they come against the psalmist, who needs divine protection in such circumstances. He lives in a situation of perpetual warfare. *Verse 3* is a combination of the ideas of Psalms 64:3 and 58:4. The tongues of the wicked are as sharp and as venomous as those of snakes.

2. *A Prayer for Protection* (verses 4-5)
The opposition of the enemies is not only verbal. It also takes the form of physical violence *(verse 4)*. The initial plea of verse 1 is

extended in this verse to emphasise the nature of the enemies' activities. They set snares for him, attempting to trap him and cause him to stumble. The adjective 'proud' *(verse 5)* is used both negatively and positively in the Old Testament. Here it describes those whose ultimate source of confidence is themselves, not God. The metaphors from hunting continue as the psalmist speaks of the attacks which have been made upon him. Psalm 10:2-11 contains the same imagery and some of the same language (such as 'arrogance', which comes from the same Hebrew root as 'proud').

3. A Profession of Trust (verses 6-8)

As is typical in appeals for help, there is a strong assertion of confidence in the Lord *(verse 6)*. The writer professes his close relationship with him, and uses that as the basis for his plea.

The Lord is the protector of his servants, shielding them from the deadly blows of the enemies *(verses 7-8)*. They have their designs set on destruction, and it is only God who can intervene to thwart them. The Hebrew word for 'plans' occurs nowhere else in the Old Testament, but its meaning here appears similar to related words in Psalms 26:10 and 37:7 ('wicked schemes'). The final clause of verse 8 is difficult. The Hebrew text simply says, 'they lift up', which the NIV interprets as lifting up in pride or arrogance. Other modern translations (see RSV, GNB, REB) link it with the next verse. The NIV interpretation makes good sense in the context. At times God does seem to allow the wicked to succeed with their plans, but this has to be seen against the broader perspective of his overall purposes for his church and kingdom.

4. A Prayer for Vindication (verses 9-11)

The context shows that this is not a personal vendetta of the psalmist against his enemies. He is a loyal covenant servant (see verse 6) who wants God to vindicate him by turning the evil of the enemies back upon themselves. The prayer is for judgment to be brought on them so severe (likened to 'burning coals', 'fire' and 'miry pits') that it will be final ('never to rise'). Some of the attacks are not physical but verbal (see verse 3), and his prayer is that such slanderers will not find a secure place in the land *(verse 11)*. They have been the hunters (verses 4-5), and now the prayer is that their own plans will recoil on them. What they have planned for others will be inflicted on themselves.

5. *Confidence in God's Judgment (verses 12-13)*
As with Psalms 54 and 64, this one ends on a note of joyful triumph.
These verses stand parallel to verses 6-7, with first person verbs commencing both sections ('I say', 'I know'). The psalmist rests assured
that the Lord will see that the rights of the poor and needy are maintained. That confidence translates into the expectation that when victory comes for the upright, they will rejoice that their lives have been
spared. At that time there will be confession that divine grace has
overcome all the enemies and that God's name is to be exalted because of his wonderful victory.

PSALM 141
A psalm of David.

Psalms 140 and 141 are closely related in language and tone. This
psalm also appeals for help, and it displays the same confidence in
the Lord. After the temple was rebuilt following the return from exile, this psalm became part of the liturgy, chanted as the evening can-
dles were lit. The practice of using this psalm in this way carried over
into the life of the early church, though John Chrysostom (c.347-407)
commented that it was chanted without the obscure parts of it being
understood. The use of rare Hebrew words increases the difficulty of
translation and interpretation. While uncertainties remain, the main
thrust of the appeal and its expression of trust in the Lord are clear.

1. *Appeal for Help (verses 1-2)*
The language of *verse 1* is typical of appeals for help (cf. Pss. 70:1;
86:1). The request is for speedy intervention by the Lord and ready
response to the psalmist's cry. The language of the sacrificial system
is used to give expression to the prayer for acceptance *(verse 2)*. It is
reading too much into the words to suggest that the idea is that prayer
replaces sacrifice. The psalmist wants his prayer to be accepted by
God just as the incense and evening sacrifices are.

2. *Prayer for Wisdom (verses 3-5c)*
In the previous psalm mention is made of the slander of wicked men
(Ps. 140:3). Now, in *verses 3-4*, the psalmist pleads that he will not
share in such use of the tongue. If God guards his mouth, then no evil
words will come from it. In addition, he asks that his thoughts and his

actions will be kept pure. He does not want to associate with evildoers, not even as much as to partake of their hospitality. It may be that the psalmist is thinking particularly of their ill-gotten gains which enable them to purchase such delicacies. By his thoughts, words, and deeds he must be marked off from those who are intrinsically evil.

The psalmist is willing to be rebuked by a good man *(verse 5a-c)*, for such rebuke is to be regarded as 'wounds of a friend' (Prov. 27:6; cf. also Prov. 17:10). When this happens it is an expression of true kindness (Hebrew, *chesed*), a sign of the strength of the bond between two people. Instead of inflicting harm on him, it is as soothing as oil on the head (cf. Ps. 23:5).

3. A Prayer for Vindication (verses 5d-7)

In consecutive psalms prayers for vindication occur (Pss. 140:9-11; 141:5d-7). On this occasion the prayer is directed against both the evildoers and their rulers. The latter are singled out because they have allowed evil to triumph in society. The desire is for them to come to a cruel end. When that happens, then the wicked will make a pronouncement, using what appears to be a proverbial saying. The idea behind verse 7 is that a farmer when ploughing turns up much that is underneath and leaves it on the surface. So the bones of the rulers will have no permanent burial place but will lie scattered over the ground.

4. Prayer for Deliverance (verses 8-10)

The psalm ends with further prayer but also with an assertion of the psalmist's settled conviction of heart and mind. His hope is in his God, to whom he looks with expectancy and in whom he finds shelter *(verse 8)*. In the face of danger from wicked men he asks for preservation in life (Hebrew, *do not empty my life*). The concluding requests *(verses 9-10)* are for safety in the face of the enemies' plots, and for the enemies to be ensnared by their own schemes.

PSALM 142

A maskil of David. When he was in the cave. A prayer.

There are many repeated expressions throughout this psalm, which give intensity to the psalmist's loneliness and grief. The title locates the psalm in the period when David was fleeing from Saul, with the cave most probably being Adullam (1 Sam. 22:1) rather than in En

Gedi (1 Sam. 24). As the final part of a trilogy of psalms, its theme
continues that of Psalms 140 and 141. In the midst of distress there is
confession of sure trust in the Lord, and acknowledgement that he
knows the whole circumstances in which his servant is placed.

1. A Cry for Help (verses 1-4)

The psalmist adopts formal language to state his initial requests, language such as would be used in addressing a superior such as a king
(verses 1-2). There is a parallelism in the Hebrew not brought out in
English translations: 'With my voice I cry out to the LORD; with my
voice I make supplication.' This emphasises both the nature of his
requests, and the one to whom he looks for help. The typical language of lament is continued in verse 2 (cf. Pss. 42:4; 62:8), as mention is made of his complaints in his distress.

To speak of the spirit growing faint describes a condition when
outward circumstances overwhelm a person (verse 3, cf. Ps. 77:3;
Isa. 57:16). David knows that his enemies have plotted against him
and laid a snare for him to trip over (cf. the use of 'snare' in Pss.
140:5 and 141:9). But in spite of his distress he recognises that his
ways are known to his God. This shift to second person speech ('it is
you') highlights his deep personal relationship with the Lord, who
understands his way. 'Way' probably means 'way out of my distress'.
When David looks to his right, the place of the helper is vacant (verse
4). No-one takes note of his situation except the Lord, who abides
when other helpers fail (cf. Pss. 109:31; 121:5).

2. A Cry from the Heart (verses 5-7)

Just as the psalm began with a repeated call, so the second section
commences with a double expression of need and confidence ('I cry
... I say', verse 5). Among men David found no place of refuge (Hebrew, manos, verse 4), but he knows that he has a place of shelter
(Hebrew, machseh) in the Lord. To make this confession to the Lord
is a recognition of his own insecurity and helplessness. 'My portion'
is a borrowing of the language relating to God's provision for the
Levites (see the comment on Ps. 16:5).

The urgency of the situation is plain from the series of cries: 'Listen
... rescue ... set me free' (verses 6-7). The 'prison' is not one in our
modern sense, but rather it is a metaphor for loneliness and despair. If
God does act in response to the prayer, then praise will follow. Though

presently separated from fellow believers, deliverance will bring renewed fellowship with them and united praise. In contrast to the enemies, God will act in tender love towards his afflicted servant.

PSALM 143
A psalm of David.

This is the last of Luther's 'Pauline Psalms' (see Introduction, p. 37), and also the last of the penitential psalms (see the introductory comment on Ps. 51). It is not surprising in the least that the apostle Paul should twice echo this psalm (Rom. 3:20; Gal. 2:16), and in both cases add the explanatory words that justification in God's sight is not by observing the law. This is an implication from what the psalm says about God's judgment, for verse 2a is a recognition that if God does judge according to works, then the psalmist will be condemned. The psalm puts the emphasis on grace and faith, and Paul clearly sees that and uses it when expounding the gospel.

1. *An Initial Prayer for Mercy* (*verses 1-2*)
As in many of the later verses, *verse 1* has similarities with other passages in the psalms. There was clearly a deep knowledge of other biblical passages which could be utilised in prayer (see the introductory comment on Ps. 86). The opening petitions resemble Psalms 28:2; 39:12; and 54:2, while mention of 'faithfulness and righteousness' recalls the character of the covenant God of Israel (Exod. 34:6). The NIV correctly paraphrases the Hebrew 'answer me' with the words 'come to my relief'.

David knows that he will be condemned if he is judged on his own behaviour and character. Not a single person is able to maintain a righteous standing before God by their own works *(verse 2)*. This Old Testament teaching is amplified in the New Testament where we are taught that God 'saved us, not because of righteous things we had done, but because of his mercy' (Tit. 3:5). Augustus Toplady described accurately this biblical understanding of salvation:

> Not the labours of my hands
> Can fulfil thy law's demands;
> Could my zeal no respite know,
> Could my tears for ever flow,
> All for sin could not atone:
> Thou must save and thou alone.

2. Present Distress and Past Mercy (verses 3-6)

The persecution the psalmist is enduring has as its aim his ultimate destruction *(verse 3)*. 'Darkness' is a synonym for the grave. The second part of verse 3 ('he makes ... long dead') appears in almost identical form in Lamentations 3:6, while the first part of verse 4 is a repetition of Psalm 142:3a. Constant persecution has had its effect, and the psalmist is at the point of utter despair *(verse 4)*.

In circumstances like these, what brings hope is reflection on the past actions of the Lord *(verse 5)*. The words and ideas of this verse are very similar to Psalm 77:11-12 (see commentary). Meditation on God's wonderful activity in the past gives confidence for the present. Encouraged by the past, the psalmist stretches out his hands as he prays to God *(verse 6, for similar expressions see Pss. 28:2; 44:20; 88:9; Lam. 1:17)*. Just as the dry ground longs for refreshing rain, so his soul thirsts for God (cf. the similar expressions of longing for God in Pss. 42:1-2 and 63:1).

3. Prayer for Deliverance (verses 7-10)

Speedy help is required, for the seeming absence of God from the situation causes the soul to pine away *(verse 7)*. When God appears to be absent, this is referred to as a hiding of his face (see Pss. 30:7; 44:24; 88:14). Frequently, as here, the plea to him is not to hide his face (see Pss. 27:9; 69:17; 102:2). The state of death is often described as going down to the pit (see Pss. 28:1; 88:4, 6).

The covenant servant has his heart firmly fixed on God ('I have put my trust', the expression of settled conviction), and he pleads for covenant mercy (Hebrew, *chesed*) to be shown towards him *(verse 8)*. The darkness of the night is to be replaced with the light of God's favour in the morning. The servant who lifts up his heart in devotion and praise to his God, also asks for guidance in the way of righteousness, a request which is repeated in another form in verse 10. These verses are very similar to Psalm 25:1-2, 4.

The request for deliverance *(verse 9)* is followed by a difficult phrase. The Hebrew text says, 'I covered', which the NIV interprets as 'I hide myself'. While many suggestions have been made, and English translations differ widely, the NIV translates it according to the context, for an expression of trust is what is expected. The section closes with a further request for teaching *(verse 10)*, putting the prayer of verse 8a in another form. Submission to God's will is required, so that life without dangers can be likened to level ground (cf. a similar Hebrew expression used in Deut. 4:43, 'the desert plateau'). A physical term is here given a spiritual application. The term 'good Spirit' is used elsewhere too of the Holy Spirit (Neh. 9:20).

4. Concluding Summary Prayer (verses 11-12)

The concluding verses re-echo the opening of the psalm. While the psalmist again acknowledges that he is the Lord's servant, yet he knows that he cannot appeal for help for his own sake. It must be for God's sake that salvation is given, for he always acts in accordance with his covenant commitment (Hebrew, *chesed*; NIV, 'unfailing love'). A servant's foes were also the foes of his covenant overlord, and so David asks God, who always acts in accordance with his righteousness, to destroy completely his enemies.

PSALM 144
Of David.

There are many similarities between this psalm and David's song when God delivered him from the hand of Saul (Ps. 18). Strong echoes of other psalms also appear. The earlier part (verses 1-10) consists of the king's personal prayer for help, asking for deliverance from the deadly sword. After a transitional verse (verse 11), the concluding section seeks blessings on the people as a whole. While the change at verse 12 is quite marked, the NIV translation correctly notes the connection between the two parts of the psalm: 'Deliver me, and rescue me.... *Then* our sons in their youth will be like well-nurtured plants.'

1. A Song of Praise (verses 1-4)

The opening exclamation of praise *(verse 1)* is a slight expansion of Psalm 18:46, while the second part echoes Psalm 18:34a. The king knows that his security is found in the Lord alone, and if victory comes in battle it is due to his assistance.

The accumulation of titles for God in *verse 2* is very similar to Psalm 18:2, except for the first one. 'My loving God' is an attempt to translate an unique title for God (Hebrew, *chasdi*, 'my steadfast love'). The expression is probably an abbreviation of the fuller expression (Hebrew, *'elohe chasdi*, 'God of my steadfast love') which occurs in

Psalm 59:9, 17. The titles highlight the character of God as the mighty Saviour, who defends the king and who gives him victory over surrounding nations.

The question in *verse 3* ('O LORD, what is man that you care for him, the son of man that you think of him?') is very similar to that in Psalm 8:4, while the answer ('Man is like a breath; his days are like a fleeting shadow', *verse 4*) summarises the thought of Psalm 39:4-5. If man's existence is of such a fleeting nature, then how utterly does he need the Lord's help?

2. *Prayer for Deliverance* (*verses 5-8*)

What is described in Psalm 18 as God's actions on behalf of David are now made the subject of prayer. Another appearance of God like at Mount Sinai (cf. Exod. 20:18-19; Deut. 5:22-27) is sought *(verses 5-6)*. The bolts of lightning are regarded as God's arrows (see the same usage in Pss. 18:14; 77:17; Hab. 3:11). The series of direct requests continue *(verses 7-8)*. The staccato effect of these prayers stresses the urgency of the need. The psalmist wants God to stoop down to him in his trouble, as he faces the might of armies around him. When the foreign leaders lift their right hands to make an oath (cf. Deut. 32:40-42), they either swear falsely or else fail to keep their word. They make a pledge, but it is intended only to bring advantage to them in battle.

3. *A Song of Thanksgiving* (*verses 9-10*)

David's response is to sing 'a new song', using this expression in the same way as in Psalms 33:3 and 40:3. The new song is in praise of God's saving action which has delivered David from the threat of death. He names himself here as in Psalm 18:50, drawing attention also to his role as a servant who exercises kingly rule by divine appointment (see the use of the phrase 'the servant of the Lord' in the title to Ps. 18).

4. *A Renewed Prayer* (*verse 11*)

This verse serves two purposes. It repeats the prayer of verses 7-8 (abbreviating it by omitting 'from on high' and 'from the mighty waters') in order to stress the urgency of his cry. It also serves to provide a link with the following verses, for if the prayer is answered then peace and prosperity will follow for the nation.

5. God's Blessing of the Nation (verses 12-15)

God's deliverance from the threat of enemy attack will result in security for the people. Sons and daughters will be nurtured in a secure environment where they are able to grow and develop. The grace and beauty of the daughters are compared to carved pillars, since it was often the practice in the Near East to have pillars carved in the shape of young women (verse 12).

God's blessing will result in abundant harvests and a great increase in flocks and herds (verses 13-14). The language reflects the covenant promise of blessing contained in passages such as Deuteronomy 28:1-14. Part of that promise was security against attack from enemies (Deut. 28:7), here stated as the defensive walls not being breached, no exile, and none of the turmoil of battle in the city streets which leads to lamentation.

The final statement is a summary of the privileged position of Israel (verse 15). The people whom God chose for his inheritance could indeed be pronounced 'Blessed' (Ps. 33:12)! An abiding covenant relationship with the Lord results in sustained blessings for his people, though the greatest blessing of all is being able to call him our Father. For the Christian, material blessings cannot compare with the privilege of being able, by the work of the Holy Spirit, to say in truth that 'Jesus is Lord' (1 Cor. 12:3).

PSALM 145

A psalm of praise. Of David.

The final section of Davidic psalms (Pss. 138-145) is concluded by a song which extols the universal kingship of God and his gracious and just provision for all his creatures. This emphasis on the scope of God's mercy is brought out in the NIV translation by the repeated use of 'all' (see verses 9, 10, 12, 13, 14, 15, 17, 18, 20). The psalm is an alphabetic acrostic, though in most Hebrew manuscripts the strophe commencing with the Hebrew letter *nun* is missing (verse 13b). However, as the NIV footnote records, one Hebrew manuscript contains it, as does one of the Dead Sea Scrolls and early translations such as the Syriac and Greek. Some other later versions, including Scottish Gaelic, have also included it. The psalm, after an initial song of praise (verses 1-2), contains four sections, with a final expression of praise to conclude (verse 21). Among all the psalms with titles, this is the only one which uses the word 'praise' (Hebrew, *tehillah*), which word also reappears in the final verse ('in praise').

1. *Praise to the King (verses 1-2)*

The language which opens this song of praise concerning the Great King and his kingdom is very similar to Psalms 30:1 and 34:1, 3. At times when God was praised by his people, language such as that in these psalms (and David's doxology in 1 Chr. 29:10-13) provided a reservoir from which appropriate expressions could be drawn. The pledge is given of constant praise which will be rendered to the King, and there is no apparent difference in meaning between 'exalt', 'praise' and 'extol'.

2. *The Splendour of God's Majesty (verses 3-7)*

Again, there is borrowed language here. The first half of *verse 3* ('Great is the LORD and most worthy of praise') echoes Psalms 48:1 and 96:4, while the second part ('his greatness no-one can fathom') is modelled on Job 5:9; 9:10 and Isaiah 40:28. The psalmist draws attention to the way in which God is distinguished from his creatures. His greatness is such that it does not come within human scrutiny, for he vastly transcends all his creation.

God's 'works' and 'mighty acts' are the subject of repeated praise, generation after generation *(verses 4-5)*. It was part of the responsibility of parents and elders to teach successive generations about the great deeds of the Lord (see the comments on Ps. 78:1-8). As the people meditated upon what the Lord had done they would be moved to praise the wonder of his actions in creation and redemption. The description of God's actions mount up *(verses 6-7)*: 'awesome works', 'great deeds', 'abundant goodness', 'righteousness'. These expressions, and those in the preceding verses, are not meant to be carefully distinguished from one another, but their cumulative effect is to draw attention to the overwhelming power and majesty of God's actions.

3. *The Glory of God's Kingdom (verses 8-13a)*

God's own declaration of his character (Exod. 34:6) once more forms the basis for praise *(verses 8-9*, see the comments on Pss. 86:5 and 103:8). The word 'gracious' comes first in the Hebrew text in order to fit the acrostic pattern. Towards all his creation the Lord shows himself as the God of abundant love and compassion.

In *verses 10-12* both human beings and inanimate creation are depicted as rendering praise to God. 'Kingdom' here conveys the idea of the universal reign of God over all creation. The 'saints' (for this term see the comment on Ps. 30:4) have the task of proclaiming the greatness of God and the glorious nature of his kingdom. The purpose of this proclamation has a missionary intent, in that all men may come to know how gracious and condescending God is. In teaching his disciples, Jesus applied the principle of God's care of the birds to show how much more his providential care extends to his believing followers (Matt. 6:25-34).

The assertion in *verse 13a* ('Your kingdom is an everlasting kingdom, and your dominion endures through all generations') puts in other words the declaration in the Song of the Sea: 'The LORD will reign for ever and ever' (Exod. 15:18), and similar words occur in Daniel 4:3, 34. Unlike earthly kingdoms, God's kingdom is not temporary but eternal. That is why generation after generation can testify to his mighty acts (verse 4).

4. *The Gracious Care of the Lord* (*verses 13b-16*)

Towards his creation the Lord shows utter dependability *(verse 13b)*. His words stand sure, and having made a commitment he upholds his creation and in this way demonstrates his faithfulness. The word translated 'loving' (*chasid*) is used here of God, whereas it more commonly is used of his loyal covenant servants (see the comments on Pss. 4:3; 12:1; 18:25; 31:23).

Verse 14 is a statement of the general and repeated actions of the Lord. He sustains those who are stumbling (see Pss. 37:17, 24; 54:4; 119:116) and restores those bowed down in distress or by humiliation (Ps. 18:6).

The language and ideas of *verses 15-16* are very close to Psalm 104:27-28 (see the comment). Both men and animals are fed from the hands of a gracious Creator who, as the heavenly Father, cares even for those who neither sow nor reap (Matt. 6:26).

5. *The Lord's Providence* (*verses 17-20*)

In the manner in which he operates, the Lord always deals in accordance with the norms he has set *(verse 17a)*. He is gracious and righteous (Ps. 116:5), and his laws are right (Ps. 119:137). *Verse 17b* is the repetition of verse 13b. While those far off from the Lord will not know his ready response to their cry (Isa. 29:13), yet to those who call in truth he is ready to respond by drawing near to help *(verse 18)*.

In *verses 19-20* the Lord's people are described by two terms used elsewhere in the Psalms. They are 'those who fear him' (Pss. 22:23; 25:12, 14; 33:18; 60:4; 119:63) and those 'who love him' (Pss. 5:11; 97:10; 119:132). Love and reverence for the Lord are fully compatible. Here the 'desire' is not for food (cf. verse 16) but for salvation from danger or distress. While the wicked are brought to destruction, the Lord preserves his own people (Hebrew, *shamar*, the same verb as in Ps. 121:7-8).

6. *Praise to the Lord* (*verse 21*)

The opening call to praise is resumed (verses 1-2), but carried a stage further. Not only will the psalmist engage in praise, but he calls on all creatures to share in it. 'Every creature' (Hebrew, 'all flesh') can refer only to humans (Ps. 65:2), but the similar phrase 'everything that has breath' describes men and animals (Ps. 150:6). Probably the NIV translation is correct, and therefore the psalm ends with an invitation not only to humans but to all living things to join in perpetual praise to the Lord.

PSALM 146

The final group of psalms (146-150) have a common feature. They all commence and finish with the expression 'Praise the Lord' (Hebrew, *halleluyah*). For this reason they were called the 'Hallel' psalms (cf. the comment on Ps. 113 for reference to the group of psalms called the 'Egyptian Hallel'). Along with Psalm 145 they were used in later Jewish practice for the morning worship in the synagogue. They bring the whole Book of Psalms to a close on a note of triumphant praise. Psalm 146 is a typical hymn of praise, with opening and closing calls to praise enclosing a description of the ways in which the Creator and King helps the needy. In the Greek and Latin versions, both Psalms 146 and 147 are ascribed to Haggai and Zechariah. The language of the psalm itself suggests that it comes from after the exile, but there is no express statement to confirm this.

1. *A Call to Praise* (*verses 1-2*)

After the initial communal call to praise, the hymn continues with the psalmist encouraging himself to praise the Lord. He then makes a vow to do so in perpetuity. While he refers to God repeatedly as 'the LORD' (eleven times in this short psalm), yet he also calls him 'my God'. It is from personal faith that he commits himself to a life lived to praise his Creator and Deliverer.

2. A Call to Trust in the Lord (verses 3-9)

Before describing God as the great helper the psalmist sets a contrast by issuing a warning against putting trust in men (verses 3-4). The theme of refusing to depend on mere men or military might is common in the psalms (see, for example, Pss. 44:4-8; 118:6-12). Human leaders are only fallible mortals, and no salvation can be found in them. Their mortality is shown by the fact that when death comes they return to the earth and their plans never reach fruition.

In verses 5-6 the psalmist sings of the happy condition of those who have trusted instead in the Lord (for comment on 'blessed', see Ps. 1:1). The God of the patriarch Jacob is equated with the covenant Lord of Israel. The title, 'the God of Jacob', is quite common in the Psalter (see Pss. 20:1; 46:7, 11; 75:9; 76:6; 81:1; 84:8; cf. also Isaiah's term, 'The Mighty One of Jacob', Isa. 49:26; 60:16). As in Psalm 121:1, reference to 'help' brings the reassurance that the real helper is the Creator of heaven and earth. Firstly, the almighty Creator has the ability to help his people because everything in heaven, earth and sea were made by him (for the phrase 'Maker of heaven and earth', see Pss. 115:15; 121:2). Secondly, he is a God who will not fail to keep his covenanted word (Hebrew, 'who keeps truth for ever'). Whoever trusts in this God is eternally blessed!

In the Hebrew text of verses 7-9 a series of participles explains further about the Maker of heaven and earth. He 'upholds ... and gives ... sets prisoners free ... gives sight ... lifts up ... loves ... watches over'. Many of the expressions used occur in other psalms, such as the opening of verse 7 which abbreviates Psalm 103:6. The reference to lifting up the bowed down occurs in this form in the Old Testament only here and in Psalm 145:14. The two final statements ('sustains ... frustrates') complete the description by stating two opposing facts. Towards the most needy in society the Lord shows compassion, but he makes crooked the ways of the wicked.

3. A Final Call to Praise (verse 10).

As the poet renews the call to praise, he echoes the words of Exodus 15:18: 'The LORD reigns for ever.' His address is to Zion/Jerusalem,

reminding her that God is the everlasting King who has chosen to
dwell with his people (see Ps. 132:13-14). That fact should bring reassurance to those whose hope is in the Lord (verse 5), and produce
from them a response to the final call: 'Praise the LORD' (Hebrew,
halleluyah).

PSALM 147

While the Greek (LXX) translation divides this psalm into two (verses
1-11, Ps. 146; verses 12-20, Ps. 147; see the Introduction, p. 25), its
unity is apparent from the parallelism throughout the sections and the
way in which the opening and closing form a frame for the central
content of the psalm. The dependence on earlier parts of the Old Testament (especially Deuteronomy 4 and Psalms 33 and 104) and the
reference to the return of the exiles suggest it was a song composed in
the post-exilic period. The most probable occasion for its composition would have been the dedication of the rebuilt walls of Jerusalem
(Neh. 12:27-43). Such a joyous time would have been most appropriate for a song calling for praise to the Lord for his great love and
favour to Israel.

1. *Praise to the Great Creator (verses 1-6)*
The opening call to praise is followed by exclamations which speak
of the worth of such praise *(verse 1)*. It is 'good', 'pleasant', and
'fitting'. While there is some similarity with Psalm 33:1-2, yet the
closest parallel to this opening is Psalm 135:3. It is quite possible to
take the Hebrew here as an emphatic statement: 'It is *indeed* good to
sing praises ...' Praise is an appropriate response, but it is also a joyful thing.

The setting of the psalm is the period after the return from exile
(verses 2-3). What happened when the exiles were permitted to return home, and the subsequent rebuilding of Jerusalem was the Lord's
work (Ps. 126:2-3). Here the psalmist looks at this as a continuing
work of healing ('heals ... binds') as the Lord deals in grace with
grief-stricken and afflicted exiles (see Ps. 137).

Encouragement comes to the people with the thought that the re-
storer of Israel is none other than the God of creation *(verses 4-6)*.
Even the stars are his, and he knows them individually. His providential work in sustaining his creation is evidence of his might and his

wisdom. One of the implications of this is that God is therefore able to intervene on behalf of his people in order to 'sustain' them (the same verb is used in Ps. 146:9). Seeing that he knows so much about things like stars so that he gives them names, how much more does he care for his hurting people. He also acts in judgment to destroy the wicked, bringing them down to the grave.

2. Praise to the Great Provider (verses 7-11)

The opening word of verse 7 'sing' is literally 'respond' or 'answer'. Praise is an excellent way of proclaiming the greatness of God. It is a thanksgiving or a confession to others of what we know of him. In Hebrew, 'make music' is the same verb as the NIV translates by 'sing praises' in verse 1. Here the mention of 'harp' links such praise with musical accompaniment.

The Creator is not only concerned with the stars (verse 4), but also with the needs of cattle and birds which he also made (verses 8-9). He easily provides the rain, which in turn helps to produce the food for both domestic and wild animals. Therefore, human strength, even military might, is no substitute for divine power (verses 10-11). God does not delight in what men can achieve. Rather, he delights in those who recognise their own weakness, and then trust in his steadfast love (Hebrew, chesed). Those who fear him (with the reverence of a child, not that of a slave; see Pss. 25:12; 34:9) have confidence in his ability to meet their needs.

3. Praise to Zion's God (verses 12-20)

In verses 12-14 Zion/Jerusalem is addressed directly, and commanded to praise her God. The reasons for this command are then given. He provides for the defences of the city, and he gives his blessings to her inhabitants. The people have rest from battle, and he gives them abundant crops so that their hunger is satisfied with the best wheat.

God's word is likened to a messenger swiftly carrying out his commands. To the earlier reference to clouds and rain (verse 8) is now added snow, frost and hail. Such wintry weather is a demonstration of God's power, before which no human can stand. But when God sends his further word, the warm breeze comes and the snow and ice melt (verses 15-18).

God's greatest gift was, however, another 'word', which involved revelation of his will for his people (verse 19). The nation whom he had made for himself was guided by the laws which he gave, so that successive generations might fear the Lord and have long life in the land of Canaan (Deut. 4:40; 6:1-2). Israel's position was unique *(verse 20)*. No other nation could claim the privilege enjoyed by Israel of righteous decrees and laws. This should have provoked envy when other nations saw how near God was to his people (Deut. 4:5-8).

After recital of all these works of the Lord, the final call fittingly is a repetition of the initial one. Consideration of God's actions in creation and redemption should lead to further praise.

PSALM 148

As part of the Psalter's grand climax of praise, Psalm 148 celebrates the honour of the great Creator. Celestial beings, heavenly bodies and earthly creatures are called to extol him. At least from the time of Hilary of Poitiers in the early church (c.315-367), many have seen this psalm as a prophetic picture of the praise which will be given to God when creation is freed from its present bondage (Rom. 8:18-21). However, the psalm does not suggest an eschatological setting. Rather, it is directed to heaven and earth – including angels, men and animals – as a call to extol the name of the Lord, and is similar to Psalms 33, 103, and 104. The concluding stanza directs attention to the people of God, who have had a king appointed for them by God.

1. *God's Praise in the Heavens* (verses 1-6)

The closest parallel to *verses 1-3* is found in the concluding verses of Psalm 103. All creatures in the heavens are commanded to praise the Lord. These extend from his angelic messengers to the sun, moon, and stars. No part of the heavens is exempt from giving praise. The heavens and the waters above (see Gen. 1:7) are to share in praise *(verses 4-6)*. The motivation for the praise is the decisive way in which they were created. God 'spoke, and it came to be; he commanded, and it stood firm' (Ps. 33:9). He brought all things into being, and set them in their place (the same verb is used here in Hebrew as in Gen. 1:17). The final part of verse 6, instead of the interpretation given by the NIV, may mean that creation cannot transgress the bounds set by God.

2. *God's Praise on Earth* (*verses 7-12*)

In general, these verses follow the order of creation in Genesis 1, coming to a climax with the references to mankind. Everything on the earth – vegetable, animal, and human – must join in the chorus of praise. Just as God commanded and everything came into being (verse 5), so does his 'word' (NIV, 'bidding') control the operations of nature.

3. *God's Praise from His People* (*verses 13-14*)

Creation is testimony to the power and craftsmanship of God *(verse 13)*. As verse 5b earlier in the psalm gave the motivation for praise, so does this verse. When creation is viewed, God's 'eternal power and divine nature' (Rom. 1:20) are evident, and so his name is exalted. That 'his splendour is above the earth and the heavens' means that the Creator's splendour far exceeds that of the creation.

Elsewhere in the psalms the term 'horn' *(verse 14)* is used of the king (see Ps. 132:17), and it makes the best sense to take it in this way here also. The provision of the Davidic family is rightly seen as God's creative act. Three terms are used to describe God's people. Firstly, they are called 'saints' (see on Ps. 30:4). Secondly, he calls the people 'Israel', and thirdly, he refers to them as 'the people close to his heart'. This latter expression is not common, though it does occur in Leviticus 10:3 ('those who approach me'). It serves as a convenient expression to denote the special relationship between God and his people. The final call to praise rounds off the majestic song of adoration.

PSALM 149

While the praise elements of this psalm are by no means unusual, yet the coupling of praise (verses 1-5) with cursing (verses 6-9) is unique in the Psalter. The nearest parallel would be the tender compassion of Deuteronomy 7 (see especially verses 7-9) alongside the judgment of God on those who hate him, both in Israel and in Canaan (verses 1-6, 9-10). It is best to understand the joy of the people being directed first to their present position. Then the psalmist points to an eschatological day when foreign powers are to be subjected to God's judgment. Present and future are linked together by God's written decree (verse 9).

1. *A Call to Praise (verse 1)*

The command to praise comes with the instruction regarding its content. The song to be sung is 'a new song'. As in Psalm 96:1 (see the comment) or Isaiah 42:10, this means more than just a newly-composed song. The phrase carries eschatological overtones concerning the final judgment, which explains its use in the Book of Revelation (5:9; 14:3). The praise is to be communal, as the worshipping people of God gather together. 'Saints' is one of the many synonyms for God's people in this psalm.

2. *Rejoicing in the Lord (verses 2-5)*

Saving acts of mercy lie behind the spiritual joy of the people. He who formed Israel into a nation is extolled as their Maker (cf. Pss. 95:6; 100:3), but also as their Sovereign and King *(verse 2)*. As the subjects experience the saving power of their King, they lift up his name in exuberant song, using instruments such as tambourine and harp to magnify their praise *(verse 3)*. It is uncertain whether instruments like the tambourine were permitted in the temple worship. If not, then this praise is some occasion outside the sacred precincts. The tambourine is elsewhere linked with dancing (Exod. 15:20; 1 Sam. 18:6; Ps. 150:4).

In *verse 4*, God's pleasure in those who fear him (Ps. 147:11) is expressed again. Two more synonyms are added for the company of believers: 'his people' and 'the humble'. The wonder of God's grace is seen in the fact that he brings to himself those who are not his people and that he makes them 'sons of the living God' (Hos. 1:8-10; Rom. 9:25-26). He grants salvation to the humble, a link in thought with Psalm 147 (see verse 6).

The saints are called to respond joyfully to this expression of salvation *(verse 5)*. Nights of sorrow are to be replaced with nights of song. The reference to 'beds' confirms the view taken above that the praise here is something outside of the temple worship. The couch drenched with tears (Ps. 6:6) is to be exchanged for songs in the night (Pss. 42:8; 77:6).

3. *Rejoicing in Hope (verses 6-9)*

The contrast between the two main parts of the psalm is very sharp, but it stems from the two classes of people being described. In verses 1-5 it is the people of God who are in view. Here it is another people (the Hebrew uses different words for 'people(s)' in verses 4 and 7), who do not acknowledge the lordship of Israel's God, and who have a sentence of judgment carried out against them. The written sentence could be one like that given in Isaiah 65:6-7. Vengeance is not man's prerogative but God's (Deut. 32:35, 41; cf. the use of this passage in Rom. 12:19 and Heb. 10:30). It is the expression of his character as the just and holy God. The picture here is of end-time judgment in which God's people will participate (1 Cor. 6:1-3). At the present time God's people conquer through the sword of the Spirit (Eph. 6:17; Heb. 4:12). The saints have a position of peculiar honour (verse 5) which shall be seen especially at the last great day of judgment. A final call to praise brings the assembled saints back to their present task.

PSALM 150

It is very likely that this psalm was composed as the concluding doxology. Whereas the earlier books which comprise the Psalter end with briefer doxologies (41:13; 72:18-19; 89:52; 106:48), the final book ends with a complete psalm which constitutes the climax of praise. Thirteen times the command is given to 'praise the Lord' (Hebrew, *halleluyah*). Just as Psalm 1 forms an appropriate introduction, so Psalm 150 brings to a close the whole collection. While the psalms traverse all the varied moods of human life, this closing one draws the songbook of Israel to a conclusion on the note of overwhelming praise of God in his worthiness.

1. *Praise in Earth and Heaven (verses 1-2)*
The opening of the psalm asks for praise in earth and in heaven. There seems to be a deliberate use of 'sanctuary' to refer to the earthly dwelling place of God, while the following clause calls for heavenly choirs to sing God's praise (Hebrew, 'in the firmament of his strength'). Heaven and earth are to unite in joyful adoration, singing of the demonstrations of his great might and majestic power. Doubtless both creation and redemption are in view.

2. *Praise with a Complete Orchestra (verses 3-5)*
The initial reference to musical accompaniment in *verse 3* is soon enlarged, as the psalmist proceeds to enumerate the other instruments,

using doubled phrases to do so. This stylistic feature adds to the feeling of movement towards a climax. The whole orchestra is involved, ranging from the shepherd's pipe to the loud percussion instruments. Mention is also made of dancing, which features elsewhere as a joyful response to God's saving power (Jer. 31:4, 13).

3. Praise from All Creatures (verse 6)

The last verse in the Book of Psalms ends with a call to all creatures to give praise to the Lord. The preceding commands are implicitly directed to Israel, as the naming of the instruments shows. Now the direction is widened to embrace not only humans but all of God's creatures who breathe. While the Hebrew expression here (*neshamah*) particularly denotes humans, yet it is used more widely of all living creatures (Gen. 7:21-22). This final command to praise in the Psalter has its echo in a vision in the Book of Revelation. John says: 'Then I heard every creature in heaven and on earth and under the earth and on the sea, and all that is in them, singing: "To him who sits on the throne and to the Lamb be praise and honour and glory and power, for ever and ever!" ' (Rev. 5:13). The concluding psalm ends fittingly with a final 'Praise the Lord!', 'Hallelujah!'

Christian Focus Publications publishes biblically-accurate books for adults and children. The books in the adult range are published in three imprints.

Christian Heritage contains classic writings from the past.

Christian Focus contains popular works including biographies, commentaries, doctrine, and Christian living.

Mentor focuses on books written at a level suitable for Bible College and seminary students, pastors, and others; the imprint includes commentaries, doctrinal studies, examination of current issues, and church history.

For a free catalogue of all our titles, please write to
Christian Focus Publications,
Geanies House, Fearn,
Ross-shire, IV20 1TW, Great Britain

THE CHRIST OF THE BIBLE
AND THE CHURCH's FAITH

Geoffrey Grogan

This book is a theological study

In the main, the odd-numbered chapters are theological. The first
five of these set out the biblical evidence for our understanding of
Jesus, while chapters 11 and 13 reflect on this theologically at a
somewhat deeper level.

It is an apologetic study

This is the function of the even-numbered chapters. They deal with
the main difficulties that have been and still are raised by those
who are interested in Jesus but are not yet committed to him. It is
to be hoped that they will also be of help to the committed. Each
of these chapters follows the theological chapter most closely related to it.

The book will be useful to ministers and theological students. It
has however been written in such a way that many Christians without theological training may be able to benefit from it, plus other
readers who have not yet come to personal faith in Christ but are
interested enough to read a serious book about him.

304 pages   ISBN 1 857 92 266 2   demy

In this wide-ranging and well-written study, Geoffrey Grogan provides a clear, scholarly and reliable account of the identity of Jesus of Nazareth. The fruit of prolonged thought about the New
Testament's teaching, *The Christ of the Bible and of the Church's
Faith* is marked on every page by clarity of exposition and reli-
ability of judgment. Here we have a careful and thoughtful sifting
of evidence and a steady pursuit of conclusions which are in harmony with it.

While familiar with trends in New Testament studies during
the past two centuries, and grateful for the work of fellow schol-

ars, Geoffrey Grogan has listened first and foremost to the witness of the apostles. He concludes that there is only one answer to the ancient question which Jesus himself asked them, 'Who do you say that I am?'

The result is this sturdy volume. Theological students, Christian ministers and leaders will find it invaluable, but any serious reader to whom Jesus of Nazareth remains an elusive figure will also come to the conclusion that this is a book well worth reading.

Sinclair B. Ferguson
Westminster Theological Seminary
Philadelphia, Pennsylvania, USA

This is an apologetic and theological study aimed at preachers, theological students, thinking Christians and interested agnostics. It succeeds in its aims admirably.

Donald Macleod
Free Church College
Edinburgh, Scotland

This beautifully-written book is a feast of scriptural analysis and argument about our Lord Jesus Christ. With profound learning but with lightness of touch, Geoffrey Grogan discusses all the main lines of the presentation of Jesus in the Bible, and then skilfully relates these to the questions that trouble people today about him. So the book is an attractive combination of Christology and apology – explaining Jesus in a way that answers modern doubts and puzzles, cleverly arranged in alternating chapters. Hearts will be warmed and heads cleared by this book – and doubt and unbelief will be turned into confidence and faith.

Steve Motyer
London Bible College

Other books by Geoffrey Grogan,

Wrestling With The Big Issues

In this much appreciated book, Geoffrey Grogan examines the principles and methods used by Paul to assess and solve the doctrinal and practical problems that appeared in the early Christian Church. Most of these problems have reappeared throughout church history, and can be found today in evangelical churches. Geoffrey Grogan is convinced that the answers to many of today's difficulties are to be found in applying to current situations the Spirit-inspired instructions of the apostle.

Howard Marshall says about *Wrestling With The Big Issues*: 'This book is remarkable for being written by a New Testament scholar in such a simple and relevant way that any reader will be able to understand what is being said and see how Paul's letters still speak to Christians today.'

Sinclair Ferguson comments that 'Geoffrey Grogan brings to his teaching, preaching and writing a life-time of study. He combines careful exposition with practical care.'

And Clive Calver says that 'Geoffrey Grogan possesses the uncanny knack of setting truth on fire: here the personality of the apostle shines through its pages; the life of a man who Christ used to transform the history of his church.'

ISBN 1 85792 051 1   256 Pages

In the Focus on the Bible commentary series, Geoffrey has also contributed the commentaries on Mark and 2 Corinthians.

Books by Donald Bridge

JESUS - THE MAN AND HIS MESSAGE

What impact did Jesus make on the circumstances and culture of his time? What is it about him that identifies him both as a unique Saviour and the greatest example of gospel communication?

Donald Bridge challenges the way we view Jesus, and our portrayal of him to the world around us. He argues that walking with Jesus today means reading his words, welcoming the impact of his personality, embracing the provision he makes for us, and sharing his good news with others.

Donald Bridge combines a lifetime of study of the Gospels with an intimate knowledge of the land where Jesus lived and taught. He has been both an evangelist and a pastor, as well as working for several years in the Garden Tomb, Jerusalem.

176 PAGES   B FORMAT
ISBN 1 85792 117 8

SPIRITUAL GIFTS AND THE CHURCH
Donald Bridge and David Phypers

First published in the 1970s, when the Charismatic Movement became prominent in British church life, this classic study of gifts, the individual and the church has been revised and expanded in light of developments since then. The authors, Donald Bridge and David Phypers, give a balanced view of a difficult and controversial issue.

The baptism of the Spirit, with its associated gifts, is a subject which has perplexed and fascinated Christians. It is unfortunately one which also divides Christians who disagree over the extent to which gifts should appear in the Church.

Donald Bridge is an evangelist and church consultant and
David Phypers is a Church of England pastor.

192 PAGES   B FORMAT
ISBN 1 85792 141 0

Reformed Theological Writings
R. A. Finlayson

This volume contains a selection of doctrinal studies, divided into three sections:

General theology
The God of Israel; God In Three Persons; God the Father; The Person of Christ; The Love of the Spirit in Man's Redemption; The Holy Spirit in the Life of Christ; The Messianic Psalms; The Terminology of the Atonement; The Ascension; The Holy Spirit in the Life of the Christian; The Assurance of Faith; The Holy Spirit in the Life of the Church; The Church – The Body of Christ; The Authority of the Church; The Church in Augustine; Disruption Principles; The Reformed Doctrine of the Sacraments; The Theology of the Lord's Day, The Christian Sabbath; The Last Things.

Issues Facing Evangelicals
Christianity and Humanism; How Liberal Theology Infected Scotland; Neo-Orthodoxy; Neo-Liberalism and Neo-Fundamentalism; The Ecumenical Movement; Modern Theology and the Christian Message.

The Westminster Confession of Faith
The Significance of the Westminster Confession; The Doctrine of Scripture in the Westminster Confession of Faith; The Doctrine of God in the Westminster Confession of Faith; Particular Redemption in the Westminster Confession of Faith; Efficacious Grace in the Westminster Confession of Faith; Predestination in the Westminster Confession of Faith; The Doctrine of Man in the Westminster Confession of Faith.

R. A. Finlayson was for many years the leading theologian of the Free Church of Scotland and one of the most effective preachers and speakers of his time; those who were students in the 1950s deeply appreciated his visits to Christian Unions and IVF conferences. This volume contains posthumously edited theological lectures which illustrate his brilliant gift for simple, logical and yet warm-hearted presentation of Christian doctrine (I Howard Marshall).

272 pages   ISBN 1 85792 259 X   large format

MENTOR TITLES

Creation and Change by Douglas Kelly (large format, 272 pages)
A scholarly defence of the literal seven-day account of the creation of all things as detailed in Genesis 1. The author is Professor of Systematic Theology in Reformed Theological Seminary in Charlotte, North Carolina, USA.

The Healing Promise by Richard Mayhue (large format, 288 pages)
A clear biblical examination of the claims of Health and Wealth preachers. The author is Dean of The Master's Seminary, Los Angeles, California.

Puritan Profiles by William Barker (hardback, 320 pages)
The author is Professor of Church History at Westminster Theological Seminary, Philadelphia, USA. In this book he gives biographical profiles of 54 leading Puritans, most of whom were involved in the framing of the Westminster Confession of Faith.

Creeds, Councils and Christ by Gerald Bray (large format, 224 pages)
The author, who teaches at Samford University, Birmingham, Alabama, explains the historical circumstances and doctrinal differences that caused the early church to frame its creeds. He argues that a proper appreciation of the creeds will help the confused church of today.

MENTOR COMMENTARIES

1 and 2 Chronicles by Richard Pratt (hardback, 520 pages)
The author is professor of Old Testament at Reformed Theological Seminary, Orlando, USA. In this commentary he gives attention to the structure of Chronicles as well as the Chronicler's reasons for his different emphases from that of 1 and 2 Kings.

Psalms by Alan Harman (hardback, 420 pages)
The author, now retired from his position as a professor of Old Testament, lives in Australia. His commentary includes a comprehensive introduction to the psalms as well as a commentary on each psalm.

Amos by Gray Smith (hardback, 320 pages)
Gary Smith, a professor of Old Testament in Bethel Seminary, Minneapolis, USA, exegetes the text of Amos by considering issues of textual criticism, structure, historical and literary background, and the theological significance of the book.

Focus on the Bible Commentaries

Exodus – John L. Mackay*
Deuteronomy – Alan Harman
Judges and Ruth – Stephen Dray
1 and 2 Samuel – David Searle*
1 and 2 Kings – Robert Fyall*
Proverbs – Eric Lane (late 1998)
Daniel – Robert Fyall (1998)
Hosea – Michael Eaton
Amos – O Palmer Robertson*
Jonah-Zephaniah – John L. Mackay
Haggai-Malachi – John L. Mackay
Matthew – Charles Price (1998)
Mark – Geoffrey Grogan
John – Steve Motyer (1999)
Romans – R. C. Sproul
2 Corinthians – Geoffrey Grogan
Galatians – Joseph Pipa*
Ephesians – R. C. Sproul
Philippians – Hywel Jones
1 and 2 Thessalonians – Richard Mayhue (1999)
The Pastoral Epistles – Douglas Milne
Hebrews – Walter Riggans (1998)
James – Derek Prime
1 Peter – Derek Cleave
2 Peter – Paul Gardner (1998)
Jude – Paul Gardner

Journey Through the Old Testament – Bill Cotton
How To Interpret the Bible – Richard Mayhue

Those marked with an * are currently being written.